Carnal Resonance

Carnal Resonance

Affect and Online Pornography

Susanna Paasonen

The MIT Press
Cambridge, Massachusetts
London, England

Author's note   In various places throughout this book I have provided URLs for Web sites that illustrate my analysis and that, I believe, will enhance the reader's understanding of what I have to say. Some readers may find these sites offensive, however, and should exercise caution in visiting the URLs. Readers should also be aware that porn sites are sometimes infected with malware that can infect a visitor's computer.

MIT Press books may be purchased at special quantity discounts for business or sales promotional use. For information, please email special_sales@mitpress.mit.edu.

This book was set in Stone Sans and Stone Serif by the MIT Press. Printed and bound in Spain.

Library of Congress Cataloging-in-Publication Data

Paasonen, Susanna, 1975–
Carnal resonance : affect and online pornography / Susanna Paasonen.
     p.   cm.
Includes bibliographical references and index.
ISBN 978-0-262-01631-5 (hardcover : alk. paper)
1. Internet pornography—Research. 2. Internet research. I. Title.
HQ471.P33   2011
306.77—dc22

                                                                2011007758

10 9 8 7 6 5 4 3 2 1

Contents

Preface

Initially, this book was to be one article in my postdoctoral research project on issues of location and interpretation in Internet research. Although it seemed obvious to me that there was much to be said about online pornography back in 2002 when I was setting out to study it, little did I know that I would be occupied with the project for years to come. By the time my first article on online porn was published, I already disagreed with some of its premises and conclusions. This experience—of disagreeing with my essays even before they come out in print—has often been repeated, and I find that forthcoming texts are already dated as my takes and stances on the topic evolve. The longer I have investigated online pornography, the more complex and interesting things have become. Things that seemed straightforward at first turned out to be much more ambiguous and in acute need of theorization. Although *Carnal Resonance* draws on my previous work on porn spam email and online pornography, it results from a process of constant rethinking and rewriting during which most things have not remained the same.

This project evolved from a neat idea for one article-length case study into a multiple-year exploration of the forms, paradoxes, and affective dynamics of online pornography. During this time, I have worked in several different research environments—the program for Media Culture at the University of Tampere, the Centre for Women's Studies at the University of Turku, the Digital Culture MA program at the University of Jyväskylä, and the Helsinki Collegium for Advanced Studies at University of Helsinki, where I was fortunate enough to be a research fellow for three years and finished the first full drafts of the manuscript. Working in the Finnish academia involves constant instability and insecurity in terms of contracts (and career), yet this environment also supports and appreciates investigations into online pornography and its less avant-garde variations. My process of thinking through online porn and its affective intensities has been shared by friends, students, and colleagues, and I greatly appreciate their insightful comments, questions, challenges, critiques, and encouragement.

A decade ago, Anu Koivunen, Mari Pajala, and I organized a conference called Affective Encounters on rethinking embodiment in feminist media studies. In hindsight, I realize that I was not quite able to grasp the diversity of issues included under the conference topic, yet I have been lucky to learn from Anu and Mari and continue to do so. *Disturbing Differences: Feminist Readings of Identity, Location, and Power,* the research project with Marianne Liljeström, Ilana Aalto, Johanna Ahonen, Katariina Kyrölä, Anu Laukkanen, and Elina Valovirta at the University of Turku, has also been an important intellectual resource and support in helping me think through ways of working with affect in feminist research. I owe much to Kaarina Nikunen and Laura Saarenmaa for the pleasurable collaborations on the texts we coauthored, the two porn books we edited together, and the discussions we have shared on and off topic. Feona Attwood, whom I met through textual collaborations, continues to impress and inspire me with her analytical insights and intellectual enthusiasm. Without these kinds of encounters and collaborations, I would not have studied porn for as long or as intensely as I have.

I would like to extend my thanks to all those who have commented on the various stages of my research in seminars, conferences, and peer review processes over the years. These drafts have occasionally been raw indeed, and with some of them, cooking has been possible only with this collegial fuel. The Association of Internet Researchers and its annual conferences have been one crucial framework and a social hub for this research. Michele White has engaged me in fascinating discussions ranging from visible panty lines to domestic filth, in addition to involving me in different networks and constellations of queer, feminist, and postcolonial Internet researchers. Ken Hillis keeps reminding me of how crucial it is to theorize online phenomena with his own stellar example, while Terri Senft has made me revisit the notion of transmission of affect with her contagious intellectual energy. Jenny Sundén, my Swedish twin, has witnessed this book evolve from scattered remarks to something more formulated and has made sophisticated comments throughout. In addition, I would especially like to thank Nancy Baym, Megan Boler, Mia Consalvo, Jillana Enteen, Charles Ess, Sal

Humphreys, Kylie Jarrett, Nalini Kotamraju, Ben Light, Sharif Mowlabocus, Lisa Nakamura, and Irina Shklovski of the AoIR crowd (broadly defined) for their enthusiasm and support. The netporn criticism conferences of 2005 and 2007 were wonderful catalysts for this project, and I much appreciate being invited to the first one by Katrien Jacobs.

The input of the editors for the books and journals that I have contributed to on this topic remains evident in the pages below, for which I am grateful. The anonymous reviewers at the MIT Press provided feedback, encouragement, and suggestions that were of great value as I was finishing the book manuscript. My editor, Douglas Sery, has been extremely organized and supportive, and it is thanks to him that the book includes illustrations. In addition to those mentioned above, I would like to thank Kati Åberg, Karen Boyle, Jordan Crandall, Nina Czegledy, Sari Elfving, Maria Fernandez, Sara Heinämaa, Amanda McDonald Crowley, Brian McNair, Sergio Messina, Emilia Palonen, Jussi Parikka, Leena-Maija Rossi, Ingrid Ryberg, Tanja Sihvonen, Clarissa Smith, Johanna Uotinen, Annamari Vänskä, and Adrianne Wortzel for listening to my trains of thought and helping me forward. Witnessing Tarja Laine's drive to finish her book on cinema and emotion inspired me to focus on completing my own manuscript and to set deadlines for making it happen. The company and friendship of the Fab Five—Mari, Tarja, Eeva-Liisa Jokela, Maaretta Tukiainen, and Ilona Virtanen—remains an ever-important anchor in the stormy seas of academe.

Soft-core pornography was introduced to Finnish national television in the 1980s. The screening of the film *Emmanuelle* in 1987 was followed by a series of X-rated films that were rendered less offensive to viewers by the pink floating hearts that were placed on top of strategic body parts. My family watched these films collectively in situations characterized by ironic distancing comments, laughter, and acute self-awareness. This overall awkwardness efficiently stripped the films of their potential titillation value while the parental regulatory gaze worked its alienating effect. These uncomfortable viewing experiences taught me at an early age that there is much more than sexual arousal to the affective dynamics of porn and that porn can also be an object of shared curiosity. My parents, Eija and Asko Paasonen, have taken great pride in my porn research, perhaps because compared to some of my previous studies, this topic is something they can relate to. I would also like to thank my sister, Sarianne, for being there with me in all those awkward moments.

Finally, thanks go to Ville Hurskainen for sharing his impressive knowledge of Internet memes. Without Ville's insights, curiosity, and volunteer research assistance, this book would be poorer indeed, and without his company, the process of writing it would have been much duller.

Research for this book has been previously published—in different shapes and forms—as "Email from Nancy Nutsucker: Representation and Gendered Address in Online Pornography," *European Journal of Cultural Studies* 9, no. 4 (2006): 403–420; "Strange Bedfellows: Pornography, Affect and Feminist Reading," *Feminist Theory* 8, no. 1 (2007): 43–57; "Irregular Fantasies, Anomalous Uses: Porn Spam as Boundary Work," in *Spam Book: On Viruses, Spam, and Other Anomalous Objects of Digital Culture*, ed. Jussi Parikka and Tony D. Sampson (Cresskill: Hampton Press, 2009), 165–179; "Good Amateurs: Erotica Writing and Notions of Quality," in *Porn.com: Making Sense of Online Pornography*, ed. Feona Attwood (New York: Lang, 2010), 138–154; "Repetition and Hyperbole: The Gendered Choreographies of Heteroporn," in *Everyday Pornography*, ed. Karen Boyle (London: Routledge, 2010), 63–76; "Online Pornography: Ubiquitous and Effaced," in *Blackwell Handbook of Internet Studies*, ed. Mia Consalvo and Charles Ess (Oxford: Blackwell, 2011), 424–439; "Labors of Love: Netporn, Web 2.0, and the Meanings of Amateurism," *New Media and Society* 12, no 8 (2010): 1297–1312, as well as in Susanna Paasonen, Kaarina Nikunen, and Laura Saarenmaa, eds., *Pornification: Sex and Sexuality in Media Culture* (Oxford: Berg, 2007), 1–20, 161–170, and in Marianne Liljeström and Susanna Paasonen, eds., *Working with Affect in Feminist Readings: Disturbing Differences* (London: Routledge, 2010), 1–7, 58–71.

1 Introduction: Carnal Appeal

"Rules of the Internet" is a list of popular catchphrases that were coined in about 2004 and posted on the image board and Internet meme-sharing site http://www.4chan.org.[1] According to well-known rule 34, "There is porn of it, no exceptions." Rules 35 and 36 further clarify the issue: "If no porn is found of it, it will be made," and "There will always be more fucked up shit than what you just saw." The rules suggest that if you can think of a pornographic scenario, theme, or style—no matter how esoteric or unlikely it may seem—then such porn will already have been made, and it will be available online. If this is not the case, then it is only a matter of time before such porn is made. And independent of how disturbing the images you may have just come across may be, there will always be much more esoteric stuff left to be seen. As tongue-in-cheek "common knowledge," the rules mark the Internet as the realm of exotic, bizarre, imaginative, and extreme pornographies that titillate and arouse but also surprise, disgust, and push the boundaries of porn as we know it. There is more than a kernel of truth to all this.

Digital production tools and online networks have led to a drastic increase in the general visibility, accessibility, and diversity of pornography—from webcams and their interaction possibilities to massive video-sharing and -hosting sites, portals, Web directories, amateur forums, torrent-sharing platforms, and communities for fringe interests. Access to porn is easier than ever, and it can be accessed for free, anonymously, and in a seemingly endless range of niches, styles, subcategories, languages, and formats that have been impossible in other media—provided that one has the necessary hardware, software, and bandwidth and skill to use them. In addition to downloading porn, users may upload and share their own image and video files, set up webcams, or gain a reputation as erotica authors.

The accumulation of easily accessible online porn has given rise to acts of regulation and policing, such as the George W. Bush administration's 2004 "War on porn," as well as broad diagnoses of contemporary culture as pornified and battling with porn addiction (e.g., Paul 2005; Leahy 2008). All this has also sparked renewed academic interest in pornography and the role it plays in contemporary media culture (e.g., Williams 2004a; Jacobs, Janssen, and Pasquinelli, 2007; Paasonen, Nikunen, and Saarenmaa, 2007; Attwood 2010b).

On the one hand, an estimated one fourth of Western Internet users access online porn, and the needs and interests of the porn industry (broadly defined) have been crucial to the development of the Internet as a commercial medium. Yet on the other hand, online porn tends to be seen as a marginal, illegitimate, and problematic sort of phenomenon—even a form of "digital pollution" (Parikka and Sampson 2009, 3). Pornography's ambivalent position as a public secret—ubiquitous yet effaced and silenced, widely consumed yet defined as miasmic filth—has fed and fueled the affective dynamics of public debates, academic studies, and regulatory practices. To unravel these connections, *Carnal Resonance* addresses online porn in a media historical framework and considers its modalities, affective intensities, and visceral and disturbing qualities. Contrary to theorizations of pornography as emotionless, affectless, detached, and cold (Sontag 2002, 55), this book explores the affective intensities that attach bodies, images, and media together and pull them apart, as well as the possibilities of studying such interconnections.

Pornography is a modern popular media genre that developed from eighteenth-century mass-produced literary fictions and graphic prints to include photographs, films, magazines, books, videos, and digitally produced, distributed, consumed, and networked images, videos, webcams, and story archives.[2] Porn is both material and semiotic: it involves fleshy intensities, conventions of representation, media technologies, and the circuits of money, labor, and affect. Pornography—whether visual, textual, or audiovisual—routinely involves elaborate and detailed depictions of body parts, bodily motions, and bodily fluids. Through minute anatomical realism, it tries to mediate the sensory and to attach the viewing body to its affective loop: in porn, bodies move and move the bodies of those watching. And if media generally aim at transferring sense experiences from one person to another, as Jay David Bolter and Richard Grusin (1999, 3) suggest, then these affective loops and fleshy motions lead to fundamental questions concerning mediation, technology, and sensory experience. As argued in the chapters that follow, this motion involves a complex nexus of flesh, generic conventions, technologies, regulatory acts, and values—factors and actors that are both material and immaterial, human and nonhuman—in and through which particular images and texts become experienced and defined as pornographic. This nexus is mapped onto, contrasted, and meshed in with the specificities of media technologies, themselves "hybrids of technical, material, social, and economic facets" (Bolter and Grusin 1999, 77), in which porn is produced, distributed, and consumed. These pornographic assemblages bring forth forms of experience, sensations of presence, and perceptions of realness.

The fleshy aesthetic of porn is combined with and supported by a tendency toward hyperbole—exaggeration—in ways of conveying sexual arousal, pleasure, and embodied differences. All in all, porn is notably fantastic in its visions of desire, stamina, and gratification knowing no bounds, in its hyperbolic depictions of social categories and scenarios where the relations between people, objects, and environments are markedly sexual. This book results from reflections concerning the modalities and forms of online pornography, the ethics of interpretation, and the affective dynamics involved in the imageries of porn, encounters with, and discussions (both academic and popular) concerning them. These investigations are intimately attached to considerations of methodology (the ways of theorizing and analyzing online porn and affect), questions of materiality (of bodies, technologies, and inscriptions), and the development and range of online pornography.

In the Realm of Abundance

Initially, my investigations into online porn were inspired by the general disinterest that the topic generated among Internet researchers, despite its centrality in terms of online economy, Web history, the everyday uses of the medium, and public debates concerning it. In the early 2000s, only a handful of studies were available, and porn—and so-called mainstream commercial heteroporn, in particular—came across as one of the most understudied areas of Internet research (for exceptions since published, see Waskul 2004; Jacobs et al. 2007; Jacobs 2007; Attwood 2010b). The challenge was crafting a point of entry to the topic—where to start, what materials to study, and how exactly to study them. This was no minor concern, considering that porn debates tend to involve a certain logic of synecdoche according to which any example (an isolated image, text, video, or Web site) can be invested with the power to stand and speak for the whole genre. When and if random examples are taken as representative of pornography as a largely imaginary denominator, the genre can be defined in endless ways and in accordance with a broad range of theoretical, ethical, and political passions and concerns (Kendrick 1996).

By choosing particular examples to study, it is possible to justify one's premises concerning the meanings, forms, and implications of things pornographic. Given the broad range of sites, webcams, communities, body styles, niches, aesthetics, and interests that are accessible online, the question is one of justifying one set of materials over another. One can choose from the products of large and well-established companies working cross-platform in a range of media (such as Vivid, Private, Playboy, Bel Ami, or Larry Flynt Publications), amateur videos, alt porn sites featuring subcultural styles, porn produced for local (geographical, national, linguistic, or ethnic) markets, extreme, artful, vintage, or humorous porn, porn for straight men, women, or couples, gay porn and lesbian porn, transgender porn, queer porn, and many things beyond and besides[3] (figures 1.1 and 1.2). There are choices to be made between Web directories, porn story archives and image galleries, interactive live shows, and streaming videos. The plethora of available porn guarantees that virtually any stance can be backed up with multiple examples supporting one's argument. At the same time, studying only one set of materials tends to say little about others.

My initial solution to this dilemma was a pragmatic one: I began archiving unsolicited bulk spam email messages advertising pornography. Rather than seeking out any particular kinds of porn, I simply archived the messages sent to me via massive spam email address databases—and since my university's email system lacked filters, there was no shortage of such material. This presented me with a vignette into everyday encounters with online porn of the commercial, mainstream, and understudied kind. For seventeen months from 2002 to 2004, I archived well over a thousand messages, and after deleting messages with faulty image files and discarding duplicates, I was left with 366 messages that comprise the starting point for

Figure 1.1
The airbrushed mainstream of http://vivid.com

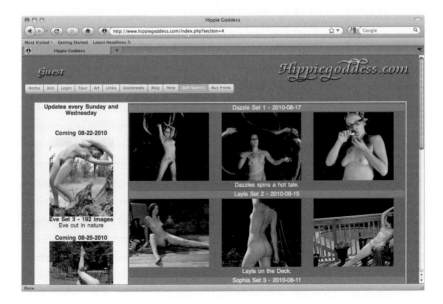

Figure 1.2
Hippie porn at http://hippiegoddess.com

this book. The landscape of online porn looks drastically different today than it did in 2002, largely due to the introduction of tubes (video-sharing and -hosting sites) and the omnipresence of amateur content, yet all kinds of content remain accessible, newer sites interlace with older ones, and themes, conventions, and styles linger on. As is the case with all studies of new media, investigations of online porn are about hitting a fast-moving target. Whatever research is done, the material will be recent history by the time the work is published. To address the contingent category of online porn, I draw on the spam material and the current (that is, 2010) versions of the sites advertised, popular video publishing platforms and file-sharing sites (e.g., http://youporn.com, http://redtube.com, http://8tube.com, http://xtube.com, http://www.xnxxx.com), Web directories and link sites comprising the top hits for search terms for porn subgenres, all-purpose porn sites (such as http://www.porn.com and http://pornhub.com), the massive amateur story archive http://literotica.com, viral videos and shock sites, and amateur forums such as http://wifebucket.com and http://www.submityourflicks.com. Because my focus is on the mainstream and popular, these sites are representative of what can be easily found and rates high in searches and visits. (At the time of writing, PornHub comprised the number one and Porn.com the number six hit for a Google search for "porn." PornHub is also rated 58 in Alexa's top global sites listing.) I engage with a range of porn sites from the perspective of a lurker rather than an insider or a community member. Participatory observation would have facilitated different analytical insights into the sites discussed, yet my focus on the freely and openly accessible is telling of the ways in which most casual users access online porn.

This book addresses the mainstream variations of online porn rather than examples of the avant-garde, the experimental, and the countercultural "building its own databases of queer and transgender pornography, and gender-fluid bodies" (Jacobs 2009, 191). This is because the mainstream remains something of a blind spot in studies of online pornography. In trying to map out how digital media tools and online platforms restructure and subvert the production, distribution, and consumption of porn, its aesthetics, its politics, and its economical underpinnings, scholars have focused on queer, subcultural, artistic, amateur, and independent pornographies. Alt porn sites featuring nonnormative bodily styles, webcam sites run by women, cybersex experiments, and more or less futuristic

versions of teledildonics do indeed broaden the definitions of the pornographic (e.g., de Voss 2002; Dery 2007b, 2007c; Kibby and Costello 2001;
Albury 2003; Villarejo 2004; Jacobs 2004; Waskul 2004; Halavais 2005; Tola
2005; Cramer 2006; Magnet 2007; Attwood 2007; Cramer and Home 2007;
Jacobs 2007).[4] At the same time, not many scholars have been interested in
the versions of the pornographic that are assumedly being subverted—the
mainstream, the standard, and the generic.

In the mid-2000s, discussions of porn indigenous to the Internet were
actively carried out under the rubric of *netporn*, defined as referring to
"alternative body type tolerance and amorphous queer sexuality, interesting art works and the writerly blogosphere, visions of grotesque sex and
warpunk activism" (Jacobs et al. 2007, 2; also Jacobs 2007). By defining
certain examples as "alternative," "amorphous," and "interesting," netporn criticism marks others as "mainstream"—which, by implication, are
distinctly categorizable, structured, and "uninteresting." The category of
"mainstream commercial heteroporn" is similarly evoked as a point of
comparison that connotes the obvious, the uninteresting, the immobile,
and things that are known without further study. Studies of commercial
porn are perhaps seen to pose few analytical and intellectual challenges,
and the more interesting examples are supposedly located at the fringes
and in the niches. The tendency to focus on the novel, the futuristic, and
the potentially avant-garde while attending less to that deemed familiar,
commercial, or predictable is a recognizable trait in studies of new media
more generally. Scholars desire to orient themselves toward things to come
and that are in the process of becoming rather toward whatever can be seen
in a rearview mirror. At the same time, the mainstream of commercial porn
has crucially affected ways of understanding the Web as a medium and the
possibilities of publishing, tracking and orienting the movements of users,
and generating profits. And although the term *mainstream* may be taken to
connote the uninteresting and the immobile, it is elastic enough to encompass all kinds of peculiarities.

By addressing the mainstream of online porn—the shapes it takes, the
ways in which it is defined, and the paradoxes that it involves—*Carnal
Resonance* investigates the discontents of the concept to chart transformations, continuities, and affective intensities in the pornographic as it is
circulated and encountered online. This leads to questions of cultural hierarchies and taste, the modalities of porn, the materiality of digital media,

affective complexity, and methodological concerns involved in addressing these issues. Considerations of affect are impossible to decouple from those of materiality—the materiality of the bodies performing in and viewing pornography; the technological objects, protocols, networks, and platforms through which porn materializes as certain kinds of objects; the materiality of perception; and the textures of pornographic images. This also means that studies of online porn cannot be confined solely to the representational, the meanings of images or videos, or the ways in which they depict and give shape to social categories such as gender, race, or class (this aspect of the representational having been one of the most important foci in studies of pornography to date). Although media historical investigations into genre, depiction, aesthetics, and modality certainly matter, studies of porn also benefit from investigations into technologies of production and distribution, affective intensities and resonances, appeal, and force. Rather than being mutually exclusive or conflicting with one another, these perspectives support one another.

Affect and Representation

Pornography is a multifaceted assemblage—a historically evolving media genre. It is a field of labor, technological innovations, monetary exchange, carnal acts and sensations, regulatory practices, verbal definitions, and interpretations. In what follows, I address this assemblage to move beyond the literal in studies of online porn and also to avoid using it as a metaphor, symbol, or symptom—of contemporary Western culture, late capitalism, cultural transformation, gender ideology, online cultures, or hegemonic forms of sexuality. To these ends, I use methods including (but not limited to) content description, studies of representation, close reading, and close looking. These investigations intersect with theoretical, conceptual, and historical considerations of affect, taste, ethics, digital media, materiality, and the pornographic. Combining considerations of modality and genre (the semiotic) with those concerning the material and the affective, this book is part of a move toward the sensory and the affective in studies of culture and media. This move has taken numerous directions, from new materialist investigations into sensation and intensity inspired by Gilles Deleuze, Félix Guattari, Brian Massumi, Rosi Braidotti, and Elizabeth Grosz (e.g., Shaviro 1993; Kennedy 2000; Abel 2007; Grusin 2010) to phenomenological redefinitions of the sensory and the mediated (Sobchack 2004; Kozel 2007; Barker 2009) and the affective intensities of reading and interpretation (Pearce 1997; Armstrong 2000; Sedgwick 2003).

As different as these bodies of work are, they have all helped to map the analytical shortcomings of textual analysis and the legacy of the so-called textual turn in cultural theory. This has also meant shifting attention away from ideology, meaning, and signification and toward the sensory, material, embodied, and energetic. By providing a conceptual framework for addressing cultural phenomena, objects, spaces, and images as texts and representations, the textual turn brought forth a certain tyranny of the semantic at the cost of the sensory and the material (Massumi 2002; Barad 2007; Thrift 2008; Hillis 2009; Liljeström and Paasonen 2010). Structuralism and, in its aftermath, poststructuralism are critiqued for their commitment to linguistic models, (logocentric) views of language as the general framework for understanding human activity, the focus on the unconscious and the Oedipal, and an emphasis on notions of lack when thinking about desire and human activity (see Braidotti 2002; Clough and Halley 2007; Deleuze and Guattari 2009). Some of this criticism stems from frustrations with the tendency of cultural theory to focus on negative critique instead of offering more life-affirming alternatives to the status quo. It is easy to agree that if the semantic and the symbolic are prioritized as the highest of analytical concerns, then a broad range of other issues and approaches are downplayed—or even framed out.

In his analysis of violent images "after representation," Marco Abel sets out to critique studies of representation as focusing on "reflections of something prior to their emergence, that is, immaterial traces of absent presences" (Abel 2007, x). Following in the footsteps of Deleuze and Guattari, Abel (2007, xi) argues for shifting attention from issues of meaning to the ways in which images work and the things that they do. Abel's critique is of representationalism—an epistemological dualism separating words from the physical world, the researcher from her object, and matter from meaning—yet it is presented as a "way out" from *representation*, as if the two concepts were synonymous. In such instances, studies of representation are seen as sharing representationalist ontology, according to which "representations and the objects (subjects, events, or states of affairs) they purport to represent are independent of one another" while "representations serve a mediating function between the knower and the known" (Barad 2007, 28,

133). Nevertheless, studies of representation, as practiced in cultural studies, start from the premise that words and images are practices with effects in and for the world. As practices that matter, representations generate both meaning and effects. In this framework, the notion of images as mirroring the world is as problematic as the view of representation as somehow producing the material world out of thin air (as perhaps best encapsulated in the biblical event of word becoming flesh)—for images are of the world and the human activity of communicating, making sense of the world, and imagining how things are or how they might be.[5]

Refusing to investigate the meaning of the images he studies, Abel (2007, 85) poses the question as one of doing: Is an image "capable to increase the power of the subjects encountering it (and being configured and transformed by it) to act, to think, to move? Or does it decrease these forces? In short, does it further the powers of living or hinder them to unfold?" This shift in focus and mode of interpretation is in line with that proposed by Deleuze and Guattari (2009, 109): "How do these machines, these desiring-machines, work—yours and mine? With what sort of breakdowns as a part of their functioning? How do they pass from one body to another?" Such reflections on doing and effects in actual images, however, are increasingly difficult to detach from questions of meaning. When addressing life forces, Abel inevitably engages in acts of interpretation, for evaluating the images' properties involves considerations of figuration and narrative, analysis of events, characters, dialog, and gestures. In other words, questions concerning the immediacy of affect and the visceral impact of images lead to the depicted, the symbolic, the mediated, and the representational. Hence critique "after representation" is difficult to tell apart from studies of representation.[6] This is telling of the methodological challenges involved in the "move to affect": it tries to move away from (or even do away with) the representational, the symbolic, and the semantic, yet when addressing cultural images, it is recurrently unable to do so.

I agree that there is a need to move beyond the exclusively semantic and to account for the affective intensities involved in our encounters with images, networked media, and the world, yet I object to the binary divisions and categorizing gestures that such a move is often associated with. As Clare Hemmings (2005) argues, the rhetoric of the affective turn tends to rely on simplified dualisms between the "old" (which is associated with social constructivism and indeed social determinism) and the "new" (which is associated with transformation, openness, and affective intensity). Hemmings (2005, 557–558) further notes that this move tends to associate feminist, queer, and postcolonial analyses of power and ideology as exemplary of the old and the constraining, as opposed to the openness and positivity of new materialism.[7] Sara Ahmed (2008, 25) similarly points out that, according to a routine claim, "feminism and poststructuralism have reduced 'everything' to language and culture, in what is often referred to as 'textualism,' and have forgotten the 'real' of the real world, or the materiality of what is given." Given that a "turn to" is always also a "turn from," the turn to affect can be critiqued for downplaying the complexity of cultural theory to date. Such erasure or aversion does not apply to all critiques of cultural theory, but it seems paradoxical that the same scholars who critique cultural theory and its textual practices for resorting to and confining itself to binary models and negativity (e.g., Sedgwick 2003, 93–94) also employ similar dichotomies when distinguishing their own theoretical stances from those they criticize. By doing so, they counter binary thinking by posing new sets of binaries in which the "activity, joy, affirmation, dynamic or molecular becoming" of new materialist criticism is juxtaposed with "the sedentary, guilt-ridden, life-denying, moralizing tone of most Western philosophy" (Braidotti 2002, 71). The rhetorical juxtaposition of the joyful and the guilt-ridden, the dynamic and the sedentary, maps out clear camps, one of which is depicted as considerably more attractive than the other (cf. Hemmings 2005, 551).[8]

According to another set of critiques targeted at studies of representation, they downplay or even ignore the technological base and make-up of media technologies, their material properties, programmability, operations, and logics of action—namely, the fact that computers "generate text and images rather than merely represent or reproduce what exists elsewhere" (Chun 2004, 27). Jussi Parikka and Tony D. Sampson (2009, 9) outline a Deleuzean framework for addressing "the material forces of culture, which not only refer to economic relationships, but to assemblages, events, bodies, technologies, and also language expressing itself in other modalities than meaning." This means stepping away from considerations of "representational analysis of phenomenological 'content'" and toward the operations of code and computational processes—even if our cognitive skills are deficient in grasping their operations when using the Internet (Parikka and Sampson 2009, 16–17).[9] Internet research that ignores the operations of the medium cannot be considered solid. Similarly, reducing the Internet to the level of the screen and its visual interfaces produces a partial perspective. At the same time, downplaying the role of phenomenological content means ignoring the interfaces and interactions that we, as users, sense and make sense of, as well as the ways in which the Internet is addressed and debated across the field of media (in terms of specific sites, videos, images, and texts).

Attempts to uncover a deeper level of processes and intensities risk foregrounding a technical "truth" concerning the Internet at the expense of the "content," which then becomes marked as being of secondary importance. In her discussion on software, Wendy Chun (2008, 301) points out how positioning it as the alleged "truth, the base layer, the logic of new media" may not help people understand the phenomena at hand on a more fundamental level. Indeed, she argues that discussions on new media tend to resonate with the story of six blind men and an elephant: since each blind man touches a different part of the elephant, each offers a different analogy for what the elephant is. The story has been used to illustrate the difficulty of talking about divinity—what transgresses the comprehensible—yet something similar is taking place in studies of new media where the effects of digital technologies—the shapes, forms, and contents of networks, the volume of interactions, and the range of user practices—far exceed the cognitive and analytical capacities of any single scholar (Chun 2008, 299–300). One scholar addresses technical protocols, another focuses on intimate networked exchanges, and a third analyzes Web traffic. Each scholar presents a thorough analysis of her topic, yet no singular perspective suffices to capture the beast of what is called the Internet. The Internet is about mediation and representation but equally about communication and exchange, technical protocols and affordances, and affective, visceral gut reaction. It is not one thing or another but an assemblage of factors and actors that cut through and build onto one another.

Beyond Reading

The "affective turn" has been identified, debated, and theorized in cultural theory for a decade (Koivunen 2001, 2010; Clough and Halley 2007), and the establishment of porn studies as an interdisciplinary field of investigation has been around for almost as long (Attwood 2002; Williams 2004a).

Nevertheless, it seems that relatively little has happened in conceptualizations of porn and its fleshy, sensuous appeal since Linda Williams's 1991 article on body genres and Richard Dyer's 1985 consideration of pornography as a genre "rooted in bodily effect" and involving bodily knowledge (Dyer 2002b, 140). Williams sees porn as analogous to genres such as slasher horror, melodrama, and comedy that aim to touch and move their viewers in embodied ways. Melodrama moves its viewers to tears and horror tries to make their bodies flinch and jump, whereas the quest of pornography is to arouse its audience sexually (Williams 1991, 4–5). As Dyer (2002b, 139) notes, "the fact that porn, like weepies, thrillers and low comedy, is realized in/through the body has given it low status in our culture."

Encounters with porn involve moments of proximity where one is moved by images and becomes conscious of the power that they hold. These intimacies may be desirable, surprising, unwanted, or disturbing, and the sense of them being "dangerously effective at moving us" (Attwood 2010b, 1) challenges established modes of analysis. Annette Kuhn (1994, 21) notes how "the capacity of pornography to provide gut reactions—of distaste, horror, sexual arousal, fear—makes it peculiarly difficult to deal with analytically." Rephrasing the question, it can be argued that these gut reactions necessitate analytical approaches and intellectual orientations that do not assume the mastery of the viewer over the image or of the user over the medium but account for the carnal dynamics and resonances at play in interactions with pornography. Working through gut reactions can teach us much about porn and its affective intensities.

The appeal of online porn is largely underpinned by its visceral and excessive modality, what might be defined as the "physical residue in the image that resists absorption into symbol, narrative, or expository discourse" (MacDougall 2006, 18). Analysis highlighting questions of meaning does not quite manage to grasp this excess and resistance—that is, the sensory, synesthetic, and visceral aspects of encountering images. It could be argued that there is little to be read from or in pornography, given the genre's commitment to exploring bodies and their interactions in detail while overriding semantics and factors such as narrative development or the nuances of dialog. Ken Hillis (2009, 27) argues that the "naturalized academic metaphor 'to read'" "points to the word, printed page, book, and political economy of text-based modes of production and distribution." For Hillis, the metaphor of reading "subsumes the unruly image under the

rational sign of the text" in logocentric manner. Using reading to describe
the analytical work done in Internet research means bypassing the differences between text and still and moving images, the ways in which they
play into each other on Web interfaces, and the ways that they are experienced and made sense of together, separately, and in hybrid ways (Hillis
2009, 27). Online porn meshes the visual and textual: videos are accompanied by textual descriptions, titles, background stories, and comments;
image galleries are categorized under headings and descriptions; and spam
email advertisements are collages consisting of images, info boxes, subject
lines, headings, links, animated features, and graphical elements. To investigate these hybrid modalities, more than one strategy of interpretation is
needed.

In the chapters that follow, the analytical focus moves between considerations of iconography, lexicon, modality, and aesthetics of online porn
to those of affective intensity, the materiality of human bodies and media
technologies, and the ways in which they build and feed on, modify, and
resonate with one another. With the term *modality*, I am not referring to
general patterns or fixed structures but to the qualities of mode, mood,
and manner (including excess, hyperbole, realness, repetition, and visceral-
ity) that play a central role in porn as its recurring characteristics. Analysis that zooms in solely on the representational aspects of a pornographic
image published on a Web site as detached from its digital circulation, its
particular materiality, the context of the site, or the forms and conditions
of accessing it (through free tour sections, with a membership fee, or as
openly accessible content) bypasses a range of factors from analysis. The
same goes for analyses of online porn and affective intensity that fail to
account for the qualities, histories, and conventions of porn. The question
is not whether to focus on one or the other but how to grasp their interplay
and interconnectedness.

As should be evident at this point, I am far from dramatically associating
textual analysis or studies of representation with lack of analytical light or
as a "dark side of digital culture" (Parikka and Sampson 2009, 5, 20). The
ways in which online porn grabs its users is a matter of affective intensity
and material forms of transmission but equally one of aesthetics, visual
style, camerawork, and forms of address. The structural (in the sense of
generic features, recurring modalities, forms of address, or lexicon) does
not suffice to explain the resonances of online porn, but it needs to be

mapped out to describe how porn is put together and what it consists of in order to see how it operates and what it affords and inspires. Resonance does not come from thin air. In studies of online porn, the level of representation and mediation is forever present, as is that of affect. Like Siamese twins, they are attached at the hip as well as the head: they share some vital organs and can be severed from one another only with a considerable degree of analytical violence and risk of harm.

What Resonates

For quite some time, film scholars have criticized scholars' inability to take seriously the visceral aspects of the media they have studied. As the embodied, sensory, and affective have been downplayed or even rendered invisible, cinema has been conceptualized in terms of language, narrative, and representation. Steven Shaviro (1993) argues that rather than distanced forms of spectating, encounters with film (and art more generally) should be seen as affective and intense encounters. This call for a shift in perspective is shared by authors who draw on phenomenology (Sobchack 2004; Marks 2000, 2002; Barker 2009), literary studies (Gallop 1988; Pearce 1997; Armstrong 2000), and new materialist critique (Kennedy 2000; Abel 2007) and who, in different ways, have identified ways of accounting for the affective and the sensory in acts of interpretation. Both cultural analyses in general and studies of pornography in particular have much to benefit from investigations into the relations of sensing and making sense (Sobchack 2004, 13). Bodily sensations and arousals matter, and their meaning is a complicated and slippery issue.

Vivian Sobchack, much like Shaviro, is interested in "carnal identification" with cinema as an event of being moved bodily before consciously processing what such experiences—the film's sounds and images—may mean. This framework sheds light on the dynamics of gut reactions and "visceral audience engagement" in pornography (Kipnis 1999, 161) that lay at the heart of its appeal and force. Given that the title of this book gestures explicitly toward Sobchack's 2004 *Carnal Thoughts*, my debt to her thinking is clear. I am, however, less inclined to conceptualize experiences of being moved in terms of *identification*—a term that is used in cinema studies as shorthand for moments of being affected but that comes with some psychoanalytical baggage and is less applicable to studies of other media forms (as discussed at length in chapter 5). Identification implies proximity but also sameness and recognition in ways that may not fully capture the experiences of online porn. By focusing on psychic processes, it also tends to downplay the sensory and material nature of the body (Kennedy 2000, 10–13). Instead of identification, I am proposing *resonance* as a concept for making sense of the movement between porn and its users. On the one hand, resonance describes the force and grab of porn—its visceral appeal and power to disturb. On the other hand, resonance is at play in how users attach themselves to porn sites, images, videos, and texts and recognize some of the carnal sensations depicted on the screen. With resonance, I want to tackle the interactive nature of such attachments, for the central question is pornography's power to touch and move us, to arouse our senses and interest alike. This is not a relation of identification in the sense of recognition of sameness, nor is it merely an issue of projection. Resonance is also the concept that Susan Kozel (2007, 24–26) introduces when describing how sensory experiences can become shared though empathy and imagination.[10] To resonate with one another, objects and people do not need to be similar, but they need to relate and connect to one another. Resonance encompasses the emotional and cognitive as well as the sensory and affective, and it points to the considerable effort involved in separating the two.

The term *resonance* carries multiple meanings across disciplinary boundaries and discursive contexts (from linguistics to physics, chemistry, electronics, and medicine). The body of meaning I am referring to involves thesaurus definitions such as "richness or significance, especially in evoking an association or strong emotion"; "intensification and prolongation of sound, especially of a musical tone, produced by sympathetic vibration"; "sound produced by a body vibrating in sympathy with a neighboring source of sound"; and "oscillation induced in a physical system when it is affected by another system that is itself oscillating at the right frequency."[11] More than a technical term, *resonance* refers to moments and experiences of being moved, touched, and affected by what is tuned to "the right frequency." Right frequencies and "sympathetic vibrations" are often discovered by accident as certain images among hundreds and thousands stick, attract attention, fascinate, and encourage future revisiting. In contrast, other resonances are experienced as disturbing and unpleasant, as revolting sorts of dissonance, as sharp shocks, or as involving a range of mixed responses—being surprised, startled, bored, amused, ashamed, bemused, and titillated. Some pornographic images have strong resonance, some have weaker resonance, and others fail to resonate at all. All resonance alters in form and intensity over time, depending on who is encountering the images, how, where, and when. As philosopher Baruch Spinoza (1992, 133) put it, "Different men can be affected in different ways by one and the same object, and one and the same man can be affected by one and the same object in different ways in different times."

With *resonance*, I am not referring to specific kinds of causal effects of pornography but to connections and movement between porn and its audiences that are always imprinted and marked by contexts and technologies of production, distribution, and circulation. This movement has no predictable direction or trajectory. As metaphorical as the term may seem, I use *resonance* to unravel the material and visceral sensations that are caused by encounters with pornography. Resonance is carnal by definition, and the sensations and vibrations that it entails are not necessarily easy to articulate or translate into language. The concept also points to the material factors of porn—the fleshy substance of the human body; the texture of images, screens, and signals; the technologies of transmission and the materialities of hardware, cables, and modems. As discussed in the following chapters, pornographic images and videos involve a complex interplay between authenticity and artifice, the indexical and the hyperbolic, immediacy and distance. At the heart of this interplay lies the physical presence and visual accessibility of its performers, facilitated by networked communications and supported by the notions of realness and authenticity associated with technologies of inscription, imaging, recording, and transmission (via photography, video, and the Internet). Such "carnal residue" is crucial to the affective registers, force, and appeal of online porn.

When writing on embodied digital experience, Anna Munster (2006, 16) argues for the "urgent political necessity" of staking out areas in which such sensations appear. Munster then progresses to address a series of new media artworks. This is an important intellectual project, yet it repeats a recurring and ultimately analytically limited tendency to contain such investigations in the framework of media art (largely representative of the technological avant-garde). Notions of materiality, bodily sensations, and relations to media technology are theorized and conceptualized in the context of art with considerable ambition and rigor—partly since the arts are seen as the terrain for grasping the "linguistically ambiguous zone" of the precognitive and affective (Kozel 2007, 16). Art may resonate with theorizations of sensation and ambiguity of meaning (and vice versa), yet much can be gained from bringing such considerations into studies of popular media culture as it is known and used by most—and not least if one sees such considerations as ones of "urgent political necessity." Otherwise, we may end up in an endless feedback loop of (media) art talking to (media) theory and theory to art while the lower tiers of culture are seen as unable to reverberate in any interesting or notable manner. This kind of loop reinforces the rather too familiar hierarchies of culture—the divisions of the high and the low, the artful and the plain trashy. Taking up the challenge, *Carnal Resonance* brings theorizations of materiality and (digital) media into studies of online porn, a media genre with considerably low cultural status, continuing popularity, and high visibility. My interests lie in thinking through affective resonance and intensity in what is considered prefabricated and mass cultural. In the framework of online porn, this involves investigations into modes of depiction (including explicit carnality, excess, and optimized visibility), public debates, cultural hierarchies (censorship, taboos, notions of shame, articulations of disgust and cultural value), sensibilities and modes of interpretation, technological horizons of possibility, and the appeal, resonance, and grab of mediated visions of sex.

Carnal Resonance conceptualizes online porn as a nexus of generic conventions, technologies, body styles, and values that, if tuned to the right frequency, has the power to affect its users in unpredictable and often contradictory ways. These resonances involve not simply sexual arousal but also sensations that include disgust, confusion, surprise, titillation, interest, dismay, shame, boredom, amusement, curiosity, and many other things. Online porn often gives rise to patterns of dissonance (incongruity and discord) rather than resonance—particularly in the form of shock porn, brutality, and Internet memes aiming to disturb (see chapter 6). Dissonance—"ultimate non-coincidence" and "total lack of symmetry" (Braidotti 1991, 14) between images and viewers—has been evident in feminist interventions in pornography. With resonance, my attempt is not so much to turn the proverbial new page in feminist theorizations of porn but to account for what the more negative points of entrance fail to cover—surprising reverberations, affective intensities, and moments of being moved by dissonance inasmuch as by "sympathetic vibrations." The two are often remarkably difficult to tell apart, and they orient ways of encountering and addressing pornography.

Discomforting Commute

In writing this book, my focus has shifted from the framework of Internet research and its methodological debates to a conceptual, theoretical, and methodological framework that draws on media studies, gender studies, philosophy, literary studies, psychology, aesthetics, visual theory, cinema and television studies, cultural studies, queer theory, postcolonial theory, material anthropology, sociology, and probably other fields that I have failed to identify. Art studies approaches play a central role in my theorizations of the modalities and registers of online porn. The focus in the individual chapters oscillates between acts of interpretation, considerations of affective force, networked communications, and possibilities of understanding pornography as a popular genre. Contrary to most commonsensical discussions, I argue that we know relatively little about online porn and that this lack of knowledge influences our possibilities to understand its specificities, appeal, and cultural power. This book adds little to bridging current knowledge gaps on the production and usage of porn. Instead, it contributes to our knowledge on the visceral appeal of porn as inseparable from its media of production and distribution.[12]

When I discuss pornography as a general category, it is on the basis of the materials addressed. The different methodological and theoretical approaches employed in the book illuminate different aspects of the research material and, through this prism, the modality and affective dynamics of online porn more generally. At the same time, the analyses explore the affordances and limitations of the methodological and conceptual routes taken (see especially chapters 4 and 5). With methodology, I refer to the tools employed in acts of analysis and the "organizing principles, motivations, and political commitments" that shape research, researchers, and objects of study (Tyler 2008, 85). As Fredric Jameson (2002, 45) argues, all methods and approaches imply and presuppose a form of theory. The presuppositions of a given method and the theoretical frameworks in which they are embedded frame the object of study, orient the questions asked, and facilitate particular forms of knowledge. Making these partialities and particularities—as well as their strengths and analytical possibilities—manifest is also an ethical effort that concerns the role and status of the researcher in pornography.

An alternative name for this book was "Curious Resonance"—a title gesturing toward the desire to learn; to scrupulous, intricate, and detailed attention; and to things that arouse interest due to their irregularity, novelty, or strangeness. This would have been an apt title since my investigations into porn have indeed been guided by curiosity, interest, and a commitment to remaining open to surprise—a methodological and epistemological stand owing to feminist theorizations of reading (e.g., Pearce 1997; Armstrong 2000; Sedgwick 2003). At the same time, attaching the adjective *curious* to the resonances of porn would have implied that such reverberations are odd, peculiar, and strange. Online porn is indeed often irregular and strange, and it aims to stand out through the novelty of the desires, kinks, and displays of bodily pliability that it showcases. However, marking the gut reactions that porn evokes as curious would have implied a viewer, Internet user, and scholar (that is, me) as someone taken by surprise and not expecting to be moved by any of it. This would surely have been a false gesture of exteriority.

Following the maxim of curiosity toward online pornography, its force, and its appeal, my aim has been to remain open to different theoretical and conceptual approaches and methodological and interpretative strategies and also sensitive to the affordances and requirements of the materials studied. Rather than forcing all examples of online porn into the same analytical framework, this book moves between different theoretical perspectives and modes of interpretation to produce a multifaceted understanding of the developments and directions taking place. The approach is rather distanced in some parts, whereas in others I move up close to tackle the resonances of porn. This is a question of both method (the ways in which we orientate ourselves toward images) and the ways in which different images offer themselves to analysis through resonance. Distance and proximity between images and viewing bodies both rise from and give rise to affective zones of encounter and interpretation, while the commute between the different positions points to the contingency and instability of such zones (Kyrölä 2010, 17, 190). Despite the differences in the analytical routes taken, this book does not amount to a narrative that progresses from one framework, approach, or conceptualization to another, assumedly more sophisticated one. Following literary scholar Lynne Pearce

(1997, 23), the itinerary can be best characterized as one of a discomforting commute where different strategies of interpretation are combined and contrasted, new ones are sketched out, and the individual strategies both support and necessitate one another (also Kyrölä 2010, 18). This commute between different methods, concepts, and approaches is evident within as well as between the individual chapters.

Chapter 2 addresses the development of online porn, the notions of filth and risk associated with the genre, and the hierarchies of taste and class that these involve. It sketches out the general context and framework for the examples discussed in the book, as well as the affective investments involved in debates on pornography (feminist porn debates included). By focusing on the figure of the porn consumer, the chapter makes evident some gaps in conceptualizations of porn consumption in so-called old and new media. Chapter 3 continues the discussion on developments in online porn by considering the role of user-generated content, amateur porn and its online distribution, gonzo and reality genres, and affective labor. These lead to considerations of the authenticity, realism, and directness that are at play in online porn and networked communications, as well as those concerning materiality and media.

These chapters pave way to chapters 4, 5, and 6 on the methodological concerns, affective dynamics, and modalities of online porn (including repetition, hyperbole, excess, and the play between proximity and distance). Chapter 4 provides content analysis of the porn spam material in terms of terminology and iconography. While addressing some of the problematic aspects of content analysis, it also points to its usefulness in mapping out the centrality of recurring aspects such as hyperbole, recognizability, and repetition in and for porn as a genre. The chapter also offers a discussion of humor, camp, heterosexuality, and queer orientation to porn that complicates interpretations of pornographic imageries. This analysis feeds into discussions on focalization, looking, and resonance in chapter 5. Countering the problems involved in the theoretical legacy of cinema studies (and psychosemiotic film theories of the 1970s, in particular) and addressing fascinations and engagements with online porn, the chapter proposes approaching its visual pleasures through the notions of resonance, rhythm, grab, and diverse forms of looking. Together, these two chapters map out the modality of online porn as hyperbolic, excessive, stylized, and repetitive while arguing that literal readings of the genre ultimately fall short in understanding its dynamics or appeal. They also address the methodological issues involved in studies of online porn (and porn and media more generally) at some length.

Building on these debates, chapter 6 provides analysis of materiality, transgression, and extremity in the framework of viral videos and extreme and shock pornography. It addresses notions of disgust and shame related to pornography and masturbation while also arguing for their centrality in the affective dynamics of porn. Notions of filth, nastiness, or sickness have a pejorative function in public discussions marking pornography as vile and worthless smut. As Michael Warner (2000, 181) notes, conceptually vacuous terms such *filth* and *sleaze* help to mark pornography and also the sexual preferences, desires, and acts depicted in it as disgusting and shameful (also Kalha 2007b, 33; Albury 2002; Langman 2004, 194; Stein 2006). Within porn, however, they take up a much more productive and positive set of meanings as indicative of extreme hardcore acts with no holds barred. In this sense, the filthy and the disgusting become both highlighted and embraced. The filthy and the disgusting resist mainstreaming and domestication, and as the chapter suggests, they help to maintain the status of pornography as a forbidden fruit that requires acts of censorship and regulation. Finally, chapter 7 continues the discussion of affective dynamics and materiality that is raised in the previous chapters while summarizing the central points of the book as a whole. The individual chapters conceptualize the productivity and force of pornography, as well as the crucial role that media technologies (and digital production tools and networked communications in particular) play in the forms that porn takes, the resonances it involves, and the experiences that it facilitates.

Vulnerability and Affective Intensity

The notion of *affect* (sensation and intensities of feeling and their circulation) figures centrally throughout the book, and it does this on different levels. I make use of theorizations of affect in conceptualizing the broad dynamics of attachment, intensity, and intimacy, as mapped out in the work of Spinoza and new materialist criticism, as well as discussions on affective labor (by Tiziana Terranova in particular). Nevertheless, my work owes most to philosopher Sara Ahmed's (2001, 2004, 2010) considerations of how experiences and articulations of affect attach people, objects, texts, and values together and pull them apart. Like Sobchack and Kozel, Ahmed works in and through the framework of phenomenology, grasping affect as embodied, lived, and social yet also paying attention to the rhetorical work that articulations of affect and emotion are put into. Articulations of affect are translations and explanations of sensation through which objects (such as pornography) are given shape and value and made sense of. The third level of, or approach to, affect involves considerations of my experiences of being moved or disturbed by the pornographic. My body resonates while I theorize, conceptualize, and speculate about kinds of resonances. There is recurrently something of a mutual resistance between me and much of the porn that I study (dissonance and noise rather than resonance), yet a scholar studying porn who is never aroused by it is as anomalous and misplaced a creature as a researcher studying comedy who is never moved to laughter or a scholar working on horror who fails to jump or flinch. It seems to me that such scholars have failed to experience and grasp the essential of what they study and that they would not be able to provide convincing analytical insights into the genre. Body genres involve carnal resonance and visceral engagement that researchers deny at the expense of intellectual rigor.[13]

At the heart of this book lies the notion of self-reflexive scholarly agency.[14] As Williams (2004b, 172) has pointed out, analysis is always directed by one's reactions and values, and revealing one's vulnerability to the materials addressed is a means of pushing studies of pornography (and broadly speaking, those of popular culture) forward. This is indeed the case. This book is motivated by my interest in and curiosity about online pornography and the passionate tone of debates on it. I am constantly moved by the images I encounter and study, and these contingent affectations are an important part of the analytical agenda. Ahmed (2004, 89) points out how "the position of 'aboveness' is maintained only at the cost of a certain vulnerability" or openness toward what is situated "below." In other words, situating oneself "above" the topics, phenomena, and materials studied is a means of escaping vulnerability and resonance as contact. Aboveness blocks from view both the power of those materials and phenomena to move oneself, as well as the ways in which this motion affects acts of interpretation. Working with the notions of affect and resonance is to no small degree about bringing vulnerability into the equation.

Affect points to uncontrollability in our encounters with porn—to a rupture between gut reactions and the fantasy of self-control, as well as the capacity of images, words, and sounds "to physically arouse us to meaning" (Sobchack 2004, 57). Carnal resonance links to ways of making sense of pornography, yet it also involves a more fundamental level of being moved and touched—and also transformed (MacCormack 2004)—by whatever one interacts with. This uncontrollability and impressionability may translate as discomfort, yet the tendency to detach oneself from the affective dynamics of pornography has also to do with the low cultural status of the genre and the highly politicized character of the debates concerning it. As discussed in the chapters below, these aspects are intimately connected to questions of taste and social hierarchies, the legacy of the "porn wars," and the affective interconnections of shame and disgust in experiences of and discussions on porn.

My investigations into "low pornographies" such as porn spam email or commercial porn sites are not about "aboveness," but neither do they involve intimate resonance by default. In many instances, the bulk of email, thumbnails, video and image galleries, and Web directories has seemed exactly that—a mass of images, links, and textual depictions that provide far more examples of tedious repetition than moments of surprise or possible affinity.[15] It has been difficult to tune into the right frequency with spam advertisements that seem to speak past me in terms of focalization, address, terminology, and iconography alike. When considering affective resonance, it is also a matter of the affordances and properties of the object that one is supposed to resonate with: "sympathetic vibrations" are by no means a given, but neither are they predictable. It is also likely that analysis of any mass of material eventually draws the researcher further away and, in the course of recurrent revisits over a number of years, loosens the affective ties between the two. Familiarity displaces the element of surprise: as the saying goes, one "becomes numbed." Visual anthropologist David MacDougall (2006, 1) describes the initial encounter with images as "undifferentiated and bound up with matter and feeling in a complex relation that it often later loses in abstraction." This, however, does not make either the initial affective encounters with pornography or latter considerations of genre, narrative, modality, or convention more "true." Neither does any "truth" lie in either gut reactions or more conceptualized viewings. Rather, such transformations and oscillations point to the affective dynamics of interpretation. Working with pornography involves constant movement between proximity and distance, moments of affectation and distanced rumination (the discomforting commute mentioned above and evident in the chapters below). This is a theoretical question concerning the role and position of researchers and their objects of research, but it also is a question about the nature of these objects: what kind of force, materiality, or agency, can be attributed to them, and what kinds of objects they are defined as being. It is no less a methodological concern, for as this book makes evident, different methodological approaches call forth different constellations of distance and proximity, "aboveness" and "implicatedness," interpretative mastery and dialogical relations.

This movement between different theoretical frameworks and modes of interpretation is also central in the sense that I wish to avoid positioning "the body" fetishistically as the basis of some kind of truth concerning porn and its affective powers (cf. Bhattachayya 2001, 37). As Michel Foucault (1990, 58–59) has famously argued, Western technologies of the self have positioned the assumed truth concerning the self in the realm of sexuality. Confessions of sexual desires and acts have meant exposing one's innermost self or "soul." Following the idea of sexuality as a more or less hidden truth concerning the self, pornography's power to move, touch, and arouse bodies would translate as pornography "speaking" the truth of these bodies and their desires. The notion of affective resonance, however, refers to a much more complex traffic between bodies performing in and consuming online porn, technologies of mediation, and conventions of representation at play. With "the body," I do not refer to notions of essence or to a surface, "text," or "the most valorized and magical of conceptual terms within the social sciences and the humanities" (Grosz 2005, 171).[16] Working with and through affect, my aim is to conceptualize bodies as both material—made of guts, bones, and blood, oriented by drives, conditioned by physical affordances, and animated by affective intensities—and as constantly engaged in semiotic activity of representation, mapping, and depiction. Debates on sexuality as either biological or culturally constructed are, in this framework, simply misplaced since the two operate in symbiosis: sensing and making sense go hand in hand (also Kennedy 2000). Following Karen Barad (2007, 3), I see the material and the textual, affect and representation, substance and significance, sensation and sense, matter and meaning as "inextricably fused together."[17] This book sets out to address their complex interplay as one of affective resonance.

When investigating online porn, I speak and write from my own, particularly located, trained, experiencing, and groomed embodiment. My affective reactions are meshed in with ethical, aesthetic, and political concerns, as well as the reservoir of pornography that I have experienced over the course of my life. Ahmed's work helps in seeing the disturbing complexity of gut reactions: sensory reactions give shape to the world around us, but they are also shaped by this same world. Countering Brian Massumi's argument on the autonomy of affect, Ahmed argues for the impossibility of telling affect apart from emotion in any clear manner. For Massumi, affect is intensity void of subjective content that is beyond narrative. Although feelings refer to individual experiences, emotions involve a "sociolinguistic fixing of the quality of experience which is from that point onward defined as personal." Emotion is "intensity owned and recognized," confined to the semantic and the semiotic and embedded in narrative circuits, functions and meanings, whereas affect is unqualified intensity that cannot be owned or recognized (Massumi 2002, 28). For Ahmed (2010, 32), emotions, as intensities, are not "after-thoughts" to the affective "but shape how bodies are moved by the worlds they inhabit." She argues that the intensities that Massumi describes as affect are "directed" as well as "qualified" or even "congealed": "this directedness is not simply about subjects and interior feeling states but about how things cohere in a certain way. While you can separate an affective response from an emotion that is attributed as such (the bodily sensations from the feeling of being afraid), this does not mean in practice, or in everyday life, they are separate. In fact, they are contiguous; they slide into each other; they stick, and cohere, even when they are separated" (Ahmed 2010, 32).

I address experiences of pornography largely through the notion of affect as gut reactions, intensities of experience, bodily sensations, resonances, and ambiguous feelings. At the same time, I realize that these are impossible to mark apart from articulations of emotion. As Ahmed reminds us, emotions—imprinted as they are with personal histories, values, politics, and many things besides—also orient ways of encountering, sensing, and making sense of the images we encounter. Ultimately, isolating affect from emotion amounts to an impossible task. With affect, I want to tackle the simultaneous "shapelessness" and sharpness of sensation. Affective sensations can be associated with and defined through numerous emotions, but such definitions simplify the intensities in question. Affects can be experienced as sharp jolts and gut feelings. Whether such a jolt is a matter of surprise, startle, disgust, titillation, arousal, shame, or any combination thereof is a different matter.

Thinking Beside

To paraphrase Eve Kosofsky Sedgwick (2003, 8), my project is not one of "thinking against" or "beyond"—that is, focusing on critiquing certain conceptual stances, theoretical frameworks, or claims. In the wake of the porn and sex wars of the 1970s and 1980s, a great deal of research on pornography has focused on criticizing other authors' premises and politics to the point that it seems that people are speaking past each other rather than trying to engage in productive dialog. Such speaking past seldom amounts to critique as a "form of intellectual work that requires engaging closely with a range of work"—in other words, critique as a labor of love (Ahmed 2008, 30). This dynamic is already encapsulated in denominators such as "antiporn" and "anti-antiporn" that position authors strictly in opposition to one another. Elizabeth Grosz (2005, 2–3) identifies thinking against as a form of dismissal that generates "defensive self-representation of counter-critique." Although my view of the possibilities of critical encounters is not as bleak as hers seems to be, I am wary of the defensiveness and binary logic that seems to accompany studies of pornography.

A similar dynamic of thinking against can be identified in new materialist critiques of the textual that frame the question as either one of affect or meaning or of matter or representation and that occasionally envision dramatic juxtapositions between their own stances and those they criticize. According to Hemmings (2005, 550), theorizations of affect recurrently "emphasize the unexpected, the singular, or indeed the quirky, over the generally applicable, where the latter becomes associated with the pessimism of social determinist perspectives, and the former with the hope of freedom from social constraint." This juxtaposition of the irregular and the regular, the new and the old, echoes the rhetorical trajectories of netporn criticism. Numerous scholars investigating new forms of sexually explicit interaction, content creation, and exchange online have argued for the need to detach digital practices from those characterizing pornography as commodities distributed in "traditional media" such as books, magazines, photographs, videos, and films (see Jacobs et al. 2007; Shah 2007; Dery 2007b, 2007c). My concern is that a categorical decoupling of new digital porn from the old and the analog—in terms of media technologies and also as cultural forms—implies that much earlier research on pornography would no longer matter in the new technological context of digitally produced, distributed, and consumed pornographies. On the one hand, technologies and media forms play a crucial role in and for experiences of pornography. They involve specificities and particularities that need to be accounted for and that are addressed at length in the chapters that follow. On the other hand, a structural division of digital pornographies indigenous to the Internet from "other pornographies" distracts attention from the fact that porn is markedly cross-platform and its products are distributed in various parallel media. Cottage-industry-style fetish Web sites for balloon sex, hippie, or vegan porn mark a departure from porn magazines or video porn, yet they may be part of publication networks that also include print magazines and video production and distribution (Albury 2003, 205). Gestures, acts, settings, and poses familiar from porn films and magazines have migrated to online platforms, troubling attempts at categorical distinction. I believe that considerations of transformation in and specificities of online porn need to be balanced with considerations of media history and genre if we are to understand how things have changed and what such transformations may effect.

My interests lie in something that could be called thinking beside, which Sedgwick (2003, 8) identifies with "a wide range of desiring, identifying, representing, repelling, paralleling, differentiating, rivaling, learning, twisting, mimicking, withdrawing, attracting, aggressing, warping, and other relations." When working on porn, much of what one writes has already been articulated in one form or another. However, given the contingency of porn (not least in its online incarnations), analytical approaches and theorizations need to be equally on the move. I also believe that research needs to try to address the moments in which words fail to grasp what resonates and moves us in our encounters with porn.

In the following chapters, I draw on the work of antipornography and anti-antipornography feminists, postcolonial scholars focusing on representation and identity politics, new materialist thinkers arguing for the "death of representation," theorizations of scopophilia, considerations of sensory attachments to images, netporn criticism, histories of literary pornography, and many other things. By doing so, I aim to make visible my debt to existing studies of pornography while also mapping out novel ways of conceptualizing the genre and its online variants. *Carnal Resonance* is about the modalities and power of online pornography—about sensory resonance, fleshy depiction, affective encounters, and the stakes involved in studying them all.

2   Bad Taste, Miasmic Forces, and the Ubiquity of Online Porn

"Internet Is for PORN!!"—a *World of Warcraft* machinima video based on the musical *Avenue Q*—was uploaded on YouTube in April 2006, and it attracted over 6.5 million views within its four first years of distribution. In the video, Trekkie Monster interrupts Kate's song about the wonders of the Internet by shouting "for porn" at strategic times. The message of Kate's enthusiastic lines—such as "The Internet is really really great," "There's always some new site," or "You can research, browse and shop / Until you've had enough and you're ready to stop"—are radically transformed by Trekkie Monster's recurring holler, "for porn": "Why do you think the Net was born?—for porn, porn, porn," the Trekkie Monster sings. The video is structured on the discrepancies between Kate's and Trekkie Monster's understandings of the medium. Applauding the speed and diversity of the Internet as an information and communication medium and claiming to hate porn, Kate accuses Trekkie of being a gross pervert because "normal people don't sit at home and look at porn on the Internet." To her surprise and horror, the "normal people" then stand up to praise the wonders of online porn in chorus: "All these guys unzip their flies for porn, porn, porn," "Grab your dick and double click, for porn, porn, porn!"

The video borrows from *Avenue Q's* juxtaposition of bawdy humor with fantasy characters modeled after the classic children's TV show *Sesame Street*, the "machinima effect" of *WoW* characters performing a light-hearted musical, as well as its take on the Internet as a medium. Like the musical, the video reiterates the piece of common knowledge that opened this book: not only is the Internet full of porn, but porn is its very reason for being (also Lillie 2004, 43–44). The video performs a coarticulation of the Internet and porn and connects the two in an intimate manner. Online porn becomes also firmly coarticulated and associated with male

Internet users: grabbing their dicks, the men are a source of disgust for Kate, as encapsulated in her exclamation, "EEEWWWWW!" For Kate, porn, its masturbating male consumers, and ultimately even the Internet become sources of disgust, whereas the "normal people" loudly express their appreciation for online porn.

A Killer Application

It is common knowledge that the Internet is full of porn and that Internet users spend considerable amount of time masturbating by their screens. At the same time, this is something of a public secret in the sense that most people (unlike the "normal people" in the *WoW* machinima video) are unlikely to mention their fondness for such activities when asked about their uses of the Internet. Instead, "normal" users tend to be marked apart from consumers of online porn, who are seen as addicts, potential perverts, or impressionable victims of the porn industry. The wide popularity and ubiquity of online porn means that the category of porn user is far from marginal or homogeneous, yet users are sheltered from exposure to porn (often in a patronizing manner). Google image searches, for example, are filtered by default as a "moderate" SafeSearch, and anyone who wants to access sexually explicit images needs to turn off the filter. SafeSearch, in its "strict" and "moderate" variations, filters out images that "contain pornography, explicit sexual content, profanity, and other types of hate content."[1] This phrasing equates sexually explicit images with hate, while the notion of safety in SafeSearch associates them with risk and danger. This rhetorical move is not unusual and reflects the position of online porn as ubiquitous yet effaced, perpetually popular yet seen as problematic filth.[2] Porn is also effaced from the listings of the most popular search terms that Google and other search engines freely publish. The Search Engine Guide listing the top five hundred search terms notes that, "Although this list is filtered, adult terms might still appear. Should you see any below, then we apologize in advance."[3] This disclaimer suggests that adult terms are potentially offensive, as are the actual search practices listed (and filtered). Ultimately, Internet users are offensive, and their activities have to be apologized for. At the same time, findings that children broadly search for porn and sex online make the news across national boundaries.[4] Although porn is recurrently marked off from the field of everyday media and its agents (consumers, producers, and distributors), such erasure is impossible to achieve because few media users are unfamiliar with porn. Furthermore, the volume and popularity of online porn have benefited pornographers as well as service providers, the companies that market broadband connections and develop software. The needs of the porn industry have driven the development of Web technologies and business practices such as hosting services, safe credit-card processing, banner advertisements, pop-ups, Web promotions, mouse-trapping (which prevents users from leaving a site), and streaming video technology (Filippo 2000, 125; O'Toole 1998, 285; Bennett 2001, 381; Perdue 2002; Lillie 2004, 47; Johnson 2010, 158–159). The revenues of the porn industry are difficult to estimate and isolate since porn is an integral part of the media economy rather than its isolated and alienated bastard relative (Paasonen et al. 2007, 6; Johnson 2010, 153–157).

Porn is a "killer application" as a form of content that is quick to migrate and easy to adapt to new technical platforms. It has been central to previous and parallel media technologies (such as photography and video) as content that is guaranteed to generate profit. As has often been observed, pornography is an engine driving developments in media technology (O'Toole 1998; Lane 2001; Filippo 2000; Perdue 2002; Jenkins 2007; also McNair 2002, 37–40; Maddison 2010, 26–27). This seems to have been the case with the Web since the needs and interests of the porn industry have played a crucial role in its development as a commercial and largely audiovisual medium. Throughout the 1990s, before the rise of online gaming and before eBay or Amazon were generating any considerable profits, pornography was recognized as the one successful form of online content production and distribution. It also seemed to suffer relatively little from the dot-com crash of 2000. Yet all this is difficult to tell when reading overviews on media history or the development of the Web. Ubiquitous as it is, pornography remains a source of concern and anxiety that seem to have grown in affective intensity as the Internet has become a mass medium and as its supply of pornographic niches, fringes, and styles has broadened over the past two decades.

The information society discourses and scholarly debates on online cultures have tended to regard pornography as an anomalous phenomenon or a social problem associated with deviance, addiction, the illogical, and lack of control (Cronin and Davenport 2001, 34; Patterson 2004, 104–105; Chun 2006, 98). The general aversion that porn is treated with reflects the values and norms attached to the Internet, its uses, and its users. After all, the figure of a rational, "information-intense" citizen who uses information networks for information retrieval and exchange—much like *Avenue Q's* Kate—is difficult to balance with the titillation and masturbatory pleasures associated with online porn (as mapped out by the chorus of "normal people" in the same musical).

In overviews on media history, pornography tends to be mentioned in fleeting references and occasional footnotes. The genre is rarely included in analyses of technological innovation or development, and it is commonly left as a topic of separate books (e.g., O'Toole 1998). Following this tradition, studies of Internet economy and history tend to pay little attention to porn (for exceptions, see Lane 2001; Perdue 2002). Until recent years, online porn was not considered a relevant, important, or appropriate research topic. To the degree that porn is "consigned to a space of supposed privacy and is not acknowledged as part of the cultural mainstream, it has become a kind of elephant in the room. We all know it is there, but its familiar poses, gestures, and secretions are often treated as unofficial knowledge" (Williams 2008, 300). These silences and aversions are understandable given the intensity of the political and religious passions in North American porn debates. This chapter addresses the affective dynamics of these debates by considering the overall low cultural status of pornography (in a range of media), the notions of filth and risk that are associated with it, and ways of envisioning its consumers.

The Internet has considerably affected the cultural visibility and accessibility of pornography. Since the 1990s, porn distribution has shifted online, and with the increase in broadband connections, consumers have anonymous access to a virtually endless range of pornographies from their homes, offices, and portable devices. The sales of digital video discs (DVDs) have suffered from the availability of streaming high-definition (HD) video, file sharing in peer-to-peer (P2P) networks, and tube sites modeled after YouTube, such as YouPorn, PornTube, 8Tube, or RedTube. Tubes feature amateur videos, clips, teasers, and trailers for commercial ventures uploaded by users and producers alike and sport thousands and thousands of new monthly uploads. The content circulated includes clips harvested from DVDs and other sites and those created by users themselves. The sales of porn magazines have suffered as porn images and porn stories can be accessed online in abundance. Although porn continues to sell, more porn is being produced than ever before, and images, videos, and texts accumulate, are rereleased in new formats, and are made available online on video sites, P2P networks, or specified platforms, its profitability has decreased, particularly for production companies. Ventures that focus on distribution (such as tubes and other video- and image-sharing sites) fare better in the current online economy.

The Internet is not "for porn" inasmuch as porn distributors and consumers make extensive use of the medium. Porn was popular in pre-Web bulletin board systems (BBSs) and Usenet newsgroups where people shared images scanned in from magazines and distributed their own homemade amateur porn (Mehta and Plaza 1997; Barron and Kimmel 2000; Mehta 2001; Dery 2007a; also Slater 1998). Nevertheless, the easy usability of the World Wide Web, especially since Netscape Navigator was introduced in 1994, marked a departure in the ways that porn was distributed and consumed.[5] The consumption of online porn requires no visits to specialty shops, and the range of products on offer is broader than any conventional shop or mail-order business could ever deliver (keep in mind "rule 34" of the Internet, which I opened the book with). Online porn consumption is anonymous and private, free material is available in abundance, and new niches and subcategories seem to surface almost overnight. No magazines or tapes need to be hidden away from the prying eyes of others. Rather, one needs to be concerned with the history, cache, and bookmarks of one's browser, files saved on hard drives, and Internet protocol (IP) addresses and credit-card numbers stored in databases.

Developments in Online Porn

Up to the mid-1990s, Web porn enterprises were small and independent, as in the well-known example of Danni Ashe's Danni's Hard Drive (figure 2.1). Established in 1995 and coded by Ashe, Danni.com initially consisted solely of pictures of the designer. As the site became popular and started generating millions in profit, Ashe hired new models before selling the site in 2004 (Mash 2004). Already established larger companies and brands, such as Playboy or Penthouse Media Group (which currently owns Danni. com), branched out online in the late 1990s (Perdue 2002, 63).

According to Wendy Chun, the success of online porn in the mid-1990s convinced "mainstream" U.S. corporations that users were willing to use

Figure 2.1
Danni's Hard Drive in 1996 (from http://web.archive.org)

their credit cards online, that online transactions could be safe, and that a great deal of profit was to be made with the Internet, which was still in the process of becoming a mass medium. In this sense, online porn fueled the dot-com craze, and other companies soon picked up on its strategies of operation and promotion. (Chun 2006, 78–79.) According to Chun's analysis, U.S. government regulation aiming at protecting homes and minors from the invasion of online porn actually pushed the commercialization of sexual content: "Verified credit cards, debit accounts, adult access codes, or adult personal identification numbers—all methods employed by commercial pornography sites in 1996—were named as adequate restrictions" for minors who tried to access online porn (Chun 2006, 110–111). Although credit-card verification was considered a "safe harbor," freely distributed content had no similar barriers of safety. Free porn or file sharing did not disappear, but age-verification systems—where users have to vouch for being over eighteen or twenty-one (depending of local legislation) and agree to watch adult content—became standard in the 1990s. Attempts at government regulation and the public attention gained by online porn "led to the pornographic gold rush" of the late 1990s (Chun 2006, 80).

The landscape of online porn evolved in the 1990s to consist of independent sites, Web rings, portals, link sites, and metasites that categorize subcategories, acts, preferences, and body styles. Users interested in free content have routinely moved from search pages and link sites to further directories and free-tour sections of pay sites, haunted by endless and often looping pop-up windows. These click-throughs have usually led to one commercial site or another. Browsing for porn involves a great deal of searching, waiting, redirecting, and balancing between the freely accessible (thumbnails, teasers, free tours) and material that requires membership fees. Before the spread of broadband connections, the aspect of waiting and delay was even more pronounced due to slow modem speeds, especially when accessing audiovisual content or high-resolution images.

Currently, a search for "gay porn," "mom porn," or "home porn" leads one to a Web directory displaying an abundance of thumbnail images to choose from and click on (such as http://www.gaymoviedome.com, http://mybestmom.com, and http://myhomeporno.com). Directory design and layout tends to be strikingly similar: there is no adjunct text to the individual images linking out from the site, and the sets of images (displayed side by side and on top of one other) are usually accompanied by sponsored links or banner ads. A click on a thumbnail image leads to another site offering a range of choices, and eventually one ends up on the free-tour section of a pay site. Click-throughs have been standard fare since the mid-1990s: they generate more traffic on the sites, which translates into advertisement income. The experience is different on tube sites, which provide free content without any click-throughs or registration requirement. Although free porn is not a novelty online, its easy accessibility and centralized distribution mark a departure from the porn cultures of the past fifteen years.

Relatively early on, sites began trying to catch the attention of those clicking through by profiling themselves through specific concepts and themes—such as sites dedicated to gonzo, blowjobs, cumshots, anal sex, large breasts, mature women, and interracial porn—and by also providing examples that catch the eye and invite curiosity. This has rendered all kinds of sexual niches and kinks considerably more visible and articulate. This visibility can also be attributed to the self-organization of sexual subcultures and their online forums. As Alex Halavais explains: "Even as we see an amazing fragmentation of interest in sexual material, we also find communities gathering around these sometimes narrow interests. . . . this extends to the most unusual fetishes. It takes very little to find 'the ultimate snow bondage and shivering site,' or a site dedicated to 'nostril exhales.' No matter how unusual the interest, there are likely others on the net seeking out company" (Halavais 2005, 21) (figure 2.2).

Sexual subcultures add to the palette of commercial porn, subcultural sites may charge membership fees to cover their bandwidth and server expenses, and niche sites may display extremities and peculiarities that remain too bizarre for the mainstream. Porn distributed in newsgroups and BBSs was difficult to index, whereas portals, metasites, search engines, links, and tags have facilitated, and indeed necessitated, the use of specific subcategories, titles, and terms for users to choose between (Chun 2006, 106). By offering novelties, sites both form new micromarkets and increase the visibility of fetishes and kinks that have previously been deemed highly marginal (also Bennett 2001, 384). This goes for the overall visibility of

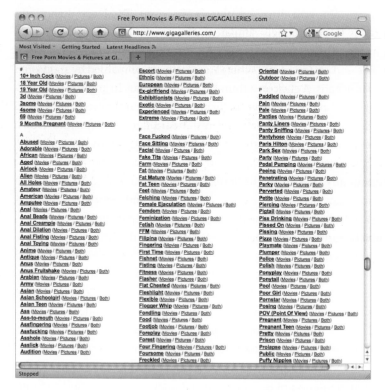

Figure 2.2
Niches named and identified at http://www.gigagalleries.com

hentai, pornographic Japanese anime that was considered too exotic for North American tastes to enter DVD distribution in the 1990s (Dahlqvist and Vigilant 2004) (figure 2.3); she-male and chicks-with-dicks porn featuring transgender bodies; and perhaps most notably, subcategories considered extreme (Sargeant 2006). Mark Dery (2007b, 135) notes that porn sites aim to grab the users "by the eyeballs" by showcasing images amazing in their novelty, eccentricity, or extremity. The use of online porn involves a considerable degree of browsing and searching in the hope of finding something novel and titillating (Patterson 2004). Extreme and eccentric imageries are a means to make users stop, stay, return, and explore the site. The bizarre catches the eye, attracts attention, and perhaps even persuades the visitor to become a paying site member.

In addition to site concepts, online-attention economy, and information architecture, the increase in niches and subcategories is connected to the expansive markets of commercialized sexual representation that have, at least since the 1990s, tried to cater to the likes and desires both "mainstream" and "deviant." As Brian McNair (2002, 206) notes, this has meant the entrance of marginal subcultures and oppositional movements into mainstream consciousness. At the same time, it has meant their

Figure 2.3
A hentai directory at http://www.pornhentai.com

appropriation and commodification. For example, handcuffs covered in fluffy pink fur are sold in women-friendly sex shops to soften the black and leathery aesthetics of bondage, domination, and sadomasochism (BDSM); depictions of mildly kinky sex appear in women's magazines; and popular forms of sex therapy encourage dress-up and power play. The mainstreaming of niches and kinks also gives rise to new boundaries and categories, as in the discursive boundaries separating the "acceptably kinky" from the "plain perverted" (Storr 2003, 208–211). Something of this kind is at play on "all-purpose" porn sites such as PornHub and Porn.com that have incorporated fringe interests and specialties into their menus (such as hentai, shemales, bondage, and squirting). By incorporating and appropriating subcategories, fringes, and subcultural styles as novelties, so-called mainstream sites aim to attract both new and returning users (Attwood 2007, 452–453).

So-called alt porn—also known as alternative and indie porn—became widely discussed in the late 1990s with its combination of the subcultural and the soft pornographic. Sites such as http://suicidegirls.com, http://www.burningangel.com, and http://gothsluts.com display female models with postpunk and Goth-style hairdos, make-up, tattoos, and piercings (see Magnet 2007; Attwood 2007; Cramer 2006) (figure 2.4). Arguing to counter the porn industry's images, ethics, and business practices, the sites offer nonconformist body styles (even if their performers are predominantly young and slim) and spaces for subcultural exchanges on music, sexuality, and lifestyle. Although the notion of alt porn involves a juxtaposition of mainstream and alternative, the boundaries between the categories are porous. The poses and gestures of mainstream porn are visible on alt porn sites (Cramer 2006, 136), and indie and alt porn sites have used tried and tested online business practices and developed them further through community features and other interaction possibilities that again have fed back to mainstream operating practices. When considering these interconnections, Florian Cramer and Stewart Home (2007, 165) call indie porn "the research and development arm of the porn industry." This may be an exaggeration, yet both mainstream and alternative sites are part and parcel of the digital economy in which subcultural production is "voluntarily *channeled* and controversially *structured* within capitalist business practices" (Terranova 2000, 39). The relationship between the two is one not of friction or juxtaposition but of complex interplay and interdependence.

Figure 2.4
Gothic alt porn at http://www.gothicsluts.com

Dualistic Categories

The Web is awash with pornographies that are resistant to most preconceived categories—sex with balloons, clowns (figure 2.5), furries (fictional
anthropomorphic animal characters), and plushies (stuffed toy animals);
porn engaging in environmental activism and displaying genderqueer bodies; and a broad variety of shoe and sock fetishisms. Under the rubric of
netporn, pornographies that are native or particular to online platforms
exhibit alternative body styles, desires, and preferences and detach themselves from the commodity logic of the porn industry (see Jacobs et al.
2007; Jacobs 2007). Scholars, artists, journalists, and activists who are interested in opening up the pornographic to surprises and repetitions with a
difference have been oriented toward grassroots-level porn experimentation rather than more established commercial ventures.

To the degree that novel, independent, amateur, and marginal pornographies question the notion of porn, they also enable points of exit
from debates on porn as either a bad or good object. This is no minor
concern, considering that popular, journalistic, and academic debates on

Figure 2.5
Catching attention at http://www.clown-porn.com

pornography remain heavily political—whether from conservative Christian, feminist, queer, or libertarian perspectives—in the wake of the North American porn and sex wars of the 1970s and 1980s. The binary logic of the debates—which were structured around the antipornography and anti-antipornography camps, moral panics, and debates on censorship and freedom of speech (Ess 1996)—continues to structure discussions on pornography on an international scale. Antipornography authors have been accused of using decontextualized BDSM imageries as evidence for their views on porn as a form of male violence against women (Rubin 1995, 245–246; see Dines et al. 2010 for counterarguments). Proporn, anti-antiporn, and prosex authors who approach the genre from a more positive angle have chosen independent, queer, and artistic projects that challenge gender norms, porn clichés, and the commodity logic of the porn industry. This has inspired discussions of online pornography as sexual self-expression that gives rise to alternative erotic imageries (e.g., Villarejo 2004; Dery 2007a; Shah 2007). At the same time, definitions of the alternative rely on and perform into being the mainstream as the otherness that is necessary for these activities, aesthetics, or preferences to be understood as departures from the norm.

Writing on alt porn and new sex taste cultures, Feona Attwood argues that they "attempt to define themselves through a variety of oppositions to mainstream culture—and especially mainstream porn—as creative, vibrant, classy, intelligent, glamorous, erotic, radical, varied, original, unique, exceptional and sincere compared to the unimaginative, dull, tasteless, stupid, sleazy, ugly, hackneyed, standardized, commonplace, trite, mediocre, superficial and artificial. In the process, a system of aesthetics is evoked as a form of ethics" (Attwood 2007, 449–450). The commercial and the noncommercial, the mainstream and the alternative continue to function as tools of categorization and evaluation at a moment when their boundaries are increasingly elastic (Attwood 2007, 453; Paasonen 2010a). Turning the question around, this book puts the mainstream under scrutiny to map out transformations that are taking place in the pornographic as it has shifted increasingly online. To do this and to understand the passions involved, it is necessary to consider pornography in the context of media history—to move back and forth between digital and analog media, the rhetorical and the material.

Miasmic Networks

Figures and percentages are tangible ways to approach online pornography, measure its quantity, and define its role in the online economy. Estimates of online porn's popularity vary considerably. The most easily accessible statistics on the volume and use of porn estimate that it comprises 12 percent of all Web sites and a quarter of all Web searches. These statistics are published mainly by sites that promote filtering software and are concerned with protecting children from exposure to pornography (e.g., http://www.safefamilies.org, http://healthymind.com, http://mykidsbrowser.com) (figure 2.6). Published on North American sites, some with conservative Christian undertones, these figures are probably inflated (cf. Slayden 2010, 54). Inflated figures feed anxieties about the ubiquity of pornography as well as consumer interest in filtering software. The sites suggest that porn is everywhere and then offer products for warding off its dangers and for protecting children (see Parikka 2005 on a similar discussion on viruses and antivirus software). Since these statistics are readily available, they are widely quoted by journalists and scholars (e.g., Phillips 2009, 196). The contagious and harmful forces of porn are equally associated with the spread of malware through porn sites, porn spam email, and P2P downloads. This risks not merely metaphorical (or mental) pollution but a powerful grab to take over computers. Hard drives can be erased, data stolen, and personal computers (PCs) turned into "zombie computers" that send out masses of spam email or even child pornography (see Haagman and Ghavalas 2005; Provos, McNamee, Mavrommatis, Wang, and Modadugu 2007).[6]

Online connections have come to present a risk of contamination that is fought with software promising to protect both home and children by keeping them safe and clean. This is already implied by the names of filtering software, such as Net Nanny, MyKidsBrowser, Safe Eyes, CYBERsitter, Pure Sight PC, and CyberPatrol. At the heart of this scenario of contamination lie the home (as a domestic space of safety, leisure, intimacy, and privacy) and the heterosexual family (which is perpetually at risk). If filtering software promises purity and safety, then pornography must stand for the filthy, miasmic, and dangerous. At the same time, contrary to the imagery of prowlers, perverts, and pedophiles who lurk online trying to reach and grab children who are accessing the Internet in their homes, the sexual abuse of children is perpetrated mainly by acquaintances and relatives. Rather than a safe haven, home can be a dangerous place (Maddison 2010, 29; also Stapleton 2010, 49).[7]

Figure 2.6
Keeping the kids safe and clean at http://www.mykidsbrowser.com

Notions of risk, danger, and contagion attached to online porn frame it as "a corrupting flood: an unrestricted abundance in the face of which people, and most especially children, require protection" (Maddison 2010, 23). Just as the uncontrollable aspects of networked communication are associated with porn, the Internet can be associated with the pornographic invasion of the home: the Internet comes to connote porn (Chun 2006, 81, 92–93). When arguments for censoring pornography are backed up with the view that sexual imagery may not only cause harm but is itself harm (Pally 1994, 71), the Internet has been defined as harmful unless properly regulated, screened, and filtered (an argument also repeated in discussions of Internet addiction). The corrupting flood of online porn holds miasmic qualities of contamination and defilement that children and the young are seen as particularly susceptible to (Kendrick 1996). This dynamic of filth, risk, and pollution is central to the discourse of moral panic that has figured in North American debates. As Giselinde Kuipers points out, porn debates in the United States are structured, on the one hand, on the principle of freedom of speech and, on the other hand, on the practices of filtering, prohibiting, and shielding. Moral panics play a central role in the "highly emotional and polarized debates, sustained media attention, the founding of organizations of distressed citizens, skewed and exaggerated representation of the nature and amount of pornography and sex on the internet and numerous attempts at government regulation" (Kuipers 2006, 390).

Moral panics envision and operationalize the figure of a child as innocent, in need of protection, and under the acute threat of moral pollution. Queer theorist Lee Edelman (2004) argues that the "image of the Child" is a cultural figure that encapsulates hopes about the future. When protecting the child, society is protecting a set of values that are related to reproductive futurism that mark sexualities deemed "deviant" as arenas of risk and harm. According to Edelman (2004, 12–13), the child is the object of compulsory empathy since what is at stake in protecting the child is the future of culture itself.

The Figure of the Child

The affective call to protect children from smut and harm online has longevity, and although its affective intensity oscillates (moral panics mark peak moments of intensity), it is far from fading. The exposure of children to materials deemed obscene has been associated with the Internet at least since the 1995 *Time* cyberporn cover article, which categorized over 80 percent of all photographs published online as pornographic. Since only few people were using the Internet at that time, the article created considerable anxiety concerning the new medium and shaped ways of understanding the exchanges that took place within it (Chun 2006, 77–80; Patterson 2004, 104–105; McNair 2002, 50). The article drew on Martin Rimm's undergraduate research article, "Marketing Pornography on the Information Superhighway: A Survey of 917,410 Images, Descriptions, Short Stories, and Animations Downloaded 8.5 Million Times by Consumers in over Two Thousand Cities in Forty Countries, Provinces, and Territories." Rimm (1995) focused on pornographic imagery that was circulated mainly in BBSs that he analyzed with "linguistic parsing software"—that is, he investigated descriptions of the images rather than the actual images. Consequently, the article makes claims about visual materials that the author has assumedly not seen. As critics of the study have pointed out, it tended to "inflate the prevalence of certain acts and underestimated others" (Mehta 2001, 696) while also suggesting that "in private, without fear of contamination or exposure, sexuality veers toward the deviant" and that "technology brings to the surface the perversity lying within us all" (Chun 2006, 84). Rimm's study suggested that the Internet is a medium in which porn abounds and in which pornographies of the extreme and deviant sort abound. The discourse of porn panic—as fueled by the *Time* article, a similar text published in *Newsweek* with the title "No Place for Kids?," and discussions surrounding the Telecommunications Act of 1996 (Chun 2006, 77)—rendered public online porn, its popularity, and its profitability (figure 2.7).

The cover image of *Time*'s 1995 cyberporn issue has been much discussed and for good reasons. The image features a young white male child, his face bluish white and lighted from below by a computer screen. Facing and looking at the viewer, the child's face expresses horror and fear: his eyes and mouth gape wide open in astonishment, and he has lifted his fingers off the keyboard, as if regretting a search term that he has just typed. This is an iconic image of childhood at risk, and the origins of the potential harm are clear. As Walter Kendrick articulates: "An androgynous, evidently hydrocephalic child stares out at you—you, the equally innocent soul who has just picked up *Time*. . . . This hapless cherub (who is all the more poignant for being very white indeed) has encountered the ultimate

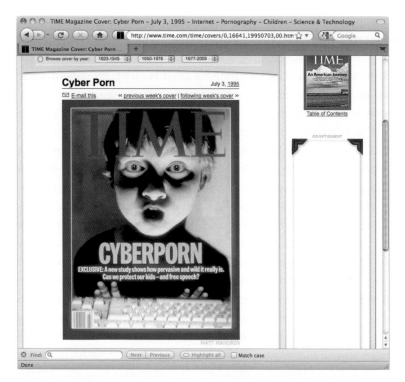

Figure 2.7
The *Time* magazine cyberporn cover of 1995 (http://www.time.com/time)

horror, sex, on the Internet" (Kendrick 1996, 254–255). This image of an endangered child is the epitome of a young person at risk, a figure that has been used for envisioning the dangers of pornography since the nineteenth century (Kendrick 1996, 262). This is "the Child who might witness lewd or inappropriate intimate behavior; the Child who might find information about dangerous 'lifestyles' on the Internet . . . the Child, in short, who might find an enjoyment that would nullify the figural value, itself imposed by adult desire, of the Child as unmarked by the adult's adulterating implication of desire itself" (Edelman 2004, 19, 21). Chun (2006, 90) identifies some unsettling undercurrents in this cover image: "The roundness of his open mouth evokes images of vagina-mouthed inflatable toys. Further, the screen's glare exposes wrinkles under the little boy's eyes, signs of premature aging, of a loss of innocence that belie his tiny hands and two front teeth." Depicted in a state of shock, the child in the cover image has gotten more than he bargained for. No longer unmarked by the adulterating implications of desire, the child has began to wear signs of adulthood, even to the point of resembling a sex doll himself. Having violated the boundaries of childhood by searching for adult content, his curious desire has now paved way for an acute risk of trauma.

Studies on online porn and children at risk have covered children's exposure to porn and the shapes and forms of child pornography (e.g., Freeman-Longo 2000; Jenkins 2001; Heins 2001; Thornburgh and Lin 2002; Levy 2002; Greenfield 2004; Kleinhans 2004; Maddison 2010). The top hits for a Google Scholar search for research articles on online porn tend to address children's (voluntary and involuntary) exposure to porn, online distribution of child pornography, and pedophile networking. These are certainly issues of concern, yet the terms *child* and *children* are strikingly featured in the top ten hits even when they are not typed. It should be noted that child porn is not readily available to regular porn users or even to avid porn watchers in any degree of abundance. I have not come across images or videos that I would identify as child porn during my years of studying online pornographies of all kinds. Teenagers and "barely legal" performers remain numerous, but children do not, for the reason that child porn tends to be distributed in closed communities attracting less outsider involvement. The recurring coarticulations of Internet, pornography, and children work to frame online pornography in highly partial terms of social harm, risk, and contamination.

Addiction and Abundance

A similar coarticulation occurs with the recurrent connections made between online pornography and addiction (Lillie 2004, 44; see Cooper, Putnam, Planchon, and Boies, 1999; Putnam and Maheu 2000; Griffiths 2000; Schneider 2000). Both articulations draw on the popular figure of porn as a corrupting force coming from outside to inside the home, "circumventing the normal family disciplinary structure, subjecting children and threatening to create deviant subjects" (Chun 2006, 87). Amazon.com's dramatic product description for Michael Leahy's 2008 book *Porn Nation*, for example, encapsulates the coarticulation of pornography with both addiction and American nuclear families under threat: "Pornography and sex-related sites make up nearly 60 percent of daily web traffic. For some of us, it's going on in our very own basements or in the den after the family goes to bed. Over twenty million Americans spend a good deal of their waking hours looking at pornography. And they won't stop, because they can't stop. At least not on their own. They are addicted."[8] Here, as in other examples of North American antiporn discourse, "porn takes on the mythic quality of a biblical plague: abundant, malevolent, mysterious—always ready to entrap the unwary, deadly in its spiral of addiction" (Maddison 2010, 19).[9]

Although the estimate in the blurb for Leahy's book—that pornography comprises up to 60 percent of all Web traffic—seems spectacular, it has been argued that due to the distribution of streaming video, pornography continues to take up as much as 40 to 80 percent of bandwidth of all Internet traffic (Thornburgh and Lin 2002, 72–73; Perdue 2002, 33–35). These estimates are from the early 2000s, and although the volume of video porn has not decreased since then, other developments—such as the increase in online gaming and the diversity of the files shared among users (including games, films, television series, software, and music)—should be considered. The more recent estimates of the volume of pornography exchanged in P2P networks vary between 1 and 18 percent of individual files, depending on the platform and the national and cultural context studied (Schulze and Mochalski 2009). Peer-reviewed studies offer moderate figures on the popularity and volume of online porn, particularly when contrasted with those offered by filtering software companies. Amanda Spink, Helen Partridge, and Bernard J. Jansen (2006) argue that pornography in 2006 comprised 3.8 percent of all Web searches compared to 16.8 percent in 1997 (also Jansen and Spink 2006). In contrast, filtering software sites suggest that the current figure is as high as 25 percent. There is little reason to doubt the perennial popularity of pornography across a range of media. The higher estimates of porn Web searches should nevertheless be taken with a grain of salt. The proportional volume of adult sites was considerable for a large part of the 1990s, but as the volume of other online content has since drastically increased, the relative volume of porn in terms of all Web sites has dropped (Coopersmith 2006, 3–4).

Like the freely available statistics on the popularity of online pornography, filtering software (which is marketed with the aid of such statistics) conflates practices like sex education, erotic poetry, and information resources for sexual minorities with pornography, equally filtering all of them.[10] The simultaneous inflation (of the volume of pornography) and conflation (of images, texts and practices under the umbrella term *porn*) is easily achieved since the methods of information retrieval and authentication are rarely explained or even mentioned. According to TopTenReviews, one of the sites offering statistics on online pornography, "Statistics are compiled from the credible sources mentioned. In reality, statistics are hard to ascertain and may be estimated by local and regional worldwide sources." This disclaimer is vague, yet the number of pornographic sites and the total volume of the porn industry on a global scale are difficult to estimate due to conflicting information: "gathering reliable data about web usage is inherently difficult because of its rapid growth, incomplete coverage of websites and poor research methodology" (Coopersmith 2006, 2; also Kuipers 2006). I would add vested interests to this list. The double movement of inflation and deflation at play in porn volume estimates are connected to political arguments and to notions of taste and value that equate porn with smut and filth and that necessitate agile acts of waste management.

Affective Dynamics of Class, Taste, and Distaste

As a media studies scholar, I understand pornography first and foremost as a marker of genre. Genre connotes agreement among producers, distributors, and consumers about the form and content of the product in question (Altman 1999). At the same time, what one person defines as pornographic is nothing of the sort for another. According to most thesaurus definitions of the term, pornography aims to sexually arouse its viewers and readers by depicting bodies, genitalia, sexual acts, and bodily fluids in attentive detail. The generic specificity of porn has been located in the images and texts themselves (what they depict), in authorial intentions (what they are intended to do and to be used for), in their effects (what they do), in audience interests (what is experienced as pornographic), and in combinations thereof. Notions of obscenity frame pornography in moral terms, casting it as immoral, damaging, and involving "prurient" (impure, lascivious, vulgar, bawdy) interests. In the United States, juridical definitions have seen porn as lacking in redeeming social or cultural value of the kind that can be found in art and erotica (Ross 1989, 181). Antiporn critiques have defined porn as a form of male violence against women, while the term *erotica* has been used to mark acceptable sexually explicit depictions apart from the unacceptable ones. In antipornography feminism, the erotic has been defined as "*sexually suggestive or arousing material that is free of sexism, racism, and homophobia and is respectful of all human beings and animals portrayed*" (Russell 2000, 48, emphasis in the original). By implication, pornography is seen to stand for the opposite—something that is indeed sexist, racist, homophobic, and void of respect for humans or animals. The euphemisms preferred by porn distributors and journalists, such as *adult content* or *erotic entertainment*, further complicate the picture, for "One person's pornography is another person's erotica, and one person's erotica can cause someone else to lose their lunch" (Kipnis 1999, 64; also McNair 2002, 43).

Writing on the histories of pornography, Walter Kendrick points out how *pornography* has been used as an umbrella term for a broad range of images, texts, and practices since the nineteenth century: "In 1857, 'pornography' meant something very different from what it now means; in 1755, 'pornography' meant nothing at all" (Kendrick 1996, 2). In Kendrick's view, a regulatory category such as pornography should not be conflated with any kind of textual particularity. For him, the term is a marker of low cultural status and taste rather than any inner dynamic, aesthetic, or "essence" that could be discovered in all things pornographic (also Attwood 2002, 94). At the same time, it should be noted that pornography is not merely a freely floating pejorative marker but also a historical and contingent popular genre that has evolved across a range of media. The genre involves idiosyncratic features—representational conventions, modalities, and aesthetics—as well as constant interplay with notions of "good" taste and sexual norms.

When it comes to aesthetic hierarchies and cultural norms, pornography has been defined through lack. Unlike erotica or art, porn is assumedly about mere showing and sexual arousal. Martin Kemp, cocurator of the 2007 Barbican show Seduced: Art and Sex from Antiquity to Now, defines the relation as follows: "The job of pornography is to do just one thing; and if it's doing anything else, it's not doing its job properly" (in Higgins 2007). According to this idea, the mode of the pornographic is limited to sexual arousal, it lacks any other kind of affective potentiality, and if it does have another potentiality, then it becomes corrupted in its original purpose. As Attwood points out, "It is the particularly explicit way in which porn depicts sex and bodies, its flaunting of boundaries, its perversity and its irredeemable 'lowness' that are often used to justify its condemnation."

Rather than mere subject matter, the low status of pornography relies on its "dirty, naughty, debasing and disgusting style or quality," as defined against more artful forms of expression (Attwood 2002, 96). Disgust is what is offensive to taste—whether in terms of palatability, aesthetics, or moral values (Miller 1997, 1). Contrary to the aesthetic thrills of the kind derived from art or erotica, porn dwells in the visceral and evokes gut reactions. There is more to the affective range and modality of pornography than meets the eye, however.

Pornography belongs to the lower tiers of popular culture (Kipnis 1999, 139–140), and this low status is intimately connected to its consistent focus on the lower regions of the body. As if echoing Attwood's remarks on pornography's low status as an issue of modality rather than subject matter, Susan Sontag, writing on literary pornography, sees the "singleminded way in which pornography addresses its readers and proposes to arouse them sexually" as "antithetical to the complex functions of literature." In Sontag's view, in pornography, considerations of language, experimentation, and artistic motivation are all subjected to carnal address, for "the aim of pornography is to inspire a set of nonverbal fantasies in which language plays a debased, merely instrumental role" (Sontag 2002, 39). This choice of words can be seen as symptomatic of the cultural status of pornography and its position in the hierarchies of literary, pictorial, and cinematic genres (which tends to be unambiguously low). It also invests pornography, its carnal registers, and its fleshy impulses with miasmic qualities to debase its means of articulation (whether this is language, image, film, or an online platform).

Starting Somewhere Different?

The discussions on pornography addressed in this chapter are predominantly Anglo-American. This is appropriate in the sense that North American perspectives have tended to dominate studies of both pornography and the Internet, and the regulatory practices of U.S.-based companies such as YouTube and Facebook (or their pornographic variations, YouPorn and Fuckbook) are of concern to a global audience. Given that my own background is Finnish and that the sex wars never really took fire in the Nordic countries (Kulick 2005), it has been challenging to negotiate my own position within the dynamics of the Anglo-American porn debates. When writing in English, my work is likely to be interpreted in this framework, even if this is not where I am entering the studies of online pornography.

The tensions and dynamics of feminist porn debates have been extensively discussed elsewhere, and I do not recap them here. Moreover, describing different stances, political investments, and premises concerning gender and sexuality means reproducing their binary logic. Such performative reiteration keeps the dynamics of the debate alive while also simplifying them. Complexities, nuances, and contradictions tend to evaporate in concise summaries of the political actions and academic debates that have taken place since the 1970s. Rather than lament the political splits that have formed and sedimented over these decades or bash antipornography feminists for their assumed lack of theoretical sophistication, I choose to shift the focus of the debate and start from somewhere different. For me, this "somewhere different" is a position of curiosity that does not presume mastery or categorical knowledge over what pornography is, what it does, or what it can do. Bearing in mind Jane Bennett's (2010, xv) remark that "If we think we already know what is out there, we will almost surely miss most of it," I decline to approach pornography as a cultural, social, or political symbol and metaphor and instead treat it as a historically evolved popular genre that, like all genres, includes certain conventions and stock features but is also volatile, contingent, and open to variation and change. This position—not assuming to know beforehand what one sets out to study, being open to surprises, and being willing to account for the complexity of the phenomenon at hand—is not a radical solution, but it is standard fare in feminist cultural studies.

For my purposes here, it suffices to say that antipornography feminists have opposed porn as a form of sexist oppression and male violence that is made by men and for men. Pornography has been said to reproduce patriarchal power relations and to contribute to the objectification of women (e.g., MacKinnon 1987; Dworkin 1989; Mason-Grant 2004; Jensen 2007; Dines et al. 2010). Other antiporn advocates oppose porn as being obscene and morally corrupt on religious and moral grounds and as being offensive in its subject matter and low cultural value—filth with the power to decay the moral fiber and family life of the nation (see McNair 2002, 49–60).[11] In contrast, anti-antipornography and prosex authors have defended First Amendment rights by resisting antiporn legislation, as well as by redefining pornography as a form of fantasy and antinormativity that is connected to radical sexual subcultures and sexual dissent (e.g., Rubin 1989, 1995; Duggan, Hunter, and Vance 1995; Califia 2000). Contrary to antipornography feminism's accounts of pornography as a singular patriarchal discourse with misogynistic effects, these critics have argued that "the sexually explicit materials called 'pornography' are full of multiple, contradictory, layered and highly contextual meanings" that are elastic and interpreted in contradictory ways (Duggan 1995, 7). Countering the antipornography discourse of porn as repulsive smut, queer and feminist prosex authors have also questioned the conditions under which sexual practices or images become marked as repulsive, shameful, or smutty to start with. Although individual contributions to the porn wars do not lack complexity or ambition, a tendency to frame pornography as either a good or bad object tends to resurface in conceptual and political takes on the genre. As the term *war* implies, opposing camps appear to be in an active conflict in which no peace agreement has yet been reached.

In both their critiques and defenses of the genre, people passionately debate pornography. They articulate disgust and pleasure, grief and empowerment. Their positions involve political, ethical, and moral concerns and arguments and also affective gut reactions, cultural hierarchies, and considerations of good taste. Antipornography writing has associated porn with feelings of hurt, sadness, anger, frustration, rage, fear, disgust, and nausea and with the adjunct political arguments of exploitation, sexism, racism, and misogyny that are seen as innate in and characteristic to pornography (Griffin 1981; Kappeler 1986; Dworkin 1989; Dines et al. 2001). Pornography has been read as both a symbol and an engine of male oppression, as in Robin Morgan's famous 1970s slogan, "Porn is the theory, rape is the practice." In this context, porn is seen as metaphorically, morally, and politically filthy.

Affect is an important analytical tool in studies of online pornography due to the visceral nature of both the imageries studied and the reactions they give rise to. Sara Ahmed's work on the circulation of affect helps to make evident that affects or emotions do not reside anywhere as such. Rather, they circulate among people, objects, and things, connect them to one another, draw them apart, and give them shape: "The relationship between movement and attachment is contingent," and "movement may affect different others differently: indeed . . . emotions may involve 'being moved' for some precisely by 'fixing' others as 'having' certain characteristics" (Ahmed 2001, 11–12). Such fixing is evident in ways of perceiving pornography as an object. Deemed disgusting, lowly, or sleazy, porn facilitates acts of distinction in which both people and other cultural products (art or erotica) are marked apart from it. This involves considerations both of cultural value and status and also of ways of imagining and figuring the producers and consumers of the cultural artifacts in question.

When designating something (or someone) as disgusting, we, according to Elspeth Probyn (2000, 131), "seek reassurance that we are not alone in our relation to the disgusting object. Through public statements, we want to distance ourselves from this uncomfortable proximity." This point has been made in anthropology for quite a while—that the "self and clean" of each social group or individual is founded on the exclusion of filth, "promoted to the ritual level of *defilement*" (Kristeva 1982, 65, emphasis in the original). Declarations that mark pornography as disgusting, filthy, and smutty are calls for others to witness our pulling away from the soiled and soiling object. This is a call for sociability, a means to "assuage doubts that we have not been contaminated, that we are not disgusting or shameful" (Probyn 2000, 131). The separation of "me," "you," and "us" from the disgusting object helps to draw a boundary against those who are willingly and actively engaging with such objects and, consequently, already contaminated by them. At the same time, the two modes of articulating disgust toward pornography—the first marking porn as something foul and offensive and the second marking it as something with the power to affect or soil other people—are not quite identical in the sense that the first grants the polluting object much more force than the latter does. For the sake of everyone, not just "the others," the disgusting object should be framed away from public view and consumption.

Articulations of disgust are central in the formulation of moral judgments, for "the disgust idiom puts the body behind our words, pledges it as security to make our words something more than *mere* words" (Miller 1997, 181, emphasis in the original). Moral judgments concerning pornography as disgusting can be backed up with and anchored in gut reactions that provide the articulations with a visceral sense of authenticity. According to Michael Warner (2000, 4), however, this is often a matter of moralizing rather than morality, for it involves dwelling in other people's shame. Hierarchies are built—between the self and others, the normal and the abnormal, the acceptable and the deplorable—by naming some people ("the others"), their orientations, and their acts as shameful or simply disgusting. All in all, the dynamics of deprecation, disgust, and shame are central to moral evaluations and moralizing concerning pornography. This same dynamic also works to support and reinforce the status of pornography as a forbidden and hence tempting and interesting kind of fruit (see also chapter 6).

Class and Disgust

Such aversion is guided by simple gut reactions or political objections and equally by class-specific notions of taste that are activated when viewers are faced with imageries that do not follow middle-class paradigms of appropriate taste and proper representation. Annette Kuhn (1994, 20–21), for example, notes how the pinup images she studied appeared "crude, tasteless and unimaginative in the extreme" and that "some degree of class-based aesthetic judgement may have been at work" in her distaste toward them. Such judgment and indignation orient research, create a position of distance (and distaste), and facilitate critiques of representation in the negative register. *Taste* is a highly carnal term in its connotations of palatability and unpalatability that are physical, instant, and unarguable (hence the truism that says there is no point in arguing over matters of taste). Since Pierre Bourdieu's work on distinction and habitus, taste has been largely discussed as a matter of class. For Bourdieu (1984, 190), taste is embodied— "a class culture turned into nature"—and is intrinsically bound up with social hierarchies and distinctions. Laura Kipnis (1999, 139) argues that the disgust exhibited by many feminists toward porn springs from a history of bourgeois desire to "remove the distasteful from the sight of society" in ways that imply a denial of the body, its orifices, and its desires. In her well-known reading of *Hustler*, Kipnis identifies the magazine in opposition to *Playboy* as representative of unruly taste and working-class distaste toward bourgeois culture and aesthetics.

Considerations of pornography as indicative of working-class sensibilities or cultures remain faithful to the cultural studies tradition of locating cultural resistance in the products of popular culture (cf. Penley 2004). By doing so, they risk giving rise to a partial understanding of the object at hand. According to various surveys of porn consumption, pornography is consumed by people from all tiers of society and occasionally even more so by those in the upper echelons of the middle-class with large amounts of disposable income (Buzzell 2005; Kontula 2008; McKee, Albury, and Lumby 2008). Sex work remains stigmatized on a global scale, but it may not be entirely correct to identify porn production as a working-class activity. Performers, directors, producers, and distributors have different backgrounds and social aspirations, and although the genre celebrates the low and nasty, this does not fully translate into a class allegory. At the same time, within pornography, class differences—like social categories more generally—are on spectacular display. It may be worth asking if associating the working class with the pornographic is a premise that orients research and brings forth particular kinds of interpretations. It can be argued that discussions on pornography give shape to, and to a degree even fix the class divisions that they postulate.

In everyday uses of language, terms such as *sick, filthy, perverse,* and *nasty* are used in unequivocally negative terms, but in pornography, they gain positive value as descriptive of hardcore action, extreme acts, and the female actors performing them. (The title of the video "Filthy Things Are Hot," rated fifth of all RedTube videos in April 2010, summarizes the point.) The spam email advertisements for the site Suck Me Bitch render this lexicon evident: "This is the downright meanest, nastiest site you'll ever find!," they exclaim and promise "freakishly messy cumshots," "More depravity. More filth. More cum. No Bullshit." The site logo of http://suckmebitch. com features a photo collage of women sucking penises, with ejaculate in their mouths and on their faces. The adjunct text further clarifies the matter: "Make her feel like a real woman. Just say the magic words . . . *Suck Me Bitch.*" The site title blinks for a maximum effect, and both the textual and the visual elements emphasize the roughness and realness of its "All amateur oral action" and "Raw & uncut real home blowjob videos." The introduction for a video featuring Allura (titled "Flea market fuck bunny") summarizes more of the site style and concept: "We found Allura down at the flea market. It's 2 pm on a tues. afternoon and this bitch is in the food court area, drunk off her ass—can you say LOSER!? . . . anyways, the friend she was with was being a total cunt because she didn't want to come back to our place. We told her to fuck off as you can see quite well in the 2nd pic. The rest as they say, is history! She was so drunk she could hardly keep my cock in her mouth without passing out!"

Allura appears drunk with heavy and almost closed eyelids. The thumb-nail images show her smiling with a bottle of beer, the camera man flipping her friend the finger, Allura displaying her anus and performing fellatio. In the largest image placed in the middle of the image gallery, she poses with her eyes closed and semen dripping from her mouth. Making abundant use of point-of-view shots, the site places the viewer squarely at the center of action from the perspective of the male performers. The intro defines Allura as a drunken loser who hangs out at a flea market food court drink-ing beer. Allura is consuming goods marked as lower class (second-hand products and beer), inappropriately and unfemininely drunk early in the afternoon, and easily persuaded into sex with strangers. She is obviously not respectable, which Beverley E. Skeggs (1997, 2005) has identified as the marker of class and gender in the British context. (As the video makes evident, Allura speaks with a British accent.) According to Skeggs (2005, 967–968), white working-class women demarcate the constitutive limit of national propriety. Associated with excessive femininity, binge drinking, and moral decay, they fail to meet the middle-class criteria of respectability, so the middle-class is able to maintain "the position of judgement to attri-bute value, which assigns the other as immoral, repellent, abject, worthless, disgusting, even disposable": "Attributing negative value to the working class is a mechanism for attributing value to the middle-class self (such as making oneself tasteful through judging others to be tasteless)" (Skeggs 2005, 977). Such a dynamic is recognizable with Allura, who, as a "flea market fuck bunny," is marked as both immoral and used goods—as out of control and out of order. As if echoing Freudian explanations of (male het-ero)sexual desire as requiring the degradation of its object, Allura and the sexual acts she performs are tied to the terminology of sickness, filth, and dirt. "That's right motherfuckers! This is the downright meanest, nastiest site you'll ever find!," Suck Me Bitch enthuses. Excessive behavior, sexual excess, and excessive femininity all conflate in a figure that connotes excess as residue, waste, and filth.

Considering pornography in a psychoanalytical framework, Elizabeth Cowie (1993, 134) argues that its attraction relies largely on its status as something that is forbidden and that "transgresses the limits and exceeds 'the proper.'" Pornography is thus "characterized not only by the now con-ventionally acceptable transgression of barriers of race and class, but by the transgression of the barriers of disgust—in which the dirty and execrable in our bodily functions becomes a focus of sexual desire." In the lexicon of porn sites, transgressions of social categories and hierarchies are accompanied by a discourse of filth as a kind of contagious, miasmic affective force that pulls people to the other side of the proper and the respectable. Similar rhetoric is also at play in antiporn discourses that mark porn as dangerous, plaguelike, and uncontrollable, which finds easy support from the terminologies of porn itself. When interpreted as instances of verbal aggression toward women, the ubiquitous use of terms such as *slut* and *bitch* work to support views of porn as violent (e.g., Bridges 2010, 46–47).

Within the pornographic, the affective forces of filth become positive and titillating. Things called *depraved*, *nasty*, and *sick* equal hardcore action with no holds barred, while terms such as *slut* or *bitch* may in fact connote a talented performer. Sanna Härmä and Joakim Stolpe (2010, 115) point to this in their discussion of "behind the scenes" videos where new female porn talent can be introduced by statements such as, "I've heard good things about her. She's supposed to be a dirty filthy little whore." Such uses of hyperbole are fundamentally reflexive and inseparable from the broader discourse of filth and scum associated with pornography. Porn sites, videos, and scenarios are promised to be dirty, excessive, depraved, nasty, and disgusting by default—and therefore exciting. The more elaborate the marks of embodied differences and the more excessive its terminology of nastiness and filth, the more hardcore the representation seems to become (see also chapter 4). In fact, the language used to describe hardcore porn is regularly "harder," "nastier," and "more vile" than the images it is attached to in an attempt to enhance their effect. Consequently, rather routine acts can be invested with the aura of extremity (Tyler 2010, 61).

On the interrelations of disgust and sexual desire, William Ian Miller (1997, 127) notes that Freud saw male heterosexuality as structured on "the desire to indulge disgust, to roll in the mud so to speak." In this framework, desire and disgust are inseparable from one another and involve the boundaries between clean and filthy and between the upper and lower classes (Kalha 2007a, 97). Miller points out that Freud's observations were culturally specific and particular to the Viennese upper middle class of the early twentieth century, where bourgeois men desired working-class young women (who were already "lower" yet young and vulnerable enough to be polluted) and prostitutes (who were already representative and even embodiments of the polluted), bourgeois women were assumed frigid, and working-class men were feared to have illegitimate desires toward bourgeois women. Upper-middle-class men "lowered" themselves by engaging in intimate interaction with "lowly" women or by degrading and polluting them (Kalha 2007a, 98–99). Freud's narrative of sexuality, marked by disgust and shame, is centrally about class (Miller 1997, 130–131).

Pornography began to evolve as a popular, mass-produced genre in the eighteenth century, when inexpensive print technology facilitated the success of pornographic books, leaflets, and images (e.g., Kendrick 1996; Hunt 1996). As media technologies evolved, porn branched out to new platforms, such as photography, magazines, film (in 16mm, 8mm, Super 8, and 35mm formats), video, and digital production and distribution. Its styles, features, and conventions have undergone considerable transformations, but certain themes—such as the transgression of social boundaries and sexual taboos or offenses against various codes of good taste—seem to persevere. Some historical, deeply Freudian tensions of disgust, shame, and desire seem to be rooted in the genre. The presence of such historical echoes might explain some of the vehemence with which notions of symbolic filth and the taboo are circulated in contemporary porn, as well as the ways in women tend to stand for the filthy whereas notions of scum do not generally sediment onto straight male bodies. As Ahmed (2004, 90–91) notes, affect sticks to some bodies, objects, and signs while it slides over others. Such sticking and sliding, again, results from historical associations between bodies and signs. It is a matter of both materiality and signification and is inseparable from the fabrics of culture and society. In other words, affect does not merely flow freely but sticks and clusters following historically constructed, yet contingent boundaries and fault lines.

Freudian echoes are explicitly anachronistic in tapping into current social categories and hierarchies, which, in their hyperbolic pornographic depictions, have not experienced drastic changes over a century. I do not see such echoes as telling of some general "structures" of male heterosexual desire, however. In fact, I find the notion of gendered structure of desire rather nonsensical in its attachment to a binary notion of difference (male and female) that grants no fluidity within the categories. The modalities and conventions of porn do not mirror male heterosexuality as some definable, monolithic point of reference (because no such point of reference exists). The association of sex with dirt and degradation is, as Marcia Pally (1994, 72) puts it, "strange reasoning," and identifying it with the desires of heterosexual men is even stranger. Different things turn different people on, as any online session spent browsing through the available subcategories of online porn is likely to show. Rather than mirroring the dynamics of male heterosexual desire, Freudian porn echoes construct a dynamic of fantasy and arousal based on transgression that tends to stretch out toward novelties and extremities. By recurrently transgressing the boundaries of social categories, good taste, and disgust, porn works to construct and reiterate them. Some of these boundaries are explicitly anachronistic, others are more or less like self-parody in their excessiveness, while yet others seem difficult to decouple from social hierarchies and relations of power. Such anachronisms give rise to temporal folds in which an early twentieth-century bourgeois sexual dynamic, with its classed deferrals and reflections of desire, is presented as seemingly endless in its expressions and variations. These folds are embedded in the hyperbolic and excessive aesthetics of pornography as its easily recognizable ingredients. Interpreting them literally as representations, reflections, or symbols of social power relations (or, say, of heterosexuality) diverts attention away from these genre-based specificities and the affective dynamics involved.

I believe that it is necessary to reconsider the question of taste and pornography as not merely indicative of social hierarchies and class divisions. First, attitudes toward porn vary across (as well as within) national boundaries and social categories (such as age, gender, profession, and religion). Although connected to social class, such differences cannot be simply reduced to it. Second, the fleshy aesthetics of pornography and the gut reactions that it gives rise to seem to operate on the level of affective, pre-cognitive sensations and orientations—the realm of carnal resonance and gut feelings. Following Bourdieu, gut reactions can be seen as exemplary of embodied and internalized class divisions. It can, however, be asked whether taste—a highly physical term that connects the gustatory with preferences over style and thereby evokes strong bodily reactions—should be considered simply an effect of social distinctions. In her work on food and taste cultures, Probyn (2000, 27) argues for less predetermined analyses of taste that also account for transformations taking place in things experienced as "tasty," of good taste, or distasteful. In her view, tastes do not merely reinforce social identities such as class positions but also work to set them in motion, and this motion cannot be reduced to any given identity categories (Probyn 2000, 27–32). Such unpredictability is also central to

Warner's (2000, 185) discussion on pornography as facilitating surprising encounters with forms of sexual desire. Pornography introduces new sexual practices, preferences, and routines. Although some of these may amount to pleasurable surprises, others are far less appealing, and yet others may be experienced as unequivocally repulsive.

Drawing on Silvan Tomkin's affect theory, Probyn investigates disgust and distaste as simultaneously primal and social. Disgust involves overwhelming closeness—the proximity of sight, smell, and touch: "the overwhelming horror that the disgusting object will engulf us, has been too close to things of which we prefer not to speak" (Probyn 2000, 131). Articulations of distaste toward pornography are associated with such risks of miasmic contagion. Disgust can be seen as bound up in social hierarchies and distinctions, but such a conflation of taste and distaste with class risks losing sight of what is being experienced as disgusting and for what reasons—for surely not all distaste springs from the same source. If feminist critiques of pornography are reduced to general notions of moral disgust or bourgeois repulsion toward the "lowly" and the embodied, it becomes much more difficult to account for the political and ethical considerations at play. Feminist objections to pornography often see the genre as disgusting due to its working practices and modes of depicting sexuality. In other words, the gut reactions that porn evokes in some scholars may be inseparable from, originate from, or be intensified by political and ethical concerns (cf. Ngai 2005). Defining this as middle-class prudishness is a means of resisting critical engagements. Negative criticism need not be the default mode of such engagements, but neither should critique be foreclosed as mere prissiness.

Active Users versus Men in Dirty Raincoats

Some discussants see pornography as a miasmic force contributing to the general sexualization of culture, and others see it as harmful to minors. Yet others identify pornography with the transgression of social norms and conventions, alternative bodily aesthetics, and carnivalesque subversive potential (e.g., Kipnis 1999; Jacobs et al. 2007). Mark Jancovich (2001) points out that much of the recent research on porn focuses on examples that are seen as "transgressive" but simultaneously construes mainstream porn as that "where nothing interesting ever happens." According to Jancovich, such distinctions come with classed underpinnings: "defined against an authentic folk culture on the one hand, and a radical avant-garde on the other," the mainstream is ultimately made to signify the middlebrow and the petit bourgeois. This line of critique draws on a tradition of mass-culture critique that has been popular since the 1950s. In this framework, mainstream porn connotes the culture industry in its standardized, mass-produced, and passively consumed products that are representative of the logic of sameness (cf. Adorno 2001, 100–104, 163–164). The principles of mass-culture critique—heavily debated for decades within cultural studies and media theory for its totalizing tendencies—seem ingrained in investigations of media culture, its producers, and its audiences. Mass-culture critique is aligned with the longer tradition of "elite paternalistic" high-culture critique in that both view pornography "as one symptom of a broader malaise produced by consumer capitalism" (McNair 2002, 50).

The porn consumer is generally perceived of as different from consumers of serious culture or mainstream media in his (for this stereotype is very much gendered male) motivations, interests, and impressionability. When addressing both pornography and media violence, researchers, journalists, and other commentators use the so-called third-person effect. That is, the people who investigate these genres rarely think that media images have the power to affect them personally. Instead, others—children, the young, and the less educated—are seen as susceptible to their impact, risk being addicted, and are in need of protection (Davison 1983; Scharrer 2002). In debates on pornography, the third-person effect resonates with cultural hierarchies and notions of value. Attwood (2002, 96) points out how "the great artist and the connoisseur whose appreciation ennobles him" is "contrasted with the porn baron and his audience of men in dirty raincoats, motivated by lust and susceptible to direct 'effects.'" When writing on the histories of pornography and media technology, Laurence O'Toole (1998, 298) evokes a similar cultural stereotype of "dirty, raincoated tossers, of hairy-palmed no-mates, of waistrels, sexist dogs, misogynists" that effectively prevents people from admitting to porn consumption in so-called polite company. These classifications and third-person effects are connected to the assumption that low cultural forms—for example, body genres such as porn and horror—lack complexity. As Kipnis (1999, 177) has it, "Pornography isn't viewed as having complexity, because its *audience* isn't viewed as having complexity."

To the degree that pornography is culturally associated with the lower classes, its consumers become a projection of fears concerning "brutish, animal-like, sexually voracious" lower-class men, their desires, and their actions (Kipnis 1999, 175). Contemporary media features more than one stereotype of a porn consumer (Boyle 2010, 144), but there is some historical evidence to back up this argument. Until the eighteenth and nineteenth centuries, sexually explicit representation was accessible only to a wealthy male elite, and as both Kendrick and McNair both point out, the expansion of visual pornography that is accessible to the lower classes meant expansion in acts of regulation and policing:

> Growing state censorship of pornography accompanied the spread of a view of all lower classes, lesser-educated individuals as akin to children, unable to regulate and control their own morality and behaviour, and thus in need of guidance from their socio-economically superior, better-educated, almost always male overlords. Women and children were seen as especially at risk from pornography—a view of the innate victimhood of these groups continues to underpin most pro-censorship opinions to this day, wherever on the ideological spectrum it sits. (McNair 2002, 51)

In discussions of online porn, references to the third person (men in raincoats, addicts, children, and the otherwise susceptible) that are familiar from studies of mass media and their assumedly passive audiences clash with notions of Internet users as active discussants, navigators, and content producers, as have been articulated since the early 1990s. When juxtaposing the uses of the Internet with those of mass media (such as television), the two perceptions remain mutually exclusive on a fundamental level. Discrepancies in identifying media users (and not merely the media) explain some of the dividing lines in studies of online porn—between the predictable, the bulky, and the potentially novel.

Porn Consumer 2.0?

Since the dot-com crash of 2000, site concepts and business models have been increasingly centered on user-generated content, social media, and community platforms. Discussed under the rubric of Web 2.0, a term made familiar by Tim O'Reilly (2005), this shift has involved the increasing importance of wikis, blogs, social software, video-hosting sites, networked collaborations, and distributed forms of production. Although media scholars have challenged the view of media audiences as passive consumers (as implied by traditions of mass culture critique) for some decades and Internet users have been seen in fundamentally active terms almost by default, the 2000s have witnessed a redefinition of Internet users as content producers, discussants, lobbyists, and lay experts. The term *Web 2.0* has been used to refer to a shift in the traditional boundaries separating experts and professionals from laymen and amateurs—or media producers from media audiences (Bruns 2008; Jenkins 2006a, 2006b). So-called user-generated content was equally central to Web 1.0 in the shape of online journals, personal home pages, chat rooms, webcams, multiple-user domains (MUDs), multiple-user domains, object oriented (MOOs), bulletin board systems (BBSs), and newsgroups where users set up forums and others joined and further developed them. In other words, online cultures have, from their very early days, been participatory and user-generated (also Bruns 2008, 3–4).

It took little skill in hypertext markup language (HTML) to set up a site in the mid-1990s, and webcams, which were inexpensive and simple to operate, could attract surprising groups of users (JenniCam was one of the most famous). Careers like Web design came to be understood as professions only after the mid-1990s (Kotamraju 1999). As Lisa Gitelman (2006, 15) points out, the categories of the consumer (or user) and producer can be notably indistinct when so-called new media are still in formation. They tend to become defined as the medium is increasingly commodified and tied to the structures of media economy. Although Web users have always been content producers, the medium has gone through considerable transformations since the mid-1990s that are technological (what could be done on and with the Web), economic, and conceptual (how content has been defined as commodities and forms of work) in character. After the dot-com crash, content production came to be seen less as a profession and more as an arena of user engagement: users would create and modify content for free and for the fun of it (see chapter 3 for a discussion of affective labor). Reframing users as content producers says less about the users, their practices, and transformations therein than it does about transitions in site business concepts and media strategies. I agree with Megan Boler (2008, 6), who defines the term *Web 2.0* as descriptive of "the corporate resonance of the technology and its users" rather than of the shapes of technology or its uses. Although these have also undergone fundamental transformations, this is not a matter of sudden disruption or upgrade.

For Ken Hillis (2009, 3), "Web 2.0 operates as a branding strategy: it asserts that new forms of social networking applications are better able to facilitate new forms of online commerce than are the established '1.0' utilities with proven commercial potential." By doing so, this branding strategy frames new applications and solutions as more advanced variations of what already has been. It also presumes users that are more active, networked, and engaged in the production of culture (including cultures of porn) in the framework Web 2.0. The term *porn 2.0* has been coined to describe the centrality of community features and user-generated content in and for online porn (Jenkins 2007; Arvidsson 2007; Mowlabocus 2010). All kinds of porn sites aim to engage their members through community features. On alt porn sites, users can interact with each other as well as with models, while performers can make public their thoughts or lifestyle preferences in blogs, profiles, and postings (Attwood 2007). In a more visible and discussed line of development, users upload content themselves. Such platforms include forums crafted by users (as has been the case on online platforms since the 1980s) and amateur sites featuring user submissions and tube sites (e.g., YouPorn, RedTube, PornoTube, XTube, 8Tube, TubeGalore, DirtyXXX-Tube, and many more).

Sharif Mowlabocus (2010) notes that community functions—such as feedback and rating options—are central to the dynamics of video-sharing sites and people's engagements with them (also Van Doorn 2010; Jenkins 2007). At the same time, the number of comments left or ratings made does not reflect the number of views. Most users are just looking, whereas those who also upload videos and otherwise engage with the site are more likely to use its interactive features. Video-sharing platforms are examples of an affective media economy in which the ideal consumer is perceived as being "active, emotionally engaged, and socially networked" (Jenkins 2006a, 20). In addition to engaging with tubes, users can use porn wikis (e.g., http://wikiporno.com/wiki/Free_Porn_Directory), search for content with a specialized search engine or directory (http://booble.com), visit movie databases (http://iafd.com), and visit versions of adult Facebook (http://www.fuckbook.com, http://www.gayfuckbook.com). Notions of Web 2.0 have become so engrained in the production and distribution of online porn that studies of video porn and its consumers or porn magazines and their viewers fail to capture much of contemporary pornography.

Contrary to the figure of men in raincoats, the Web is awash with sites that combine pornography with lifestyle and invite porn users to share their preferences, likes, dislikes, and porn images and videos of themselves. This figure of an active, social, and reflexive porn consumer is difficult to balance with the imagery of addicts or "hairy-palmed no-mates." Although some active users have turned into producers, users mostly lurk and look rather than share videos or discuss them. Interacting, rating, or uploading files is a possibility but is not the default form of engagement. These two figures of porn consumers (active versus passive, content producers versus addicted consumers) are mutually incompatible, while the media they use also become juxtaposed as "passive" (magazines, books, VHS, DVD, or Blu-ray) versus "(inter)active" (online platforms). Such juxtaposition of media forms and their consumers is misleading and also reflects the ideological premises associated with studies of so-called new and old media. Porn consumers using VHS or DVD are as articulate about what makes "good pornography" as are discussants on online forums (Albury 2003, 201; McKee 2006; McKee et al. 2008). People are addicted to porn online and offline, amateur porn production has a lively history predating the Web, and the same people access and use pornography in a range of media (DVDs, magazines, and online platforms are not mutually exclusive).

At the same time, online porn consumers remain objects of moralizing statements that claim that users are soiling themselves and simultaneously putting their computers at the risk of malware and other disruptions in the networked flow of information. As Jussi Parikka (2005) points out, "moralizing judgments are targeted against users who copy pirate games, download software from dubious BBS's or net sites, or, as is often mentioned, visit pornographic websites." These "unhealthy" or plain "dangerous" users risk the safety of the network and make it necessary for others to engage in acts of filtering and to invest in antivirus software.

The Elasticity of the Mainstream

The uses and experiences of pornography are embedded in economic, material, aesthetic, social, and technological frameworks that vary drastically by media type, online forum, and media format. Amateur image swapping one-on-one differs from distributing the same images in newsgroups, uploading them to an amateur porn image gallery, or using them in a personal profile of an adult dating site. The Internet is no mere "platform" or "container" for pornography that takes up the functions of magazines, DVDs, or VHS tapes (although it does also do this). Rather, "sexual desires are being mediated through the pleasures of the technology itself, and the particular fantasies it has to offer" (Patterson 2004, 119). The attraction of online porn is about the porn and the Internet as a medium as well as about the ways in which the two intermesh in the possibilities and promises of interaction, anonymity, realness, and transparency. The interaction of bodies, interfaces, and network technologies gives rise to particular kinds of expectations, experiences, and resonances (Lillie 2002, 37–41; Uebel 1999; Reading 2005).

At the same time, arguments on the specificity of online porn need to be considered critically, given that it comes in all shapes and forms. In addition to pornographies that are indigenous to online platforms, a considerable volume of porn is repurposed in several parallel media, including DVDs, video-publishing platforms, image galleries, mobile Internet applications, and print. Peer-to-peer networks—where users upload, seed, and download files outside organized distribution systems—have challenged the conventional meanings of media usage and perhaps even the very notion of porn (Phillips 2009). Yet what is exchanged in such networks exemplifies not only the novel, independent, and amateur but to a far larger degree professionally produced porn that has been originally distributed on DVD or VHS or on pay sites (Lillie 2004, 58). This was already the case with Internet relay chat (IRC) and newsgroup exchanges (Slater 1998, 99). Digital and networked technologies have opened up new forms of circulation and exchange while also incorporating and appropriating familiar aesthetics, commodity forms, and practices of usage. Porn spam email, for example, represents new forms of distribution, yet the experiences it offers and the services it promotes are difficult to identify as radically rupturing the conventions of porn. As mentioned above, all kinds of novel pornographies are defined and marked against the denominator of the mainstream as the quintessentially mass cultural (dull, predictable, bulky, and passively consumed). At the same time, the notion of the mainstream itself has been left with little analytical attention. What is this thing called "mainstream commercial heteroporn"?

A person who is inexperienced with online pornography might type in the URL http://www.porn.com. This might be one of the most expensive domain names in use. (The current record holder, www.sex.com, was sold in 2006 for the reported price of $14 million.) The user who accesses www.porn.com would find a site described as "Porn—Free XXX Tube Videos and DVDs & Porno Pics" (figure 2.8). Porn.com offers access to images, videos, and DVDs in forty-six different categories (at the time of writing, these included some 2.5 million images and 32,000 videos), live sex cams in forty-eight categories (each of these offering from one to over four hundred camera sites to choose from), some 20,000 porn star profiles, as well as exclusive sites and content available to paying members. Porn.com can be browsed for free, but only thumbnails of images and short teasers and trailers of the videos are accessible without a membership fee. It is large and glossy in style. Given the accessible URL, general focus, considerable volume of content, and commercial nature, it is fair to consider Porn.com a mainstream porn site.

When looking closer at the categories and subcategories found at Porn.com—including "Softcore," "Blowjobs," "Anal sex," "Insertions with food," "Dwarves," "Squirting," and "Uniforms"—the mainstream starts to seem nebulous. In fact, mainstream online pornography opens up as an endless

Figure 2.8
The subcategories of http://www.porn.com

register of niches, fringes, styles, and preferences in terms of sexual acts, fetishes, body shapes, ethnicities, ages, and props. Some of these (such as "Anal sex," "Blowjobs," "Big cocks," "Housewives," and "Cum shots") are better represented than others (such as "Anime," "Escorts/hookers," "Pregnancy," "Food fetishes," and "BDSM"), but the mainstream involves a plethora of options to choose from and navigate between. A relatively minor category such as "Uniforms" (1,640 videos in total) gives rise to an entire taxonomy of subcategories—"Business Suit" (466), "Cheerleader" (197), "Fireman" (7), "Maid" (99), "Maintenance" (0), "Medical Wear" (73), "Military" (101), "Nurse" (177), "Police" (51), "School" (423), and "Sports" (46). This range reflects both the particularity of sexual preferences and also the ways in which some uniforms (cheerleader, school, and nurse) have been more "pornified" than others (sports and medical wear) through their ubiquitous presence in pornographic scenarios. (At the same time, the overwhelming popularity of business suits remains puzzling.)

The visibility and clear articulation of subcategories facilitated by indexing and categorization provide users with faster access to the imageries of their choice and give them a plethora of brands and alternatives to choose from. Browsers are not used merely to search for *porn, nudity,* or *sex*—even if these terms do have perennial popularity among the most popular search terms. Users search for specific acts, scenarios, shots, and styles—such as mothers I'd like to fuck (MILFs, i.e., mature women), messy cumshot galleries, barely legal teens, interracial orgies, and sock fetishism. Porn.com is representative of the mainstream as commercial, bulky, and catering primarily to a male heterosexual market, but it also points to an acute need for more nuanced definitions of the notion. What is at stake is not only the elastic and ephemeral nature of the alternative and the mainstream but the very notion of pornography—what it encompasses, how it can be defined, and how it is experienced.

3   Amateur Wives and the Attraction of Authenticity

The transformations effected by Web distribution and digital production tools on pornography—its aesthetics, its economical underpinnings, and the experiences and resonances that it facilitates—cannot be understood apart from the shifting notions of amateur and professional. What was formerly hierarchical is currently elastic. As pointed out in the previous chapter, amateur production videos and images shared online have challenged the dominant role of commercially produced porn and contributed to decreased profits for the industry. The notion of active Internet users who busily produce content on Web 2.0 platforms has also challenged the familiar stereotype of porn consumers as passive addicts. This chapter investigates the elasticity of the categories of the amateur, mainstream, professional, and commercial by considering reality and gonzo porn, amateur videos, photos, and stories. The examples of amateur porn addressed can be seen as mainstream in the sense that they have been harvested mainly through Web directories, link-through paths, and metasites—the sites that are most easily found when searching for amateur material. Other examples represent well-known amateur production and spam email advertisements.

From Amateur to Gonzo and Reality

The history of amateur porn includes the written word, photography, home movies, and video, and it has remained relatively invisible (outside aficionado circles) due to challenges of distribution. Cameras were first marketed to middle-class households in the late nineteenth century. Amateur markets broadened into 16mm cameras in the 1920s, 8mm the following decade, and Super 8 in the 1960s (Slater 1991; Zimmermann 1995). Producing porn on film presents specific challenges since the images and films need to be sent out for developing, and they are subject to unwanted outside observation. For this reason, Polaroid cameras, which had self-developing film and were relatively expensive, became popular in the production of amateur porn in the 1960s, the same decade that witnessed the launch of the first portable video cameras (McNair 2002, 39). Sony introduced the PortaPak in 1967, and it was used by artists and video activists rather than amateur pornographers. Not until the 1980s did video cameras and videocassette recorders (VCRs) transformed domestic porn video production, and the first wave of amateur porn surged as "millions of people bought their first home video camera and budding film-makers decided to make their own pornography" (Esch and Mayer 2007, 101). The digital imaging technologies of the 1990s and 2000s built on this development and took it to new directions with the introduction of inexpensive scanners, digital still and video cameras, easy-to-use image-manipulation and video editing software, and Web hosting services. In his studies of Usenet alt.fetish newsgroups, Sergio Messina (2006) associates the "amateur revolution" with the digital production tools of the late 1990s. Equipped with digital cameras and Internet connections, amateur pornographers started to use online forums to exchange their images (and videos, when bandwidth increased) and established and joined groups in which people shared similar interests, tastes, and preferences. Although these do-it-yourself (DIY) and self-organized newsgroup activities took place outside the mainstream distribution routes of pornography, amateur activities have been increasingly channeled to Web interfaces and easy-to-use publishing platforms. Current publishing forums suggest that user-generated content is seen as a resource and source of profit since the dot-com crash, that low-fidelity porn is appealing and has claims to authenticity, and that the overall palette of online porn is greatly diversified.

In the 1980s, amateur videos were shared with others through swap-and-buy services, and despite difficulties in distribution, amateur porn gained attention with its sense of authenticity and occasional intimacy and damaged the sales of commercial porn. Because money was to be made with amateur content, the porn industry soon integrated it into its product line, and the amateur came to connote "a bunch of long-serving members of the industry cooking up a show 'at home,' yet marketing like it was part of the original pioneering amateur spirit" (O'Toole 1998, 180; also McNair 2002, 39). Amateur porn inspired the genre known as *gonzo*, a term that was coined in the late 1980s and early 1990s. Like gonzo journalism, which was based on participatory observation (taking drugs when reporting on drugs, sleeping on the streets when writing on the homeless), gonzo porn is largely directed and shot by the people performing it, and it makes extensive use of point-of-view (POV) shots that allow the viewer first-person visual access to the action taking place. Like amateur porn, gonzo involves hand-held and shaky cameras that are held close to the performing bodies. Rather than full-body shots, viewers are offered close-ups of sexual action. The videos generally lack narrative and scripted dialog, they are shot in mundane locations, and the performers' bodies are mostly not enhanced according to the excessive and stylized "porn star" body aesthetics. Florian Cramer (2006, 136) associates gonzo with "white-trash body performance in the vein of *Jackass*," implying that the realness of gonzo is filtered through class-specific body styles. According to this perspective, the reality of gonzo is similar to reality as performed on reality TV. Yet gonzo is much more than this, for the genre is recurrently identified by critics as encapsulating arguments of porn as male domination, female degradation, and blatant misogyny with its elaborate use of human (female) toilet bowls, cum swapping, double penetrations, and overall roughness (Jensen 2007; Maddison 2009; Johnson 2010, 159). Gonzo, then, stands for the truly hardcore.

Although gonzo has its own star producers and performers—such as Rocco Siffredi, Max Hardcore, John Stagliano (aka Buttman), and Belladonna—it makes wide use of semiprofessional or semiamateur performers. This is taken a step further in reality porn, which became popular in the early 2000s primarily on online platforms (although the success of DVD series such as *Girls Gone Wild* should not be underestimated). If amateur video porn fed into gonzo, then gonzo fed into reality porn in the 1990s. Today, gonzo tends to connote extremity and extreme nastiness that is often heavily scripted and staged, while reality porn is somewhat ubiquitous. Much like early gonzo, reality porn involves staged scenes and scenarios presented as real and accidental actual events, and characters often address the camera directly. Professionally produced, it emulates the style and feel of amateur productions and lays claims to the amateur status of its performers (particularly the female talent). Reality porn may or may not include POV shots, and in many instances, it is more distanced than gonzo in its field of vision. It is also relatively inexpensive to produce due to lack of settings, costumes, props, scripts, or high-quality production tools.

Striptease Culture?

The high visibility of gonzo, reality, and amateur porn reflects shifts in the pornographic content production on the Web and the attraction and centrality of "the real" in media culture (Esch and Mayer 2007). The pornographic has grown ever more diverse as the Web has facilitated easy-to-use modes of distribution and sharing that are also business concepts. At the same time, media culture has witnessed the rise of so-called ordinary performers, reality and confessional media genres, and amateur production. Brian McNair (2002, 88) has identified this development as a striptease culture that is characterized by "media activity by people who are, at lest when they start out, amateurs and non-celebrities—'ordinary' people, to use that label of convenience for the moment." Striptease culture is characterized by the media visibility and public activity of nonprofessionals who often share details of their sexuality and reveal their feelings and their bodies in the public eye. Reality television, docusoaps, and webcams are exemplary of a confessional striptease culture (McNair 2002, 88–103; Plummer 2003; Attwood 2010a). With the reality programming of the 1990s, so-called ordinary people gained unprecedented visibility on television while also becoming minor celebrities through shows such as *Big Brother* and *Survivor*. Kate O'Riordan (2002) connects the rise of reality television and personal webcams to the redrawing of the boundaries of privacy that people draw as they position themselves, their intimate acts, and their domestic places in front of the camera for others to observe.

The first well-known webcams were not pornographic, although Jennifer Ringley of JenniCam (1996–2004) occasionally paraded around naked and had sex with her boyfriend while the camera was running. But it did not take long for more explicit webcams to emerge, including surveillance-camera-style reality sites, voyeur cams, and toilet cams. Despite their mutual differences, such camera sites brought together the notions of realness and immediacy that have been associated with both the Internet as a medium and porn as a genre (Bennett 2001, 387–388). The sense of realness is crucial to porn across a range of media because the (at least seeming) realness of the acts creates a sense of authenticity and grabs the audience. The attraction of online porn owes much to the sense of immediacy that it facilitates. Amateur porn videos and webcam streams are both associated with a perceptual "absence of mediation or representation"—the illusion that the technologies of mediation have disappeared and that the user is allowed direct and somehow authentic access to the objects depicted (Bolter and Grusin 1999, 70). This directness may require a degree of suspension of disbelief, yet a sense of realness is crucial to online porn, peer-produced (amateur) content, and reality genres more generally.

Much has happened in the media since the early 2000s to support diagnoses of striptease culture and the reorganization of the mediated boundaries of the public and the private. Reality TV programming has remained successful, social media and its peer-produced content have boomed, and so has amateur porn (a development discussed under the rubrics of Web 2.0 and porn 2.0). Ruth Barcan associates the appeal of homemade video pornography—like that of reality television—with a taste for the ordinary that is also a reaction to "the glut of glamour media images." As a style that cuts across the field of media—the Web, TV, advertising, cinema, and music clips—reality carries associations and expectations of truth and intimacy (Barcan 2002; also Dovey 2000). In pornography, the look and feel of nonprofessional, amateur production—marked by shaky camerawork, low image quality, poor lighting, and awkward, untrained performers—has similarly worked to enhance a sense of "truth" and authenticity that is central to the genre (cf. Citron 1999, 17; Zimmermann 1995, 144; Paasonen 2010c). In her study of TV talk shows, Laura Grindstaff (2002, 31) argues that to be heard in public, so-called ordinary people must speak in terms of emotion and personal experience, as this is their assumed arena of knowledge and credibility. Furthermore, "ordinariness is associated with emotional expressiveness rather than emotional restraint" (Grindstaff 2002, 38), and talk show "money shots" consist of moments of affective intensity and expressiveness, such as guests breaking into tears or verbally and physically attacking each other. Some of the appeal of amateur porn draws on these connections between ordinariness, realness, and lack of emotional restraint through which amateur images are invested with a sense of authenticity and directness that is different from professionally produced ones (figure 3.1). If porn shows bodies performing as if on a stage by default, then amateur images promise peeks to the off-stage, the intimate, and the authentic.

Realness and Presence

The liveness of webcams—whether webcam shows or twenty-four-hour streams—connotes the real and the authentic in ways that help to efface the level of mediation (the fact that "whether or not these images are

Figure 3.1
Amateur feel at http://www.myhomeclip.com

real, they are still generated from code, rather than simply relayed") and frame both webcams and the Internet as windows into the intimate lives of people (Chun 2006, 103; also O'Riordan 2002; Snyder 2000). Moments of intimate exchange take place as people look directly at cameras, chat with each other, upload images to be shared with others, or create new ones in response to those posted by others. The sense of connectedness, inter-activity, and presence facilitated by network technologies renders online porn specific in the resonance it entails between the bodies displayed on the screen and those located at the keyboard. As Wendy Chun (2008, 318) points out, as real-time images such as those provided by webcams refresh on their own and point elsewhere: "they make our networks seem transparent and thus fulfill the promise of fiber-optic networks to connect us to the world, as do real-time stock quotes and running news banners." This fundamental promise of connectivity, transparency, immediacy, and presence is facilitated by networked communications. Ken Hillis (2009, 131–132) similarly argues that webcams are seen to exceed representation as traces of the original and extensions of the person behind the screen. Webcam images are experienced as traces "of an actual human being located elsewhere"— that is, as indexical signs of presence—while the interplay between camera operators and their audiences involves desire for "someone so near yet still so far because just out of material reach" (Hillis 2009, 14, 210).

Webcams allow for visual and auditory access to people, spaces, objects, sites, and acts. They bring these into view across geographical distance yet are equally about a sense of distance. The lack of physical proximity gives rise to a sense of safety and control: the connection can be easily broken off, tabs can be closed, and new ones opened. Consider, for example, Chat Roulette, which attracted broad media attention and popularity soon after its launch in 2009. On Chat Roulette, users connect to one another randomly via webcam, sound, and text, quickly clicking from one person to another. The vistas catered on Chat Roulette are very much about naked bodies— penises and, to a lesser degree, breasts. This is a spectacle of immediacy, presence, and contact but equally one of abrupt disconnection, distance, and solitary exhibition. Anna Munster (2006, 8–9) sees discontinuities as being characteristic of digital sensory experiences that cross the "thresholds between here and there, continuous and differentiated, corporeal and incorporeal." The people, acts, and things seen are virtually rather than factually present, and their materiality can be accessed only through sight and sound—the texture of the image and the resonance of sound (figure 3.2). In any case, sensory gaps always remain.

The bodies of people performing in porn come close indeed, as skin, pimples, and bruises are exposed in zooms and highlighted with the aid of flashes. At the same time, this visual proximity is accompanied by a sense of detachment and distance that is characteristic to the resonances of online porn. Linda Williams (1989) has famously identified pornography as concerned with "the frenzy of the visible"—the attempt to make visible, document, and bear witness to bodily pleasures, body parts, and sexual acts. Representational conventions such as "meat shots" (shots of penis entering the partner's body), "money/cum shots" (ejaculation on the partner's body), or "cream pies" (shots of ejaculate in a vulva or an anus) are key examples of such frenzy of the visible as an imperative to document what is taking place, to verify sexual arousal and climax, and to document it in visual means. These conventions are also amply used in amateur porn (Van Doorn 2010). Annette Kuhn (1994, 26) similarly argues that photography

Figure 3.2
Webcams promise directness (http://www.dacams.com)

"draws on an ideology of the visible as evidence," according to which the camera is a neutral recording tool for the world as it is. As records, photographs are offered as authentic, direct, real, and true. Such pictorial realism is the crux of porn—from amateur, gonzo, and reality sites to the glossier interfaces of Porn.com. Camera technology gives the viewers augmented visual access to the minute details of bodies and their orifices (Sargeant 2006). Driven by the frenzy of the visible, such reflective attention to minute detail results in a carnal cartography of sorts where body parts become not only visible but also somehow "known."

The Rise of the Amateur

The aura of authenticity that is found in nonprofessionally produced pornographies—similar to that of so-called home media (Chalfen 2002)—is noteworthy in the role that it plays in the range of online pornographies. This aura translates as realness, immediacy, and presence that feed into the resonances and affective intensities of online amateur porn. The amateur, as currently understood, is a creation of the late nineteenth century, when the concept of leisure was developed as time that was separate from work and as cameras and film were first marketed to nonprofessionals for domestic use (Zimmermann 1995, 5; also Slater 1991). According to the distinction between the professional and the amateur, "while the professional conducts activities for work, an amateur labors away from work, in free time or leisure time" (Zimmermann 1995, 1). Amateurs have, for well over a century, recorded primarily the private sphere of the home and the family, and amateur porn is no exception to the rule.

Wife Bucket (http://wifebucket.com) showcases amateur images and videos updated by users and site members. The visual landscape of Wife Bucket is populated mainly by wives but also by their husbands, other partners, and swinging groups of people. As in family snaps, people (mainly women) pose mainly in domestic locations—bedrooms, living rooms, kitchens, bathrooms, and gardens. The images are predominantly shot by the "wife's" partner, which creates multiple levels of intimacy. In most examples, the women smile at and flirt with the camera as they would with their partner. Some show their tongues, and others mockingly flip the finger. These kinds of exchanges are not common in commercial porn. Amateur images and videos shot during sexual acts tend to make use of POV shots and subjective camera (particularly in blowjob videos) as the lens becomes the eyes of the husband. Since cameras are held close to the action, the soundscape becomes one of heavy breathing, the sound of bodies smacking into one another, people moaning and uttering random words. Since there is usually no music, the sound intensifies the sense of proximity and immediacy, bringing the viewer close. It is equally common for participants to place the camera on a stand while performing in front of it. Videos shot with a stand involve little camerawork. The framing is broad enough to grant the performers a degree of motion, but there are no close-ups, zooms, or pans to structure the video and to create altering degrees of proximity, distance, and visibility. The video camera witnesses and records what is taking place, much like a surveillance camera would, while the sounds generally remain faint.

Understood in relation to its hierarchical opposite, the professional, the amateur is associated with spontaneity. While professionalism connotes skill and quality (staging and manufacturing images), amateurism is defined through lack thereof. Amateur shots may be off-focus, thumbs may block the frame, and the lightning may be either too dark or too harshly bright. Amateur representations are invested with some documentary value, as their authors are assumed merely to record things with the technologies available to them rather than skillfully manufacture or manipulate them. Consequently, their shots are coded as truthful, authentic, and somehow less manufactured than professionally produced images—a variation of *cinéma vérité*, if you like (Citron 1999, 17; Zimmermann 1995, 144). In online amateur porn, these notions of realness and directness are mapped onto the notions of directness that are associated with both pornography as a genre and the Internet as a medium.

Traces and Likenesses

By rendering sexual acts, body parts, and bodily fluids visible, hardcore porn insists on its status as presentation—that the acts shown are also done "for real" and not merely simulated or acted out and that its images have an indexical relation to the acts in question. In Peircean terms, porn images function as both icons and indexes. According to Charles Sanders Peirce (1991, 181–183), an icon is a sign that stands for its referent through likeness. Icons are representative, as in the classic example of a passport photograph. An index is a trace—a sign that is created by the presence of the signified (like footprints in the snow or a photograph caught on film through the mechanical movement of the shutter and the rays of light on film). Pornography sports the "authentic presence" of arousal and orgasm with the aid of the documentary powers of photography and cinematography by promising to convey indexical traces of the events that have taken place. At the same time, any first-year media studies student will point out that pornography hardly just "records" the acts performed for the camera. Porn scenarios are scripted, acts follow generic patterns (as "numbers" such as double penetration, girl-on-girl, or facial cum shot), and action is staged, performed, and lighted for cameras that are positioned under, in front of, and between the performers for optimized visual access. Scenes are choreographed for ultimate visibility, which leads to stylized positions and poses that are repeated from one image and video to another. As Feona Attwood (2010a, 239) notes, over the years, "this version of the pornographic 'real' has come to be understood as formulaic and predictable," and it is associated with "performance, the spectacular and artificiality, unconvincing representation and 'fake' sex." The raw, grainy, and mundane imageries of gonzo, reality, and amateur porn have countered these aesthetics with their claims to the nonspectacular and real.

Rife with generic conventions of their own, amateur, reality, and gonzo pornographies remain attached to the register of the quotidian and the mundane. On Wife Bucket, people pose on living room sofas and carpets, on kitchen tables and beds, surrounded by discarded clothing, magazines, fluffy toys, and used dishes. The women generally sport little glamorous makeup, and marks of clothing worn and recently removed are often visible on their skin. Some images include a date tag that anchors the shot in a particular point in time. Such homespun images highlight pornography's general commitment to authenticity—the *ça-a-été* ("that has been") that Roland Barthes (1981, 77) saw as the fundamental witnessing function (indeed, the essence) of photography as traces and records of things that were once placed in front of the camera's shutter. With photography and cinematography, the iconic and the indexical became increasingly difficult to tell apart, and the two remain intermeshed in the age of digital imaging (Hillis 2009, 110). According to Thomas Elsaesser (1998, 207), "the indexicality of the trace is so bound up with the iconicity of the likeness that it has, in some ways, confused these categories." These categories seem to have become intimately blurred with the technologies used for distributing, consuming, and, in many cases, producing online porn.

Although technologies of imaging deployed in porn have moved from the photochemical to the digital, notions of presence, authenticity, and witnessing remain central, independent of the techniques deployed. Photos, videos, and webcams highlight the realness of what they depict, as if offering proof that such acts have taken place: particular bodies show off their properties, rubbing against and penetrating each other, and actual bodily secretions are displayed. The viewer is then offered the opportunity to witness all this from her virtual front-row seat. On the one hand, pornography typifies characters, signs, and gestures of arousal and pleasure (a point addressed further in chapters 4 and 5). On the other hand, its attraction is also tied to pictorial realism and evidence of sexual pleasure captured by the camera. This results in an awkward balance between the hyperbolic and the documentary as porn both lays claims to realness and draws quotation marks around the images that supposedly function as documentation.

The Flipside of Glamour

Film scholar Emily Shelton identifies porn as the alternative or flipside to Hollywood glamour: "In its self-presentation as a fantasy totally besotted with the material pleasures of the image, pornography depicts itself as a secret glimpse of the hard-core sleaze behind the airbrushed products of studio publicity, making no attempt to disguise the bruises on the legs of its hair-sprayed starlets nor the rather obvious signs that the beds on which all sex is taking place are not on studio sets but in seedy Los Angeles motel rooms" (Shelton 2002, 123). Shelton proposes a dialectical relationship between Hollywood and the San Fernando Valley (the hub of U.S. porn production). This kind of dynamic does not, however, characterize pornography more broadly (internationally or across different media). It can be argued that Shelton overestimates the power and appeal of Hollywood as a fantasy machine, given that the cultural role and position of cinema is drastically different today than it was in the 1950s during the last golden years of the studio system. Pornography is not nor has it ever been simply a question of film culture—especially when considering its recent developments. As a markedly cross-platform genre, pornography appears on the printed page as well as on all kinds of screens (cinema, television, computer, and mobile devices). Film studies have been and remain an important context for studies of pornography, but (as I argue in chapter 5), this context also comes with some problematic premises and implications that hinder rather than facilitate attempts at understanding the nexus of contemporary online pornographies.

Production companies (such as Vivid) that operate in the San Fernando Valley and are known for their high production quality, gloss, and glamour use makeup to hide the bruises and pimples of their performers, which was less the case with earlier porn producers (on Vivid, see Slayden 2010). According to Cindy Patton (1991, 375), in the 1980s, the "documentary aura" of 1970s hardcore porn films "complete with wrinkles and wayward pubic hairs" gave way to increasingly stylized, polished, and airbrushed video productions. This shift from the ordinary and the nongroomed to the fantastic and the surgically enhanced lead to a stylized, even drag-queen-like look of North American video porn actresses of the 1990s as "permatanned, waxed, bleached, artificially enhanced with silicon" (Härmä and Stolpe 2010, 113). This body aesthetic is critiqued for being "'unrealistic,' since it favours silicone implants, taut aerobicised loins, fake tan, false nails, big hair and Brazilian waxes, over the 'natural' attributes of everyday women" (Albury 2003, 204; also Rooke and Moreno Figueroa 2010, 227). Combined with pornography's tendency toward hyperbole, these fantastic qualities conflict with the claims for the documentary and the authentic. According to Barcan (2002), the rise of reality porn can be associated with the desire for authenticity and realness.

Amateur porn is distributed on many different forums, including pay sites, P2P networks, and newsgroups. Wife Bucket is a pay site operated by the Web master http://seemybucks.com, which also runs the Wife Bucket sister sites Cum on Wives (http://cumonwives.com), See My Girlfriend (http://seemygf.com), and See My Boyfriend (www.seemybf.com, addressed to a gay audience). The sites use similar layout and design templates and profile themselves in opposition to "boring plastic porn" (http://seemygf. com) and "boring plastic gay porn" (http://seemybf.com) with their promises of real homemade material and amateur performers. The thumbnail images advertising the sites' contents tend to follow familiar routines with their blowjobs, cum shots, meat shots, and other bodily displays. Some female performers approximate the flirtatious "dirty looks" of commercial porn, and others close their eyes, grin, and grimace in ways that do not conform to conventional porn. Especially on sites featuring "wives" (rather than girlfriends), the performers are no longer in their twenties or as thin and groomed as women are on most other pay sites (gonzo and reality included). The sites mark themselves apart from the mainstream and its (plastic) body styles, performers, and contexts of production while constantly drawing on its visual reservoir of poses, positions, and scenarios. This is rather literally visualized in Wife Bucket images that show people having sex while watching porn on a TV or computer screen. This recurring visual theme depicts domestic spaces (living rooms and bedrooms) as sites of both porn consumption and production.

Sergio Messina explains the attraction of amateur porn through its realness. According to him, in mainstream commercial porn, people perform by "using all the props of professional productions: lights, backdrops, make up, editing, special effects, etc." In contrast, amateur pornography involves "pictures of real people with real desires, having real sex in real places" (Messina 2006). Porn stars are marked apart from "real people" as "plastic and fake, constructed by fantasy, unnaturally endowed and giving a false impression of how sex is performed" (Härmä and Stolpe 2010, 113). Contrary to this figure of artifice, the amateur stands for what is real. McNair (2002, 108) identifies a similar dynamic and attraction at the heart of striptease culture as "the real thing"—not an "occasion for parades of gamine supermodels and designer-trained Adonises, but of imperfectly ordinary people with perfectly ordinary perversions and sexual idiosyncracies." Amateur porn revolves around notions and promises of real bodies, real pleasures, real people, and real places. Contrary to professional actors and performers, amateurs are assumed to merely "do it" (Patterson 2004, 166). Rather than being motivated by money, they make porn for fun and share it for the reason that they like to be seen (Jacobs 2004; Messina 2006). For Messina, online amateur porn is realcore as opposed to the familiar categories of hardcore and softcore:[1] "Realcore is all about the reality of what you see, the truth of these images. It's about the desire to see someone doing something because they like to be seen. They're filming it because you are part of the game as well. You're the audience. They get horny because someone is getting horny over them" (Messina in Dery 2007a, 24).

Messina sees the relationship between the producers, performers, and audiences of amateur porn as dialogic and based on shared or at least interconnecting pleasures and networks of desire. Understood this way, amateur production circumvents many, if not all, problematic aspects of the porn industry, such as its artificial glossiness, the working conditions of its performers, or its principles of profit generation. Amateur videos and images are recurrently framed as reflecting the desires of the people performing in and shooting them. At the same time, family snaps and home videos have, throughout their history, been posed in, staged, edited, and manipulated (Kuhn 1995). Amateur imaging has been governed by conventions concerning what is appropriate or necessary to record and what qualifies as a good photograph and film (Zimmermann 1995). As Michele Citron (1999, 13) points out, while the people in front of the camera connect directly to those behind the lens by looking at the camera, their poses are not necessarily expressive of their own desires or preferences.

Amateur practices are inseparable from the dynamics of intimate relationships and arrangements and their tensions and hierarchies. This makes it difficult to interpret amateur imageries as directly telling of the personal desires or preferences of the people performing, for the desires involved may well be those of the people behind the camera. This issue links also to matters of distribution. Although sites usually insist that the person uploading files has permission to do so from the people depicted in the images, it is enough that the person argues this to be the case. Informed consent may be the basic ethical point of porn production and distribution, yet some sites imply that no consent has been secured in terms of distribution. "Ex-wife" and "ex-girlfriend" sites (such as http://myexgf.com, http://exgfpics.com, http://creammygirlfriend.com, http://formergirlfriends.com, and the aptly titled http://revengetv.com) are based on the concept of sharing homemade porn shots of former female partners without their knowledge or permission. In other words, the sites present vengeful fantasies of payback where intimate moments are exposed and the women are evaluated in terms of their looks, personality, and sexual skill. Aside from the issue of how real such vengeful postings are, the popularity of this fantasy undermines the assumption that the people performing in online videos do so simply because they want to be seen. The question is also one of how and by whom one is seen, who chooses to upload the images, and who controls their circulation.

Working for Love

The divisions between amateur and professional pornography involve complex yet dualistic notions—such as authenticity versus artifice and the homespun versus the commercial. These divisions also involve differences in motivation: amateurs assumedly do what they do for the love of it (as the Latin root of the word, *amare*, "to love," suggests), and professionals are motivated by money. The boundaries become blurred in amateur porn, however, because some sites offer (modest) fees for the videos and images that the users upload, and many more others require (less modest) membership fees for accessing them. All this renders "labors of love" a form of commercial sex, and their performers become something like sex workers— a label that comes with a degree of social stigma. Unlike most sites, See My Girlfriend pays for the user submissions:

We're looking for girls and couples to submit photos and videos to us! (over 18 years old only).We want to see "real life people" "girls next door." You don't need to be a super model.

If you're a girl, show off your body to us! If you're a couple, we're looking for hardcore snaps of those intimate moments. Be creative and make money! . . .

We pay per picture and per minute for video. For hardcore photos, we pay up to $2 per image. For nudes, up to $1 per snap. . . . Also, we pay out big bonuses for really great photos (hardcore like BJ, cumshots, hot sex, or hot masturbation / posing photos. Be creative!).[2]

In addition to these fees, submissions with the best ratings receive small prizes (such as a one-month full membership, a $50 Amazon.com gift certificate, or $100 in cash). In return, users grant the site "a non-exclusive, fully-paid, world-wide, royalty-free license" to distribute the images and videos they submit in virtually any variation, medium, or format license-free and for an unlimited amount of time.[3] These images can be accessed for a monthly membership fee of $24.80. Payments are organized through CCBill.com, a large online credit-card and check payment processor established in 1998 that runs transactions for thousands of sites. Sites offering amateur porn for free gather revenues from sponsored links, ads, and premium membership fees that allow more functions than visitor status. Because the producers of amateur videos are in most cases not compensated for what they upload, the main asset of the sites—the images and videos—are free (or in the case of See My Girlfriend, nearly free) content for the hosting site. The sites generally take no responsibility or liability for the content that they host (this being the responsibility of the people who submit it). This practice can be seen as a kind of gift economy—in which users upload their videos or pictures and videos for fun and for free (perhaps paying for a membership fee and waiving copyright protection) and the hosting site makes a profit from selling advertising space and access and possibly holds the copyright to any further distribution. For users, such a gift economy leaves them with little control over the fruits of their own labor. For the site, this kind of participatory culture is obviously lucrative.

Online publishing forums shape and condition amateur practices in ways that are not merely technical in the sense of concerning specific media formats, image resolution, length, or overall quality. The number one hit for a Google search on "amateur porn," http://www.youramateur-porn.com, insists that the videos uploaded by users need to be legal (they must not include illegal sexual acts, such as animal sex, child porn, or performers under eighteen), void of spam, and saved in mpeg, mpg, avi, asf, or wmv format. Furthermore, videos "below 1 minute or with bad quality are not accepted/posted," and there must be "no single men or dicks on the videos. Only women, pairs and groups." The emphasis on female bodies and heterosex is equally evident in top-hit amateur video sites such as http://www.burningcamel.com, http://amateurporndump.com, http://

myhomeclip.com, and http://eroxia.com, which do not limit their subject content in these strict ways and also feature gay content. Female users who enjoy the sight of "single men or dicks" need to migrate to gay porn sites, as such content would assumedly disturb straight male consumers. When gay porn is included in the available subcategories, it tends to link out to another site.

The video categories on amateur sites are similar to those of commercially produced videos, and they are organized alphabetically in categories such as "Anal," "Asian," "Big Boobs," "Blowjob," "Couples," "CumShots," "Drunk Girls," "GangBang," "GroupSex," "Handjobs," "Hardcore," "Interracial," "Lesbian," "Mature," "MILF," "PublicSex," "SoloGirl," "Teen," "Voyeur," "Webcam," and "Wives." The categories may be more specific (as on http://www.yuvutu.com or http://www.submityourflicks.com) or completely missing. Perhaps paradoxically, amateur porn that is shared online needs to fit into already established subcategories to be recognized as porn. At the same time, it needs to differ from the commercial and the mainstream as something that is more authentic, homespun, direct, intimate, real, and raw. In his study of a hundred amateur videos distributed on http://www.youporn.com, Niels Van Doorn (2010) argues that they evoke a sense of authenticity through poor technical execution (such as poor camerawork, image quality, and sound quality) and through a display of ordinary and imperfect bodies. The videos may include interruptions—dogs barking, cameras falling off stands, phones ringing—that highlight their unstaged nature. At the same time, the performers reiterate familiar porn conventions in their poses, gestures, and positions, acts performed, garments worn, and words uttered. In effect, a categorical separation of amateur videos from mainstream or commercial porn is difficult to achieve on several levels. The differences are clear in working practices, motivation, and pay, but the categories blur as amateur content becomes a commodity on online platforms. This content can be freely uploaded or sold to users, and its availability suggests that rather than being a category alternative to the mainstream, the two tend to conflate.

Porn.com—which is a mainstream commercial site by default—offers amateur porn as one subcategory, but it also links to a sister site, http://You.porn.com, where all material is "submitted by real people." Another sister site, http://gay.porn.com, displays content in thirty-four categories and follows design outlines that are almost identical to the main site. In contrast, the layout of You.porn.com tries to evoke a sense of amateurism with explicit references—a background image that resembles messy hardboard, fonts that approximate messy rawness, and a design that includes images of a small digital video camera and a pile of VHS tapes—to the low tech and the homespun (figure 3.3). A sense of the self-made, DIY, authentic, and amateur as crafted through visual means is also clearly spelled out: "forget cheesy scripts, perfect lighting, professional makeup or HD quality, this is real fucking the way it was meant to be enjoyed! It's all-original, amateur-made porn that has never been made public . . . until now! Join today and get instant access to the largest collection of raw, authentic homemade videos on the Net. Submitted by real people, these are the private-life vids of wives, neighbors, ex-girlfriends, couples and swingers!"[4]

ProAms and Affective Labor

Gonzo, amateur porn, and glossy video porn all give rise to different carnal resonances with their audiences. But amateur and professional (or mainstream) should not be mapped as somehow mutually opposing categories, and the promises of realness should not be associated with the

Figure 3.3
The "raw" design of http://you.porn.com

noncommercial. Such categorizations have become increasingly convoluted and nebulous. Gonzo and reality sites regularly employ professional amateurs (ProAms)—porn performers who perform as amateur for a living. Constance Penley (2004, 321) identifies ProAm porn as fake amateur films "in which recognizable professionals, even stars, would play ordinary folks clowning around the house with their camcoder." This definition of ProAm is actually more descriptive of gonzo and reality. Kevin Esch and Vicki Mayer (2007, 102) define ProAms as people who work in reality and gonzo porn while perhaps try to break into the industry as full-time professionals. The women in gonzo and reality sites who are described as "amateur" and "off the street" can in most cases be best described as ProAm. In many instances, the sites include links to model agencies that cater to the industry. These agencies offer porn consumers with suitable physical qualities the possibility of becoming paid performers on reality sites like the ones that they themselves frequent.

In extrapornographic contexts, the concept of ProAm has been used to describe the participation of people with professional skills in activities such as software development, design, sport, video editing, and knowledge production. ProAms do not identify their activity as work and question the division of the field into professionals and amateurs (Bruns 2008, 202, 234). In discussing the rise and meaning of the ProAm, Charles Leadbeater and Paul Miller (2004) see them as transforming the innovation, development, and distribution of cultural artifacts. Following Henry Jenkins (2006a), this development can be seen as exemplary of the participatory culture in which media users are also active content producers who challenge the hierarchical divisions of professionals and laymen.

The blurred boundaries of amateurs and professionals are evident on a number of levels in online porn—in cottage-industry sites that grow into profitable businesses, in amateur performers who turn into "micro-celebrities" (Senft 2008), and in online story archives with peer rating systems, competitions, and community features (Paasonen 2010b). Gonzo and reality porn have been available for some time on pay sites, whereas throughout the 1990s, amateur porn was found mostly on Usenet newsgroups. The situation has since changed, and many file-sharing sites, video publishing platforms, and specialized sites are now available. Some amateurs have ended up running their own pay sites, and others continue to upload their files for free. In any case, the familiar categories of the commercial and the noncommercial have lost much of their analytical edge in describing such developments. Sex worker advocate and author Audacia Ray (2008) critiques the hierarchies of value implied by divisions such as commercial and noncommercial. As she argues, free sites that promote open publishing do not necessarily stand for a "higher form of porn" than ones that charge membership fees. The sites do, however, offer different positions for their producers and performers. Some work for free within the principles of the gift economy, covering bandwidth and server expenses themselves, while others work for money that can be spent any way they choose. For Ray, identifying free sites as "good" and pay sites as somehow "less good" is problematic since the open accessibility of content says little of their ethics or principles of operation. At the same time, amateur porn has been firmly associated with gift economy as labors of love distributed and enjoyed for free and for the fun of it (in opposition to what is seen as the commodity and profit-driven modes of operation of the porn industry).

One way to unravel these connections is to consider amateur porn both in terms of the content and the work that goes into producing it. Italian autonomist Maurizio Lazzarato (1996) introduced the concept of immaterial labor to describe work that produces "the informational and cultural content of the commodity." Such labor is no longer performed in the factories, and its outcomes are not tangible objects but rather services, information, text, sounds, images, or code. The concept of immaterial labor has been widely picked up to describe forms of work that are about the production culture and the production of value that is "dependent on a socialised labour power organised in assemblages of humans and machines exceeding the spaces and times designated as 'work'" (Terranova 2006, 28). The space of work is not the factory or even an office. The practices of work and leisure are blurred, and immaterial labor takes place collaboratively with the aid of network technologies. Michael Hardt and Antonio Negri (2001, 293; 2004, 108) identify two forms of immaterial labor. The first produces "ideas, symbols, codes, texts, linguistic figures, images and other such products"—such as HTML, videos, images, and stories. Amateurs who upload their videos are engaging in immaterial labor, as are the people who operate the sites. The second form of immaterial labor is affective labor, which produces (and manipulates) affects, social networks, and forms of community. In the case of pornography, such affective labor includes affective investments and attachments to specific sites and platforms and the exchanges taking place on them (Lindgren 2010; Whisnant 2010). The "labors of love" involved in amateur porn tap into the affective dynamics of sites as community platforms and interaction forums. This is something that the sites themselves explicitly encourage. See My Girlfriend, for example, offers numerous examples of the kinds of images that the site invites users to upload (figure 3.4). In some of these, women pose and give blowjobs while holding signs that say "I love seemygf.com." In others, the message is written on their bodies. These confessions of love are encouraged (and rewarded), and they work to anchor the images in a specific framework of the site as a brand and an object of affection. Not surprisingly, the same practices are invited at Wife Bucket, which holds a competition for the best fan sign image (with the text of "I Love Wifebucket"). Everyone who enters a competition receives free membership for up to a year, and gift vouchers and small money prizes are handed out to winners.

Tiziana Terranova (2000, 33) identifies "voluntarily given and unwaged, enjoyed and exploited" labor as characteristic to the Web, digital economy,

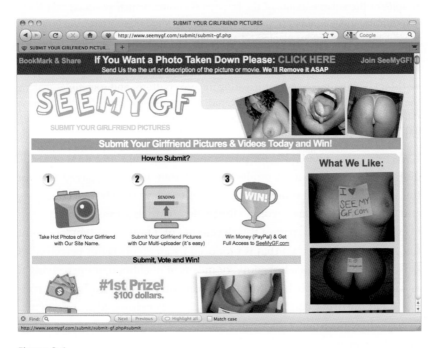

Figure 3.4
Guidelines for submitting files on http://seemygf.com

and contemporary media culture at large. Activities such as chatting or blogging are not necessarily recognized or experienced as work, yet they are forms of labor in the sense of creating "monetary value out of knowledge/ culture/affect" (Terranova, 2000, 38). Affective engagements and attachments are evident on social networking sites and in online communities where users are attached both to each other and the style, feel, and architecture of the specific platform they use. Although it might be attractive to associate affective labor as a development that is characteristic of Web 2.0 and its commercial underpinnings, Terranova (2000, 48) points out that the same practices were ubiquitous in pre-Web online exchanges: "Within the early virtual communities, we are told, labor was really free: the labor of building a community was not compensated by great financial rewards (it was therefore 'free,' unpaid), but it was also willingly conceded in exchange for pleasures of communication and exchange (it was therefore 'free,' pleasurable, not imposed)." She nevertheless argues that this seeming freedom results from an artificial separation of then and now:

In spite of the volatile nature of the Internet economy (which yesterday was about community, today is about portals, and tomorrow who knows what), the notion of users' labor maintains an ideological and material centrality that runs consistently throughout the turbulent succession of Internet fads. . . . Users keep a site alive through their labor, the cumulative hours of accessing the site (thus generating advertising), writing messages, participating in conversations, and sometimes making the jump to collaborators. . . . Such a feature seems endemic to the Internet in ways that can be worked on by commercialization, but not substantially altered. (Terranova 2000, 48–49)

As Terranova (2000, 39, 49) points out, newsgroups and BBSs (and the desire for creative content production that they involved) paved way for the Web cultures and online economies of today in which free, collective, and affective labor has become effectively channeled into business practices.[5] Amateur porn is part of this development. On the one hand, content (images, videos, and text) that is produced by amateurs is not perceived of as work in the sense of a task, duty, or means of livelihood, for perceiving it as such would ruin much of the motivation and pleasure involved in creating it. On the other hand, this content is actively being sold and circulated in ways that are virtually impossible for its creators to control. This does not mean that such labor would be exploited by commercial parties (although this may also be the case) or that this form of labor is an alienated one (as some autonomist critics might suggest). Rather, a new vocabulary is needed for addressing the complex meanings of amateur and commercial porn beyond the kinds of easy dichotomies (amateur versus professional, noncommercial versus commercial, independent versus mainstream) that we have tended to use.

Increasing Opacity of the Medium

For some, the platforms of Web 2.0 mark an emancipation of users as publishers, creators, and discussants. Others point out that the possibilities for lay users to interact with and shape the medium are more limited than they were fifteen or even ten years ago. Although in the late 1990s a basic mastery of HTML (and perhaps a few touches of the cutting-edge, such as Java-Script) was sufficient for setting up a Web site that matched professional criteria, this is no longer the case.[6] Code has grown increasingly complex and requires specialized skills. Rather than building their sites (such as the personal home pages and online journals of the 1990s) from a scratch, users now use of customizable templates and social media applications (such as Blogger, YouTube, Facebook, PhotoBucket, and Flickr) when publishing their images, videos, texts, and music. By doing so, users operate with ready-made templates and site architecture that they can influence only to a small degree. The threshold of online publishing, participation, and customization is lower than ever before. At the same time, users have less access to the technical basis of the medium in the form of code. Although the term *Internet* can be used to refer to the online practices of both 1994 and today, the medium that is referred to has been radically transformed (Gitelman 2006, 8). When I started using the Internet in 1994, email was used via Telnet, and documents were retrieved with Gopher. By the time I started using Netscape Navigator the following year, the landscape had already changed radically through the introduction of Web browsers with graphical user interfaces and hyperlink structures. The differences between the technical affordances of Netscape 2.0, which was launched in the autumn of 1995 (and the sites one could access at that point in time), and the Web as it was used in 2010 are equally or even more striking.

It is noteworthy that the best-known amateur porn "success stories," much like Danni Ashe's Danni's Hard Drive, were launched quite a while ago. The site http://wifeysworld.com has been in operation since 1998, following the newsgroup success of "Wifey's" Polaroid shots posted by her

"Hubby" (figure 3.5). Heather Harmon of http://ideepthroat.com launched her Web site with husband Jim in 2000 (but despite promising constant updates and live webcam shows, I Deepthroat has not been updated since 2005). The two sites remain perhaps the best-known success stories of amateurs who became entrepreneurs and ran their own sites. The sites can be seen as fair-trade porn in the sense of being detached from the working practices of the porn industry and driven by the desires of the performers/producers themselves. This is strongly suggested in Harmon's "about me" background information:

I am 24 years old. I am 5´ 7 inches tall and weigh 115 lbs. I have sandy blonde hair and green eyes. I have been married for 1 year and am very happy. I really like to show off, and am turned on to show off my body and to know people like watching me perform sex acts!

This is my first experience in the adult industry. My husband and I are running the whole site ourselves. We work very hard to make this exactly what our members want. SUPER DEEPTHROATING! Things are going very good. Recently we opened our Online Web Store, IDTStore.com!

I like to dance, go to the beach, go camping and go boating. I workout regularly and try to take good care of my body.

My husband and I got started doing this by performing on Ifriends. Ifriends is a website that offers live webcam shows to viewers. At first we we [sic] nervous, but that wore off real fast. Soon our fans were telling us that we should start our own site.

Well, we took their advice and started learning about html and website building. We new [sic] nothing about websites except how to type in a URL before starting all this. We are learning more everyday!!⁷

This background information gestures toward authenticity on multiple levels. First of all, the site is defined as motivated by the desires of Heather, who likes to be seen and finds public displays of sex exciting. Her likes, hobbies, and preferences are described in a manner that is similar to a dating site or a personal home page from the 1990s. Second, the site is motivated by a dialogical and interactive relationship with her audience—the fans. Third, the site is defined as a homespun venture run by the couple with no previous expertise in either HTML or the porn industry. The immaterial labor of such sites has meant that homes become sites of porn production, code work, and interaction with fans and other subscribers. As immaterial labor, sex with one's partner gives rise not only to bodily sensations but also to webcam streams, still images, and data archives framed as consumables. The domesticity, authenticity, amateurism, and realness involved in such sites are about the production of affective labor that creates intimate

Figure 3.5
ProAm performance on http://wifeysworld.com

resonance with the users and attaches them to the site. The sites produce not merely porn but also sociability in chat sessions, interactive forums, texts, looks, and poses targeted at users.

The success of ideepthroat.com owed much to Heather Harmon's deep-throat oral sex skills but even more so to her enthusiastic girl-next-door performance style and the homespun concept of the site. Like other micro-celebrities who run their own webcams, Harmon actively engaged and interacted with her fans and site members by starring in eight live weekly webcam shows and additional chat sessions. As Theresa M. Senft (2008, 26) points out when writing on micro-celebrity, "on the Web, popularity depends upon a connection to one's audience, rather than an enforced separation from them." This goes especially for webcams, where amateur and independent porn entrepreneurs market their own persona as much as videos, images, and webcam shows. Micro-celebrities chat, blog, and make use of social networking sites to engage in personal communication with their fans (Senft 2008, 25). This also is, to a degree, the case with porn stars (of the DVD kind) in general. Porn stars routinely interact with their fans at conventions, on occasional tours, on Web sites, and in chat sessions. But although contact with a fan base is important to porn stars, their appeal is not as dependent on constant interaction and feedback as is that of Web-based ProAm micro-celebrities.

New amateur sites may still mushroom overnight, yet today there is an abundance of material to navigate through, and it is considerably more difficult for new content to stand out or even become visible. The abundance of freely accessible videos and new uploads also poses challenges to new enterprises. And as code has increased in complexity, it is more difficult for people to set up a functional site with only introductory knowledge of HTML. Amateur porn has been to a large degree channeled into image and video galleries and hosting sites that are run in a rather organized manner. So although content is easier to publish, distribution is much more difficult to control. The transformations that the Web has undergone as a medium directly affect what so-called lay users can do with it. In their well-established performances of amateurism, Wifey and Hubby as well as Heather and Jim Harmon are already ProAm.

Working for "the love of it" is also evoked as the motivation of the female Wife Bucket employees who are introduced in the site blog[8] (figure 3.6). The three women presented in images and brief bios include Rebecca, an early member and avid swinger who became the first employee of the site. Currently age thirty-eight, she gained celebrity on the site with her images. According to her introduction, she was known for loving sex and was invited to work as support manager in 2009 (the year in which the site was launched). Emily, a stay-at-home mom—and also a site member, "active swinger and exhibitionist who loves to show off for the camera"—works as Web content manager and is responsible for adding new content on the site. Both women are presented with both headshots and more explicit submissions of their own. Content editor Cammy, the third staff member introduced, is described as a party girl and an active swinger. The introductions frame the women as insiders who love both sex and the site and whose submissions are loved by other site members.

Meanwhile, beyond customer care and content maintenance, the people who own and operate the site remain faceless and anonymous. As immaterial laborers working for the site, Rebecca, Emily, and Cammy also play a crucial role in the field of affective labor by writing a blog where users can learn more about the site. They provide Wife Bucket with a sexy, female, and swinging face that helps to tie the staff, the members, and the site

Figure 3.6
Visualization of the Wife Bucket community in the site blog (http://wifebucket
.com/blog)

together with strands of love, desire, and affection. What lies behind this
face is much more opaque. The site insists that "All proceeds from member-
ships on our site go back into maintaining it with super fast servers, support staff and of course content prizes!" This claim detaches Wife Bucket
from the interest and imperative of profit making and replaces it with the
notions of labors of love and servicing the community (as one of affective
ties). Whether the motivation is love or money or both remains for the user
to interpret. Nevertheless, this framing and the amateur feel of the images
and videos help to detach Wife Bucket as a community from porn sites as
commerce—despite the monthly membership fee of $24.80.

Matters of Media and Materiality

Married couples and their domestic surroundings lay at the heart of amateur,
semiamateur, and ProAm porn, particularly in its North American manifestations. This goes against pornographic fantasies that are characterized by

the erasure of the external world (social relations, work, or politics) and by detachment from the social or material textures of everyday life (Rival, Slater, and Miller 1999, 301). In contrast, the social and material textures of everyday life are the very stuff that amateur porn is made of and are key parts of its attraction as recognizable, authentic, and somehow real in its depictions of desire and pleasure. In his study of Victorian literary pornography, Steven Marcus (1964) famously coined the term *pornotopia* to describe the utopian aspects of the genre, its excessive depictions of sexual acts, and its abundance of bodily displays. Pornotopia is an imaginary nonplace that can be geographically located anywhere but exists ultimately only in the readers' imagination. This is a fantasyland of flowing desire that, separated from the confines of physical location, promises the freedom of fantasy without the burden of excessive detail (Marcus 1964, 269). The mundane domestic pornotopias of amateur porn are far from lacking in "excessive detail" of the kind that Marcus addresses, however. In fact, the domestic spaces where women and couples pose and perform are rife with detail—curtains, wallpapers, lamps, vases, dolls, fabrics, carpets, paintings, books, souvenirs, clothes, dishes, bottles, family photos, sofas, chairs, tables, TV screens, candles, knickknacks, Bibles, exercise equipment, and more. The visual landscape is a mundane and usually cluttered one that is recognizably domestic and familiar from family snaps and home videos.

This texture of domesticity combines with the feel of the images—bodies exposed in bright light from flashes, filmy faces, surprising acts of framing, bodies moving in and out of focus—to cut through images shot by different people in different places and at different moments. The carnal resonance in question cannot be uncoupled from the texture of domesticity, the traces of everyday life, and the products of material culture that decorate, surround, or even litter the images. As I encounter such images, the material residue of the images—both the materiality of the performers and that of lived environments—lingers on and touches me. Eve Kosofsky Sedgwick (2003, 17–19) points out that the term *feeling* carries with it a sense of proximity, contact, and touch. For her, affects become attached to material objects, ideas, and sensations that connect different material bodies. In the case of online porn, materiality is an issue of representation, subject matter, aesthetics (textures of domesticity included), as well as one concerning the materiality of the images themselves.

The physical aspects, formats, textures, and makeup of images resonate in different ways, and they give rise to different sensations and experiences. Hence, "it is not the meanings of things *per se* that are important but their social effects as they construct and influence the field of social action that would not have occurred if they did not exist, or . . . if they did not exist in this or that specific format" (Edwards and Hart 2004, 4, referencing Alfred Gell). It matters how objects feel since such "feeling" gives rise to different kinds of attachment and resonance. The feel, tactility, and texture of pornography are intimately tied to its technologies of production and distribution—whether the high definition and texture of 35mm film, the grainy authenticity of gonzo and amateur videos, or the apparent immateriality of digital images, videos, and texts that consist of zeros and ones and are open to virtually endless remodification. A photographic print can be touched; its surface becomes marked with fingerprints, creases, folds, and other signs of wear; and it can be carried and handed over to other people. There is a certain uniqueness to photographic prints as objects. Film and video involve more distanced forms of viewing, and their images—projected on a screen or made sense of as a flicker of pixels—are much less tangible. Tapes and rolls of films are firmly material objects that can be grabbed and held, compared to digital image files that are stored as data files, easily downloaded and uploaded, saved as aliases, deleted, renamed, and circulated further. Porn stories printed in a book, read on a screen, or printed out on paper all involve a different materiality as relations between people, words, media formats, and experiences of reading. The same goes for digital images. Nevertheless, as Laura U. Marks (2002, 163) notes, "Digital and electronic images are constituted by processes no less material than photography, film, and analog video are."

Although it seems obvious that digital image formats facilitate a range of sensory encounters and dynamic relationships, they have been recurrently characterized in terms of loss (of image quality, tactile qualities, and the object's specificity) in comparison to photochemical prints. According to Joanna Sassoon (2004, 190–192), for example, with digital images, the attention shifts from photographs as material objects to visual surfaces—from the complexity of the material to a pure focus on subject content—as images are stripped down from their existence in space and time to flat digital copies. Thinking beyond the framing of loss, digital photographs have a specific kind of materiality and social life (owing to hardware, cables, hubs, and wires) that is inseparable from the ways in which they are experienced and interpreted. N. Katherine Hayles (2003, 267) points out that digital texts (and images) exist as processes (rather than objects) that involve "data files, the programs that call these files, and the hardware on which the programs run, as well as the optical fibers, connections, switching algorithms and other devices necessary to route it from one networked computer to another." Digital images do not exist anywhere as such before their materialization on the screen as the necessary programs are activated. These processes, again, involve differences:

> Consider, for example, the time it takes images to appear on screen when they are being drawn from a remote server. Certainly the time lag is an important component of the electronic text, for it determines in what order the user will view the material. Indeed, as anyone who has grown impatient with long load times knows, in many instances it determines whether the user will see the image at all. These times are difficult to predict precisely because they depend on the individual computer's processing speed, traffic on the Web, efficiency of data distribution on the hard drive, and other imponderables. This aspect of electronic textuality—along with many others—cannot be separated from the delivery vehicles that produce it as a process with which the user can interact. Moreover, for networked texts these vehicles are never the same twice, for they exist in momentary configurations as data packets are switched very quickly from one node to another, depending on the traffic at the instant of transfer. (Hayles 2003, 275–276)

The issue, then, is not the immateriality of digital images but their different materializations and the processes involved in these materializations. The performance capacities of hardware, the settings of software, download speed, and the volume of Web traffic all contribute to the sensory properties of digital images as ones with a specific informational structure (Hayles 2003, 274–276; also Manoff 2006). These sensory properties are also issues of the texture and feel of the images as they materialize in different media.

Between and across Media

Clips of 1980s video porn starring John Holmes can be easily accessed on video-sharing sites (figure 3.7). The clips carry the grainy texture and low sound resolution of VHS, their colors are often faded, and some of the hiss and noise of the original VHS tape may be evident in both image and sound. The digital file in question remediates video porn of the vintage and analog kind and carries traces of its technical specificity, but as a digital copy,

Figure 3.7
A vintage John Holmes video on http://www.youporn.com

it has a different existence. The video clip can be accessed at any point, downloaded, and distributed further. In the framework of a video-sharing site, it is part of a database and searchable through specific keywords (such as Holmes, video porn, or 1980s) and hence a different kind of object of knowledge. When watched on a video-sharing site or downloaded from a P2P network, the video differs from one that would be watched on television screen attached to a VCR player.

These differences concern format. A digital flv, mpeg, avi, or swf video file differs from one that is divided into numerous small files distributed in a peer network and downloaded as torrents (while simultaneously seeding and uploading the same video for other users to access), and it differs even more from an analog and linear video recording that is stored on magnetic tape. The videos are accessed in different ways, and there are clear differences in how they can be shared, copied, and modified. Furthermore, these different material incarnations (in terms of file formats and technical platforms) facilitate different sensory engagements and acts of usage (from watching to downloading or seeding), tactile engagements, and resonances. A streaming video watched online is embedded in particular site-design and information architecture, and it is accompanied by links, banner ads, and possible rating and commenting tools. The video also looks different depending on screen resolution, size, and color contrast—that is, it materializes in different ways in acts of viewing. A video shared in a P2P network can be endlessly copied and redistributed, while videotapes wear over time and may even break. When watched on a computer screen, the grainy qualities of video porn connote VHS and perhaps even media nostalgia. At the same time, this is no longer the same video because video cannot be "completely encoded into digital media" (Hayles 2003, 270).

The Internet is markedly multimedial in the sense of being rich with traces of other media forms, such as videos, newspapers, magazines, journals, and radio. Writing in the late 1990s, Bolter and Grusin (1999, 208) even suggested that "the ultimate ambition of the web designer seems to be to integrate and absorb all other media." Some of the functions of other media have branched and shifted to online platforms, and these online variations are already different creatures. Online newspapers are constantly updated, their archive databases can be searched, their stories are accompanied by videos and banner ads, and affective debates are carried out on their discussion forums. Users participate in queries and discussions independent of their physical location, while their movements and activities are automatically tracked. As Chun (2006, 122) notes, the "constant involuntary data exchange crucial to any user-controlled exchange of human-readable information" is "disastrous to any analogy between print and the Internet" as media forms. Reading an online newspaper makes the activity of reading—choosing some articles and topics while disregarding others—visible as data. Furthermore, the materiality of the activities of reading on a screen differs in obvious ways from reading a newspaper that is made of paper and ink and spread on a table or lap. The relationship is not one of sameness, of reproducing one medium in another, but one of incorporation (of newspaper as a media form) and transformation (of technological basis and functions).

Bolter and Grusin (1999, 197–200) argue that the Internet remediates the functions and aesthetics of previous media from television and video to animated film, surveillance cameras, radio, and the telephone—gradually and to varying degrees. As a communication medium, the Internet connects to media as historically distant as the telegraph by facilitating nearly instant communication across the globe. New media can be made familiar (or domesticated) through analogies to previous media, and familiar forms of representation and interaction help to bridge differences in technological makeup (no matter how radical these may be). At the same time, these analogies have shortcomings in not allowing for differences in materiality and technological horizons of possibility. There are differences in how media operate and function as technologies and technological assemblages and in what kinds of interactions they facilitate or demand on the part of users. Similarities in representation do matter, for this is the level of engagement that is familiar to all users, but this is not all there is to intermedia relationships. The Internet involves specificities—the technical protocols, network structures, file formats, databases, software, and hardware contributing to what we understand as the Internet—that cannot be reduced to other media. The Internet is not instrumental in the sense of functioning as a transparent "window on the world." It is "windowed itself—with windows that open on to other representations or other media" (Bolter and Grusin 1999, 34). Furthermore, "Even when attached to glass tubes, computers do not simply allow one to see what is on the other side but rather use glass to send and receive light pulses necessary to re-create the referent (if one exists)" (Chun 2004, 27). Rather than a channel or a platform (in a neutral sense of the term), the Internet is more like an assemblage of material artifacts, technological standards and protocols, information architecture, practices (of design, economy, and commerce), community features, forms of communication, conventions of representation, and experiences of user engagement.

Materializations

Format and content questions can also be posed as a matter of materialization. Bill Brown (2000, 4) argues that when an object is understood as a thing, this is less about naming the object than it is about a particular subject-object relation. Understanding objects as things with certain potency—others might call it agency or force—makes it possible to see how they "organize our private and public affection" (Brown 2000, 7). In other words, things matter. Developing further Brown's idea of subject-object relations, Hayles (2009) argues that materiality results from physicality and attention—from objects and entities being grasped, used, and sensed in certain ways. Karen Barad (2007, 35) similarly considers matter as "a dynamic and shifting entanglement of relations, rather than as a property of things."

All this helps to see materiality as contingent in its perceptual nature (cf. Bennett 2010). Objects have properties (such as mass, weight, or texture). Materialization is about how these properties are perceived, how people orient themselves toward the objects, and how the objects resonate. Materialization is also a matter of affective dynamics.

The materialization of images on Wife Bucket can be mapped through various routes, the first of which involves their technologies of production. The images are shot with a digital camera in mundane locations such as private residencies, swingers' clubs and gatherings, motels, gardens, cars, and nude beaches. As digital files made of zeros and ones, the images are, on the level of the representational, rife with indexical and iconic traces of what has appeared in front of the camera—of bodies, details of material culture, and textures of the spaces depicted. The images materialize not merely as digital files—for this would be an abstract materialization, indeed—but as shots interpreted through the codes of amateur imaging and home media (that is, directness, authenticity, realness, and recognizably intimate resonance). They are embedded in textures of domesticity that have a particular feel.

The image files are then imported to a computer (with the aid of wires or Bluetooth) and perhaps treated for color contrast and size in image-manipulation software (in many instances, the eyes or other facial features of the performers have been disguised with the obvious aid of blurs, pencils, brushes, and other editing tools). After being saved on a hard drive, the files are uploaded to Wife Bucket, where users agree to the terms and conditions of publishing and provide identification information about the performers before copying the file on the server operated by http://seemybucks.com. On the site, a note or other pictures submitted by the same user may accompany the individual images, but they are also made available without such contextualization. Once uploaded, the images enter a social circulation that is uncontrollable in its directions. One can ask for images to be deleted, but there is no way to completely erase an image after it is made available. As content that is accessible on a pay site, the images have already materialized as commodities. Ultimately, the images materialize as users click on hyperlinks and download the files, interact with their texture and feel, make sense of them in the context of the site, and perhaps find points of resonance with them.

These materializations are framed by the technologies used for accessing them—laptop computers, desktop computers, cables, wires, modems, keyboards, mice, and screens—that involve a particular sense of connectedness and detachment, intimacy and distance. Illuminated by a computer screen (constantly refreshing, slightly flickering, and illuminated against a white background), easily copied and forwarded, the images both originate from and detail a particular time, moment, and space as iconic and indexical traces. At the same time, they travel across geographical borders with the tenacity particular to digital files in a computer network. This tenacity and ubiquity involves particular viral resonance: the images can be accessed again and again as copies without originals.

The experiential effects of digital media are underpinned by their technological makeup (hardware, software, cables, scripts, protocols, both tangible artifacts and the fruits of immaterial labor). This, however, does not mean losing sight of what is depicted on the screen and how. According to Hillis (2009, 263), "part of the seduction of digital flows from the affective materiality of the digital sign/body"—that is, from the bodies represented on the screen that carry traces of affective materiality. This sense of presence—based on the intermeshing of the indexical and the iconic and facilitated by the nearly instantaneous speed of networked communications—makes it impossible to decouple the semiotic from the material. The videos on Wife Bucket are not seen in real time, yet they are equally laden with a sense of presence, largely since "grainy moving images have become a marker of the real" (Chun 2008, 316) (figure 3.8). The videos and still images resonate through looks directed at the camera that often seem to involve a great deal of intimacy and are suggestive of relationships and affective dynamics between the people in front of and behind the camera. Sporting the semiotic signs of amateurism and authenticity as traces of what has taken place and been recorded with varying degrees of skill and effort, the images resonate in a mundane and intimate mode that invites a curious and titillating gaze but does not allow a comfortable sense of distance. Such closeness can be sensed as disturbing, but it is also where much of the attraction of amateur imaging lies.

Domestic Pornotopia

The contingent materialization of images through perception is guided and framed by the site and the rhetoric it deploys. This is something of a distanced spectacle that follows the general guidelines of pornographic

Figure 3.8
Domestic pornotopia in the Wife Bucket blog

hyperbole. Individual submissions are categorized largely in terms of what kind of wife is posing or shown in them. On the front page of Wife Bucket, one finds "Blind Folded Wife," "White Wife," "Naked Muslim Wife," "Homemade Wife Slave," "Wild Wife," "Skinny Wife," "Amateur Army Wife," "High Class Cuckold Wife," "Cheating Wife," "Young Teenage Wife," "Naked Wife," "Amateur Latina Wife," "Pregnant Wife," "Unemployed Wife," "Stranger Fucking Wife," "Chubby Wife," "Insane Wife," and more. Such labels create a sense of an objectifying distance that works against the intimate resonance of some of the images.

The image galleries available on the front page make this focus equally evident. The women depicted in the thumbnail images (and there are women in every picture) are described as wives, mature hookers, and MILFs but with considerable variation. The accompanying text provides more detail: "The Original Amateur Wife Site! 100% Real Amateur Women having sex with husbands, swingers and strangers. Wife Bucket is the biggest and best site featuring nothing but Real Wives, MILFs, Amateur Sluts, Chuckolds, and Leaked Pictures and Videos. Over 30,000+ Pictures and 1,000+

Videos of amateur women is currently available on our site with new material added daily! See what REAL women do behind closed doors. We have tons of lonely cheating wives, business women, naked teachers, and even school lunch ladies!" This taxonomy guarantees diversity and variation while situating the women within the confines of marital ties. Whether the women transgress the principles of monogamy or perform within them, they remain wives. Male bodies (of husbands, boyfriends, friends, swingers, and strangers) are present, but the visual spectacle of female bodies dominates the landscape.

Wives are equally prevalent elsewhere. On Porn.com, the category of "housewives" has the second largest number of videos listed under it (the first is cum shots, and the third is blowjobs). This may seem surprising, yet it is less so when the illustrious history of "the wife" in porn is considered. The American stag films of the 1940s trooped "an army of handymen, milkmen, grocery boys, icemen, radio (and, later, television) repairmen, door-to-door salesmen, bill collectors, census takers, sex researchers, meter-readers, tramps, and burglars," all visiting the home of "the frustrated, lonely, horny housewife" (Di Lauro and Rabkin 1976, 92). Ever since, the housewife has been a popular pornographic type—and trope—in stories, glossy magazines, and adult films and in amateur, reality, and gonzo porn.

The figure of the family home as pornotopia, as opened up on Wife Bucket and numerous other file-sharing sites, marks a departure from the notions of home as a safe haven that is in need of protection from the pornography that threatens it from the outside (addressed in chapter 2). The discourse on filtering software envisions the home and the family as pure, clean, and requiring acts of screening to guarantee its safety. Meanwhile, in amateur porn—whether written, visual, or audiovisual—domestic spaces are settings for sexual scenarios that are shared with others through online platforms. Kath Albury (2003, 208) points out how online porn is "often represented as a perverse outsider, forcing its way into suburban homes," independent of the fact that "the suburban bedroom may already be a pretty perverse zone." The thought is difficult to avoid when browsing through the seemingly endless image and video galleries of amateur porn in which family living rooms, kitchens, bathrooms, backyards, and bedrooms are documented as settings for hardcore action, BDSM scenarios, blowjob sessions, and casual poses. If porn does not merely enter the home but also originates from it, its miasmic filth becomes ambiguous and difficult to do away with (as something that moves from the home to the world outside and back again). Turning the notion of "clean domesticity" around, it can be argued that porn is domestic and has been so throughout its manifestations in different media (see Juffer 1998; Lillie 2002). Porn has been consumed largely within the home, and amateur porn production has a long history, even if it has become much more visible recently. Furthermore, the home is also a site of pornographic fantasy—a pornotopia in its own right.

Ultimately, protecting the family from porn means protecting it from itself and its own members and—centrally—protecting the ideal notion of family that has a random connection to lived and felt realities. Without the symbolic notion of clean family life, the low-fidelity displays of home-grown sex (and all kinds of incest fantasies) that are shared online would have much less appeal. Fences around the clean home become boundaries to transgress, while clean bodies and neat family spaces call for all kinds of nastiness. This becomes clear when reading selections from Literotica (http://literotica.com), an amateur story archive that was established in 1998 and currently hosts over 200,000 individual submissions. On Literotica, readers can rate and give feedback on submissions, and top stories are listed separately. Stories can be entered into numerous competitions (such as monthly and yearly winners and Earth Day and Valentine's Day contests), and they are also ranked according to their number of reads. The site involves peer rating, feedback, and support (as in the form of volunteer editors) and community features such as a bulletin board, chat forum, and personal ads. This elaborate site has been operating for more than a decade. It is a site of both affective and immaterial labor on which authors and readers interact and contribute to both for the love of a "good story" and fondness for the community (see Paasonen 2010b).

The stories are divided into thirty-two categories, the most popular of which include "Erotic couplings" ("Wild one-on-one consensual sex," 31,068 stories in August 2010), "Incest/Taboo" ("Keeping it in the family," 22,108 stories), "BDSM" ("Bondage, D/s, and other power games," 17,210 stories), and "Loving Wives" (with "Tales of adventurous married women & their mates," 16,704 stories). The first category is an umbrella term for diverse heterosexual activities happening in twos, and the three others involve transgression in different ways—the incest taboo, the limits of vanilla, and matrimonial ties. The figure of a wife has perennial popularity in Literorica stories, particularly in the categories of "Loving Wives" and "Group Sex" ("Orgies, swingers, and others"). "Loving Wives" stories routinely open with a description of the wife's looks, as described by the husband, and as the story unravels, the woman has sex with other men—through mutual agreement, on her own initiative, or as set up by the husband. The stories are not merely about swinging couples who indulge in their mutual whims and desires. They also address voyeuristic tendencies, sexual exploration, jealousy and possessiveness, feelings of sexual frustration and inadequacy, and the suspension or transgression of moral conventions and codes of decency. By doing so, they invest sexual activities with the complexity of affect and psychological motivation (feelings of interest turned to fear, jealousy, humiliation, and pleasure and feelings of disgust turned to affection) that are often focalized through the perspective of the husband.

The "Incest/Taboo" and "Loving Wives" stories involve a density of meanings concerning marriage, family, and sexuality. The incest taboo prohibiting sexual interaction between close members of the family is one of the more fundamental interdictions that some anthropologists have defined as universal (see Levi-Strauss 2004; Leach 2004). James B. Twitchell (1989) even sees it as an organizing principle of Anglo-American culture. As such, the incest taboo is a source of considerable anxiety and an object of emotional investment. Literotica stories are galvanized by the taboo and acts of transgressing it. The family home turns into something of a pornotopia as siblings have sex with each others, parents, friends, and parents of friends ("Service") and as generational gaps are bridged when granddaughters lose their virginity to their grandfathers in gangbangs featuring five of his closest friends ("Grampa's Girl Friday"). These are not homes that require SafeEyes or CyberNanny to ward off the miasmic forces of online porn that attack the safety of private spaces but are their flip side—sites of excessive taboo acts and hyperbolic transgressions.

Moderate Excess

The MILF is a product of U.S. popular culture, and it connects to fantasies concerning mature women and the dynamics of matrimony and extramarital sex. The MILF figures prominently in reality and amateur porn but is also used interchangeably with "mature" on all kinds of sites. Introduced to the broader public in the 1999 movie *American Pie*, which featured young men lusting after mature women (mostly the mothers of their own friends), these "mothers I'd like to fuck" have since become the subject of many porn sites (such as http://milffox.com, http://milfbank.com, http://milf-movs.com, http://themilf.net, and http://milfshake.com). Mature women have become more prominent in online porn due to the rise of niches and subcategories but also due to consumers' desire for alternatives to "hot teens" or "barely legal" performers. The MILF, much like the more recent cougar, is a figure of sexual experience, active desire, and sex with no strings attached. *Cougar* refers to divorced women who are interested in younger men, but the MILF is more ambivalent a category. MILFs can be married or divorced, in their 20s, 30s, 40s, or 50s, as long as they have children. Building on and feeding back to the American porn trope of the housewife, the MILF is also a means of articulating anxieties and tensions concerning matrimony and sexuality.

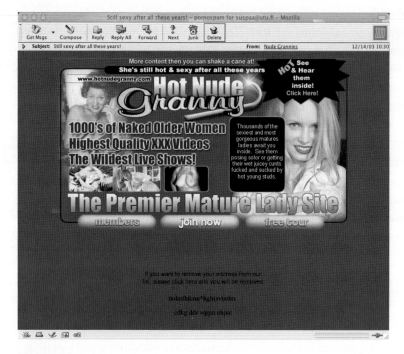

Figure 3.9
Spam email advertisement for Hot Nude Grannies (2003) and the flexibility of age categories

The MILF is strongly presented in the porn spam material I collected in 2002 to 2004, such as MILF Hunter, MILF Riders, MILF4U, M.I.L.F. Search, M.I.L.F. Seeker, and Mom's a Slut! The ages of the women (and men) who pose for the sites generally range from the late twenties to the early forties. Age differences between the parties are clearer in the more recent subcategory of GILFS ("grannies I'd like to fuck") (such as http://www.tubegranny. com and http://www.gilfporn.com), even if some of the "hot grannies" appear to be in their forties (figure 3.9). The MILF is also in active use in sex dating sites such as MILF4U.com (currently http://bangmatch.com) that advertise in-person encounters. The message body is dominated by an image of a blonde woman in her forties who is dressed in black underwear, lying on a bed with a leopard-print bedspread, and looking astutely at the camera. Above, a small, round image with a red frame (showing a man seated by a desktop computer with one hand on the keyboard and the other at his crotch) is crossed over. The site promises possible matches with "100,000 sex-starved women." The women are listed under several categories, such as Mamateurs ("REAL Moms who think they're amateur porn stars!"), Matures ("Sexperienced woman!"), Horny Housewives ("Desperate to get away from the housework!"), Cheating Wives ("Don't get enough cock from their husbands!"), and Next-Door Neighbors ("Pretty girls, Sexy ladies, REAL MILFS!").

These are scenarios of trespassing ("Fuck somebody's wife tonight!") but also fantasy landscapes of female sexual availability and willing serviceability ("They've got pussy pics, sexual fantasies and really personal descriptions so you know who they are and what they're good at [oral sex, doggy style, cowgirl, etc.] before you get laid"). The advertisement includes testimonies that assumedly are written by male users who describe and evaluate their sexual experiences with the women they met through the site ("She fucked like a race horse"; "FUCK she could suck the cock off a race horse"). The emphasis is on realness: "100 percent Horny, 100 percent Amateur, 100 percent Real. We have every intention of getting you laid. Our female members are motivated by their own sexual needs. They want to fuck and they want to do it now" (EZCheating.com, currently http://bangmatch. com). Below this declaration of female sexual agency, a hyperlink provides a different kind of promise for the implied male recipient: "Your next door neighbors by day . . . Your sexual fuck slaves by night." Like MILF4U, EZCheating coins fantasies of accessible, no-strings-attached sex with "next door neighbors" who get nasty and, paradoxically, motivated by "their own sexual needs," end up as "sexual fuck slaves."

The figure of the MILF has traveled from a mainstream teen comedy to ProAm gonzo and reality porn, amateur sites, porn stories, and online dating sites. Like the wife, the MILF promises alternatives to the glossiness and bodily conformity of regular porn. She connotes realness, accessibility, and authenticity. At the same time, the notion of "the real" in contemporary (audio)visual pornography comes in multiple modalities that both build on and contest one another. As Feona Attwood explains,

Realness may be expressed by the extent to which the action is divorced from emotion or everyday life, or conversely the extent to which it is connected to these; it may be held to depend on the authenticity of the producers or the direct responses of the consumer; on conventions of "liveness," "nastiness," or lack of aesthetic and technical varnish; on the effective staging of conventional and recognizable porn elements; on psychologization, personalization, or politicization; on how faithfully it represents the desires of individual performers, communities, or subcultures; on interactivity; on how boldly it asserts or refuses sex and gender difference, or on how dramatically it upholds or transgresses representational and sexual norms and categories. (Attwood 2010a, 240)

Things are convoluted, indeed. As pornography has been increasingly departmentalized, its different pockets and niches operate with different notions of authenticity and realness that may be political, aesthetic, economical, representational, or any combination of these. The attraction of amateur aesthetics becomes understandable in and through the nexus of pornographic "realnesses." This realness is relational—a matter of representational conventions, camera technologies, values, subgenres and their interconnections, experiences and sensations afforded by media technologies, and affective intensities involved in the production and consumption of pornography. The sense of realness in online porn is tied to notions of directness—the visual and auditory accessibility of physically distant people and events (and the more tangible access to products for purchase) that are associated with the Internet as a medium. What is physically distant remains so even when it is accessed or interfaced with online. Physical distance can be bridged through image, sound, and text, yet it remains and may give rise to a feeling of safety and control. The consumers of online pornography remain by their computers (whether at home, in the office, or somewhere else), anonymous, and visible as IP addresses, movements tracked with cookies, credit-card information, and visitor and member logins. Isolated behind the screen, users navigate from one site to another, browse, search, follow hyperlinks, and choose certain images, videos, and stories for downloading and closer inspection.

Bodies Stretched and Failing

Amateur images stand for the authentic, real, and the removal of the hyperbolic excess that characterizes much of contemporary porn. Its aesthetics, like those of gonzo and reality porn, can be seen as a reaction against the artificial and fantastic aspects of commercial porn. At the same time, the fantastic continues to have its own appeal, and porn sites regularly introduce into their diet acts that were once deemed extreme. The hyperbolic seems to have a perpetual presence in commercial hardcore: "Hardcore pornography is about the depiction of literal excess; about multiple penis plunging into one asshole or one vagina (or even both) about orgies about the world's biggest gang bangs and facials in which a dozen or more men shoot their genetic material onto the grinning faces of starlets as cum slathers their foreheads, cheeks, chin, lips, and teeth. The sheer unremitting quantity becomes an object in itself. Nothing can ever be enough" (Sargeant 2006). Jack Sargeant's description of pornographic abundance and excess—hyperbolic and pornographic in itself—refers both to the modality of hyperbole as central to the genre and to its development during the past decades. It can be argued that as pornography has grown increasingly demanding in terms of the acts it features, the division between amateurs and professionals has also become one of bodily skill, ability, and threshold. Acts such as double anal or ass-to-mouth (ATM) sex, for example, are not the most common of sexual acts exhibited in amateur porn galleries. These acts are spectacular in their physical demand level and threshold, and their extraordinariness grants them additional added value.

In one recurring amateur video theme, attempts at anal sex are halted by—or carried out in spite of—screams of pain. Unlike the eloquently functioning bodies of commercial porn and anal penetrations taking place with seemingly no lubrication or warm-up, amateur bodies regularly fail to comply. They do not always desire, perform, or enjoy according to generic scripts and choreographies. These "failures" increase the sense of authenticity and realness associated with amateur videos and help to set them apart from commercial productions. In commercial porn, scenes featuring acts that fail may be included in DVDs as extras and bloopers, and they are also compiled online to be enjoyed separately from the films themselves. In such clips, remixes, and mashups, performers fall off sofas during action shots, complex positions fail and people fall over, and the flow of action is disrupted as people start laughing, pause, and rearrange themselves. Although amateur failures point to the assumed realness of the sex acts recorded on camera, professional bloopers point out the acted-out nature of skillful porn performance. Once the performers have rearranged themselves, smiles tend to disappear and relaxed bodily postures are replaced by knowing and stylized poses, gestures, and expressions optimized for the camera. Nevertheless, in their displays of acts that do not comply with the smooth operations of commercial porn, both bloopers and amateur clips broaden notions of what porn is, what it involves, and how it is performed and consumed.

Author and porn film director Tristan Taormino (2008) calls porn performers stars because they are "sexual athletes" who are able and required to perform acts that seem unlikely or even physically impossible for most people. For Taormino, porn performance involves pushing the boundaries of what bodies are considered able to do, and this professional skill should be acknowledged and appreciated. This is a valid point even if one is not considering the more extreme subgenres (such as the gangbang videos and sexual marathons discussed in chapter 4). In a perpetual search for novelty—for something different to show people and have people pay for—the imageries of commercial pornography have grown increasingly fantastic. Double penetration has become standard fare in heteroporn, double anal is no longer a rare specialty, and the more demanding and elaborate group choreographies of double-vaginal, double-anal (DV/DA) sex (that is, the two abovementioned acts combined) have grown increasingly recognizable. Such acts stretch the bodily capacities of the female performers, and they raise questions of ethics and labor—namely, what the female performers act out, on what conditions, and at what expense as their bodies are stretched to the boundaries of their carnal affordance (cf. Boyle 2008, 46). Separating amateur porn from the professional, these are the kind of acts that one should not try at home.

4   The Literal and the Hyperbolic: Mapping the Modalities of Online Porn

If porn is considered one of the lowest forms of popular culture (Williams 1991, 2), then porn spam—or junk email—would in all likelihood be considered the lowest of the low (figure 4.1). Amateur porn may retain some status as peer practice and even "folk culture," but spam email connotes the bulky and the commercial. Some of this is already implied in the explicitly meaty term *spam*, referring to the processed, canned pork luncheon meat product that has been manufactured by Hormel Foods in the United

Figure 4.1
Spam advertisement for http://www.orgasm.com (2003)

States since the 1930s and that has been a staple element of everyday diets in Great Britain since World War II (see Parikka and Sampson 2009, 1–2). Spam is industrial and bulky. Consequently, things labeled *spam* lose their individual character and become representative of a mass or pulp. By both describing and orienting attitudes toward unsolicited email, the labels of *junk*, *bulk*, and *spam* circumvent considerations of aesthetic qualities.

It is therefore not surprising that some researchers are disturbed by the linking of porn and spam. Alex Halavais (2005, 19–21) sees the connection as buttressing the derogative and value-laden terminology of *scourge*, *sleaze*, and *filth* that is associated with porn and as steering focus away from alternative, amateur, and independent pornographies. For Katrien Jacobs (2007, 2–3), spam is corporate debris and represents the technological push of consumer culture that has no connection to more experimental and subcultural endeavors (such as nerd porn, dyke porn, tranny porn, and bear porn) that provide possibilities for rethinking the genre in question. Although this may be the case, all kinds of pornographies—their differences as well as points of contact—need to be addressed beyond the (contingent, largely blurred and random, yet common, hierarchical, and regulatory) divisions of the mainstream and the alternative and of the commercial and the noncommercial if we are to understand developments in the field.

Spam email comprises an estimated one third to two thirds of all global email traffic, and seasonal estimates have been as high as 80 percent. After the filtering carried out by service providers and individual users, the mass of spam in anyone's inbox may be less overwhelming, yet it remains an integral part of everyday Internet use. The volume of spam increased steadily in the mid-1990s as more organized ventures replaced chain letters and random mass mailings (Cranor and LaMacchia 1998, 74; also McWilliams 2005). Spam promotes everything, including mortgage bargains, fast access to drugs (like Cialis, Viagra, and Valium), ready-made college diplomas, lottery award notifications, and commercial porn sites. In terms of online content and Internet use, spam email represents the mundane, the banal, and the largely undesired. The spam messages that I address here are all in English and appear to originate from North America, although this location is separate from the physical location of globally distributed spam servers. Spam address databases are mined from various Web sites (or in the case of viruses, from email clients) rather than demographic data, as is the case with postal junk mail. Attached personal greetings, if any, are haphazard.

Yet the massive global circulation of spam implies that the messages occasionally "arrive" in ways that are intended by the sender and attract users to click on their hyperlinks (Cranor and LaMacchia 1998, 74–75).

Online Porn in Figures

Pornography is a contingent genre that is divided into endless subgenres that share certain family resemblance but that also differ significantly from one another. Unlike Walter Kendrick (1996), I do not see pornography merely as a regulatory category through which the ruling classes have historically tried to regulate public access to materials deemed dangerous or seditious for the masses (or the underclass). Pornography comes with its own specificities, idiosyncrasies, and modalities that need to be accounted for if we are to understand the role that it plays in contemporary culture and the ways in which online practices have shaped and transformed the pornographic. This chapter begins with a descriptive account of spam messages that is intersected by considerations of representational histories and interracial porn, hyperbole, recognizability, transgression, and spectacle in and for pornography. This material is followed by a discussion of the methodological and epistemological issues that are related to content analysis and interpretation, the role of camp and humor, and the recurrent modalities of porn.

When I first considered spam email, I wanted to address the mass of it, which would have been impossible to accomplish by picking some advertisements for analysis and disregarding others. My chosen strategy was content analysis. I coded the messages in terms of subgenre, performers (for example, by gender, ethnicity, approximate age, mode of dress or undress, and hair style), acts performed, the terminology used (for women, men, genitalia, sexual acts, and the action in general), as well as the ways in which the sender and the recipient of the message were marked (such as how the sender was identified and whether the greetings or invitations were of a general or personal nature). Within the different categories, further details emerged. Penetrative sex, for example, could be vaginal, anal, or double and could involve objects, fingering, fisting, or masturbation, while cum shots (external ejaculations) could be directed at a female partner's face, mouth, breast, or other parts of the body.

The most popular singular sex act depicted in the spam messages is oral sex, which is presented in 59 percent of all the advertisements (217 out of

366) (figures 4.2 and 4.3). Heterosexual coitus is featured in 39 percent, cum shots in 22 percent, and male-to-female anal sex in 16 percent of the messages in total. Oral sex is depicted in 502 individual images. Penetrative vaginal sex visualized as "meat shots" of a penis entering a vagina is the second most popular act, followed by cum shots, girl-on-girl acts, variations of foreplay, group sex, and male-to-female anal sex. These are followed by female masturbation, vaginal insertion with objects, and diverse niche practices, such as squirting, bondage, bestiality, fingering, fisting, and double penetration.

Within the oral sex category, the overwhelming majority of acts (79 percent) involve fellatio (a female performer giving oral sex to a male partner). In 11 percent of the oral sex acts, both parties are female; in 5 percent, the active partner is male; in 2 percent, women are performing with animals; in 1 percent, bisexual acts are depicted with several male performers; and in 2 percent, transgender acts are shown in various combinations. Fellatio is by far the most widely repeated sexual act in spam material as a whole.

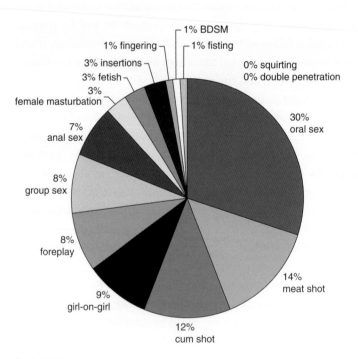

Figure 4.2
Sexual acts visualized in spam messages

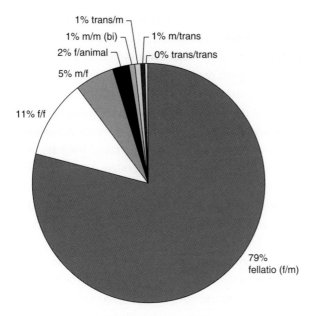

Figure 4.3
Depictions of oral sex and their active or passive partners in spam messages

It is often complemented by cum shots (207 instances in total), the majority of which are targeted at the female partner's face (93), mouth (73), and breasts (21). Ejaculation is also presented as evidence of female orgasm: female ejaculations are depicted in 6 percent of all cum shots. All this is predictable, given that male orgasm remains firmly at the center of contemporary porn images, as other content analyses have shown (McKee et al. 2008, 65–68). Furthermore, oral sex was a perennial favorite in (audio) visual pornography well before the era of online networking. An estimated 37 percent of American stag films included fellatio in the 1920s; around 50 percent did so in the 1930s; 70 percent did so in the 1950s; and close to 100 percent did so in the 1970s (Di Lauro and Rabkin 1976, 100). The situation remains somewhat similar in online porn. Out of all the videos published on Porn.com in February 2010, 17 percent were categorized as cum shots, and 12 percent as blowjobs. These two categories and the all-American category of housewives (13 percent) listed the most content. Cum shots were established by 1977 in porn films as a somewhat technical, compulsory, and highly visible sign of sexual climax that both verifies male sexual pleasure and culminates the sexual act (Williams 1989, 93–95).

Writing on gay video porn, Richard Dyer explains the popularity of cum shots through their role as evidence: "The goal of the pornographic narrative is coming; in filmic terms, the goal is ejaculation, that is, visible coming. If the goal of the pornographic protagonist (the actor or 'character') is to come, the goal of the spectator is to see him come (and, more often than not, probably, to come at the same time as him). Partly this has to do with 'proof,' with the form's 'literalness,' as Beatrice Faust puts it, with the idea that if you don't really see semen, the performer could have faked it (and so you haven't had value for money)" (Dyer 2002b, 144). For these reasons, cum shots are also referred to as "money shots." Although external ejaculation has traditionally been associated with the contraceptive method of *coitus interruptus*, in its cinematic and videographic reiteration it has become an important pornographic trope that is divided into numerous subcategories and that has virtually endless image galleries, video listings, and Web sites dedicated to it (Moore and Weissbein 2010, 81). The category of cum shots on Porn.com includes some 38,000 videos divided into numerous subcategories depending on which body part is being ejaculated on and what other activities the videos entail: these include "Ass" (1,597 videos), "Back" (154), "Chest" (234), "Face" (18,544), "Feet" (176), "Hands" (591), "Pussy" (625), "Stomach" (908), "Swallow" (10,165), "Swapping" (720), and "Tits" (4,181). Cum shots, preferably targeted at the partner's face or mouth, function as indexical evidence of male sexual climax. As these video listings illustrate, they are also key fantasy figures in their own right.

Heterosexual Structuralism

Of all the characters presented in the spam messages, 72 percent are female. These women are thin (98 percent), young (92 percent), and white (66 percent) and have long (84 percent) and blond (48 percent) hair. The predominance of female performers is not unexpected, given that the female body in various stages of undress and exposure has been the main focus of pornography from eighteenth-century graphic prints to photography, magazines, film, video, and beyond. This is also the case in amateur porn. Addressing amateur videos on YouPorn, Niels Van Doorn (2010, 425) identifies them as making use of a "normative mainstream 'pornoscript'" that highlights "sexual difference as the primary source of heterosexual visual pleasure, which is predominantly experienced from a male subject posi-tion."[1] Don Slater makes use of a similar term, "pornonormativity," when discussing the repetition of heteroporn conventions in IRC porn exchanges. The aspects of "pornonormativity" include the recycling of sex acts, body types, fetishes, and kinks familiar from so-called mainstream porn, deeply gendered self-representations ("young blonde bombshells and well-hung dudes"), heteronormativity (the absence of gay sex), depictions of female bisexuality (girl-on-girl sex), and the policing of "pariah sexualities" that are seen as illegal or otherwise too kinky (Slater 1998, 99–103). Spam mate-rial can be seen as "pornonormative" in that it includes no ads for gay porn yet plentiful displays of girl-on-girl action. Examples of "pariah sexualities" such as bestiality and urophilia are nevertheless included in its palette, and as discussed later in this chapter, its depictions of transgender sex compli-cate any overarching analyses of heteronormativity.

Similar broadening of the palette is evident on Porn.com and PornHub. The latter's video listings are topped by the generic categories of "Big Tits" and "Hardcore," while the categories of both gay and shemale porn offer no content and link to an external site, 8Tube. The diversification of the palette should not lead one to underestimate the predominance of certain body aesthetics, sexual acts, and representational conventions over oth-ers. Contingent "pornoscripts" have taken shape over numerous decades, even centuries, and although the range of pornography has grown increas-ingly diverse in terms of its themes, preferences, target audiences, and body styles, the female body engaging in heterosexual acts remains firmly at its center. Pornography by and large is made with male heterosexual consum-ers in mind (cf. McNair 2002, 43). As Simon Lindgren (2010, 184) notes in his study of online porn fandom, the porn audience conversing online is a male homosocial one: "Men watch porn to be men, together, in a social and cultural context where the most important elements are—in [Stephen] Strager's words, 'masturbation,' 'male pleasure,' and 'reductive female categorization.'"

These notes on the male homosocial framing of porn and the focus on categorizing female bodies and performers reverberate with the porn spam material. In addition to the visual focus on female bodies, women are described with a far wider range of adjectives and nouns than men. Most popular terms for women include *girl, slut, babe,* and *lesbian,* followed by *woman, chick, bitch, whore, virgin, lady,* and *honey.* The range remains similar in the selection of adjectives that includes *hot, teen, sexy, young, nasty, sweet, innocent, hungry, starved, dirty, nympho,* and *naughty*. The emphasis is firmly on youth (*girl, teen, young*), sexual experience (*slut, lesbian, nasty*), and desirability (*hot, sexy*) balanced with notions of "sweetness" (*babe, sweet, innocent*). Women are described with nouns in 410 accounts, whereas there are only 49 similar descriptions of men. The terminology used for men is much narrower and more homosocial in tone: they are referred to as *guys, men, studs, mates, buddies, dudes,* and *brothers*. As a rule, men are not defined with other adjectives than *horny* except when describing their penises. Here, the range of terms is rather uniform: the most popular terms for male genitalia are *big, monster, huge, over 12 inches, fat, thick,* and *massive* (others include *gigantic, long, hard, enormous, abnormal, colossal,* and *large*) (figure 4.4).

The terminology helps to depict heterosex as a game involving clear-cut differences. The choice of adjectives resonates with, envisions, and elaborates on gender as a binary structure made of mutually opposing shapes and sizes. The spectacularly massive and gigantic male organs are juxtaposed with diminutive female genitalia that is *tight, tiny, little,* and *small*

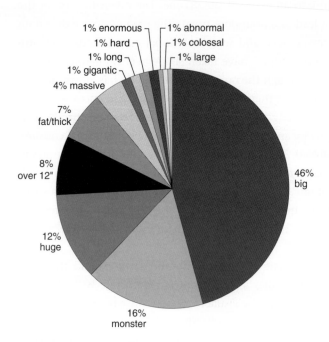

Figure 4.4
Adjectives for male genitalia in spam messages

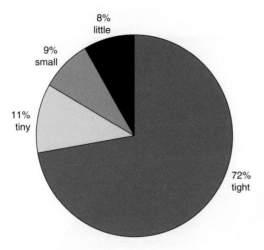

Figure 4.5
Adjectives for female genitalia in spam messages

(figure 4.5). Such extreme juxtapositions—familiar from the promotional material of porn sites, videos, and erotica—creates a particular vocabulary for heterosex. In addition to the general terminology of *fucking, sucking, banging,* and *swallowing* that comprises two thirds of all the terms used for sexual acts, the lexicon broadens to an elaborate detailing of the tight and the frictional, with verbs such as *stretch, stuff, nail, punish, give hard, pound, gag, torture, rip, split open, exploit, choke, dilate,* and *chug* (figure 4.6). The choice of adjectives for sex emphasizes the nasty and the hardcore, including *extreme, shocking, nasty, filthy, bizarre, freakish, kinky, amazing, perverted, raw, sick, insane,* and *rough.*

Large male genitalia are presented as key attractions in advertisements for the sites 14 Inches, Big Cock Sex, Big Dick Mania, Freakish Cocks, Her First Big Cock, Megacock Cravers, Monster Cock Farm, Record Sizes, and Shocking Cocks. The ads predominantly use meat shots, which are supported by firmly hyperbolic invitations ("Watch colossal cocks split tight holes right open," Big Cock Sex; "Discover April's Big Dick Addiction When she gets fucked by a Big nasty donkey dick in her tight pussy!," Big Dick Mania) and descriptions ("Tight teen twats violated by monster-size cocks," "Dirty Cunts Split Open with Monster Cocks," Monster Cock Farm). As I have argued elsewhere (Paasonen 2007, 52), the ads invite users to visit the

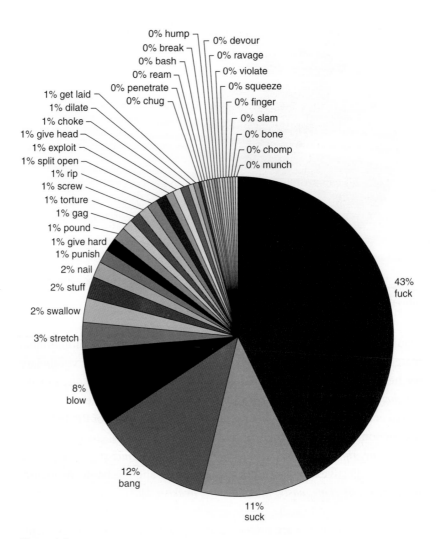

Figure 4.6
Terms for sex in spam messages

sites of penises-as-spectacle where men proudly display their genitalia for viewer gratification. Although the presence of female performers remains central to the ads in anchoring the displays of spectacular male genitalia in the framework of heterosex, the ads do, at least to a degree, mark a departure from the visual centrality of female bodies. The women have exaggerated expressions of surprise, startle, and shock, given that the main emphasis is on the extraordinary capacities of the penises. At the same time, these penises-as-spectacle are defined as *monstrous, abnormal, nasty,* or even belonging to another species, such as donkeys. The penises are marked as exceptional, awesome, and overwhelming, while the sexual acts they engage in are described in rather violent and frictional terms.

According to the culturally predominant notion of gender as a binary structure involving "the opposite sexes," female and male bodies are seen to complement each other all the way to their interconnecting genitalia (Richardson 1996, 7). Such "heterosexual structuralism" envisions genders as mutually opposing yet complementary to each other and interconnected by heterosexual desire (Butler 1993, 90–91). As if faithful to the logic of heterosexual structuralism, pornography zooms in on body parts marked as primary signifiers of gender difference, such as genitalia, breasts, buttocks, long hair, and red painted lips.[2] Gender differences are defined as primarily sexual and as culminating in the presentation of genitalia (Kuhn 1994, 34–37). Laura Kipnis (1999, 200) suggests that heterosexual pornography "creates a fantastical world composed of two sexes but one gender, and that one gender looks a lot more like that what we think of (perhaps stereotypically) as 'male.'" For Kipnis, porn concerns a fantasy of complete sexual commensurability where both men and women are ever willing to engage in sexual acts outside intimate commitments and where what is pleasing to the male partner is also pleasing to the female. This notion of pornotopia is recognizable in the examples addressed in this book, yet it is noteworthy that they also render highly visible the frictions and incommensurability involved in its scenarios. On the one hand, the women function as mirrors of male desire (for example, when begging male partners to ejaculate on their faces), yet such "friction-free" exchanges are knowingly disrupted by descriptions of heterosex as acts of *stretching, nailing, torturing, ripping, splitting open, choking,* and *exploiting,* on the other. In the examples presented above, heterosexual structuralism seems stretched to the point of dysfunction. Signs of gender difference are heightened and exaggerated to such a degree that heterosexual coitus becomes a near-impossible play of colossal penises and the tiniest of vaginas. Much remains familiar in comparison to amateur porn sites addressed in the previous chapter, yet the modality is much more firmly one of hyperbole.

Racial Boundaries and Historical Echoes

Gender is far from being the only social or identity category depicted through hyperbole, for differences in terms of age, class, ethnicity, and nationality are highlighted with equal vigor. In advertisements for interracial porn, the juxtaposition of "huge penises" and "tiny vaginas" is backed up with and amplified by spectacularly contrasted skin hues. From the visual display of pale white flesh and brown skin tones to textual exclamations and site titles, the ads conjure up a theater of juxtapositions (Hall 1996, 18) in which both gendered and racialized differences are played out as something of a Manichean allegory (Gates 1986)—that is, as divided into mutually opposing, exclusive, and hierarchical poles: "Sweet and cute girls take black boners!" (White Pussy Black Cocks); "Cum and see this young slutty couple as they fuck and suck on huge black monster cock!!!" (Monster Cock Farm). The thumbnail images in Web directories for interracial porn—such as http://interracialxporn.com, http://bwmovies.com, http://interracialpornclips.com, and http://bestinterracialmovies.com—depict (predominantly although not exclusively white) women posing for the camera and performing fellatio on black men and couples standing side by side and engaging in coitus and anal sex. The blackness of the male performers implies that the term *interracial* in fact connotes black men.[3]

The names of interracial porn sites—such as White Pussy Black Cocks, Black Cocks White Sluts, Black Bros White Hoes, White Meat on Black Street, Dark Meat White Treat, or Black Cocks White Twats—encapsulate clear-cut differences and hyperbolic juxtapositions. The titles have an uncanny resemblance to *Black Skin, White Masks* (*Peau noire, masques blancs*), the title of Franz Fanon's classic 1952 analysis of gendered and racialized subject positions under colonial rule. I would even suggest that the titles are connected by more than mere academic wordplay. In *Black Skin, White Masks*, Fanon (1967, 110–111) argues that blackness has been defined in relation to and through its difference to whiteness, through stories, anecdotes, and metaphors, such as "black magic" and "animal sexuality." In the colonial

Figure 4.7
The spectacle of race: spam advertisement for http://blackonwhite.com (2003)

order, both the attraction and danger of black men were located in the
sexual, and the black man was ultimately identified as a monstrous penis:
"He *is* penis" (Fanon 1967, 126, 170, 177). A similar dynamic seems to
be at play in spam messages envisioning "Big black cocks stretching tight
teen pussies!" (Jungle Fever) and "Fucking white holes with some big black
poles!" (Black Bros White Hoes).[4]

In fact, depictions of race, ethnicity, class, and nationality in porn are
rife with historical echoes to the point of seeming to be overdetermined
by them. When addressing historical echoes in North American interracial
porn, Linda Williams (2004c, 270, 272) argues that it provides spaces for
exploring tensions, histories, and fantasies that are otherwise silenced by
official color blindness. Interracial porn references a broad spectrum of stereotypes and sexual taboos that draw on and interlace with histories of slavery and (as is evident in sites such as Black Bros White Hoes, White Pussy
Black Cocks, and Black Cocks White Sluts) historical stereotypes and taboos
concerning sexual relations between black men and white women. Following Georges Bataille, Williams reads the recognition and violation of taboo

as a central attraction of pornography that involves both desire and fear. In acts of transgression, taboos are made visible and recognizable, and this also makes it possible to rework them. Aiming to detach interracial porn from the label of racism, Williams (2004c, 281, 284–286) argues that porn scenarios and fantasies necessitate the recognition of, rather than belief in, racialized stereotypes. Considered in this vein, the stereotypes recycled in pornography can be seen as both inflated (that is, hyperbolic) and deflated (in terms of their effect or people's belief in them).[5]

This is one way to approach the recurring subgenre of interracial amateur porn in which white, predominantly North American women paint messages on their bodies before and during sex with black men, marking—and indeed advertizing—themselves as "nigger whores" and "sluts for black cock," drawing arrows to their genitalia with the message "black cock only" and referring to their preferred sex partners as "niggers." Hyperbolic terminology evokes historical echoes, anchors the women in the porn lexicon of sluts and bitches, and frames the sexual activities as knowing performances and reenactments of the historical taboos they reference. Interracial porn sites seem to reference markedly anachronistic taboos and racial discourses that are parts of a different historical era. There is little taboo against people of different ethnic and racial identifications having sex together (now a common practice), yet through the process of recycling and reenactment, such taboos are given a kiss of life. Historical restrictions and depictions are revived in contemporary pornography as echoes that have undergone transformations while still remaining recognizable. Regulation and practices of everyday life have changed, and these historical taboos have been reenacted out of context and yet still resonate. For the anachronistic taboo to continue to be recognized as one, the visual depiction of sexual acts is supported by and organized through hyperbolic articulations of difference.[6]

A Colonial Adventure

Consider, for example, a site called Indian Roadtrip (http://v2.indian-road-trip.com). It advertises promises of "amazing Indian sluts wet, ripe, and ready for action!!," "the nastiest and most exotic Indian women," "luxurious Indian tight kitties," "young sex starved jungle jewels," "taboo Indian sex acts that give them continuous orgasms," and "gorgeous INDIAN SLUTS revealing their genital jewels." The site design combines text with an image collage that blends the silhouette of the Taj Mahal, an orange and yellow background connoting sunset, a large map of India, a series of pin-up poses and more explicit shots, images of a digital video camera, and a figure of a thin, balding white man penetrating a young dark-haired woman. Indian Roadtrip uses historical tropes in the way that it envisions taboo acts and the transgression of ethnic and national boundaries. The point of view is that of white male travelers who, equipped with cameras, explore the wet and ripe mysteries of female Indian sexuality and record their findings for users to share in return for a membership fee. The site presents a form of travelogue, a narrative form that has historically envisioned adventures of white protagonists in exotic lands, which, like their people, are presented as mysteries to be solved (Said 1994, 202–203). The site's advertisements evoke both the colonial figure of India as the crown jewel of the British empire and the trope of female genital jewels, and both are put forward as available for picking in the "exotic jungle" of India.[7] As José B. Capino argues, residual dynamics of colonial desire linger on in Asian pornography that caters primarily to North American consumers. These residual dynamics "resurface out of Asian porn's evocation of the figures of colonial encounter and, more important, of the historical and political resonances of Asian and Caucasian sexual relations" (Capino 2006, 207; also Shimizu 2007).

The discovery of historical echoes and hyperbolic displays of race and gender in online porn requires relatively little analytical effort. Although it cannot be reduced to these histories, it also cannot be decoupled from them, for this recycling keeps histories alive as well as subject to challenge. In porn, displays of difference are spectacular, characters are types, scenarios are highly repetitive, and all this involves a large degree of self-consciousness. Promising to show sexual acts and pleasures exactly as they unravel, porn pays little attention to its protagonists as other than types. This two-dimensional aesthetic is organically supported by the abundant use of stereotypes.

Capino (2006, 214–215) points out that the "bawdy, ridiculous, and carnivalesque humor" used in promoting Asian porn videos (like that of the spam ads and sites discussed in this chapter) is notably reflexive. Exaggeration and hyperbole produce a sense of "heightened artificiality," and the films themselves involve tongue-in-cheek acting—stylized performances of race and gender in which roles are taken up with glee and an attitude. Like Capino, I believe that analysis of racial spectacle needs to take seriously the excessive elements and registers of pornography and not merely lament over the violence involved in the recycling of colonial, racist, and sexist fantasies. By highlighting artificiality, it is possible to step away from studies of representation as a recurring—and ultimately predictable—discovery of oppressive structures, hierarchies, and relations and instead to consider the imageries from a different perspective and perhaps better account for their attraction.

Beyond the Literal: Notes on Method

All this is crucial when considering the analytical possibilities of studies of representation. Such investigations make visible the historical layers involved in apparently simple depictions and their connection to broader discourses concerning sexuality, identity, social proximity, and distance. Interpretations focusing on insistent repetition and the use of stereotypes, however, may risk both predictability (for example, by rendering individual images as rearticulations of sexist, classist, or racist ideology by default) and unhistorical assumptions that provide no space for change, difference, or variation (Shohat and Stam 1994, 199). In the course of their constant recycling, repetition and reiteration, stereotypes change, are questioned, and remain open to acts of appropriation and interpretation. At the same time, content analysis, studies of representation, and considerations of stereotypes (the methodological approaches applied above) orient attention toward the repetitive and the familiar—to what is accentuated and highlighted in porn with gusto.

An analysis of examples of online porn, particularly spam email material, reveals that the general premise of the genre (as allowing all kinds of scenarios, acts, resonances, and desires) seems recurrently exhausted by the repetition of predictable, hierarchical, and hyperbolic exaggeration of differences (ones based on gender, age, class, and histories of racism). To the degree that such questions of boundary management are central to studies of representational histories and discursive genealogies, it can also be asked whether the trajectories of interpretation applied have been implicated and oriented by the desire to uncover these (rather explicit) dynamics. Studies of representation have often identified cultural images as either supporting or challenging prevalent understandings of groups of people. Things depicted on the screen are seen as shaped and marked by histories of representation and by the social hierarchies that they are entangled with. This is not a form of disinterested critique but one that, by focusing on how images are made to matter, tries to map their role in and for making sense of the world and of individual and social identities.

Studies of representation were, for a long time, my comfort zone, yet this comfort has begun to crumble. My growing discomfort with this former zone of comfort has to do with the fundamental paradox that analyzing cultural phenomena requires participation in their construction. When setting out to investigate a case study, such as "race and gender in porn spam email," analysis of representation frames characters and scenes through social categories, systems of representation, and historically contingent referents (such as race, class, age, and gender). Individual characters become reduced to these categories (as representative thereof), and the categories mapped out are performatively produced into being as recognizable points of reference (of categories that precede their representation). Dorothea Olkowski (1999, 2) argues that a system of representation "operates by establishing a fixed standard as the norm or model." To the degree that studies of representation resort to such models and norms, it does "no more than register a complaint against the norms of language, images, and social and political structures." Although I see a point in registering such complaints against the images that we constantly interface with, there are limitations to forms of critique that first describe and identify the workings of ideology and then set out to map these operations. Representational categories may be unstable (Olkowski 1999, 3), yet analysis invests them with a sense of stability (that can then be either subverted or destabilized in acts of representation). By resorting to the categories of representation that it seeks to question, research may even lock down the meanings and affordances of the images studied. Traces of other images are always present, yet research needs to do more than merely state these connections.

Guided by the question of meaning—that is, "What does this mean?"— analysis may impose meaning onto the examples it studies (as always meaning one thing or another by default). Thus, pornography can mean all kinds of things: some see it as camp and play; some as degradation, violence, and harm; others as cultural resistance and identity work; and yet others as a symbol of the moral decay of Western societies. Writing in the framework of visual anthropology, David MacDougall (2006, 1) notes that forcing meaning on things can "blind us, causing us to see only what we expect to see or distracting us from seeing very much at all." The question of meaning orients research, shapes an analytical horizon, and may not go very far in helping to unravel the appeal and affective resonance of what we study. In *Anti-Oedipus*, Gilles Deleuze and Félix Guattari (2009, 109) criticize the focus on meaning and suggest a shift from the question "What does it mean?" to "How does it work?"—that is, to texts and images as producing certain effects and being amenable to certain uses. As Fredric Jameson (2002, 7–8, 13) notes, this involves a new (immanent, antitranscendent, hermeneutic) method for reading texts—and looking at pictures—in terms of asking what they do rather than looking for their "inner essence" as encapsulated in the question of meaning. According to Jameson (2002, 45), a "criticism which asks the question 'What does it mean?' constitutes something like an allegorical operation in which a text is systematically *rewritten* in terms of some fundamental master code or 'ultimately determining instance.' On this view, then, all 'interpretation' in the narrower sense demands the forcible or imperceptible transformation of a given text into an allegory of its particular master code or 'transcendental signified.'" I take this to mean that acts of interpretation involve specific theoretical and ideological underpinnings that orient, regulate, and shape the ways in which the objects of research are seen and are "rewritten" in acts of interpretation. To a degree, then, researchers tend to find what their premises orient them to seek out, and as the object of research is processed through the given framework, it becomes a different kind of object. For Jameson, this is the case with all interpretation involving questions of meaning. One finds what one is looking for, as the mutually incompatible readings of pornography accumulated over the past decades make more than evident.[8] Porn spam messages can be read as referencing colonial narratives and histories of racism or, alternatively, as reflexive and camp performances that create a sense of artifice and disbelief. Both routes of interpretation are as valid as they are partial. As cultural studies scholars know, meaning always depends on context. These routes of explanation frame the affective appeal of pornographies in different ways, for the transgression of historical taboos gives rise to intensities of feeling that are different from the recognition of camp or drag elements in porn performance.

Analysis and Distance

Content analysis was initially developed for interpreting written and spoken language in accordance with ideals (such as quantification and objectivity) that were derived from the natural sciences (Rose 2007, 59), and it assumes a certain distance between the researcher and the things being researched. In this sense, content analysis discloses considerations of the affective dynamics involved in encounters with pornography. The researcher looks, counts, categorizes, and reports on the findings, seemingly without being affected by the images or influencing the analysis with her own affectations. In content analysis and other forms of grounded theory, the researcher theorizes on the basis of the research material. As an epistemological stance, this means not approaching research material through a preconceived framework. Yet content description is always also a matter of interpretation, and it is filtered through the values, premises, and personal investments of the researchers involved. What one scholar identifies as violent pornography, another does not, and these differing interpretations influence both the coding and the results. And although some might label the ubiquitously popular sites featuring "teen" and "barely legal" young women as child porn, others would decline to do so (Mehta 2001, 699–700; Bridges 2010).

With porn spam email, the excessively fleshy images and the brightly colored captions, close-ups, and exclamation marks can be coded and presented as pie charts (see figures 4.2 through 4.6). In the process of analysis, the object of study is transformed, and its power and affective force become difficult to conceptualize. Spam messages are rich in small images, their resolution is low, their details are mostly difficult to decipher, and images overlap with other images, text fields, and graphical elements. Identifying features such as the performer's ethnicity or age requires work, even imaginative work. In many cases, such aspects cannot be identified or can be guessed at best. Percentages and charts have the appeal of clarity and order, yet the process of analysis that gives rise to them tends to be messier.

Pornography aims to create proximities between viewers and images, whereas content analysis is efficient in obscuring these proximities. Both content analysis and studies of representation can be critiqued for being based on and giving rise to a distance between the images studied and the one doing the study. Marco Abel (2007, xii) argues that representation "draws a line between the judging subject (the critic) and the judged object (the image)." When studying pornography, such a distance may create a comforting sense of safety as the imaginary line keeps the body genre and the carnal reactions that it evokes at bay. By doing so, the distance may keep the researcher from asking some crucial questions concerning the genre and its affective force—unless this force is considered a theoretical one or involves other people besides the researcher herself (as in the third-person hypotheses discussed in chapter 2).

Eve Kosofsky Sedgwick (2003, 123) has critiqued contemporary cultural theory for its paranoid tendencies. If we already know that, say, pornography works to reinforce social hierarchies, then what can studies of such hierarchical arrangements tell us that we do not already know? According to Sedgwick, Paul Ricoeur's hermeneutics of suspicion has become widespread enough to be understood as "nearly synonymous with criticism itself." This, again, "may have made it less rather than more possible to unpack the local, contingent relations between any given piece of knowledge and its narrative/epistemological entailments for the seeker, knower, or teller" (Sedgwick 2003, 124). In Sedgwick's (2003, 126) view, such "paranoid' inquiry has become dominant enough to block from view other interpretative practices, ways of knowing and making sense of the world—it has in fact become a "uniquely sanctioned *methodology.*" Paranoid reading implies a compulsive will to knowledge through uncovering and revealing the hidden workings of power. On the other hand, these have been known from the start, since "paranoia requires that bad news be always already known" (Sedgwick 2003, 130). Paranoid reading is generalizing and relies on "vigilant scanning." It also tends to be tautological in that it "can't help or can't stop or can't do anything other than prove the very same assumptions with which it began," and this proof may then "be experienced by the practitioner as a triumphant advance toward truth and vindication" (Sedgwick 2003, 132, 135). Brian Massumi (2002, 12) identifies a similar tendency in critical thinking to disavow its own inventiveness: "Because it sees itself as uncovering something it claims was hidden or as debunking something it desires to subtract from the world, it clings to a basically descriptive and justificatory modus operandi." The compulsory gestures and movements of scanning, uncovering, and revealing lead to circular argumentation in which surprises are unlikely and negative critique abound.

When rereading the passage from Sedgwick, I am struck by a sense of recognition in terms of the research that I read and that I write. Content analysis of porn spam material has pointed to how categories of gender and race are exaggerated and juxtaposed with one another. It has also rendered the heterosexual structuralism of porn terminology and iconography strikingly evident in ways that serve an analytical purpose. At the same time, it can be argued that such structuralism hardly necessitates much revelation after three decades of feminist critiques that have identified pornography as overwhelmingly "racist, classist, ableist, and heterosexist" (Mason-Grant 2004, 86). This is something always already known. When encountering new examples of pornography, it is easy to categorize them in relation to those seen before rather than to remain open to moments and possibilities of surprise. Since such classification is the starting point of coding in content analysis, individual examples are divided into predetermined categories.

All this considered, the spam pie charts shown in figures 4.2 through 4.6 deserve more attention. For me, the effect of the charts' themes, acts, and terminologies is both visual and rhetorical. When I first presented the pie charts during a conference talk in 2004, I had to resist an urge to giggle. The charts seemed like offbeat variations of the charts that researchers use to summarize data or findings, and the presentation format of percentages and wedges seemed mismatched with their referents (the terminology of *sucking, humping,* and *dilating*). At the same time, the charts seemed far removed from the actual material discussed. A feeling of absurdity about this disconnect has never quite left me. The charts provide easy visual access to a relatively broad and multimodal set of materials, and they capture much of the grammar of commercial pornography and its advertising. At the same time, they are paradoxical in the way that they transform explicit sexual representations into tidy graphics. The ample visual landscape of body parts and bodily fluids is simply effaced. As visualizations, the pie charts translate pornographic material into something easily distanced and approachable, and when faced with them, it is easy to resort to the position of an outside observer. While summarizing key aspects of spam material, they also render invisible those examples that do not quite fit their categories. By doing so, they produce an illusion of coherence that does not account for variation or elements combined in surprising ways. Given that such odd moments are the most memorable ones in the spam archive as a whole, much seems to be lost.

Ultimately, I feel that content analysis is constrained by notions of distance and mastery over the material in ways that set limits to its usability in my studies of online porn. Coding and cataloguing instances is a distanced form of interpretation that orders the material studied while securing the researchers' power to pin down its meanings. All this does not facilitate an interactive relationship between the researcher and the researched, and it constrains ways of imagining and forming different kinds of relationships between the two (Pearce 1997, 14). It may also work to efface possibilities of surprise from acts of interpretation. Content analysis, as I have deployed it, is valuable in mapping out regularities and recurrent elements in porn, but additional analytical tools are needed to grasp the ambiguity and plurality of the material studied.

Sedgwick (2003, 145–146) suggests reparative reading as an alternative to paranoid investigations that are devoid of surprise. Paranoid and reparative readings produce different relationships between the reader and the text. Unlike the generalizations of paranoid readings, reparative reading is partial, geared toward positive affect, imaginative close reading, and moments of surprise and does not aim at unequivocal outcomes. Scholars with more Deleuzian inclinations might refer to this as the "irreducible singularity" of the event of reading. Literary scholar Lynne Pearce (1997, 11–15) has phrased the question as one of "hermeneutic" and "implicated" reading. Hermeneutic reading focuses on the ways that texts position readers and the meanings interpreted from the texts. In contrast, implicated reading considers reading to be an interactive activity that includes a wide range of emotions and is far less certain in its "results." Like reparative reading, implicated reading implies proximity, uncertainty, and the possibility of surprise: it is guided by fascination and curiosity.

Sedgwick and Pearce are not alone in reframing reading acts as proximities and intimate discoveries rather than discoveries of ideological effects (that already were known beforehand). As different as their respective critical projects are, Jane Gallop's (1988) embodied reading, Nancy K. Miller's (1991) personal criticism, Pearce's (1997) implicated reading, and Sedgwick's (2003) reparative reading are all forms of theorization that account for the affective power and material force of the texts studied and that also insist on openness toward the surprising, the uncertain, and the unpredictable. These approaches are not too distant from Massumi's (2002, 12–13) discussion on affirmative methods that, contrary to the tradition of critical theory engaging in the modality of negative critique, embrace their own inventiveness and involve enjoyment taken in conceptualization and writing. Massumi (much like Karen Barad) argues against the notion of exteriority—that is, scholars who situate themselves as outsiders to what they study and who fail to account for the effects and productivity of their own actions. I agree.

The remainder of this chapter moves toward moments of surprise and uncertainty in spam material. I address the forms and functions of humor and camp in and for porn, as well as the shifting meanings of heterosexuality to complicate the interpretations offered above in pie charts and to tease out some of the complexities involved. The discussion on humor is followed by conclusions concerning the modalities of porn, as mapped throughout this chapter, and the importance of addressing them beyond their seemingly obvious or literal aspects.

Porn: Not a Laughing Matter?

During my years of studying porn, I have been frequently asked the question, "But how can anyone take it seriously?" The question suggests that porn is too excessive, artificial, self-referential, or ridiculous for anyone to take it seriously enough to spend years trying to untangle its aesthetics, conventions, and resonances. Indeed, the ample use of camp aesthetics, practical jokes, intentional puns and gags, exaggerated types and stock characters, word games, and parody in porn challenge attempts at uncovering hidden levels of meaning and set its hyperbolic and excessive imageries in a new light. The senders of porn spam messages are often (122 instances) female porn artist names, such as Joyce Juicycunt, Julie Puckerlips, Wendy Asspump, Melissa Ducock, Sucking Sonja, Nicole Humpme, or Myra Lovesdick. The two male names are Homer Humping and Dick Director. The artist names resemble those in use in porn film production. Andrew Benjamin's lighthearted book *Pornification* (2006) provides examples and suggestions for tweaking mainstream film titles and actor names into such "pornified" versions (*The Karate Kid* becoming *Bukkake Kid* and Britney Spears *Britney Rears*). These Leslie Nutcrunchers, Connie Cokloves, and Joleen Cuminrubits have their ancestors in Harry Reems, the male star of *Deep Throat*, and stag film characters such as Hard Penis, Lotta Crap, and Minnie Womb, who worked at the Fuckem Right studios at *Strictly Union* (1919), and Bill Hangnuts of *A Stiff Game* (1930s) (Di Lauro and Rabkin 1976, 59, 66–67).[9] Although artist names have been an obvious means of maintaining actors' anonymity, they have also added to the overall over-the-top and as-if modality of pornography since its early days.

Constance Penley sees pornography as involving unruly laughter and a disregard of bourgeois codes of good taste or proper demeanor. In a North

American framing, Penley (2004, 310) associates porn with white-trash looks, tastes, and sensibilities, which all involve a shameless flaunting of trashiness. For her, bawdy humor, exhibitions of bad taste in clothing, make-up, and language are a means of challenging mainstream middle-class norms. In the trajectory of interpretation employed by Kipnis and to a lesser degree Penley, pornography is invested with a transgressive potential to disrupt normative notions of taste and class. Karen Boyle (2008, 46) sees this as a question of a reading strategy—"that is, it is the viewer who is transgressive, who rejects the middle-class construction of 'taste' in openly celebrating 'trash.'"

As these examples illustrate, there is little consensus on the role of humor and laughter in pornography. According to Nina K. Martin (2006), comedy and sexual acts are rarely combined in porn. Despite the abundance of titles that are puns on titles of Hollywood films, she sees humor as too disturbing to be broadly used in porn, as it clashes with the seriousness with which sexual acts are depicted. Jokes, gags, and puns are inserted into the narrative as separate numbers that occur between, rather than during, sexual acts. The few films combining comedy with pornography that Martin (2006, 199) identifies are parodies pointing out the ridiculousness of generic porn conventions. At the same time, porn parodies do not undermine these conventions but "*solidify and reify*" them "by highlighting their ubiquitous presence" (Martin 2006, 196). By repeating the conventions that they make fun of (stock characters, standard routines, and compulsory numbers), porn parodies do not transform the genre (Martin 2006, 199). In other words, Martin sees these repetitions as producing no difference but rather more of the same. Susan Sontag (2002, 51) shares this view when she argues that porn is not a form that can parody itself: parody is a common form of pornography, but it always remains pornography. I doubt that the denominator of pornography is quite as set or solid as Sontag and Martin seem to assume. Although pornography is a genre (literary, cinematic, pictorial, mixed-media, networked, and beyond), it is one as a result of categorizations and negotiations between producers, distributors, consumers, and legislators. It has certain characteristics, but its boundaries are far from being set.

Martin is looking for pornography that repeats things with a difference—for example, by undermining the centrality of the penis and male climax or involving scenes where characters burst out laughing. I sympathize with

Martin's argument in the sense that one of the more exceptional and memorable examples of porn spam email involves such laughter. An advertisement for Fisting Party! (a site that longer exists) consists of three images and white text against an orange background. The first image is closely cropped and features a young woman with brown hair and latex gloves smirking at the camera with her left hand inserted in another woman's vagina all the way to the wrist. She is leaning close to the woman's body while a caption reads, "Smile—you're on fisty cam!" The second image shows a young woman kneeling on a bed with her back to the camera, looking over her shoulder with her left hand inserted in her anus to the knuckles. "Young and willing 18 year old handfuls!," the caption exclaims. The pink wall in the background resonates with the woman's pale white skin. With a slightly tense smile, her expression is nevertheless self-contained, even proud over this display of bodily pliability. The third image features five women against a pale blue background. In the center, a woman with red hair is kneeling on a table with her back to the camera. She is naked, and the sole of her left foot occupies a central position in the bottom left corner. Next to her, a woman is grinning widely in a red latex corsage and vinyl gloves, pushing both her hands between the woman's buttocks. Two women, who seem to be laughing out loud, support the kneeling woman from under her arms. Their mouths are open, eyes closed, chins raised, and heads partly turned away from the camera. The fifth woman is hidden behind the others.

These are not typical porn pinup poses. These are grins, not smiles; proud displays rather than invitations; laughter instead of seduction. In fact, this is the only instance in the archive of 366 messages that displays laughing women. The women performing are young and wear little makeup, and their bodily styles reference independent and subcultural porn productions. In spite of—or perhaps due to—the women-only action, the caption asks, "Did this happen on your bucks night? Make it happen now!" This somewhat feeble address frames the women as performing for male viewers. These images were reproduced in a more elaborate advertisement for the same site, along with conventional poses of topless women gazing at the camera, opening their mouths, smiling, and sucking on lollipops. The bottom of the message features images of group sex and heterosex, as well as screen shots of affiliate sites. The captions of the three above-mentioned images remain the same, yet the header "The Biggest Names in Porn Fucked and FISTED!" produces a drastically different kind of framing and dilutes some of their amateurish feel of directness. The ad is a visual bricolage of images in contradicting styles and tones, the blonde young woman posing in the foreground with a pink angora hat, a belt, and little else looks invitingly to the camera and provides the collage with a focal point.

The first ad for Fisting Party! stands out due to the body language and smirking enthusiasm of the female performers, and as a viewer, I remain curious about it. The images are staged and posed with viewers in mind, but the laughter in them is shared with the other performers rather than with viewers. Fisting may be a marginal theme in the spam ads dominated by blowjobs, meat shots, and cum shots, yet in terms of the paraphilias featured, these images are not the most exotic. As sympathetically as the ad resonates with me, I am wary of celebrating it as an example of subversive laughter mainly because I do not share Martin's basic argument. Her search for laughter and comedy elements embedded in porn film narratives leads to a literal and limited interpretation of the role and potential of humor in pornography—one that operates with the implicit ideal figure of transgressive, subversive, and narrative porn modeled after feature films. The argument is specific to porn films and difficult to adjust to online video clips that generally feature sexual acts without much narrative.

I would also question the argument that humor necessitates narrative or even a narrative framing of some kind. File-sharing platforms and amateur sites are rife with images and videos of rubber ducks and plastic dolls inserted into vaginas, candles pushed into anuses, and penises decorated with foodstuffs for comical effect. The Wife Bucket "infamous cock-dog" photo, for example, shows a woman posing as if she were to have a bite of a hot dog, looking at the camera with her jaws open. In her right hand, she is holding a "hot dog" that consists of a penis enclosed in a bun and seasoned with ketchup and mustard. Such visual puns are shot, shared, and distributed for fun, and their ongoing presence questions generalizations concerning the interrelations of humor and porn. Rather than understanding the relationship between the two as fixed and pornography as something of a monolith, the question needs to be posed as one of subgenres, their aesthetics and visual practices, and their platforms and forums of distribution. The attraction of amateur content owes, among other things, to the light-hearted feel of play—of "just goofing around." In amateur porn, intrusions and interruptions connote authenticity (Van Doorn 2010,

421–422, 426), yet they are also enjoyed as numbers of their own, as in the sixty-eight-second video "Intruder Alert"[10] distributed on "gross-out sites" (this genre is discussed in more detail in chapter 6). The video consist of short clips of amateur porn shootings that are interrupted by pets: a kitten jumps on a man's crotch during sex, a dog starts licking a man engaged in anal sex, a curious dog enters the scene of fellatio. Such visual puns and genital gags (of varying degrees of explicitness and extremity) are widely available.

Camping Around

The hyperbolic modality of porn—those colossal penises and tiny vaginas, starved nympho sluts and horny dudes—already borders on self-parody. Capino (2006, 214–215) points out the hyperbolic absurdity of marking out "the oriental": some of these camp performances even evolve into displays of "Asian drag." Camp, however, involves not merely ironic distance and criticism but also fondness, appreciation, and humor. In other words, its registers of pleasure are not confined to "the righteous rush of negative critique" (Penley 1997, 3) that characterizes much of the academic debate on porn (and feminist analyses in particular) and lurks behind parody as a form of commentary. The history of camp is founded in urban gay cultures, yet it has, since Sontag's 1964 essay "Notes on 'Camp,'" been used to describe a more general urban sensibility—a love for the unnatural, artificial, and extravagant, the "off," "things-being-what-they-are-not" (Sontag 1999, 53, 56).[11] For Sontag (1999, 54–55), camp lies both in attitudes and sensibilities (ways of looking): it tends to draw quotation marks around the objects that it engages with. This gesture is simultaneously ironic, detached, distanced, and loving in its embrace. In Sontag's view, camp is innocent, naïve, and unintentional. When "self-parody lacks ebullience but instead reveals . . . contempt for one's themes and one's materials . . . the results are forced and heavy-handed, rarely Camp" (Sontag 1999, 58). Perhaps paradoxically, camp can be either naïve or wholly conscious (Sontag 1999, 59). It is a "tender feeling": "Camp taste is, above all, a mode of enjoyment, of appreciation—not judgment. Camp is generous. It wants to enjoy. It only seems like malice, cynicism. . . . Camp taste is a kind of love, love for human nature. It relishes, rather than judges. . . . Camp taste identifies with what it is enjoying" (Sontag 1999, 65).

For Sontag (1999, 60), camp "incarnates a victory of 'style' over 'content,' 'aesthetics' over 'morality,' of irony over tragedy," and it is fundamentally antiserious. Porn camp—that is, displays and articulations of camp sensibility about the cultures and histories of pornography—extends from the valorization of vintage pornographies and porn stars to the knowing referencing of retro styles (such as the body hair of 1970s films or the frizzy perms of the 1980s) and exaggerated performances of "innocence," "surprise," "shock," and "lust." Porn camp embraces what is bad, excessive, artificial, and of poor taste and low cultural status. Sontag's (1999, 55) list of items in the canon of camp includes "stag films seen without lust." Why should they be seen without lust? Perhaps lustiness would bridge the distance between the film and its viewer and dissolve the mutual detachment that is necessary for camp as an aesthetic practice. I discuss the notion of aesthetic distance further in chapter 6, but it suffices to say here that for Sontag, camp attitude is one of detached distance. Camp, again, "is love for the old as such. It's simply that the process of aging or deterioration provides the necessary detachment—or arouses a necessary sympathy" (Sontag 1999, 60). This notion reverberates with the recent cult and camp status of 1970s porn films that were shot on 35mm film—the so-called golden era of porn and its chosen masterpieces—as well as that of 1980s video porn. The notions of camp, cult, and retro have also supported the lasting celebrity status of male porn stars such as John Holmes and Ron Jeremy (Shelton 2002).

The question "But how can anyone take porn seriously?" implies that porn is camp and therefore that considerations of its modalities, affective intensities, ethics, and politics are ultimately misplaced and literal and fail to see porn as "auto-deconstructive, always reflecting its own artificiality and excess." Consequently, those who criticize porn "are the ones who 'don't get it' and fail to understand its carnivalesque dimensions. Camp sensibility seems to go well with porn since camp serves to create distinctions and celebrate the inappropriate and the low while being aware of the cultural hierarchies at play" (Paasonen et al. 2007, 15; also Epley 2007). In other words, camp, both loving and reflexive, works to ward off critiques that are targeted at its objects. Camp protects pornography from critical considerations in its insistence on the nonserious, the stylized, and the exaggerated. This nonseriousness is nevertheless selective, for although the frame of camp tends to reject questions of power or politics, it is both ironic and dead serious in its loving attachment to its objects (Kalha 2007b, 61). Furthermore, camp is both a sensibility and also a strategy of interpretation that can be knowingly deployed. I would argue that camp is very much a textual approach in its focus on the interpretations and preferences of the spectator toward the camp object (a film, story, image, or Web site). Considerations of the material contexts of production and questions of ethics do not fit well in this framing. Camp protects porn by isolating it as a question of aesthetics, interpretation, sensibility, and style: the carnalities of the performers and viewers are not part of its agenda.

Debates on humor, comedy, camp, and pornography are exemplary of how research tends to find whatever its theoretical premises point it toward (Jameson 2002; Sedgwick 2003). Those reading porn as camp find camp moments of exaggeration and artifice, whereas those investigating the interconnections of the film genres of comedy and pornography may find few satisfactory examples of such genre hybrids, given that the moments of laughter that can be found fail to meet the criteria of satisfactory or transgressive hybrids. It would be useless to argue over which meaning or reading is most correct and which ones are erroneous. As I see it, moments of laughter involve both proximity and detachment, and they cannot be resolved in a question of meaning. People laugh and fail to laugh at different jokes, allusions, camp moments, or ridiculous experiences.

"Idiotically Comical"

The philosopher and film scholar Slavoj Žižek (1998) sees explicit sex acts and appealing narrative as mutually incompatible. For Žižek, ecstatic sexual acts are impossible to represent, since the outsider observer's "sober" gaze perceives them as amusing and excessive. I take this to mean that pornography can show what people do but cannot grasp or mediate what they feel in any direct or immediately carnal (haptic, olfactory, or gustatory) manner. Excessive gestures and expressions involve an attempt to mediate something of these sensations. The acts performed, the performers' facial expressions, the sounds made, and the scenarios enacted may all resonate with their viewers—and this resonance is necessary for porn to be experienced as sexually arousing—yet the viewer is ultimately an outsider looking in.

Žižek's claim (1998, 26) that it is impossible to combine narrative with sex acts "showing it all" leads to the paradox that a spontaneous human activity (sex) is represented in an extremely codified and formulaic manner. Given that he defines expressions of pleasure and desire in pornography as "idiotically comical," it can be argued that this analysis speaks of the effects of cultural hierarchies of value where porn stands firmly for the bulky and the insipid (Žižek 1998, 25). It may well speak more of the author's nervous uneasiness when faced with the sexually explicit than of the laws and dictates of narration in general (Williams 2004a, 5–6). Nevertheless, Žižek's discussion of "insiders" and "outsiders"—the people performing and those watching—can be useful when unraveling the difficulties involved in conveying and mediating desires and bodily sensations. It may also come in handy when thinking about the modalities of porn as they are performed and experienced. At the same time, it is necessary to consider what renders someone an outsider when interfacing with porn. Are all viewers outsiders by default, or is the question more one of orientation and affective resonance through which one becomes (or fails to become) open to being moved and affected by images?

Considering the latter option, being outside is a position that can be chosen to a degree, for people orient themselves in different ways when watching porn. Watching porn in the classroom or an office to study it means situating oneself as an observing outsider, resisting the power of the images, and focusing on their formal properties and contextual ties. Watching porn for sexual arousal is a different matter altogether. Here, idiosyncratic articulations of pleasure and arousal and stock characters and scenarios are far less disturbing. For the one taking analytical distance, the excessive and hyperbolic depictions of bodies, sexual desires, sensations, and acts may teeter on absurdity (Capino 2006, 208), whereas for the one watching the same imageries in quest of sexual arousal, those depictions may simply facilitate masturbation. The questions here are of pornography's power, of the dialogical relationships between images and viewers, and of the viewer's willingness to play along with and orient herself toward the images.

Considering pornographic depiction as comical by definition is one means of maintaining distance and managing the affective resonances involved in one's encounters with it—keeping them at bay, so to speak. Consider, for example, the video "Save for Work XXX," which was developed by the Viral Factory for Diesel and seeded online as an advertisement celebrating the brand's thirtieth birthday in 2008 (figure 4.8). The video gained modest success as viral marketing for Diesel. The 120-second video includes short clips from 1980s hardcore video porn featuring meat shots, blowjobs, handjobs, and masturbation. These are then combined with animated features that hide the genitalia and turn hardcore action into nonsexual (and markedly innocent) activities, such as musical sessions, basketball practice, and pottery making. The expressions of the performers suggest concentration, seriousness, or abandonment to their sensations. In the viral video, the performers' body parts are covered with animated pieces of clothing, drums, harmonicas, guitars, accordions, and even koala bears. The mechanical body movements and focused facial expressions are associated with activities such as DJ-ing, dialing a telephone number, riding a horse, playing pinball, and eating corn and candy. The video plays with the low-fidelity retro aesthetics of video porn, such as big hairdos and mustaches, generic expressions, and stylized positions.

The witty viral video is an extreme, even ironic example of what Žižek identifies as something that is "idiotically comical" to the outsider's sober gaze. For someone watching the video, it is quite impossible to establish

Figure 4.8
Diesel's viral video, "Save for Work XXX" (http://www.youtube.com)

resonance with the acts performed on the screen as porn. The viewer is presented with a series of fast clips from the middle of action that have been
reframed and remodeled in a highly ironic manner. The viewer is an outsider by default, one who recognizes the presence of porn conventions and
clichés, enjoys the inventive use of animation effects, and remains firmly
at a distance. This intentional framing results from script and editing—a
form of laughing at and with retro porn that makes it difficult to approach
the images as pornography that is intended to or has the capacity to arouse.
Titillation gives way to an appreciation of the clever execution and perhaps
to a camp fondness for the retro styles at hand. This form of humor works
through distancing and renders the clips of vintage video porn something
else than pornography by stripping them of their affective force. When
genitalia and genital fluids are replaced with animated figures, the "nasty"
turns "cute" and amusing.

Jokes, Surprises, and the Contingency of "the Straight"

A different sense of distance is involved in the gonzo and reality sites that
make extensive use of practical jokes. The spam advertisement for the site
Pity Fuck includes two images (figure 4.9). In the first, a red sports utility
vehicle has apparently just run over a man sitting in a wheelchair on a
parking lot. Above the image, an exclamation frames the action: "Shocking!" In the second image, a naked blonde woman is straddling the man as
he sits in a wheelchair (he is white, blonde, relatively fit, and in his thirties
and looks rather hostile) in what appears to be a private residence. The text
next to the first image says, "Find out how this," and next to the second it
says, "Leads to this." The site title, Pity Fuck, includes a smiley face image
showing a crooked smile.

On http://www.pityfuck.com, the man using a wheelchair is introduced
as Joey B, and he is shown performing various scams (as blind, physically
disabled, accident victim, paralyzed, stupid, and "campus retard") to engage
women ("victims") in sexual acts. In this combination of MTV's television
show *Punk'd* and hardcore gonzo, the joke is scripted as being on the unsuspecting women, yet the whole scenario is offbeat and peculiar. The plots of
gonzo porn tend to revolve around luring women into sexual acts, as is the
case with Pity Fuck. In the spam ad for the site Tranny Surprise, the practical joke is played on a male performer:

Figure 4.9

Spam advertisement for http://www.pityfuck.com (2003)

You have never seen anything this funny. We get these guys and we set them up for the fall. We take them out and let them pretend they are picking up a normal hot chick and even get them to invite her back to our pad. We let them get comfy and when they make their move that's when the fun starts. You should see the looks on their faces when they pull her panties off and find a cock. It just doesn't get any better than this. Check it out. . . . This shit will fucking blow your mind, just like it did to the guys who pulled these chicks [*sic*] panties down and was [*sic*] shocked to find a cock!!!

In this homosocial scenario, men lure other men into intimate contact with transgender "chicks."[12] The framing as a practical joke (that is invisible in other spam ads for transgender porn sites, such as Shemale Schlongs, Sexy Transsexuals, She's Got a Dick!, Tranny Zone, and Tranny House) produces comic relief (figure 4.10). It assures viewers that the men who end up performing sexual acts for the camera have "no idea" that their partners are transgender, that they are merely regular guys interested in "normal hot chicks," and that the same also applies to the viewer himself. In these examples, the category of heterosexuality becomes elastic and stretches to include men having anal sex with transgender people as "straight enough."

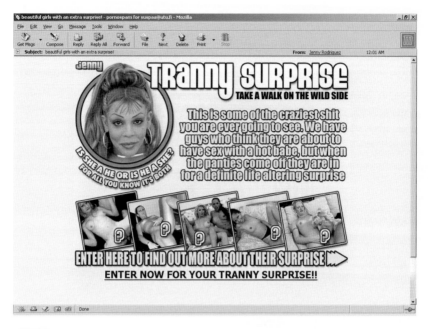

Figure 4.10
Spam advertisement for http://www.trannysurprise.com (2003)

The moment of the reveal—the "shocking" discovery of a woman's cock—
is not the climax of the story, however, as it might be in candid camera
shows. The thumbnail galleries of http://www.trannysurprise.com show
the "hookup," "the reveal," fellatio (performed by "the chick"), and anal
sex. On the one hand, the "pornoscript" at play is a familiar one. On the
other hand, the all-too-familiar porn lexicon becomes rearranged in inno-
vative ways as users are promised access to images and videos of "hundreds
of cute girls with big cocks hiding in their pants."

The frame of a practical joke ("You have never seen anything this
funny") is a means to introduce shemale, chicks-with-dicks pornography to
a mainstream audience. Transgender porn has been produced for decades
in South America (Brazil) and Southeast Asia (Thailand), yet until its online
distribution in the 2000s, it catered mainly to a specialized niche audience.
The mainstreaming of the niche is telling of the overall fragmentation of
the pornographic but also of the fundamental elusiveness of the marker
of "mainstream heteroporn." On http://www.trannysurprise.com, heteroporn stretches to accommodate the display of men licking the anuses of,

performing fellatio on, and being anally penetrated by transwomen. The framing of a practical joke evaporates as the emphasis shifts to the gallery of the thousands of "trannies" on display. Here, the body aesthetics are mainly ones of high femme: long hair, make-up, scanty feminine clothing, revealed silicone-enhanced breasts and round buttocks, and flirty smiles. However, there are also flat breasts, and beauty queen looks are displayed side by side with masculine square jaws. In comparison to markedly queer examples, such as Morty Diamond's film *Trannyfags* (2003), a genderfuck movie starring four gay transmen, Tranny Surprise represents the commod-ified and the commercial. At the same time, the body styles, acts, and possi-ble titillations it entails are not reducible to any one notion of normalcy or normativity. Not quite heteroporn, not marked as gay, queer, or of special interest, the site suspends such notions and hovers somewhere in between, as a fantasy of perpetual sunshine and elastic desires.

As is standard in gonzo and reality porn, Tranny Surprise lays claim to the realness of its videos. Claiming that "this little honey is straight off the street" and that "we were just going down to shoot some pool when we see this hottie bending over that table," it suggests that the crew comes across one transwoman after another by surprise and then simply decides to make some porno. Like the framing of a practical joke, this claim gives rise to a strong sense of "as if," as it envisions a pornotopia where straight men make hardcore porn with chicks with dicks who are ready and willing to perform for the camera and who can be found on a street, in a bar, or at the beach in abundance (the site currently features some seven thousand "girls"). Such a pornotopia would seem unlikely in the United States, and it is therefore noteworthy that the videos are often shot in Brazil. While Tranny Surprise makes use of terms such as *preop*, the performers may not be planning further gender reassignment surgery. They could be more accurate described as *travesti*, a term used in Brazil for men identifying as homosexual yet adopting female names and body styles, taking hormones and injecting themselves with silicone to fashion themselves as feminine objects of male desire—this highly marginal social group works mostly as prostitutes (Kulick 1998, 5–6). The travesti are not cross-dressers, but nei-ther do they self-identify as women or as being in the process of becoming one. The site itself is not framed through travelogue or sex tourism. Some captions mention Brazil as the location, yet the sunny vistas, palm trees, pools, and hotel rooms depicted in the videos could just as well be situated in California or Florida (where Reality Kings, the company running the site, is based). The exoticness of trannies is not further emphasized through the highlighting of national or linguistic differences: these are present but far from hyperbolic.

Queering the Straight

Heteroporn tends to make use of repetitive and familiar scripts, conventions, lexicon, and iconography. To the degree that it focuses on and scrutinizes body parts marked as primary signifiers of gender difference (genitalia, breasts, or faces), this scrutiny would seem to become frustrated at transgender sites where no "truth" of gender as decipherable from bodies as either male or female can be found. In fact, the play of uncertainty, scrutiny, discovery, and wonder becomes an end in itself. "Is she a cross-dresser? Pre-op? Post-op?," Tranny Surprise asks of each "latest tranny." Users are invited to interpret and compare the images and videos and to enjoy the exhibit of "best of both worlds" (as an ad for Sexy Transsexuals puts it). In many ways, these are perfectly self-contained pornographic bodies—high femme with a penis. Transporn is easy to define as queer in its display of nonnormative bodies, sexual acts, and fascinations. However, labeling such examples as queer in opposition to straight or as alternative rather than mainstream creates a false sense of neat departmentalized order. Within the porn industry, performers and other porn professionals tend not to obey divisions of the straight and the queer. Consider, for example, the ubiquity of straight "gay for pay" performances in gay porn. Heterosexual women write slash fiction (depicting romantic and sexual relationships between fictional characters of the same sex) falling under the category of gay erotica, while women straight and queer watch gay porn and straight men enjoy variations of girl-girl action, dyke porn, and shemale action.

If heterosexuality is seen as a normative monolith, then virtually any breech of its boundaries—whether fetishes, kinks, or acts understood as somehow taboo—can be categorized as queer. In this case, the concept of queer becomes broad enough to encompass any act or preference seen as a digression. By the same token, "If everything a man and a woman do together counts as 'straight,' then the term 'straight sex' could describe almost any activity" (Albury 2002, vii). Categorical definitions of what sexual acts or pornographic displays mean fix them in unhelpful ways. Since queer is about the antinormative, it always carries with it the assumption (and more or less a definition) of the normative, as it is articulated in regulatory discourses (such as legislation, sexology, and religion) and as it is experienced and lived in practices of everyday life. The normative is what queer is not or what is not queer—a point of demarcation reiterated into being in articulations of queerness. This is not to say that the normative would be a figment of queer imagination, perpetually revealed in the paranoid quest for uncovering it. Normative categories (gender, race, sexuality) are not paranoid fantasies of the scholarly sort but are sociocultural operations with effects and reverberations that are lived and felt.

As Sara Ahmed argues, the normative is a question of exhausting regularity and repetition: "an effect of the repetition of bodily actions over time, which produces what we can call the bodily horizon, a space for action, *which puts some objects and not others in reach*" (Ahmed 2006, 66, emphasis in the original). This is a matter of bodies that appear to be straight and "in line" in their orientation, and bodies oriented toward the so-called opposite sex have considerably more space to engage in all kinds of acts and activities. It takes some effort for straight bodies to become queer, whereas such regularity is out of grasp for bodies that are differently oriented and fail to "line up" (Ahmed 2006, 66–67). Straightness is naturalized by attaching it to notions of decency, conventionality, directness, and honesty so that it "moves *without any deviation* toward 'the point' of heterosexual union or sexual coupling" (Ahmed 2006, 70, 78, emphasis in the original). What occurs in such couplings or between the bodies that are seen as "in line" is a secondary concern in terms of the dividing lines of straight and queer orientation.

The challenge of critical work (in the productive rather than the pathologically negative sense) is to question the categories that one works (or is made to work) with. This means thinking beyond the kinds of models that rely on fixing their points of reference (such as the straight or the mainstream) in order to grant mobility to others (such as the queer or the alternative). Consequently, it is necessary to consider apparently monolithic concepts, such as mainstream heteroporn, as fields of activity and potentiality where all kinds of constellations are possible. In addition, heterosexuality should not be conflated with heteronormativity. Some forms of heterosexuality (like monogamous relationships involving matrimony and procreation, which are sanctioned by the church and the state) have a more prominent and normative status than others (such as nonreproductive or nonmonogamous heterosex). Writing back in 1984, Gayle Rubin argued that sex is perceived of through hierarchical arrangements of "good" and "bad sex." Good ("normal, natural, healthy, and holy") vanilla sex is practiced by heterosexual people of the same generation in a monogamous relationship, preferably marriage, at their home for reproductive and noncommercial purposes, without the aid of pornography, fetish objects, sex toys, or role-playing. Whatever falls outside these parameters becomes bad ("abnormal, unnatural, sick, sinful, 'way out'") sex that is practiced by or with transvestites, transsexuals, fetishists, and sadomasochists for money and possibly in cross-generational assemblages (Rubin 1989, 280–282; also Albury 2002, 67–68). Queer theorists Michael Warner and Don Kulick have sketched out similar topologies of good and less good sex. For Warner (2000, 1–5), the division is between acceptable sexual practices (which are seen as benign, pleasant, and wholesome) and bad ones associated with shame (such as gay and lesbian sexualities, BDSM, and fetishism). Writing in the Swedish context, Kulick (2005, 208) defines good, healthy, and natural sex as "socially approved, mutually satisfying sexual relations between two (and only two) consenting adults or young adults who are more or less sociological equals. It must not involve money or overt domination, even as role-playing. It should occur only in the context of an established social relationship." Whatever falls outside these parameters (the commercial, kinky, and promiscuous) is defined as less wholesome.

This is not the whole picture, however. Rubin (1989, 282) argues that an imaginary line is drawn and maintained between good and bad sex because only a very small portion of sexuality can actually be sanctioned as "good" or "healthy." Sex practiced by unmarried heterosexual couples, promiscuous heterosexuals, masturbators, or lesbians and gay men in long-term relationships fall in something of a no-man's land that is not quite good and not quite bad either. With its depictions of noncommittal and nonreproductive sex acted out for money (with some exceptions), porn resists this topology and blurs its contours. It may be geared toward kinks and fetishes, and its aim is to drive people to masturbate, yet it is regularly watched at home by couples in long-term relationships. This is especially the case today, more than twenty-five years since Rubin's article was initially published, as the Web is awash with amateur porn made by couples, and as pornography has, in many Western countries (like Finland, my own country of residence), become mainstreamed as sexual stimulation for couples and the lonely, sex education for the young, and a field of entrepreneurial exploration for women (see Nikunen and Paasonen 2007; McKee et al. 2008; Paasonen 2009).

The instable, contingent, and porous category of heteroporn can be used to complicate and trouble understandings of heterosex as something that is somehow already familiar and known and to bring out its inconsistencies, hierarchies, and tensions. This may be more difficult to achieve if the straight is understood according to its thesaurus definitions as the opposite of the diluted, mixed, disordered, disorganized, or twisted—namely, as what is inflexible, invariable, solid, straightforward, uncurled, undeviating, undistorted, uninterrupted, unswerving, unadulterated, categorical, decent, neat, tidy, moral, outright, plain, and pure.[13] In such a dynamic, fluidity, diversity, unruliness, and mobility in the sexual (as encapsulated in the term *queer*) necessitate and postulate rigidity and fixity as its opposites and points of comparison (Ahmed 2000, 84). "Queering the straight" necessitates both accounting for the diversity of things definable as straight and challenging the binary model in which the categories are being laid out in the first place. All this does not mean turning a blind eye toward the practices of normalization and normativity at play within the sexual (quite the opposite). Rather than a property of specific objects, it makes sense to consider queer as an orientation (Ahmed 2006) toward them—an activity of questioning and making strange that refuses to work with and start from oppositional binaries such as "us and them, in and out, gay and straight" (Hillis 2009, 211). Understanding queer as orientation rather than as a matter of ontology, the question is not whether a site such as Tranny Surprise is queer or straight (a debate with some ontological dimensions) or whether heteroporn may or may not include queer moments (for this depends on the interpretation). Rather, sexual depictions and activities need to be considered outside the framework of fixed identity categories. A queer orientation to pornography involves analytical curiosity and openness that does not start from or resort to binary models.

Repetition and Hyperbole

As contingent as they may be, binary categories are difficult to ignore when studying porn. Browsing through, looking at, and reading online porn in the volumes that I have during the past eight years or so have made it evident that women and men occupy rather different positions in porn. Contrary to recurring gestures of male homosocial bonding, this imaginary landscape is populated by "amateur sluts" (to quote an advertisement sent by Nicole Nutlover for the site Filthy Cocksuckers). If taking a literal approach to this lexicon and the heterosexual structuralism at play in it, its meanings and perhaps also its effects would seem to be obvious. However, given that the aim here is to open up pornography and its modalities—to move beyond the literal and to account for the complexities, affective intensities, resonances, and modalities at play—analysis should stop here.

Even cursory glances at online porn make evident the overwhelming popularity of "straight" scenarios in which women are dominated and somehow under control, yet this standard, nearly hegemonic pornoscript does not exhaust the available options. The style, feel, and setting vary from one video to another, between different sites and community formations, and it would be highly misleading to lump them all together as representative of male domination and female submission as the ultimate porn fantasy. The combination may be exceedingly popular, but there may also be more to the matter than meets the eye. The hyperbolic depiction of social categories—such as gender, race, age, and class—intertwines with sexualized relations of domination and control. The roles of the hunter and the prey and of the con and the conned are easily recognizable and clear-cut (especially in gonzo). But the concepts of control or domination, as deployed in porn imageries, are not automatically synonymous with those of power. Because there seems to be an easy conflation of the concepts, more attention ought to be paid to their differences—as well as to their interconnections—in discussions of pornography.

All kinds of porn revolve around scenarios and fantasies of domination, and the positions and roles of the virgin and the seducer, the student and the teacher, and the slave and the master reappear in different variations. This does not mean that all (more or less fantastic) displays of domination and control should be seen as reiterations, representations, or evidence of social power relations. Here an analogy to BDSM may be useful, for pornographic scenes can be thought of as sessions where the partners take up roles and positions that are then acted out according to certain rules, negotiations, and norms. The roles played out do not reflect the positions of the partners outside the sessions in any simple or direct manner. A submissive position taken in a session does not translate into disempowerment outside its confines, nor does dominance imply a position of authority or power in other areas of everyday life. There is no general causality between sexual desire and social hierarchies or between scenes of domination and social relations of power, even if these seem to be insistently aligned and conflated in pornographic depiction.

If one considers the denominator of media genre (such as porn) as a matter of rapport between media producers, distributors, and consumers, then it can be argued that a similar contractual logic extends to pornographic imageries themselves. Different popular genres operate with different inner rules and logic. The stock formula of romance, for example, involves strong, masculine men who are softened by romantic love (Radway 1984). Although porn is undoubtedly concerned with "explicit representation without narrative, devoid of all but the minimum of dramatic context" (McNair 2002, 70), its scenarios have a logic of their own. In the absence of relationship constraints, commitments, and responsibilities, men are "always erect, women always eager for sex," and in acts involving coercion, "no" tends to mean "yes" (McNair 2002, 40): "there are no material cares or dangers (including disease); no enduring commitments; performance is unproblematic; desire is inexhaustible, as is desirability (everyone is desired and included). Bodies neither fail, nor make non-sexual demands. Nothing external challenges the integrity of 'the sexual'" (Rival et al. 1999, 301). At the same time, these conventions—as familiar as they are after having been circulated for decades in porn magazines, books, films, and videos—are also recognized as such and resisted for being too formulaic and not real enough (Attwood 2010a, 240). As pointed out in chapter 3, amateur porn challenges many of these definitions with its display of wives and husbands and bodies that fail to perform.

When conceptualizing the modalities and styles of porn, any generalization is easily countered with numerous examples that resist such attempts, turn the conventions around, and operate with a drastically different logic. This is inevitable, given the range of things that are placed under the umbrella term *porn*. At the same time, particular modalities—such as excess and hyperbole—cut through a range of pornographies in ways that demand analytical attention. Scenarios of control, submission, and domination meander through all kinds of pornographies, and they have been used to illustrate arguments of porn as a form of degradation (of women

in particular). According to a familiar—and literal—strategy of interpretation, porn both mirrors and reproduces social hierarchies and relations of
power. Although social hierarchies are undoubtedly displayed in porn scenarios with gusto through the display of various stereotypes, a great deal
of nuance, diversity, and complexity is done away with when positioning hierarchical relations of power as the outcome of analysis. Since this
has been known to be the case from the start, analysis amounts to the
kind of "triumphant advance toward truth and vindication" that Sedgwick
discusses. This is not to say that there would not be space for critique in
the imageries of porn. I argue that critical analyses of pornography would
benefit from considering relations of control as tied to social categories,
not literally as expressions, mirrors, or symbols of social relations of power
(and as abuse thereof) but as central to the dynamics of porn, for this is a
somewhat different issue.

Dyke porn (http://gooddykeporn.com and http://cyber-dyke.net)—that
is, lesbian porn addressed to lesbians rather than audiences interested in
girl-on-girl scenarios of the kind depicted as standard porn numbers (see
Kangasvuo 2007)—is rife with BDSM and plays with control and domination. The same can be said of gay porn, a much more commercial field of
production with a longer history and well established conventions. Consider, for example, the numerous pay sites hosted by http://nats.gaygravy.
com. On http://www.bearsfuckboys.com, older bears (men who are heavy
and hairy) are on top, and "tight & unspoiled" younger men are at the bottom. The setting is somewhat similar on http://dadsfuckboys.com, where
"twinks" (men who are young, thin, and hairless) get "nailed by huge studs,"
and on http://thugsontwinks.com where "thugs prey on gullible white ass."
Teachers initiate "twinks" into sex on http://myteachertaughtme.com, on
http://www.creamfilledtwinks.com young men take "huge loads up their
asses!," and on http://www.coverhisface.com ejaculate is targeted at faces.
The terminology of victims is at play on http://www.twinksinpain.com as
"twinks" are "jammed with huge cocks and toys till they scream of pain."
Locating domination as central to the dynamics of porn and identifying
recurrent strands in how tops and bottoms are positioned does not mean
that such relations of control would be predetermined or fixed or that they
would somehow fix their viewers (into positions that would be either sadistic or masochistic). The roles of dominant and submissive partners vary and
change across the axes of gender, class, and race. Individual characters may

shift between the positions, but these are seldom ambiguous. This is perhaps best exemplified by the "first time" story category on Literotica, where older women seduce younger women and men, older men seduce younger men, and younger women and men seduce older women and men. In the stories, men, women, and people of undefined gender find pleasure in submission (as a route to uninhibited expression of and enjoyment in sexuality), domination, romance, and noncommittal sex. Bosses and teachers of different genders pressure employees and students of different genders to submit to their wicked wills, and employees and students do the same with their bosses and teachers.

Pornography is among the most generic of popular genres, and its conventions do not change overnight (Arthurs 2004, 43). Although online pornographies have stretched the conventional notions of what porn is, what it looks like, and what it can do, the overwhelming majority of sites, images, stories, and videos owe some of their attraction to formulaic familiarity—the comfort of repetition, settings, acts, and iconographies that are recognizable in an instant. Social categories are made explicit in and through the performers' bodies, while their mutual differences are exaggerated in interracial porn, the subgenre of "barely legal," intergenerational porn where young women have sex with men in their sixties, the discovery of Indian genital jewels in Indian Roadtrip, or sites focusing on "trailer trash whores" (http://www.trailertrashwhores.com or http://www.dixietrailertrash.com) (figure 4.11).

Online porn—whether still images, YouPorn videos, full-length view-on-demand films, webcam encounters, or porn stories—uses types rather than characters and displays acts rather than complex narrative trajectories. The same can be said of porn in general. All this leads to a certain predictability in terms of action, settings, possible plot, and characters that seem to be coined with a limited selection of templates. As is the case with the templates used in designing Web sites (or HTML email messages of the kind addressed in this chapter), elements can be removed and new ones added, texts can be rescripted, and styles changed. A sense of repetition is difficult to escape as promises of perpetual novelty are countered with the presentation of familiar and predictable scenarios. This is also evident in the facility with which Fanon's discussion of the black man's penis, theorizations of orientalism, or the erotics of colonialism have found their illustrations in the spam advertisements. In other words, spam email has provided me with

Figure 4.11
Hyperbolic age: http://oldgonzo.com

textbook examples of theoretical arguments coined over different decades and in different disciplinary frameworks and addressing different historical moments and geographical regions. The distance separating the research material from the specificity of the research literature seems to disappear in ways that do not facilitate actual interpretation. The Indian genital jewels or "black gangbang squads" displayed in the ads seem absurd yet too literal in their reiteration of representational histories to be simply experienced as parodies.

This is a question of the affordances of the spam material (which remain limited), strategies of interpretation (what I choose to emphasize when trying to make sense of them), and the resonances that take place between the two and shape the analytical process. Although the ads may not quite add up to subversive laughter, they are markedly artificial and denaturalized and make use of jokes and puns that further challenge attempts at literal reading. Boundaries and categories of race, ethnicity, and nationality are rendered hyperbolic and fetishized to make the acts of crossing them as spectacular as possible. This is not the case only with heteroporn. Gay porn involves its own range of types, such as bears, cubs, twinks, and daddies, and is hardly alien to spectacular displays of race, class, and age (Mowlabocus 2007, 69).

I am not the first to note that pornographic choreographies (particularly mainstream ones) are largely repetitive and rely on conventionalized formulas (Miller 1989, 150; Kuhn 1994, 38). According to philosopher Elizabeth Grosz (2006, 197), "pornography can only function as such in so far as it is ritualized, fundamentally repetitive, a series of infinite variations of a very small number of themes." She sees pornography as resistant to and refusing innovation as it "relies on its formula, its theme, its script, to induce its desired effects through a more or less guaranteed pathway" (Grosz 2006, 197). Although the history of pornography and the range of available pornographies online and offline point to considerable innovation, much remains to be said of its formulaic repetitiveness. Richard Fung's (1991, 160) note on gay porn—that "there is such a limited vision of what constitutes the erotic"—continues to apply to examples of online porn. Lynn S. Chancer (1998, 77) argues that pornography "manifests a rather remarkable and ironic homogeneity amid its apparently rich and ultracommodified diversity." I both agree and disagree. On the one hand, the generic conventions of porn are rigid, and their repetition can be traced across different subgenres, niches, and media. But on the other hand, this need not lead one to minimize the diversity of porn. My argument is that analyses of pornography's lexicon or iconography should not be limited to literal cataloguing. Recognizing pornographic images as stereotypical and repetitive or their chosen terminology as predictable requires little analytical effort since the circulation of standard types and stock characters is the stuff that porn is made of. Instead, one should ask whether there is more to these choreographies in terms of the overall modality of porn—and online porn in particular—that needs to be accounted for.

First, online porn is primarily occupied not with narrative (character development or motivation) but with sexual scenarios and the anatomical aspects of its performers. Fantastic in its display of desire, stamina, and gratification, it also lays claim to a certain kind of realism in its minute attention to detail (cf. Hardy 2009). Second, and in connection with the previous point, in porn, embodied differences, desires, and pleasures as conveyed through bodies are rendered instantly recognizable—and hence accessible to the viewer as something to relate to. Third, this involves both repetition (for things to be recognizable, they need to be familiar to a degree) and exaggeration (meaning that there is little room for ambivalence).

Narrative has been and remains central to pornographic literature, short stories, erotica writing, and porn films, but photographs and graphic representations involve static displays. Videos viewed online tend to be brief (usually equaling one episode or less of a porn film) and have little in terms of narrative. People commonly simply enter the frame and start having sex. Throughout its multimodal history, pornography has made use of knowingly exaggerated types (rather than characters), formulaic plots, and excessive gestures. The stock characters (such as the plumber or the horny housewife) and easily recognizable scenarios of video porn (such as "the horny housewife surprises the visiting plumber") are exemplary of the formulaic. With the increased popularity of amateur porn, explicitly scripted frameworks may not be equally dominant, yet types remain central also to its dynamics. Spam material is rife with stock characters and types from "bar bitches" to "hot Latinas," ghetto gangstas, horny rich housewives, and girls next door innocently dressed in white. All this involves artificiality, detachment, and knowing play with the conventions of pornography that resist literal interpretation.

Excess and Transgression

To generalize, porn depicts fantasies about social relations turned quintessentially and even exclusively sexual. Embodied differences are made explicit and overplayed with notable determination. In the realm of porntopia, the size of male genitalia and the intensities of arousal, desire, and pleasure know no bounds. The women are hot and starving, and the men perpetually horny. Kipnis (1999, 202) associates porn with a desire for plenitude: it "proposes an economy of pleasure in which not only is there always enough, there's even more than you could possibly want." The sense of abundance and indeed of excess has grown even more acute due to the accumulation of images, videos, stories, links, and sites. Video publishing platforms feature thousands and thousands of titles and image galleries list equally numerous available alternatives. Link sites, Web directories, and metasites make categorizations even more evident with their hundreds of key terms and thumbnails. There is a virtually endless range and number of sites, webcams, and niches to navigate among, DVDs to purchase, and videos to download. Online pornotopia is abundant and impossible for any single user to map completely. The feel of endless alternatives and opportunities plays no minor role in the attraction of online platforms where something new, exciting, extreme, and titillating is proposed to be always just a click away (Patterson 2004, 110).

Perhaps the most literal examples of pornographic abundance and excess can be found in gangbang videos that have, since the *World's Biggest Gang Bang* (USA 1995, directed by John T. Bone) aimed to transgress the boundaries and affordances of female embodiment. In *World's Biggest Gang Bang*, Annabel Chong had sex with 251 men (falling short of the intended number of 300), and the video gained considerable popularity.[14] Later projects include *Gangbang 2000* (1999), with Sabrina Johnson having sex with over 700 men; *The World's Biggest Gangbang 3: The Houston 500* (1999), where Houston has sex with over 620 men without interruption; *World Record Anal Gangbang* (2004), with Victoria Givens having (nonlubricated) anal sex with 101 men; *50 Guy Creampie* (2004), where 65 men ejaculate in Jenifer's vagina and anus; and the list goes on (*Creampie* alone has at least nine sequels). These "record-breaking" films defy the limits of human—and more specifically, female—physique in their marathon performances, seemingly endless rows of participants, and a plenitude of bodily emissions. Writing on the notion of orgy, Karl Toepfer (1991, 10) argues that almost any physical pleasure (or desire) is "never enough": the threshold of "enough" is seldom reached, let alone transgressed. This explains the position of the orgy as an object of fantasy of what is "more than enough"—a utopian figure of abundance, excess, and gratification. The gangbang videos are explicitly about sexual abundance and excess, yet they can never depict or reach the utopian state of "enough," for each record can also be broken.

Both such sexual marathons and the routinely hyperbolic depiction of embodied differences and social categories in porn involve the drawing and transgressing of boundaries. Once a boundary has been set—whether this is one concerning the number of acts performed or taboos regulating appropriate sexual acts and sexual partners—it can also be breeched. Norms of taste and morality are regularly turned over, inside out, and upside down in pornography. In the stories published on Literotica by the tens of thousands, taboos are broken and class hierarchies overcome as strangers engage in spontaneous sex, characters enjoy acts exciting in their

novelty or extremity (anal sex, deep throat, group sex, or BDSM), and find
themselves in unpredicted situations after they are overcome by lust. Porn
published in a range of media involves both the highlighting and crossing
of boundaries, and sexual arousal and pleasure are promised to grow ever
more intense as new acts are tried out and as habitual norms are exceeded.
Bataille (1986, 63–64, 107) famously points out that taboos and prohibitions exist in order to be broken, that all boundaries can be crossed, and
that transgression both makes these prohibitions and boundaries visible
and strengthens them. Boundary crossing necessitates a line or norm that
is redrawn in the act of crossing (Bataille 1986, 36; also Foucault 1998, 73;
Ahmed 2000, 84).

Ultimately, the notion of pornography as either being subversive or
reproducing existing norms or hierarchies is simplified. Such dualistic logic
aiming to pin down the meanings, orientations, or effects of pornography
obscures its particular modalities. As Laura Rival, Don Slater, and Daniel
Miller (1999, 297–299) argue, theorizations of the transgressive potential
or nature of sexuality presume sexuality as being something separate from
mundane life and normative sociality. In Bataille's eroticism, for example,
"sexuality is placed outside of and in opposition to society." Such detachment enables the viewing of sexuality as a subversive force, but it "has very
little to do with what passes for pornography today" (Rival et al. 1999, 299;
also Cowie 1993, 134). As is the case with other areas of commercial sex,
the production, distribution, and consumption of pornography is about
the circuits of money, technology, and culture. Pornography is overwhelmingly mundane and ubiquitous in the Western countries. It is part of the
everyday media landscape rather than a radical disruptive force—even if
numerous critiques of the pornography's mundane nature, particularly in
the United States, tend to depict it as such (i.e., Paul 2005; Leahy 2008;
Levy 2005).

Transgression, as addressed by Bataille, is not best suited to describing
the cultural position of sexually explicit images or their force in transgressing social boundaries, taboos, and conventions. At the same time, the logic
and idea of transgression remains pivotal to the inner dynamics of pornography (a point further discussed in chapter 6). In porn, the boundaries of
race (and racialized taboos), the extreme gender differences (those colossal penises and miniscule vaginas), and the hierarchies of class and race
are painted with the broadest of brushes and presented with exclamation

marks to depict the acts of transgressing them in the most spectacular vein possible. Taboos are broken and boundaries transgressed time and time again and with gusto.

This transgression has been central to pornography since its early days. Pornographic narratives of the eighteenth century were printed in the same shops as revolutionary literature, and classic works of the era—such as those by the Marquis de Sade—have been seen as analyses and critiques of dominant institutions of morality mocking the codes of decency, the clergy, and the powers that be (Bataille 1986; Hunt 1996; Laqueur 2003). Later pornographies have been equally identified with a desire to break free from the shackles of bourgeois norms and ideals. However, the more mass-cultural and "militantly 'tasteless'" the genre becomes, "the more difficult it is to see pornography's historical continuity with avant-garde revolution-ary art, populist struggles, or any kind of countercultural impulse" (Penley 2004, 312). This may have to do with the fact that studies of pornography's subversive edge have, from Bataille to Sontag and beyond, focused largely on literary pornography and occasionally on examples of the 35mm film pornography of the 1970s. Newer examples—with the notable exception of alt porn, indie porn, and netporn (see Jacobs et al. 2007; Jacobs 2007; Paa-sonen 2010c)—have seldom been identified with any potential for cultural resistance.

Pornography combines minute anatomical realism with hyperbolic depiction to find points of resonance with its viewers. This is done not through narrative or character construction but through a different modal-ity—showing in close-up, pointing out things in capital letters and with exclamation marks, and displaying characters as types to the point of ren-dering them caricatures. The resulting imageries routinely fail to meet the criteria and conventions of good taste, emotional credibility, or good sto-rytelling. As I argue further in the remaining chapters, in porn, irreverence to social codes regulating appropriate behavior is programmatic, and its attraction stems largely from its ability to disturb such codes (also Kipnis 1999). In other words, the incorrect becomes dogmatic. The genre operates in the register of gut reactions and aims to get under the viewer's skin in one sense or another. Following this principle, unsolicited porn spam email uses explicit images and hyperbolic captions in an attempt to get the recipi-ents' attention and, by moving them, to arouse their curiosity and interest to the point of driving them to visit the sites advertised.

All this is a question of affective intensity. By addressing spam advertisements or porn sites only on the level of the semantic or the semiotic (that is, terminology, narrative, and lexicon), it is possible to outline (or uncover and reveal) some degree of structure. At the same time, some see structure as "the place where nothing ever happens, that explanatory heaven in which all eventual permutations are prefigured in a self-consistent set of invariant generative rules" (Massumi 2002, 27). Recurring modalities, styles, and terms are the building blocks of porn, and understanding what porn is made of remains crucial to analyzing its reverberations. Considerations of structural issues should not be seen as implying totalizing fixity but as involving a discomforting commute between modes of interpretation. Above, this commute has aimed to account for the dynamics of humor and the instability of the categories of gender and sexuality that are being constructed and reiterated in porn. The modality of porn involves hyperbole, excess, repetition, and stylization. Displays of embodied differences or relations of control follow the fault lines of social hierarchies but often as spectacular, hyperbolic variations. Hyperbole both grounds these depictions in social hierarchies and creates a sense of detachment, a kind of fantastic "as if" that literal interpretations fail to grasp.

5 Visual Pleasures: From Gaze to Grab and Resonance

From amateur videos to spam messages and porn stories, pornographic scenarios are depicted from a particular perspective—either that of an outside observer (in videos, represented by a cameraman or a camera placed on a stand) or of one person (as in point-of-view shots)—or from a mixture of numerous perspectives. These points of view are crucial in terms of the modality of porn and the affective dynamics that it involves. To unravel these connections, this chapter takes a somewhat unusual route. Starting with considerations of focalization and perspective through the prism of porn spam email, it moves on to address the limits of theorizations of scopophilia and voyeurism, as developed in film studies, in and for studies of online porn. Outlining alternatives to psychoanalytical theorizations of looking and the dynamics of identification that they entail, I address the appeal of online porn through notions of resonance, oscillation between presence and distance, tactile modes of looking, materiality, grab, and the appeal of online porn. Once again, as if illustrating Pearce's notion of a discomforting commute, the analysis and conceptualization in the first part of the chapter is highly distanced, even structuralist, whereas the latter part moves close—perhaps too close for comfort.

"Cum Inside for These Hot Girls and More"

When working on spam email, I have been bemused by the ways in which my (imaginary) penis is addressed. In the spring of 2004, messages advertised stretching devices, pumps, and pills to make the penis grow ("suspaa, increase your dick weight"; "the miricle [sic]) for your penis"; "amplify your cock today"), porn to gain erection, drugs to maintain it, handbooks to hypnotize women to have heterosex with ("Learn the 2 Minute Hypnotic technique that lets YOU have any woman you want"), and products to increase the flow of sperm ("cum like a porn star") (figure 5.1). The gendering at play in porn spam has been equally overt.

As email messages, spam advertisements have a sender, a recipient, and a subject line, and as advertisements they invite the recipient to see, watch, enjoy, and visit the sites that they promote. To use the mode of content analysis, 55 percent of the messages address their users on a general and nonpersonal level to visit the site or to subscribe to a membership (with calls such as "click," "look," or "join"); 31 percent resort to a slightly more personal address ("you can experience," "you should participate," "can you imagine"); while 14 percent get even more personal ("lusty women are waiting for you," "command me," "empty your load on her face"). As references to the recipient's assumed genitalia make evident, the target of personal address is male ("spank your monkey on our liveshow slut's face"). This terminology frames the sights advertised as something meant "just for you" and invites the viewer to an intimate relationship with sites and their performers (O'Riordan 2002, 45; White 2006, 24–25).

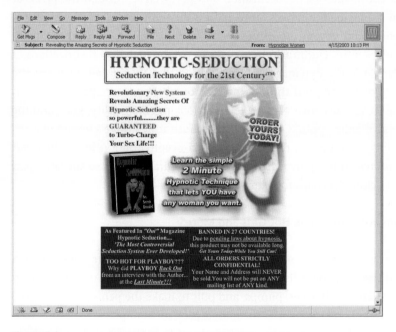

Figure 5.1
Hypnotic seduction technologies, spam advertisement from 2003

The sender is marked female in the majority of the messages, and the subject lines often frame the message as a direct invitation or comment, such as "He wanted me to lick his dick and I could stay for 5 days" (from Jessica Bending), or "Yes the guys tell me my Latin bootie takes the cake" (from Regina Finebooty). In most cases, such subject lines promise a "female perspective" on the site concept and the scenarios advertised: "Why would this jerk offer me money out of the blue to strip," wonders Lisa Deeps in the ad for Street Blowjobs ("Girls Eating Meat on the Streets!"). In the message body, Bob Incognito ("the experiment mastermind") explains that he walks "the streets, malls, coffee shops, where ever" and tries "to pick up hot gals who are hurting for money" (figure 5.2). According to the site concept, Bob pays the women for oral sex and records the acts with a camera hidden in his eyeglasses. "VAVOOM GIRLS LURED INTO SHUNNED ACTS ON FILM!!!," the message exclaims. Street Blowjobs is exemplary of several trends in reality and gonzo sites that frame the action depicted as "real" and the female performers as caught on camera "unawares." This is a recurring theme, especially in the ads for sites run by the Miami-based company Reality Kings, which has produced and promoted gonzo and reality porn since 2000. Reality Kings sites—such as Big Naturals, Cum Fiesta, We Live Together, MILF Hunter, Tranny Surprise, Mega Cock Cravers, In the V.I.P., 8th Street Latinas, Mike's Apartment, Captain Stabbin, and Street Blowjobs—are somewhat overrepresented in the spam material as a whole (comprising 45 messages out of 366).

Since the camera is positioned at the eye level of Bob Incognito, his field of vision becomes that of the viewer, who sees the action unfolding as if through his eyes. This use of POV shots is suggestive of focalization, as defined by literary scholar Gérard Genette in his studies of narratology. *Focalization* refers to the perspective from which a given narrative is depicted—that is, the events are shown unraveling from a particular point of view (Genette 1986, 185–188). In literature, focalization concerns the *I* of the text, whose sensations, perceptions, and thoughts are brought closest to the reader. In cinema, focalization is achieved mainly through camerawork. The Street Blowjobs site is an example of external, rather than internal focalization—for although viewers share Bob's field of vision, they are unlikely to learn much about his emotions or inner life.

To continue in narratological terms, the narrator (the all-seeing voice telling the story) in most messages either is invisible or refers to the site (as

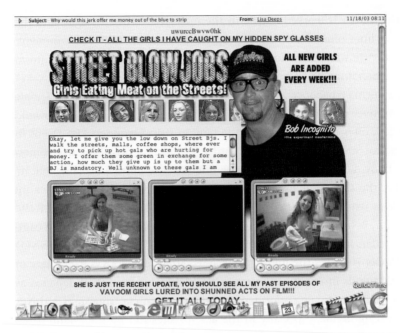

Figure 5.2
Bob Incognito in a spam advertisement for http://www.streetblowjobs.com (2003)

us). The *us* and *we* refer to individual protagonists and groups performing on the sites. In contrast to the wide use of female sender names and the visual spectacle of female bodies in the images, the narrators are mainly gendered male.[1] Of all the male figures shown in the messages, 65 percent are present only as penises with the rest of their body framed out. This convention of "faceless penises," combined with the abundant use of POV shots, aims at effacing the distance between the male performer and the viewer (also Bridges 2010, 38–39). In an explicit act of focalization, the recipient is offered the possibility of occupying the point of view and fantasy position of the male performer: "You and I both know little girls like big dicks! They act afraid of the anaconda in our pants but we both know they can't wait to get it inside of their tight little holes! They ride those giant cocks with their sweet little cunts and then wait for the cum when you're done" (Big Dick Mania). The juxtaposition of "us" and "little girls" and of "big" and "tight" follows the lines of heterosexual structuralism, while both the narrator and the recipient are marked as in the possession of frightening "anacondas." The recipient is invited to join in the spirit of anonymous male homosociality through intimate forms of address such as "You and I" and "our pants." Through the figure of "little girls" who both are afraid of and also desire the penile anaconda, the message proposes a great degree of elasticity between "those giant cocks" and the ejaculating member assigned to the recipient.

Suspension of Disbelief

Chloe Woida (2009) argues that mainstream online porn seems "as if made for someone else," and hence possible sexual arousal is haunted by a sense of distance. In porn spam email, this kind of "speaking past" takes the shape of male homosocial invitations and references to the recipient's penis. Yet there are some gaps in these male homosocial forms of address. Advertisements for MILF sites, for example, routinely mock husbands for their small penises and lack of sexual bravado. The husbands remain absent as other than disappointing sexual partners. Consider, for example, MILF Hunter's "Mission Summary": "Imagine the look on my face when my buddy the poolman told me he needed me to fill in for him and go clean some horny rich bitches [sic] pool. I guess her millionaire hubby has a 3 inch cock so I [sic] volunteered my 10 incher and stuffed her pussy in the shallow end." The action is focalized through male eyes, but these belong to the MILF hunter, seeker, or rider with more sexual prowess than the husband. Husbands are constantly mocked for their inability to satisfy their wives, and even the size of their genitalia becomes a joke. In one ad after another, MILFs are described as "sex starved" and finally getting what "her husband wasn't giving her!!!"

According to Constance Penley (2004, 320), pre-1970s pornography involved jokes at the expense of the men. In stag films targeted at a male audience, men are subject to practical jokes, women express their disappointment in men's sexual stamina and skill, and men even lose control of their penises (Penley 2004, 314, 316–317). Nina K. Martin (2006, 193) suggests the opposite to be the case in contemporary porn. Since porn emphasizes the overall "awesomeness" of the penis—which is, then, no laughing matter—humor disturbs and disrupts its fantasy scenarios. In particular, "delicacy is required in order to represent women laughing *and* desiring in the regimented world of porn" (Martin 2006, 201, emphasis in the original) for the reason that the joke might be on the men. In contrast, MILF

Hunter renders men and their penises subject to ridicule by other men. In a mocking gesture toward three-inch penises, the hunter exposes his ten-inch weapon, and while the husbands fail sexually, the hunter prowls and gratifies their sex-deprived wives. The juxtaposition of levels of virility creates a rupture in the male homosocial modality that is otherwise characteristic of the spam material and, to a degree, that of heteroporn porn generally. The viewers are no longer a group of men who are unified in their interests and activities (to have sex with women in varying constellations) but something of a hierarchical arrangement in which the "rich hubby" residing in the "mansion" (described as the location of the sexual action) represents class privilege and low sexual performance. The substitute pool guy, a temporary manual laborer, rates low in the hierarchies of class but represents desirable, masculine heterosexual performance (as a "real man"). This dynamic reverberates with Kipnis's (1999) argument that pornography mocks and resists class-based signs of successful masculinity. In porn, education, money, and upper-class status are of little help, and elitism surfaces only to be mocked.

In a hyperbolic display of military masculinity, the protagonist of MILF Hunter is styled as a G.I. Joe character with camouflage make-up and a military helmet (figure 5.3). The site's camouflage wallpaper and the dots of its logo are marked with stars, giving it a military flair (perhaps suggesting the title *M*A*S*H*). Each new video features the same man who, since the spam advertisements of 2003, has grown older and is more "mature" than several of the MILFs he currently interacts with. The reality/gonzo framing remains the same, but the feel is decidedly that of ProAm. Types, scenarios, and roles—such as the "MILF" and the "hunter," the "rich bitch" and the "stand-in pool boy"—are played with a degree of reflexivity, as if in inverted commas.

Like MILF Hunter, Street Blowjobs claims realness for its amateur performers and nonstaged scenarios. It is also equally fantastic in the perpetual repetition of the same trick played on perpetually unsuspecting women— week after week, year after year, and in one video after another. Repetition necessitates a degree of suspension of disbelief, of "playing along" with the proposed scenarios regardless of how unlikely or familiar they may be. Both the free tour pages of http://www.streetblowjobs.com and email ads for the site describe each video with a set of four to five images. These provide glimpses into Bob Incognito's encounter with his "latest catch" (meeting,

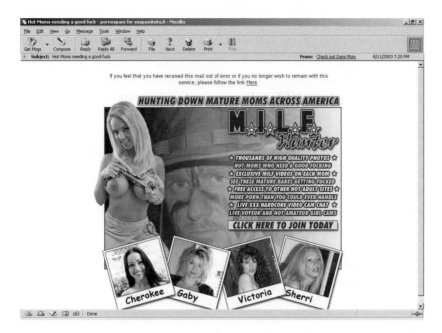

Figure 5.3
The military butchness of MILF Hunter (spam advertisement from 2003)

persuading the woman to perform sexual acts in exchange for money, and evaluating the session). The images might show fellatio, coitus, cum shot, and occasionally the "catch" looking directly at or posing for the camera, money exchanging hands, or close-ups of the woman's body. The images bring the female performers close to the viewer—particularly through their looks directly at the camera—and provide some idea about what the videos (accessible to members) will reveal. Meanwhile, Bob remains invisible except for his penis and an image of a man with spyglasses embedded in the logo collage of http://www.streetjobs.com. In the thumbnail galleries, Bob Incognito becomes a highly fluid persona represented by penises in a range of shapes, sizes, and skin hues. This flexibility and ability to inhabit numerous embodiments makes Mr. Incognito a point-of-view concept and perspective rather than a character or a persona.

By laying claims to the realness of their settings and characters, gonzo sites depict mundane spaces as potential grounds for sexual action while downplaying their obviously staged and scripted aspects. Street Blowjobs and MILF Hunter attempt to bridge the gap between everyday life and the excessive fantasy realm of pornography. Streets, parking lots, shopping malls, libraries, and motels—all mundane, accessible, and familiar environments involving little glamour—become sites of pornotopia as anonymous nonplaces that are both anywhere and nowhere in particular (cf. Marcus 1964, 268–269).[2] In the Street Blowjobs ads of 2003 and 2004, the image quality is grainy and comes with some documentary aura, whereas the site today declares that it is "now in full digital HD." The low-fi gonzo aesthetics have given way to optimized visibility and high resolution, but the site still insists on the realness of its imageries as documentation of what has taken place. Notions of realness have become detached from the aesthetics of amateur video (as grainy and shaky), but they remain firmly associated with both the assumed amateur status of the female performers and the mundane locations in which the videos are shot.

Reality and gonzo sites routinely suggest that the women performing are unaware of being filmed or that they agree to the acts in exchange for money that nobody intends to give. It requires little effort to note that such concepts involve not only male homosocial forms of address but also sexual fantasies played out from a male perspective (it is hardly breaking news that heteroporn might involve male fantasies of female sexual serviceability). Reality and gonzo sites combine this pornotopian formula with hierarchical arrangements of "hunters" and "prey" and of the "masterminds" and the "conned" in repetitive ways. The audience is invited to look at scenarios that are framed as "real" and "authentic" yet that display a great degree of scripted artificiality and require a major suspension of disbelief. For those trained in cinema studies and feminist film theory, their repeated formulas, focalization, POV shots, and visual spectacles of female bodies echo discussions on scopophilia (sexual pleasure involved in looking) and the male gaze as debated since the mid-1970s. The pleasures of looking undoubtedly lie at the heart of pornography's appeal and its principles of visual access and maximized exposure. What kinds of pleasures these are and how they are conceptualized is, however, a different matter.

Scopophilia and the Controlling Gaze

In her now classic 1975 article, "Visual Pleasure and Narrative Cinema," Laura Mulvey argues that in addition to identification, the dynamics of film spectatorship involve scopophilia, the pleasure of looking, and the adjunct processes of voyeurism and fetishism. To the degree that scopophilia is about a gaze that is both curious and controlling, it forms the basis for looking at another person as object. Objectification, again, signifies voyeuristic gazing as sexual stimulation through sight. For Mulvey (1988, 68), Hollywood cinema is structured by a threefold male gaze—that of the camera, the audience, and the characters. All three gazes involve positioning the female characters as objects and construct female bodies as spectacle. Men are the bearers of the look, while women are left with the task of holding the look, playing to and signifying male desire (assumed to be heterosexual): "the woman displayed has functioned on two levels: as erotic object for the characters within the screen story, and as erotic object for the spectator within the auditorium, with a shifting tension between the looks on either side of the screen. . . . A woman performs within the narrative, the gaze of the spectator and that of the male characters in the film are neatly combined without breaking narrative verisimilitude" (Mulvey 1988, 62).

In Mulvey's model, the woman stands for the lack of a penis, and scopophilic pleasures involved in looking at women are underlined by castration anxiety. The display of the woman as object is a source of both pleasure and potential displeasure, and this dilemma can be resolved in two ways. The first option, that of voyeurism, is to reenact the original trauma by demystifying the mystery posed by the female, "counterbalanced by the devaluation, punishment or saving of the guilty object." In this sense, voyeurism is associated with sadism and control. The second solution, fetishistic scopophilia, is to disavow castration by turning the female figure into a fetish that is reassuring rather than dangerous. The woman becomes an object as her body parts (lips, legs, hair, etc.) are fetishized as substitutes for the penis (Mulvey 1988, 64). In the scopophilic model, the work of fetishization is always the same for the reason that sadism is assumed to lie "at the root of all patriarchy, pornography, and dominant narrative cinema" (Williams 1989, 42).

In one online porn thumbnail gallery after another, the female body is positioned squarely at the center of action as a visual feast, while the eyes of the male performers may become interchangeable with the look of the camera and the spectator's field of vision (through POV shots and focalization). It could be argued that Mulvey's discussion of male gaze in the "show girl" performances in studio-era Hollywood cinema reverberates with such displays and that the plots of reality and gonzo sites where women are made porn performers against their will or knowledge are voyeuristic and underpinned by the dynamics of sadism and control. In porn, bodies are also routinely presented as fragmented. Although individuals, couples, or groups engaging in sexual acts are depicted in full-body shots, attention to detail central to the genre calls for close-ups and zooming in. And since the female body is the visual focus of heteroporn, this fragmentation and stylization might be seen as exemplary of fetishistic scopophilia (cf. Mulvey 1988, 65).[3] Examples of both modes of structuring vision and depicting the female body (voyeuristic, objectifying distance and fetishistic proximity) can be easily found when browsing through video galleries. I am not convinced that identifying such structures of vision provides the analytical means necessary for mapping out the modalities of online pornography, however, let alone experiences of interacting with it.[4] Mulvey's remarks may similarly resonate with the imageries of online porn, but there is also a strong sense of mismatch.

Perhaps ironically, Mulvey's article on visual pleasure speaks very little of pleasure as other than product of ideology. There is certainly little consideration of cinema as not only a visual but also a visceral medium (Kennedy 2000; Sargeant 2004). Steven Shaviro (1993, 12) argues that to prove "the *systematic* nature of patriarchal oppression," Mulvey constructs a "phallic paradigm of vision that is much more totalizing and monolithic than anything the films she discusses are themselves able to articulate." This totalizing model then renders all forms of encountering images and narrative as subservient to scopophilia. As Elizabeth Grosz (2006, 198) points out, the scopophilic model enables two modes of looking—the look of the voyeur (the active mode) and the exhibitionist pleasures of being looked at (the passive mode). Meanwhile, pornography can be glanced at in a number of ways, modes of looking alter and change, and in addition to looking, a range of other sensory engagements and affectations is taking place.

The Specificities of Media

The role of media technology also needs to be considered. As viewers, we do not only look through the medium to the acts and scenarios depicted, but as Jay David Bolter and Richard Grusin (1999, 81) argue, "we look *at* the medium or at a multiplicity of media that may appear in windows on a computer screen or in the fragmented elements of a collage or a photomontage. We do not gaze; rather, we glance here and there in various

manifestations of the media." The Web facilitates a sense of transparency—
or in Bolter and Grusin's terms, a sense of immediacy—in its real-time
applications in particular, but experiences of online porn are fundamentally mediated. On tube sites, videos can be browsed by category (subgenre,
date of upload, tags, popularity calculated in terms of user ratings or the
number of downloads), banner ads invite the user to click and navigate
further, and small windows pop up advertising intimate webcam sessions.
In addition to the screen, keyboard, and mouse, there are multiple windows
and frames, and the fascination of the images unfolding on the screen is
difficult to tell apart from fascinations with the medium (cf. Bolter and
Grusin 1999, 83). Looking at this medium, we may occasionally feel as if we
are looking through it, yet this sense of transparency is a momentary one
that is framed by screens, windows, links, and menus and that depends on
cables, wires, and modems. Such a desire for connection and transparency,
again, is not best captured in the notion of the gaze.

Several things surface from all of this. First, I argue that the notion of the
gaze is too easily used as a conceptual template for analyzing representations and ways of encountering them across a range of media. The historical specificity of Mulvey's analysis is lost if and when the male gaze is seen
as a general visual order and dynamic of looking.[5] Second, given that the
gaze is always gendered male, the female is left with the position of exhibitionist and masochistic object of a spectacle. At the same time, it can be
argued that pornography involves the objectification of all performers—in
different ways and to different degrees. The bodies of women, men, and
the transgendered are depicted in close-ups and exhibited for the viewers
to scrutinize. Pornography is about depicting people as both sexual subjects and objects—and also as assemblages of anonymous, interpenetrating
flesh in motion. Objectification is merely one possible mode of encountering and experiencing these images, and it does not exhaust all available
options.

Third, a more complex understanding of looking at online porn is in
order. Recognizing certain representational conventions or clichés, such as
the homosocial dynamics, does not mean that the viewer is simply hailed
or interpellated into a certain visual-ideological order. Through focalization, certain forms of interaction with pornography and insights into its
imageries are highlighted without limiting other modes of looking. Grosz
(2006, 108) proposes a typology of looking that does not merely draw on

"the vast apparatus of projection, identification, fetishism, and unconscious processes" that align the gaze with sadism and a desire for mastery. Modes of looking such as the "seductive fleeting glance," "laborious observation," "a sweeping survey," "the wink and the blink," exemplify a plurality of possible visions that dictate "how objects are seen and even which ones are seen" (Grosz 2006, 109). Film scholar Jennifer M. Barker (2009, 37) similarly points out that we, as viewers,

might touch the film gently, with a placid and undemanding gaze, but we can also touch the film aggressively, with a searching look and keen ear that palpate and investigate the film. This palpating touch may be affectionate, as we linger appreciatively over the details of the film, or challenging, in the sense that a viewer's attention examines the film for weak spots, errors, and implausibilities.

There is no reason to assume that there would not be equally diverse and shifting forms of looking at online porn. Ultimately, the problem lies in identifying looking with control, distance, and mastery through the psychoanalytical notions of voyeurism and scopophilia, as well as in associating relations of control, as depicted in pornography, with the control of the viewer. It is in no way given that the pleasures of looking need to involve control, let alone sadism. Fourth, the issue of media technologies, affordances, and idiosyncrasies needs to be considered.

Approaching the question from a different perspective, it may just as well be that the "pure and unadulterated pleasure of simply allowing images and sounds to be in control—allowing the process to take over as in a dream" (Burnett 2005, 10) explains more of the visual pleasures derived from screen-based media. Perhaps the point is precisely not to be in constant control or to exercise visual mastery but to enjoy the texture and rhythm of the images unfolding and to be impressed by them. This kind of abandon, often intersected with distanced observation, would seem to characterize ways of looking at pornography for sexual arousal. Yet no matter how willing one is to be moved and impressed, arriving at such abandon necessitates finding images and videos that resonate. Even more important, such abandon is not always easy to achieve.

Although online porn is intimately tied to the histories of porn films and videos, it has gone beyond the limits of these media. As Wendy Chun points out, scholars using film as their point of departure in studying online porn tend to assume that it "has an all-engrossing visual impact": "Fiber-optic networks, however, both enable and frustrate this all-pervasive visuality: visuality, the camera, and the gaze are *effects*," and the invisible workings of online porn are "more significant, and its visual impact less than that of cinematic pornography" (Chun 2006, 124). In other words, much more is going on than gazing at a screen—including the structures of search, the strategic uses of metadata and links, the JavaScript used to coin pop-ups or to lock in users, and user statistics gathered through cookies. A focus on the exclusively representational renders these fundamental principles of operation invisible. These operations and conditions are, as Chun argues, particularly evident in porn sites that pioneered the use of click-throughs, pop-ups, mouse traps, and Web rings and continue to orient and manipulate the movements of users in elaborate ways. The porn user is promised an endless range of options to choose from, yet the sites' operations reveal this freedom of choice as a software construction (Chun 2006, 124–125). These operations are impossible to miss, they contribute much to the experience of online porn, and they frame moments of visual engagement (whether intense and all-engrossing, casual, or haphazard). I agree that addressing the workings of Web sites beyond the visual and the template of the cinematic is important. The visual appeal of the Web is drastically different from that of cinema. But from the perspective of the user, it is not necessarily lesser. The Web is a markedly and, with the increase in high-speed connections and bandwidth, increasingly visual medium. Furthermore, accounting for the visual engagements and exchanges taking place online—including live webcam streams, amateur porn videos, and stylized fetish performances—does not mean conflating them with those of cinema or television or turning a blind eye to the technological specificities of the Internet and its visual landscape.

Visual Control and the Grab

It is impossible to decouple Internet "spectatorship" from other ways of interacting with the medium in tactile ways—placing hands on the keyboard, clicking the mouse, turning eyes to look at the screen, attaching a computer to a network, interacting with digital files, databases, software, search engines, and other users, and automatically sending data about one's activities (see White 2006). The cognitive relationships that users form with technologies mark online platforms apart from other media forms (cf. Uebel 1999). We do not merely look and listen but choose, pick, fast-forward, download, upload, bookmark, browse, click, read, and write—among other things—and the structure of the sites both orients and conditions what we do or can do with them.[6] In her discussion of webcams, Theresa M. Senft conceptualizes this visual and tactile dynamic through the notion of the grab. As a visual dynamic, the grab is an alternative to voyeurism or the gaze. According to Senft, on the Web, "spectatorship functions less as gaze than grab. By 'grab,' I mean to clutch with the hand, to seize for a moment, to command attention, to touch—often inappropriately, sometimes reciprocally" (Senft 2008, 46). The grab describes a media landscape that is characterized by user-generated content and the blurred lines of users and producers, and it differs in important ways from the operating principles of broadcast media and screen fiction. Both camgirls and participants in a reality TV shows perform "the ordinary" in front of the camera (as examples of striptease culture). However, the images of TV show participants are chosen, edited, and filtered through production processes involving directors, editors, and producers. Webcam girls film themselves while also interacting with their audience (Senft 2008, 45). The systems of production are different, as are the technological platforms, user operations, economical underpinnings, and forms of interaction.

As Senft also points out, the audience for webcams engages with their images in a somewhat random manner. Rather than watching webcam streams every hour throughout the day, they grab pieces of it (sometimes concretely by taking screen grabs). This form of viewing may involve the pleasures of being in control of the images, but people make use of the images for a variety of purposes. Once images, videos, stories, and webcam streams are made available online, they are out of the producers' control as users grab images, perhaps link or incorporate them to other sites, share them, and frame them with comments of their own (Senft 2008, 47). With the concept of grab, Senft captures some of the complexity of online visual production, circulation, and consumption. The grab can also be extended to discussions beyond the visual dynamics of online exchanges—to the ways in which users are grabbed as their movements are tracked and as their routine tasks are saved and analyzed as data. Chun (2008, 323) refers to this grab by largely invisible networks and technologies that envelope us as *capture*—a term that is similarly tactile and mundane in its connotations. Users grab images and technologies by which they are grabbed in return. Some of this grab can also be considered in terms of resonance. Whatever grabs, resonates: it demands attention and has the power to move and touch the one interacting with it. The grab can be experienced as disturbing, arousing, or surprising. Depending on the affective resonance, users may turn away from the images or move even closer to be moved and impressed.

In her discussion of webcam girls, Michele White (2003, 21–22) points out that these women only "ambivalently connote Mulvey's 'to-be- looked-at-ness'" in the sense that they are actively in charge of what the cameras show. Furthermore, she argues that the "webcam spectator is situated in a place where voyeurism is constantly promised, yet theoretically uninhabitable, because the viewer has relinquished a distanced position" (White 2003, 23; also Senft 2008, 45). As users knowingly engage in the dynamics of seeing and being seen on webcams, reality television, and amateur porn sites, their access to visual control is far from assured. As something implied and invited, this voyeurism is, in fact, no longer voyeurism as such. Consequently, scopophilia becomes something of a game knowingly played. The performers know that they are being watched, they may pretend to be unaware of this, or they may actively engage with and pose and perform for the audience. Viewers are aware of the performative nature of "hidden camera" shots but decide to play along by orienting themselves in a particular way (which could also be defined as a suspension of disbelief).

Historically, pornographic images and texts have made extensive use of the dynamics and the trope of voyeurism as sexual interest related to witnessing people's intimate functions (whether sex, confession, or modes of undress) in secret and without their knowledge. The position of voyeurism depends on realism: "the force of these images stems from their 'transparency,' from the ways they seem to move beyond representation to reference through our own visceral reaction to them; yet the extreme realist quality of visual and textual pornography is a style that denies being one" (Chun 2006, 101). The fantasy of voyeurism is one of direct visual access, and although pornographic depictions of voyeurism are rich in conventions and formulas, the promises of transparency help to efface the sense of the representational. This quest for transparency and immediacy finds easy resonance in the format of webcams (particularly as hidden cams) that promise to show what is taking place without any acting, camerawork, or editing. The site http://voyeuraddiction.com ("Spy on unsuspecting girls now!") is advertised as the number one voyeur cam site. Featuring "upskirt shoe cams," "dressing room cams," "bathroom cams," "hidden toilet cams," "two-way mirrors," and "unsuspecting girls caught on camera," it offers ample and literal examples of sadistic scopophilia and visual control. However, given that users are invited to watch, their position is not exactly one of voyeurs. Furthermore, webcams "mimic voyeurism in order to create indexicality and authenticity within a seemingly nonindexical medium" (Chun 2006, 103). In other words, as familiar visual dynamics are acted out on online platforms, they go through transformations that necessitate changes in the conceptual frameworks through which they are analyzed.

Hidden camera sites, webcams, and video galleries offer plentiful instances of visual control, yet there is much more than voyeurism to the visual landscape and resonances of online pornography, and, as Chun suggests, their voyeurism may be a matter of mimicry. Recognizing voyeurism as a pornographic fantasy and trope is one thing. Associating all online porn with voyeurism in a wholesale embrace of a psychoanalytical framework is a different matter altogether. It may just as well be that viewers do not want to be in control of the images unfolding but take more pleasure in being overwhelmed by them. And perhaps they do not identify with the characters engaging in performances of domination and submission on the screen. The images may also resonate in a different register.

When criticizing antipornography feminists for their "mythic reading" of pornography, Walter Kendrick (1996, 230) sees it as analogous to psychoanalysis in that "its conclusions are irrefutable and always the same." Applying this polemic to the uses of Mulvey's model in studies of online porn, one might argue that they result in predictable conclusions that can be envisioned even before studying any particular set of materials. This psychoanalytical framework (actually, Mulvey's approach is more representative of psychosemiotics and so-called screen theory) seems to constitute what Jameson (2002, 45) identifies as "something like an allegorical operation in which a text is systematically rewritten in terms of some fundamental master code." In other words, the trajectory of interpretation seems to result in predictable outcomes (that are articulated in terms of voyeurism, scopophilia, sadism, and narcissism).

Ruth Barcan (2002) associates the attraction of reality genres with the dynamics of scopophilia. Although voyeurism is central to the pleasures of watching amateur porn, performing in it involves exhibitionism (also Calvert 2000). McNair (2002, 89) makes a similar argument about striptease

culture as involving audience members with inclinations toward voyeurism and performers with an exhibitionistic streak who reveal (and perform)
intimate and confessional details of their lives, feelings, and sexualities.
Such broad cultural diagnoses aim to capture the new context where "ordinary people" have access to micro-celebrity, public confessions are increasingly common, and people reveal both their emotions and their bodies in
public. People like to watch, be watched by, and perform for others. I nevertheless doubt that the concepts of voyeurism and exhibitionism are the
most apt for charting out such tendencies and transitions in media culture.
First, grounded in psychoanalytical theories, the concepts risk envisioning
a culture at the brink—or at the throes—of mass pathology. Second, to the
degree that the concepts cover and connect a range of practices (Facebook
profiles, webcams, XTube videos, television shows like *Big Brother*, strategies
of tabloid media, therapy culture, and beyond), they also conflate them.
This makes it difficult to account for their mutual differences, tensions,
and discrepancies (whether in terms of media technology, aesthetics, or
economy). Third, when used as broad labels, voyeurism and exhibitionism
overdetermine individual acts and activities while positioning the people
who act them out into fixed and predetermined roles and dynamics. As
such, they enable easy answers to the complexities of contemporary media
culture and its producers, consumers, and imageries.

As the discussions above have already implied, I believe that identification, a notion that is central to conceptualizations of scopophilia in film
theory, falls short of explaining the experiences of viewing online porn.
Scopophilia facilitates narcissism as recognition/misrecognition in which
viewers both temporarily lose their ego and reinforce it through identification with figures on the screen (Mulvey 1988, 59–61). The discourse of
identification is dominant in cinema studies to the point of having gained
commonsensical status, and encounters with all kinds of pornography are
routinely discussed as involving identification (e.g., Williams 1989; Shamoon 2004; Patterson 2004; Moore and Weissbein 2010). Martin (2006, 194),
for example, argues that in porn, viewers have "a necessary close identification" with the bodies on the screen. The centrality of identification in
studies of porn owes to the legacy of both literary studies and cinema studies and their focus on narrative.[7] In the tradition of cinema studies, spectatorship has been largely discussed on an abstract level as textual positions
produced by the text. Mulvey's theory of the three gazes, for example, has

little connection to empirical viewers and their practices. In formulating alternatives to the textual and psychoanalytical notions of spectatorship, Jackie Stacey (1994, 25) argues for the need to account for alternative readings, multiple meanings, fluid identifications, and erotic viewing pleasures. Furthermore, she argues that identification has "been used as a kind of commonsense term within some film and literary studies, referring to a set of cultural processes which describe different kinds of connections between spectators/readers and fictional others" (Stacey 1994, 130). Reframing the question as one of fascination, Stacey opens up these connections as ones involving transcendence, aspiration, inspiration, and mirroring and suggests that identification is by no means an automatic process that requires similarity between the self and the characters depicted. Situations, clothes, settings, props, movements, and bits of dialog can all be experienced as fascinating: they can all resonate.

On gonzo, reality, and amateur sites, users may witness sex acts from the perspective of one of the performers, and action is often focalized through POV shots. This does not, however, necessitate identification with the characters in the sense of "jumping into their skin." As Peter Lehman (2006, 89) points out, "rather than lose themselves in identification with the fictional bodies on the screen, porn spectators direct their attention to their own bodies. It is hard for someone to masturbate without knowing what she or he is doing." Being aroused by pornography means having a heightened awareness of one's body, one's bodily sensations, and the transformations occurring in them. Furthermore, as Kipnis (1999, 197) argues, identification does not mean that one likes what one sees or wishes to emulate it: it "may be ambivalent, or based on relics and repressions from the past. All that it means is that something hooks you about the scene, and you don't necessarily know what." We do not always know why certain video clips, images, scenes, or moments grab us while others fail to. In Kipnis's discussion, identification translates as appeal, attachment, and fascination in ways that could be addressed as resonance. As I see it, such fascination and resonance need not be seen as matters of identification.

The Question of Narrative

Richard Dyer (2002b, 142) argues that although pornography has been defined through its lack of narrative, narrative is, in fact, its very basis. Even short loops tell a story, no matter how minimal it may be. Narrative has played an important role in literary pornography, stag films, and the 35mm films of the 1970s that occasionally are assigned the status of classics (see Paasonen and Saarenmaa 2007). The form of narrative cinema, somewhat marginal in terms of inter- and cross-media histories of pornography, has gained close to normative status as the criterion of "good pornography." When writing about the "golden age" of porn in the 1970s, Linda Williams laments the later developments in video porn and beyond: "pornography itself would devolve in the following decade into the parallel universe of mostly cheaply made, badly acted, and aesthetically impoverished sucking and fucking shots on video" (Williams 2008, 128). In Williams's account, the failure of pornography to become more like mainstream narrative cinema resulted in and contributed to poor technical and aesthetic quality. This comment is surprising coming from an author with impressive knowledge about the history of screen pornography, a tradition in which narrative has by no means been the most important theme but that has, from its origins, focused on sucking and fucking shots. In this continuum, the narrative films shot on 35mm are an anomalous, exceptional development rather than a case of pornographic form reaching its pinnacle. Perhaps Williams is after a different kind of resonance with pornography, one based on narrative development and character construction. Or perhaps she is nostalgic about the format of film, its visual richness and haptic qualities. One can only speculate.[8]

Posing the 1970s as a golden age of pornography in a more general sense is certainly debatable since video allowed the expansion of the porn industry and the mainstreaming of audiovisual pornography for home consumption. Super 8 and 8mm projectors were sold to households, but the domestic circulation of porn films was marginal until the 1980s (Greenberg 2008). Seeing the form of narrative feature film as an aesthetic or a technical norm is problematic in that it renders all later developments as inferior variations (rather than accounting for the developments on their own terms). Similarly, adapting a model of spectatorship from cinema studies to Internet research comes with fundamental problems. Watching a narrative film, for example, is a different form of activity than following hyperlinks, doing searches, and uploading and downloading videos online. The fact that pornography is projected onto a cinema screen (of varying size), watched on a TV or computer screen, or watched on the screen of a mobile device and therefore is screen-based does not mean that different media can be conceptualized through same conceptual tools or that the experiences and resonances they give rise to are the same. There are obvious differences in watching a stag film on a cinema screen or on one's laptop at home (in terms of the social setting, privacy, and intimacy), watching a porn video on a DVD or VHS player attached to a TV screen, or browsing through Web sites with thousands of videos available for download and webcam sites to choose from. The experiences of pornography are always mediated and conditioned by particular technical set-ups and media forms. The sense of privacy and connectedness varies drastically, as does the form of experiencing and using porn, the materiality of the medium, tactile engagements with it, and the resonances that it affords.[9]

There is also reason to ask whether character construction and narrative have ever been crucial to porn. Jennifer Lyon Bell (2001, 42) argues that sexual arousal is best achieved through the use of stock characters, since complex and contradictory characters evoking different kinds of emotions tend to disturb the viewing experience and derail sexual arousal. Hence "nuanced characters may actually detract from a film's ability to generate sexual desire. In this, I believe that pornography differs from other mainstream genres: More 'character engagement' is not necessarily better, when the goal is generating sexual desire" (Bell 2001, 42). Stock characters and scenarios are functional in that they enable quick transition to the sex act itself: "once the scene is set, pornography can get down to real action" (Kuhn 1994, 45). Sontag (2002, 51) makes a similar argument by pointing out that pornography prefers "ready-made conventions of character, setting, and action," and types instead of individuals. The reader's (Sontag is discussing literary pornography) sexual arousal is dependent on having the "inner life" of the characters remain undeveloped and their sentiments undisclosed, for only "in the absence of directly stated emotions can the reader of pornography find room for his own responses" (Sontag 2002, 54).

According to an argument often repeated, good pornography "tells a good story," resembles a regular feature film, and has real characters and proper dialog. I fail to understand why story, characters, and dialog would be criteria of quality. Although these aspects are recurrently used in high-production-value videos designed for the couples' market (Tyler 2010, 58), the case might be the opposite. After all, many people fast-forward through dialog and background stories in porn films.[10] Video pornography consists largely of episode films (compilations of more or less connected scenes). This episodic nature is even more pronounced in DVD productions that may be three hours long. In films with a narrative frame, action routinely consists of "numbers" (oral, anal, girl-on-girl, masturbation, threesome) that, much like the dance numbers in musicals, tend to disrupt any narrative flow (Williams 1989, 48–49). Video clips distributed on file-sharing and video sites consist of numbers with little narrative framing. In thousands and thousands of videos, people just get down to action, and considerations of narrative are bound to fall short of explaining either their form or appeal.

Contrary to the requirements of narrative and character building, pornographic scenarios necessitate little motivation or building. For example, it is not necessary to explain why people would like to perform the acts they do or why they would want to act them out with these particular people: they just do. The only necessary motivation is for the performers to be in the same space. This does not render pornography somehow lower or inferior as a genre but suggests that it is different in its principles of operation. I therefore agree with McNair's (2002, 41) statement that if porn has an aesthetic, "it lies in the extent to which a text succeeds in its erotic ambitions—a quality largely independent of such elements as plot, script, character development, or production design." Good pornography is whatever turns on its viewers, gives rise to carnal resonance, and moves the bodies of those watching.

Grab, Resonance, Rhythm

I would like to propose some key concepts for addressing the appeal of online porn outside the framework of voyeurism, scopophilia, and the cultural form of cinema. Rather than gaze, the dynamic of vision involved in online porn ranges from the multiple aspects of the grab (as discussed by Senft), to the different looks mapped out by Grosz ("seductive fleeting glance," "laborious observation," "a sweeping survey," "the wink and the blink"), as well as the pleasures of being overwhelmed and impressed by the visual that Ron Burnett addresses. Rather than narrative, I suggest that porn may be more an issue of rhythm as movement with particular tempo. Finally, rather than identification, the question could be phrased as one of resonance, and this is more than a mere poetic metaphor. Like Zabet

Patterson (2004, 166), I see resonance as somatic and somewhat involuntary moments of proximity with characters and bodily performances on the screen. This resonance can be further intensified by the (assumed) amateurism of the pornographers and the sense of directness they give rise to. However, unlike Patterson, I do not consider this an issue of identification by default.

Online porn involves narrative elements, scenarios, and frameworks (such as reality and gonzo plots), as well as much more abstract kinds of motion and rhythm. The narrative elements frame events and envision a certain dynamic between the performers, yet this is not the thing that most viewers find most appealing or important in porn. The sexual acts and detailed displays of body parts are spectacular in themselves. This spectacular display has only a random relationship to narrative, while the ways of experiencing it cannot be reduced to notions of identification. The notion of rhythm refers to the tempo of pornographic action—the individual scenes and acts taking place within them. Like narrative, rhythm and tempo involve movement, but they do not necessarily add up to a story. According to standard structure repeated on YouPorn, RedTube, and PornoTube, a heteroporn video starts with the introduction to the female performer, who presents her body and touches herself or is touched by a male partner. This slow tempo is followed by "numbers" such as fellatio, coitus, and anal and double penetration. The rhythm speeds up and slows down again in intervals until the final crescendo and climax of cum shot(s). This rhythm may be accompanied by music, although this is rare in reality and amateur videos.[11] Given that people generally watch more than one video when visiting a tube site, the practices of online porn consumption can also be conceptualized through the notion of rhythm more generally. Rhythm oscillates from slow to fast and back again, extreme close-ups are followed by distanced vistas, and viewers move from one video to another, encountering both repetition and novelty.

Focalization, as actively employed in pornography, should not be easily conflated with identification (as discussed in film studies), which is dependent on character construction and narrative. Viewers certainly can identify with porn performers in the sense of imagining themselves in the center of action, and this kind of proximity is both invited and supported in heteroporn for male viewers through focalization and address. I nevertheless suggest that the concept of resonance may be more helpful in describing such motion and orientation. The use of stock characters embodying clichéd "social types" (or depending of interpretation, stereotypes) would seem to build a certain distance between the spectator and the characters. These types are acted out with some degree of exaggeration and by highlighting their artificiality. In online videos where character construction is a minor concern, performers merely "get it on." Identification in the sense of sameness seems too large a term for describing encounters with the characters and the possible pleasures derived from them. Moments of intimate resonance tend to be of the fleeting kind—fascination and interest shifts from one shot, scene, site, video clip, performer, and act to another. Through resonance, something grabs and moves me, and its power to move me makes me question my sense of mastery over what I view.

Grosz (2007) discusses arts as something that produces and generates intensity—"that which directly impacts the nervous system and intensifies sensation." Art "is the art of affect more than representation, a system of dynamized and impacting forces rather than a system of unique images that function in the regime of signs." Art submits its materials to intensity and sensation with no predetermined format, hence affecting the bodies of people. Johanna Ahonen (2010, 122) argues that for Grosz, art turns vibrations—life forces—into sensations. Although Grosz (2007) refuses to create a definition and hierarchy of art, she does separate art in certain terms from material production that generates "pre-experienced sensations, sensations known in advance, guaranteed to affect in particular sad or joyful ways." This marking apart of the artful from other forms of cultural production (mass culture, popular culture, and entertainment) as meriting conceptual interest and intellectual attention recurs in contemporary discussions on affect and materiality. On the one hand, this is a question of the properties and affordances of different objects—the ways in which they resonate, the kinds of encounters they invite, and the modes of analytical engagement they facilitate. On the other hand, this marking apart of the artful from the prefabricated involves the reiteration of cultural hierarchies and the premises of mass culture critique in which some objects are marked as more worthy of intellectual engagement than others. This has to do with presumptions concerning the objects' properties and affordances based on their position in the hierarchies of culture. Experimental installation art and amateur video clips on RedTube, for example, have different kinds of affordance, yet the sensations derived from the video clips cannot necessarily be known in advance and cannot be guaranteed to have particular effects on their audience.

Mixed Feelings

When thinking through the affective dynamics and resonances of porn (whether online, offline, or somewhere in between), it is crucial to note that fascination and sexual arousal do not foreclose experiences of disgust, amusement, dismay, or even boredom. These affective intensities coexist and, in many instances, support and necessitate one another. In other words, bodily resonance can run alongside and together with critical considerations and resistance toward the imageries consumed. Jane Gallop (2005, 97) points to this when writing about the "creepiness" of being turned on and being inspired to masturbate when reading Marquis de Sade's *Philosophy in the Bedroom*—a book that provides ample opportunities for feminist critique. Considering that Sade's style of writing is visceral, indeed, in combining torture with philosophical reflection, the mixed reaction of "creepy arousal" is not unexpected (cf. Cramer 2006, 133). It is also present in other encounters with porn, and some feminist critics have titled such "disturbing, or traumatic, or unpleasant, or scary, or confusing" forms of sexual arousal as dysrotic as opposed to erotic (see Dines et al. 2010, 18–19). I would suggest that mixed reactions, moments of creepy arousal, and surprising resonance are characteristic of encounters with pornography and other body genres as well as a range of media images. In a Deleuzean framework, such creepy moments would be exemplary of the "unpredictable autonomy of the body's encounter with the event, its shattering ability to go its own way" (Hemmings 2005, 552). These make evident the phantasmatic nature of the ideal of the modern (rational) subject who is able to control his or her body and affectations.

I have found myself in tears over the goodbyes of Meryl Streep and Robert Redford in the emotional climax of *Out of Africa*, the release of Michael Jackson after his 2005 trial, the weddings of Prince Charles and Camilla Parker-Bowles, numerous track and field award ceremonies, and the highlight moments of *Extreme Makeover: Home Edition*. This may be because—in novelist Frank McCourt's memorable phrasing—my "bladder is too close to my eye." These moments of being moved have often involved rather cursory engagement: I have been watching television when eating dinner, reading a newspaper, or entertaining my cat. As such, they represent the precognitive and the affective, physical responses to moving images rather than emotional encounters in the sense of being definable or conceptualized. However, these gut reactions are also impossible to draw apart from the knowledge of context, genre, and modality by which they have been oriented. My susceptibility to the power of popular media is hardly peculiar since films, media spectacles, shock sites, Internet memes, and television shows all involve a knowing and intentional affective address. Their attraction and appeal is dependent on the affective resonance they aim to evoke.

The concepts, plots, and themes of porn sites may add to visceral responses and bodily sensations, but they may have a disruptive effect or little effect whatsoever. Moments of resonance can be found with individual scenarios, gestures, and movements. It is not presumed that viewers will pay attention to narrative, characters, or their development. At the same time, porn positions the viewer as an outside observer witnessing bodily acts and displays at a distance. The lack of physical contact between the viewer and the image is "constitutive of whatever our relation to these images may be" (Williams 2008, 16–17), yet the bodies and acts on the screen are at the same time intimately close and available for scrutiny. With the notion of carnal resonance, my aim is to capture some of this dynamic in which moments of proximity surface in encounters between the spectator and the depicted (whether characters, acts, sounds, close-ups, or something else). Resonance may involve recognition in the sense of being able to relate the acts shown to one's own experiences and sensations. Resonance touches and moves the viewer's body without a need for sameness—between the viewer and the performers, the viewer's sexual preferences and the acts performed, or her fantasies and the onscreen scenarios. Experiences of pornography may involve rhythm rather than narrative—resonance felt in the body rather than identification as an imaginary sameness that melts away the boundaries between the self and the characters on the screen. Less than gaze, these may be occasions of glance and grab that vary and alter in intensity, focus, and attention.

Working with the Resonant: Further Notes on Method

In terms of analysis, the disturbing power of porn is slippery, and it evades gestures of analytical grasping and grabbing. Considering this power in terms of the qualities of images is one means of gaining some hold of the slithery matter. When contemplating on images that have grabbed me in particularly intense ways, I have found myself rereading Roland Barthes's ruminations on the effect of photographic images, particularly the category of images that fascinate and injure, prick, bruise, and puncture one's body, which he titled *punctum* (Barthes 1981, 26–27; also Fried 2005, 539). Punctum, which Barthes separates from images involving shock and manipulation of the viewer, is unintentional and unpremeditated, and it resists being pinned down and known—for what can be named cannot truly prick (Barthes 1981, 32, 45, 51). Whatever pricks cannot be translated into language, in contrast to *studium*, descriptive and banal images that lack detail and knowingly aim "to inform, to represent, to surprise, to cause to signify, to provoke desire" (Barthes 1981, 27–28; Fried 2005, 542). Pornographic images intended to arouse and depicting sexual acts and genitalia in minute detail fall into this category by definition as too literal and full of shock (Barthes 1981, 41).

Barthes's divisions concern the visual qualities and properties of photographic images—the experiences and interpretations that they allow, enable, and call forth—but also their intentions and functions. At the same time, his categorical dismissal of pornography as single-minded is rather totalizing and draws on cultural hierarchies that separate the artful (erotica) from the mass-cultural (porn) (Williams 2004a, 6).[12] This dismissal is based on assumptions concerning the genre and its visual modality rather than on studies of actual pornography. The exclusion of the pornographic from the realm of punctum also goes against the definition of punctum as unintended experiences separate from authorial intentions. Although images can be invested with intentions and functions, these do not dictate ways of encountering and experiencing them. As something that fascinates and injures and causes effects through the body, punctum would seem to describe something of the affective resonance and, indeed, the power of pornography. At the same time, it (unlike the erotic) remains excluded from the category.

A similar dynamic is at play in Laura U. Marks's discussion of haptic and optic images. For Marks (2002, 2–3) haptic images are encountered along the skin as well as through the eyes. They encourage "a bodily relationship between the viewer and the image," and encounters with them do not "require an initial separation between perceiver and object that is mediated by representation" (Marks 2000, 164). For Marks (2002, 15), haptic images depend on "limited visibility and the viewer's lack of mastery over the image." Inviting "a small caressing gaze," they draw the viewer close and as such are erotic in contrast to pornography that is defined by optimized visibility (Marks 2000, 163; 2002, 6). Haptic images have certain properties that give rise to particular kinds of resonance and intimacy—ways of looking and experiencing through a caressing gaze rather than voyeuristic control or mastery. As is the case with punctum, their effect is more direct than that of representational images: they escape mediation. Although Barthes defined punctum through its effects more than its aesthetic properties (for these definitions remain rather loose), Marks sees haptic images as indirect. For the former, punctum is accidental and unintentional, whereas for the latter, the haptic is both a visual quality and a strategy that is knowingly adopted by artists (Marks 2002, 16). The materiality of the image is a question of authorial creation—the ways in which the artist has actualized it (Marks 2002, 149). The haptic, like punctum, is defined through its difference to the pornographic, a class of images that comes to represent something that is already known, that invites no caressing gaze, and that lacks the power to bruise and puncture the viewer's body.

Images have specific properties, affordances, and materiality that are conditioned by their media of production and circulation and that invite and facilitate certain kinds of experiences, intimacies, investigations, and resonance. As discussed throughout this book, porn operates in the oscillating registers of hyperbole and authenticity, predictability and visceral encounters, and it involves a complex commute between distance and proximity, gut reactions, distanced observation, curious glancing, incredulous blinking, insistent grabbing, and haphazard glimpses. Haptic images offer a pure surface to view through extreme close-ups—a definition that would seem to reverberate with how porn is "able to zoom in and focus on the body, and especially the genitals, in minute details and present the flesh enlarged to proportions that are impossible to see in actual sexual encounters" (Sargeant 2006). Such contemplative proximity intersects with much more observational shots. In Marks's terms, the modulation is between haptic and optic visuality. Contrary to a haptic emphasis on materiality, texture, embodiment, and touch, optic visuality "privileges the representational power of the image" and perceives of it as an object that facilitates a sense of distance (Marks 2000, 163). I do not argue that pornography involves haptic rather

than optic imaging (for clearly this is not the intimate modality that Marks
has in mind), but the ways of experiencing pornography move between
different visual registers and modes of looking as attention shifts from the
close-up details of bodies, rhythms, and resonances to whole-body or long
shots, surprising juxtapositions, and ruptures.

Optimized visibility and extreme close-ups are about both clinical distance and exposure as well as particular "landscapes" of flesh that viewers can almost touch and feel through the texture of the images. Generic,
theatrical, and spectacular depictions of bodily orifices, liquids, and acts
in extreme close-up draw viewers closer, while repetitive, exaggerated, and
distanced conventions work to push them away again. Proximity surfaces
(or fails to surface) from encounters with the image, its resonance, and its
materiality that are always conditioned and indeed structured by media
technologies, their specificities, and the practices of using them. To address
such proximities, one needs to be open to being touched, moved, and vulnerable to its resonance. At the same time, I cannot simply choose what
images, Web pages, or videos I want to resonate with or to resonate with me
or what kind of resonance I might experience.

Affectations

When addressing sensations and affect, film studies scholars have written
about films that they have been personally touched by (e.g., Shaviro 1993;
Marks 2002; Sobchack 2004; Abel 2007; Barker 2009; Laine 2010). By doing
so, they have been able to combine analysis of the more formal aspects of
film (narrative, editing, character construction, cinematography, the use of
music and sound) with considerations of their own affectations, fascinations, and embodied entanglements (after all, one has firsthand access to
only one's own sensations). At the same time, the cinematic examples discussed tend to be representative of art house and modern classics: Shaviro
writes on Cronenberg, Romero, and Jerry Lewis; Vivian Sobchack on Jane
Campion and Itami; Jennifer Barker on Tarkovski; and so on. This is a question of moments of being moved and of personal preferences and tastes
(that are linked to expertise and the canons of film culture). Meanwhile,
recollections of being touched and moved by pornography—which lies at
the "lowest of the low" in the hierarchies of culture—remain few and far
between.[13]

Working with and through one's own sensations is a means of making research more accountable and ethical. It also involves some challenges, such as those related to generalization. Other people may not recognize the resonance we ourselves feel. There is no guarantee that others will be moved by the same images, scenes, and moments by which we find ourselves impressed or that they will recognize the resonances we try to describe. As Gallop (1988, 53) points out in her discussion of reading de Sade, something that fascinates me "could leave another reader cold. What I assumed was a general desire, a 'normal' attraction . . . turns out to be my peculiar tendency, my perversion." Sensations cannot be generalized as an account of images, intensities, or properties. Sensations are also where methodological (and epistemological) differences become manifest between authors who argue for closer close reading and caressing gazing and the more Deleuzean theorists of affect and intensity. The calls for increased closeness with images—as voiced in material anthropology, phenomenology, and feminist literary studies—reverberate with projects such as Marco Abel's (2007, xiii) interest in how images and texts "configure our ability to respond to, and to do things with, them," but these also differ from one another.

Abel (like Shaviro and Grosz) does not address affect as personal in the sense of being experienced in specific bodies. Instead, affects are forces that cut across and connect different bodies. Abel (2007, 6) makes this clear when writing on the differences between the images that capture life forces and those that merely represent them. The first involve sensations and affect (as presubjective), and the latter are about narrativization (logic) and subjective feeling. According to Abel, phenomenological accounts of affect fail to address the level of force. At the same time, he discusses films and novels that have affected, moved, and fascinated him (Abel 2007, xvii). When these are posed as examples of abstract pre- and nonsubjective affective resonance and force, his own sensations become generalized as nonpersonal affective intensity. As Katariina Kyrölä (2010, 8) argues, there is a risk of losing sight of the specificity and particularity of viewing bodies and their cultural conditions: "If there is no locatedness, corporeality is easily stripped of its political and ethical gravity" (Kyrölä 2010, 130). In contrast, scholarship that is informed by theories of "thinking through the body" and situated knowledge addresses sensing, self-reflexive, and largely autobiographical bodies that are fundamentally implicated in the interpretation they produce. Pearce, Gallop, and Sedgwick start from a different place in that the affect they conceptualize is not autonomous but experienced in particular bodies.

Ultimately, working with affect poses the methodological question of affordance—whether it is possible to address intensities and force without resonating with specific objects that have particular properties and affordances. The answer would seem to be negative, and the same goes for investigations of personal affectations in general. What, then, can be made of examples that fail to resonate and leave the observer indifferent or cold? These kinds of images surely comprise the overwhelmingly majority of pornography and visual culture. Do they merely fall off the agenda? I have been recurrently "touched by the substance and texture of images" (Sobchack 2004, 65) and also aroused (sexually and not merely "to meaning") when working with online pornography.[14] However, focusing exclusively on such moments and examples would require me to frame out most of the material addressed in this book. Pornography routinely fails to resonate: its dissonance may just as well leave the recipient disinterested or bored.

This is especially the case after years of working on the same material: moments of surprise are rare, and little of the initial curiosity is left. The first encounters with an image may be characterized by interest, surprise, and even titillation of the kind that is lost in the course of contextualization and interpretation. Analysis brings with it a sense of familiarity and predictability Analysis brings with it a sense of familiarity and predictability. Affective intensities are diluted, and they change shape as surprise turns to predictability, boredom, but perhaps also fondness. Authors writing in the framework of new materialist critique have been largely interested in immediate sensation. When writing on cinema, Shaviro (1993, 26) argues that its images "confront the viewer directly, without mediation"—meaning that one is impressed and moved by the images unfolding and responds to them viscerally before interpreting them as symbols of any kind. Abel (2007, 10) is similarly interested in the force of images to "produce effects *prior* to their inevitable narrativization, their eventual territorialization onto the plane of representation" and to "affect me before the narrative apparatus of capture organizes them for me." These interests are in line with Deleuze's view of art as "less a representation than an experience of the sensible" (Hillis 2009, 264)—as immediate sensation rather than reflection thereof.

At the same time, media images have been produced through processes of scripts, storyboards, shooting, and editing. Images are conveyed and materialized through particular media technologies: they are crafted, produced, and represented, even if eventually they may be sensed in terms of gut reactions. The images and videos we encounter online are always recorded with particular technologies, are almost always edited, and are circulated on specific platforms and in formats that set limits to how we encounter them, sense them, and make sense of them in the first place. They are already organized for us through specific technologies and cultural codes. Perhaps paradoxically, analyses of images as directly touching and affecting the viewer that aim to do away with mediation also do away with the materiality of the medium, its working practices, its technical conditions, and its affordances. In my view, media studies that ignore the work that media do (mediation as particular conditions, conventions, practices, modes, and intensities) and the work that goes into the production of media are bound to fail in grasping their object of study.

Unlike Abel (2007, xvi), I do not believe that it is possible to choose to reinhabit "the moment before subjective interpretation, that is, the moment of the event . . . itself." One can reconstruct something of the initial and undifferentiated encounter with an image, but one cannot relive or reinhabit it by simply deciding to do so. This would requite a subject who is in control of her cognition and master of her emotions. It would also require the possibility of accessing affect (irreducible and unpredictable intensity and force) in similarly undifferentiated ways. Affective dynamics change in the course of recurring viewings, and these dynamics are not for the viewer to master. As Susan Kozel (2007, 18) points out, it is problematic to assume that we can reach the prelinguistic and "shake off our inscription by language and culture" in analytical work unfolding through language. The prereflection cannot be reached through reflection as such. The challenge is to loosen analytical frameworks based on language and meaning enough to accommodate ambiguity and fluidity and to give rise to new forms of thought (Kozel 2007, 19). This does not mean visiting or accessing the prereflective inasmuch as holding on to its traces and sensations in acts of making sense.

Material Close Looking?

As bodily knowledge, carnal resonance requires viewers to get close enough to the image to be moved by it and to account for its "uncontrolled and uncontrollable" aspects (MacDougall 2006, 7). Such affectation results from encounters between bodies (whether human or animal, bodies of objects or thought) and connects them. As Tarja Laine (2010) argues, film (or equally, a Web page, an image, a video, or a text) can be seen as an event that gives rise to sensations, affectations, and ways of understanding. Acknowledging moments of being impressed or overwhelmed is both a methodological matter and an ethical question. The kind of material close looking that I wish to propose as an methodological approach to studying pornography involves sensitivity (to the material properties of the images, texts, and sounds studied) and attentiveness (to their modalities, their resonances—in terms of texture, feel, subject matter, and aesthetics—and the physicality of their production and mediation).

Consider, for example, an individual image that I came across when searching randomly for amateur porn. Starting from a Web directory and clicking through a series of image links, this search led me to a Wife Bucket image shot in a living room. Among the hundreds of porn images I looked at on that particular day, this one arrested my attention, grabbed me, and inspired me to investigate the site further. The image shows a white man and white woman engaged in coitus on a duvet on a living room floor covered with red wall-to-wall carpeting with a floral pattern. The man is on top with his legs spread and his scrotum and tan lines visible to the viewer. Below him, we see the woman's legs dressed in fishnet stay-up stockings and a part of her buttocks and labia. The long curtains of the room are drawn, and the lighting is intimate, complete with candles. In contrast, the image, in all likeliness taken with a stand and automatic settings, uses a flash that highlights the paleness and faint redness of the couple's skin. The room is decorated with furniture made of dark wood, a dark gray fireplace, arrangements of dried and artificial flowers, a decorative statue, a large TV screen, a stereo system, a subwoofer loudspeaker, a DVD player, and a VCR. A VHS tape is placed on top of the subwoofer, and DVDs are piled under the player. A sweatshirt is thrown onto a chair, and boxer shorts and other pieces of discarded clothing are visible at the edge of the image.

What grabbed me in this image was not the act depicted, for the missionary position is unexceptional among online porn's more exotic tableaus. Rather, the grab involved the overall texture of the image—the sharp flash, hairy legs, pink skin, flowers, textiles, and furniture. As discussed in chapter 3, such tangible domesticity is characteristic of Wife Bucket images. This tactile grab—direct and haptic—is impossible to decouple from the optic layout of the image. The couple is at the center of the image, on display, and the man is facing a TV screen showing hardcore porn. I was drawn to the presence of mediated sex in the production of amateur porn (and, as viewers, we see both instances at the same time) and hence more conceptualized and contextual considerations of the image. The TV is tuned to the pay channel TV1000 and shows a white woman kissing a large, erect, black penis. Sitting on the TV, there is a smaller screen—perhaps a baby monitor or perhaps a screen used for watching the videos that the couple makes.

This is not an image capturing or conveying life forces. It is motion stopped still—sex deprived of intensity. As a laconic kind of a pornographic image, it states the act of penetration. The image is posed and designed, yet haphazard, taken as it is with an automatic shot. It is at once random and precise in the details and the mundane textures of everyday life that it conveys. When considering the image and its grab, divisions of the haptic and the optic, punctum and studium are of limited use, as the images slips through such categorizations. It offers possibilities for numerous "readings"—of the mediated feedback loops of porn consumed and produced, of the visual economies of amateur porn, of habitus and interior decoration. At the same time, the texture and feel of the bodies—the woman's slightly flabby buttocks pressed under the man and the man's hairy buttock line—cannot be read and refuse to "mean." These visual registers are both about the affordances and properties of the image and about modes of looking at it. All this is underpinned by technologies of production and distribution—digital cameras, PCs, modems, and servers—through which it is possible for the image to materialize in acts of consumption (see chapter 3). Resonance is descriptive of what disturbs, tickles, or confuses in such materializations—what moves us in a particular way in specific images and technological assemblages.

Caught between the Senses

As an act of translation and mediation, close looking is not confined to describing one's sensations and affectations (which, in any case, largely escape such attempts). It accounts for the properties of the image—its modalities, textures, and styles—in an attempt to figure out what it affects and how it works. When working with affect, it is both possible and necessary to commute between different perspectives—from modes of affective address to considerations of aesthetics and acts of contextualization. It is both possible and necessary to oscillate between optic and haptic modes of seeing—the first involving distance and the latter drawing the viewer too close to see properly. In the course of analysis, one needs to hold the image close and remain open to its force, yet one also needs to push it further away to sense (and make sense of) its other properties. As the methodological frameworks and modes of looking shift, the image moves with them, as do the interpretations made. Considerations of the image's texture, its feel, or the resonances that it evokes by no means foreclose considerations of technological affordances, contexts of production and distribution, generic conventions, or representational histories. Rather, these all feed into each another as particular materializations through which images gain weight and power (to move people through and with resonance). This is a discomforting commute, indeed—movement between different forms and positions of analysis, between proximity and distance, resonances with the image and the flows of one's own processes of interpretation and writing.

Another way to approach the question is through Barthes's reflections on reading and criticism. For Barthes (2007, 40), reading involves desire toward the work: "to read is to desire the work, to want to be the work, to refuse to echo the work using any discourse other than that of the work." Reading is an intimate relationship in which the reader attaches herself to the text and surrenders to its rhythms and styles. In the context of pornography—a framework that Barthes probably would have refused to consider as an example—this kind of "reading" involves desire for carnal resonance and openness to being moved and aroused. Writing in the mode of affectation and sticking close to the resonating object mean description as well as writing that itself borders on the pornographic. I was once asked if it upsets me that people may be sexually aroused when reading my essays on porn. My response was negative—no, this would not bother me too much—even if I was surprised that this might be the case (for surely those reading with the intent of arousal can find more gratifying texts to interface with). Thinking more closely about it made me less surprised, for writing on pornography and, in most cases, not being able to illustrate the text with any kinds of images (as these are often considered too explicit and possibly offensive), one is ultimately left with the option of description (which is already an interpretation). When something cannot be shown but can only be described, it gains affective stickiness and intensity and becomes if not exactly a kind of a forbidden fruit then at least a potentially titillating object. In this sense, writing on porn with any sense of closeness or describing images in detail is, to a degree, also an act of writing pornography.

I also gave some thought to the matter when negotiating illustrations for this book. I wanted to include illustrations to render my examples more understandable and to provide readers with the possibility of comparing my interpretations with their own (even if monotone images on a printed page are admittedly a far cry from the colorful multimedial Web interfaces studied). I also wanted to circumvent the trajectory of desire involved in detailed writing about what cannot be shown (the forbidden and hence titillating), yet I was equally aware that much of the material I discuss is difficult to adapt as illustrations for an academic book. Visual explicitness and extremity might well work against the writing by attracting and inviting titillation, shock, and affective responses of the kind that no form of scholarly prose can imagine competing with—and many readers might choose not to engage with such a book. The outcome is something of a middle-of-the-road solution of images that illustrate the points I am trying to make yet are not explicit in their carnal details. This also means that some of the images I address at length—such as the Wife Bucket image discussed in this chapter—cannot be included in the sample of images. This, again, leads back to the question of description and titillation in academic prose. Close description retains something of the resonance of the original images, yet the transformation from the visual to the textual—distilled through scholarly cognition—is also an act of hiding and veiling that transforms its object. Rather than merely translating the visual into the textual, the researcher writes into being a different creature. For Barthes (2007, 40), the only response that a "pure reader" in love with the text could produce would be pastiche (when the reader is so embedded with the resonances of the text and desires the text so much that it becomes impossible to depart from it). In contrast, criticism involves a different desire, one felt toward one's own language. The critic is not merely in love with the text she studies but to a far greater degree attached to language and the pleasures inherent in the act of writing.

Kipnis (1999, 161) argues that porn speaks through visceral audience engagement, while Barthes was interested in how the objects of photography speak. Literary scholar Isobel Armstrong (2000, 117) argues that the body speaks through affect: "A noticing of affect is a noticing of the body which *speaks*, both confirming ownership of the body by consciousness and disowning consciousness—*my* body; *it* speaks." As I have suggested elsewhere (Paasonen 2010a), bringing these lines of thought together would make sense when investigating the "stickiness" of pornography as a resonating object of affective attachment. Considering the question further, it is nevertheless necessary to ask if such resonance involves speech at all or if the reverberations in question are in a different register. The metaphors of speech, text, and reading need to be reconsidered, as do their applicability to studies of both photography and pornography. Pornography, the object of photography, and the body do not speak—that is, they do not communicate through linguistic means—and their forms of communication are not defined by or confined to the semantic. This is also the reason why the buttocks and thighs in the Wife Bucket image addressed above are not primarily a matter of meaning.

Reading or close reading, as practiced in art studies, are rarely explicated as specific methods. In fact, they may be more an issue of craft that one learns by doing and following examples set by others.[15] Consequently, there is the risk of putting forward looking as an alternative to reading without addressing the methodological differences between the two activities (or their epistemological and ontological reverberations). In methodological terms, it is likely that reading images has often been a matter of looking and articulating one's descriptions and interpretations through text. Acknowledging the status of images as nonlinguistic entities that operate in a different register of meaning and experience than texts bound to specific structures, it is fair to say that *reading* is not the best term for investigating them, as is suggested in chapter 1. But although one may not be able to read an image, it is certainly possible to write about it. If porn tries to show how carnal sensations feel, then interpretation involves textual translation of the interactions taking place. Much is necessarily lost in acts of translation from one sensory regime and modality to another. When writing about porn, words often seem to fail to grasp what grabs: descriptions pin down scenarios and scenes while also translating them into something literal and fixed, knowable and certain.

Sensory Translations

Considering carnal resonances as speech in which objects that are not invested with linguistic skills become articulate is to a large degree an act of ventriloquism (that is, speaking on behalf of something that does not speak). Such "speech" by and large refers to one's own interpretations and sensations of the resonating object, for the one interpreting the reverbera- tions does the speaking by translating the sensory to the linguistic. The carnal resonance of porn involves the viewers' ability to recognize and expe- rience the sensations, movements, and positions depicted on the screen in their own bodies. At the same time, translations from the carnal and the tactile to the visually perceived and the linguistically articulated are never fully accomplished. There is a perpetual gap between how things look and feel and how they can be described. Porn mediates the intensity of bodily sensations and interactions. In terms of the sensory experiences of sex, this mediation is by necessity partial and lacks the tactile, gustatory, and olfactory. The warmth, smoothness, or hairiness of skin, the heat of breath and bodily cavities, the feeling of bodily weight, the stickiness and taste of sweat—and the smell of this all—are represented through visual, tex- tual, and audiovisual means. Mediation cuts down the range of the sensory (what can be mediated) and also creates a sense of distance by displaying the acts performed on the screen. Compared to the physical proximity (and possible intimacy) involved in sex, mediations thereof ultimately fall short.

Writing on pain, Elaine Scarry (1985, 5–6) identifies it as resistant to language: pain remains inaccessible for words, as do other people's experi- ences. The dilemma is familiar from other physical practices on which— as Niklas Largier (2007, 14) puts it—"*words go around.*" Largier sees bodily practices as analogous to pictures in the sense that both can "never be fully translated into words." Paraphrasing Scarry, Largier argues that both physi- cal sensations and images show "a fundamental resistance to language": "Their 'meaning' withdraws from view as soon as it is named, for the action itself does not aim at any sort of meaning, but rather at what *might* be said, yet *cannot* be said, insofar as its significance is never fulfillable in a word" (Largier 2007, 14–15, emphasis in the original). Like pain, sexual arousal and pleasure can be known only with and through the body. They do not aim at meaning for their importance lies largely outside significa- tion. A double resistance to language can be found in pornography—one springing from both the carnality of the scenarios performed and recorded and another from the general modality of photography. At the same time, language has a perpetual and highly visible presence in captions, lines, ter- minology, hyperlinks, exclamations, names, and titles. The verbal orients, supports, highlights, and frames the visual and ties it in specific interpretive frameworks (cf. Armstrong 1998, 2).

The movement and translation taking place between the performed, the mediated, and the sensed in pornography bring me back to the notion of carnal resonance. One way to put this is that as people experience and experiment with embodiment, memories, and imprints—of bodily sensations, pleasures, and their associations to people, incidents, locations, and moments—accumulate and change over time and give form to somatic archives or reservoirs. The depictions of bodies (touching, stroking, licking, sucking, grabbing, penetrating, and spanking each another), bodily liquids, body parts, facial expressions, sighs, and grunts that are conveyed in porn may find resonance with these archives as reverberations experienced in the body. This is particularly the case with sensations, textures, and motions that have been previously experienced. Watching pornography, I can relate to variations of fondling, licking, and penetration with little difficulty despite the obvious differences between the acts performed on the screen to those that I may have engaged in. Movement (of bodies) and taste and feel (of mouths, fingers, genitalia, skin, body hair, saliva, and semen) are easy enough to sense (and not merely to make sense of) for people who have experienced them, yet these somatic traces are never identical to those witnessed in pornography.

Somatic archives are about affection in the sense discussed by Henri Bergson (2007, 60), for whom affection is "that part or aspect of the inside of our body which we mix with the image of external bodies." In other words, sensation and perception are closely tied together, and they involve movement between and within bodies (mine and those on the screen). The body is shaped by historically layered skills, experiences, and sensations that bring forth particular ways of relating to other bodies and reverberating with them (also Kyrölä 2010, 193). Kozel (2007, 26) discusses this as resonance that is based on our assembly of senses and varied experiences and that allows for empathy with mediated (or fictional) experiences and acts. The notion of somatic archives also comes close to that of kinesthetic empathy—that is, feeling sensations in one's body that are similar to those watched on the screen or in front of oneself. In kinesthetic empathy, the sight of other people moving calls forth responses in one's own body (Laukkanen 2010, 131). To a degree, such empathy is central to the "body genres" discussed by Williams and Dyer that aim to move the viewers' bodies. This motion is largely precognitive, based on the capacities and affordances of the body, for the "roiling mass of nerve volleys prepare the body for action in such a way that intentions or decisions are made before the conscious self is even aware of them" (Thrift 2008, 7). As I see it, this is not a modality of identification with characters or narrative but one of corporeal, fleshy relationality and resonance.

In porn, the stickiness, heat, smell, and touch that are integral to physical acts become mediated through visual and auditory means as movement, rhythm, and sound. This mediation creates a degree of "hygienic" distance while the other senses linger on as synesthetic traces and echoes. Massumi (2002, 35) sees affect as synesthetic and "implying the participation of the senses in each other," for "the measure of a living thing's potential interactions is its ability to transform the effects of one sensory model into those of another." Vision is never "purely vision" but embedded in a multimodal nexus together with hearing, touch, and proprioception (Massumi 2002, 145–146; also Sobchack 2004, 67–68). The synesthetic intensities of porn are not separate from other modes of cognition. These intensities, however, are markedly pronounced and pivotal to how pornography works on, in, and through bodies (both the bodies mediated on the screen and the bodies encountering them). The synesthetic lies at the core of the pornographic as "synesthesia proper to vision" that touches "as only the eyes can touch" (Massumi 2002, 158).

In the case of unfamiliar acts or body parts, looking at porn concerns a more fantastic level of imagining how things might feel. Such imagining is based on previous experiences of feeling, touching, and sensing other bodies, textures, tastes, and movements that provide visual-tactile feedback (Massumi 2002, 158). Yet this is not only a question of recognizing things through or in terms of the familiar since the body constantly learns and becomes surprised as its sensations, palates, tastes, and somatic archives alter. As Nigel Thrift (2008, 2) puts it, "the human sensorium is constantly being re-invented as the body continually adds parts in to itself: therefore how and what is experienced as experience is itself variable." Experiences of watching porn shape and influence one's contingent somatic reservoirs (as resonance, titillation, dislike, curiosity, or exercises of imagination), while these archives in return orient ways of looking at and sensing pornography.

The notion of somatic archives may also help explain moments where the resonance between porn and its viewer disturbs or halts interest and potential arousal. Consider, for example, the act of deep-throat sex. Famously introduced to a mass audience in Gerard Damiano's 1972 film *Deep Throat* through Linda Lovelace's skill set, deepthroating has since become something of a staple feature in pornography (in its amateur, gonzo, reality, and glossier variations). Thumbnail galleries are rife with images of female performers getting their "slutty throat fucked," "throat fucked hard," or "throat jammed" (to use some examples from Porn.com blowjob video gallery). As a spectacular variation of fellatio, deep-throat sex has broadened into variations of throat, face, and skull fucking in which the female partner takes up a more passive role (as a "fuckee" rather than the "sucker"). Because deepthroating requires suppressing the gag reflex, which is not easy to achieve, deep-throat imageries often involve gagging (as a penis is pushed down the throat), as in the examples "blond gag girls love to gag on a dick," "Latina stunner loves to be gag fucked," or "gorgeous coed gets moist when she gags" (a search for the term *gag* on Porn.com produces some 800 hits).

Gagging during fellatio is commonplace—a sensation not necessarily pleasurable for the person performing it that, in porn, points to extremity and "going all the way." Gagging resonates with my somatic archives as something of a stated fact. This happens, it causes varying degrees of discomfort, and it distracts from the matters at hand. From the perspective of the gagger, it is an issue of disturbance rather than titillation. When adding a further layer of asphyxiation—for example, by holding the woman's nose while she is performing deep-throat fellatio or grabbing her by the throat, as happens in oral sex videos—my discomfort as viewer grows through my ability to relate to sensations of suffocation, the excessive proximity of another body (inside and next to oneself), body heat, saliva, and the lack of air. The case would be different if I was into erotic asphyxia, and my inability to enjoy such scenarios does not imply that other people would not be able to do so. My point is that somatic archives facilitate particular resonances with pornographic imageries and their carnal acts. These resonances can give rise to discomfort, sexual titillation and arousal, anger, disgust, disappointment, and many things in between. This could, following Sobchack, be called carnal identification in the sense that somatic archives enable me to imagine how the acts could feel. Attachment to acts and scenes is nevertheless of the fleeting kind, moving as they do between detachment and resonance: carnal proximities of this kind remain contingent.

In porn, a great deal is lost in the translation between how things feel, how they look, and how they are being depicted. Not only are acts staged and performed for optimal visual access (at the expense of positions possibly producing more stimulation and less physical strain), but a whole range of sensory stimuli escapes mediation. Given the centrality of touch and skin contact in sex, such untranslatability is not a small issue. Carnal resonance is a means of overcoming some of this gap by evoking fleshy memories and emphatic sensations in the viewer that can please, displease, or do both at the same time. Affect is visceral, multisensory, and untranslatable. The modality of pornography—visceral in its own right—involves attempts at intersensory translation that aim to move and touch those engaging with it. It is not about depictions of affect finding their expression on and in bodies on the screen inasmuch as it is about carnal address overriding the dictates of narrative, grabbing the viewers, and disturbing their sense of mastery.

6   Absolutely Disgusting: Shock Sites, Extremity, and the Forbidden Fruit

As discussed above at some length, the mass market for pornography has been fragmented as the Internet has facilitated an unprecedented spread and diversification of available content. In addition to the radical expansion of online amateur porn, this has meant the increased visibility of so-called extreme imageries and acts. Bukkake (ejaculation by several men onto one person's face), ATM, DV/DA, coprophilia (play with feces), or coproflagy (eating feces)—all porn niches previously displayed mainly on specialist fetish sites—have grown more recognizable and available.[1] As the palette of online pornography widens toward new niche markets, the mainstream is constantly divided into new subcategories. and the overall visibility of fetishes and extremities increases in the process (Patterson 2004, 106–107; Bridges 2010, 37). Lauren Langman (2004) identifies extreme subgenres as aggressively sexist "grotesque degradation" and as emblematic of a crisis of masculinity in late capitalism (also Maddison 2009). For him, the genre "provides fantasy realms of hypermasculinity in which women are not simply objects of male lust, but are systematically degraded in retaliation for their assertiveness"; hence, this is a symbolic backlash of a kind (Langman 2004, 202). In a Freudian framework, desire and degradation go hand in hand, and "bad sex"—that is, sex of the forbidden, dirty, and nasty sort—is good (Kalha 2007a, 90–91). Seen from this perspective, extreme depictions translate as the lowering and pollution of the object of desire in acts that are "dirty, obscene, degrading, ugly, or bestial" (Kalha 2007a, 110) and hence good porn.

Consider, for example, the promises of "Nasty Girls Getting Down and Dirty!!," "Sick & degenerate hardcore!," and "Amazing, bizarre, nasty XXX!!!" in a spam email advertisement for Spunk Farm, an animal porn site. The lexicon of the "nasty," "dirty," "sick," and "degenerate" frames the site as "amazing," "bizarre," and attractive in its extremity and associates the acts visually depicted in the ad with degeneration, sickness, and plain nastiness. This chain of association works to frame the site advertised as an extreme and taboo-defying case of sexual performance. The coarticulation of image and text guarantees that the things depicted visually are also echoed and amplified through textual means, creating a sense of hyperbolic nastiness. The ad for Farm Girls (apparently run by the same company) deploys similarly hyperbolic rhetoric:

Forbidden XXX hardcore

Banned in over 51 states.

You've never seen *anything* like it!

Nasty, desperate country girls who will do anything for cock. The bigger the better! NOTHING is too TABOO for these young sluts.

THE MOST SHOCKING & UNBELIEVABLE SEX ACTS.

The female performers become identified with taboo desires and acts with no holds barred. This realm of unbridled "animal passions" is juxtaposed with notions (both promises and threats) of censorship, illegality, and banning. These become guarantees of the transgressive, shocking, and unbelievable nature of the acts featured, while also marking them as forbidden fruits of a kind. The nastiness and dirtiness advertized culminates in close-up photos of female faces engaging in sex with animals. Here the "nasty girls," more than the animals, become figures for the taboo.[2] As Jack Sargeant (2006) points out, the figure of the nasty girl is central to contemporary hardcore that aims to constantly push the boundaries of what can be acted out and shown on the screen: nasty girls act out nasty things (from ATM to cumswapping and beyond). In her discussion of TV docuporn, Karen Boyle (2008, 45) argues that extreme acts are constructed as the excesses of female sexuality "not for the purposes of arousal but of disgust as women are reduced to lengthy checklists of increasingly extreme acts that they will or will not do or have done to them." Once the female performers become the locus of the disgusting, the nasty, and the excessive, it may become easier to ask "How can they do that?" rather than to inquire after the conditions of labor and production that have led to the acts being performed and recorded in the first place. As a pornographic figure, the nasty girl is a source of disgust, titillation, and desire. Lauren Berlant (2006, 21) points out that investments in objects or scenes of desire "and projections onto them are less about them than about a cluster of desires and affects we manage to keep magnetized to them." So when "we talk about an object of desire, we are really talking about a cluster of promises we want someone or something to make to us and make possible for us" (Berlant 2006, 20). What are, then, the nasty girls of porn performing as objects of desire? And what kinds of desires and affects are magnetized to all this nastiness?

The dynamics of disgust give rise to relations between the performers, the viewers, and the pornographic object that is pulled closer and pushed away—that is kept at a distance and yet stubbornly comes close and gets under one's skin. If the nasty and the filthy are used in porn as positive denominators and "any kind of dirty thing your sick brain can imagine" (XTRM Liveshows) is an invitation to enjoy hardcore, then the case is not one of distance as turning away but more one of shared sickness and dirtiness. It seems that porn requires and thrives on articulations of disgust and that such articulations are knowingly sought out, evoked, provoked, and formulated by both the producers and consumers of porn (cf. Tyler 2010). As long as its imageries have the potential to upset at least someone, porn can conserve some of its transgressive and forbidden aura. Without potential disgust and vexation, this aura would be considerably less impressive and effective. I suggest that nasty girls and extreme and bizarre pornography make explicit the dynamics of interest and disgust that are central to the genre.

This chapter addresses the interconnections of interest, disgust, and shame through a discussion of viral videos and shock porn sites that are representative of the markedly "nasty." Although these examples are less mainstream than some of the examples discussed above, they do have considerable cultural visibility and force in galvanizing and sticking affect to online porn in general. Viral videos—like Internet memes more generally—gain broad attention and occasionally also long-term fame as users share video links with each other, invite new people to watch and react to them, record their own reactions, circulate both the reaction videos and the original video link further, and comment on and discuss the videos in online forums and also in TV, radio, newspaper, and magazine articles. Shot in Brazil and featuring two women, a cup, and one minute of coprophilic play, "2 Girls 1 Cup" became famous in 2007 (figure 6.1). Accompanied by Hervé Roy's romantic "Lover's Theme," (Roy is remembered from the theme song for the softcore film *Emmanuelle* from 1974) the two women

Figure 6.1
The seemingly innocent beginning of "2 Girls 1 Cup" (http://www.2girls1cup.com)

first kiss. Next, one of them defecates in a cup, and the other eats feces and then vomits into the first woman's mouth. In "Japanese Eel Soup," which became famous in 2004, a woman inserts small eels into another's anus and, as they are pushed out, catches and eats them. Such videos—like "2 Guys 1 Horse" (2005), a thirty-second video showing anal penetration by a stallion, which led to the death of Mr. Hands, the human performer in question—are extreme and definitely grab users by the eyeballs.[3]

Dwelling in Disgust

Although people are generally reluctant to disclose their uses of and preferences for pornography in casual everyday exchanges and face-to-face encounters (anonymous online forums being a notable exception in the detailed descriptions of preferences and arousals that discussants indulge in), viral videos are very much about social circulation. The videos that are discussed and circulated in public represent the extreme and the bizarre, and sexual arousal generally plays a minor role in the titillations they evoke or at least in the reactions that people openly share with others. Like masturbation, the sexual pleasures derived from porn are often associated with shame. All in all, shame plays a central role in the affective dynamics of porn, which include sexual arousal, embarrassment, disgust, laughter, interest, and many things beyond. Shame, like disgust, both links and gives shape to hierarchies of taste and norms of acceptability.

Affect theorists Silvan Tomkins (1995b, 54) argues that "There is literally no kind of object which has not historically been linked to one or another of the affects." In other words, the objects in his affect system are "free" in that any object can be attached to any affect and vice versa: "The object may evoke the affect, or the affect find the object" (Tomkins 1995b, 55). Writing centuries earlier, Baruch Spinoza (1992, 133) articulated a similar idea by stating that "what one man loves, another hates, what one man fears, another does not"; that "one and the same man may now love what he previously hated and may now dare what he previously feared"; and that "one and the same thing can at the same time be good and bad, and also indifferent" (Spinoza 1992, 153). Tomkins nevertheless argues that a child learns disgust as a primary negative affect through feces, from which parents tend to recoil. Hence, feces stand for what is, on a fundamental level, disgusting rather than volatile in terms of affect (Hemmings 2005, 560). In their investigations of disgust, both social historian William Ian Miller and phenomenologist Aurel Kolnai identify tight connections between disgust and the embodied, biological, sexual, and material and associate the affect of disgust with particular material properties and textures. Both see disgust as primarily oriented toward embodiment and especially the excessively carnal—whether rotting flesh, sexual abundance, or "crawling, pullulating maggots" (Kolnai 2004, 2). For Kolnai (2004, 39), disgust involves an undesired proximity that necessitates turning away from and distancing from the object of disgust—a gut reaction that is similar to vomiting, through which the offending object is forcefully vacated. Disgust is immediate and sensory: it is experienced by smelling, touching, or seeing its cause in the rancid, filthy, sticky, excessively soft, or oozing object (Kolnai 2004, 31–32, 48; Miller 1997, 19). Various objects of disgust concern the sheer surfeit, the "indecent surplus of life" (Kolnai 2004, 55). They are excessively organic and fleshy, tactile and sticky, and involve the gustatory system, sexuality, reproduction, and defecation. Both Kolnai and Miller place the sheer surfeit of life, procreation, and mortality squarely at the heart of the disgusting as bodies are entered, exited, and consumed. Sticky, stanching, liquid, and oozing objects represent both mortality (the organic and biological) and vulnerability (of bodies and their boundaries) (cf. Nussbaum 2001, 347). These definitions come close to Julia Kristeva's (1982, 4) discussion of abject as something that signifies the border of existence (feces, corpses) and "disturbs identity, system, order. What does not respect borders, positions, rules. The in-between, the ambiguous, the composite." Abject is what encroaches the boundaries of the self.

According to Bataille, dead bodies, excrement, and sexual acts deemed obscene are all experienced as disgusting. The dead body represents nothingness and decay, similar to excrement in its surfeit and residual character: "The sexual channels are also the body's sewers; we think of them as shameful and connect the anal orifice with them. St. Augustine was at pains to insist on the obscenity of the organs and function of reproduction. 'Inner faeces et urinam nascimur,' he said—'we are born between faeces and urine'" (Bataille 1986, 57–58). The viral videos make particularly evident the dynamics between food, excrement, and sexuality; the sexual and alimentary channels; and the body's sewers. "2 Girls 1 Cup" displays an elaborate play with feces eaten, vomited, and rubbed onto bodies; "Eel Soup" zooms in on squirming eels that are inserted into and then exit a woman's anus; while "2 Guys 1 Horse" is all about the excessive size of horse genitalia compared to the dimensions of the human anus. The feces, eels, and anal insertions and excretions displayed in these viral videos summarize Kolnai's thoughts on the swarming, slimy, oozy, flabby, and dirty excess of life and Miller's discussion on the "soup of life"—the stinking, viscous, oozing, festering, scabby, disgusting, and murky cesspool of eating, defecating, mating, reproducing, death, rot, and rebirth (Miller 1997, 18). Following Miller (1997, 80, 85, 96), the videos display things that disgust through sight, smell, or touch. At the same time, keeping in mind both Tomkins's separation of affect and object (that is, any affect can be attached to any object and vice versa) and the fact that the videos have been produced as pornography (with the intention to arouse), their visual landscape is open to a range of affective dynamics beyond disgust. The videos bring the excessively carnal and visceral up close through sight and sound that may, through synesthetic resonance, bring forth something of the olfactory and the haptic.

Sight and sound are the senses that involve most distance between the subject and the object or phenomenon perceived. They have also tended to stand at the top of value hierarchies concerning the five senses. Since antiquity, vision has dominated the sensory hierarchy, followed by hearing, while below them follow the "grosser" senses of smell, taste, and touch (Connor 2006, 12; Serres 2008). The lower that one goes in the sensory hierarchy, the closer the object perceived comes to one's body (skin but also bodily orifices). For Immanuel Kant, the "near senses" were suspicious because they were capable of serving merely "lower sensual pleasures," whereas the more distanced senses (sight and hearing) were "capable of mediating pure, and therefore more noble, aesthetic pleasures" (Gronow 1997, ix, 132). Vision, the "highest" of the senses, is certainly central to pornography, yet the genre is very much concerned with mediating the more "base" senses of touch, smell, and, to a smaller degree, taste (the senses serving "lower sensual pleasures"). In audiovisual pornography, the senses involving closer proximity to the sensed object (whether a human body, an object, or something else) are depicted and mediated through vision and hearing. "The higher senses" are rendered subservient to the "lower" ones and to the carnal intensities of porn.

Although Miller associates disgust with some tactile and olfactory qualities, he differs from Kolnai in not defining disgust as something innate to its objects (even if he does associate disgust with certain tactile and olfactory properties). Rather, disgust results from a more complex nexus of social norms, hierarchies, intimacies, and desires that it also maintains and constructs. Since disgust sticks to what is seen as morally objectionable, it is linked to filth both figurative and material—not only to feces, bodily emissions, and rotting corpses but also to what is seen as morally objectionable and hence disgusting and shameful (Cohen 2005, viii, xi). Viral videos seem to bring these two registers of disgust together by depicting acts deemed perverse as sexual paraphilias (coprophilia, bestiality) and hence figuratively filthy, by reveling in objects deemed materially filthy (feces, anuses), and by displaying all this in the framework of pornography, a genre regularly identified as morally vile.

Eating and defecating are both connected to the cycle of life and the sense of mortality. As the two ends of the alimentary system, the mouth and the anus are literally connected to one another (Miller 1997, 96). However, since the anus is, according to Miller, "the essence of lowness, of untouchability," neither the anus nor feces can be licked or otherwise touched with the mouth, unless the person in question delights "truly in turning himself and the world upside down, taking his pleasure from total indulgence in self-defilement" (Miller 1997, 99–100). Even a brief glance at contemporary online porn produces too many counterexamples to be listed here: rimming ("eating ass") is a standard video and image category in both straight and gay porn, "water sports" are commonly featured in all kinds of videos, and ATM is a recurring practice. In viral videos such as "Eel Soup" or "2 Girls 1 Cup," the performers literally wallow in feces, secretions, and—in Miller's view—self-defilement. Eating feces, in particular, presents Miller with an extreme form of the disgusting, an act so extreme and vile that it is hardly imaginable: "People do not eat feces as a joke, even as a sick joke; what they do is talk about eating it or ridicule people who do eat it" (Miller 1997, 118). In this perspective, eating feces—and, in all likelihood, the anal eel activities featured in "Eel Soup"—stand for the uttermost point of disgust where the self and the world are turned upside down and inside out. Sargeant (2006) similarly points out that sexual coprophilia is a rare preference practiced in private and mainly in secrecy: "Even the few that confess enjoying 'brown showers' do not admit to eating raw shit, either their own or that of somebody else. The practice is considered to be too dangerous, too unhealthy, and too disgusting. Even amongst the radical sexual communities many find that it stinks of excess, as if desires and fantasies had limits." Viral videos owe their appeal exactly to such limits and hyperbolic acts of transgressing them. In viral videos, people have anal sex with stallions and eat live eels popping straight from another person's anus. People do not merely eat shit but enjoy eating brown showers of vomited shit. The abject is not merely displayed but rendered as a spectacular display.

Shame and Filth

Just as food turned bad is spit or vomited out, people tend to move away from a body or mass that is experienced as disgusting. Disgust involves distancing oneself from the object or removing it altogether. In contrast, shame, another one of Tomkins's basic affects, has to do with hindered desire, interest, or excitement. Shame is about desire for proximity and its deferral rather than a desire for distance (also Probyn 2005). According to Tomkins, shame results from interest being deferred or blocked—for example, from being rejected, mocked, or disapproved of by someone we wish to be recognized and approved by. People in shame feel inferior and experience failure both in their own eyes and in the eyes of others (Tom-kins 1995a, 399–400; also Ahmed 2004, 103–105). Although shame and disgust differ from each other both as physiological reactions and affective dynamics, they both assume the activation of interest or pleasure, which they then disable (Tomkins 1995a, 84). Shame and disgust also link to and reinforce one another and structure different relations between peo-ple, objects, and values. Sally Munt (2007, 2–3) defines *shame* as a conta-gious and particularly sticky emotion to which other sensations such as envy, hate, contempt, humiliation, and disgust are easily attached. Sara Ahmed has explored the ways in which disgust and other affective invest-ments bind together and pull apart bodies, properties, and objects. Disgust involves the separation of the lower and the higher, the self and the other, the marking of both the boundaries of culture and those of the self (also Miller 1997, 50):

It is not that what is low is necessarily disgusting, nor is sexuality necessarily dis-gusting. Lowness becomes associated with lower regions of the body as it becomes associated with other bodies and other spaces. The spatial distinction of "above" from "below" functions metaphorically to separate one body from another, as well as to differentiate between higher and lower bodies. . . . As a result, disgust at "that which is below" functions to maintain the power relations between above and be-low, *through which "aboveness" and "belowness" become properties of particular bodies, objects and spaces.* (Ahmed 2004, 89, emphasis in the original; also Tyler 2006)

With pornography, articulations of distaste, disgust, and disapproval are attached to the acts shown, to the people acting them out, to the people producing and consuming porn, as well as to porn as a genre with low cultural status. Writing on the French context, Carolyn J. Dean (2000, 43) remarks how commentators on pornography have, since the early twenti-eth century, used the affective register of "suffocation, disgust, and nausea" when describing its effects. However, nausea has "gradually became less a description of pornography's effects than a metaphor for its vertiginous circularity" (Dean 2000, 46)—that is, for its bodily movements and its ways of affecting its viewers. The coarticulation of pornography together with disgust and filth has been efficient in marking out the cultural role and position of pornography, as well as associating it—and its performers, acts, and consumers alike—with shame (Warner 2000, 181; Stein 2006).

The shame and disgust that are associated with porn are inseparable from the bodies, sexual acts, and bodily fluids that it depicts in vivid detail.

Andrea Dworkin argues that notions of obscenity basically draw on a (mis) understanding of bodies—and female bodies, in particular—as filthy. Filth, again, is excrement "from down there" (Dworkin 2000b, 24). Martha Nussbaum (2001, 348) similarly notes how "disgust properties are traditionally associated with women, as receivers of semen and as closely linked, through birth, with the mortality of the body." Women stand for the excessively physical and immanent. And because "'she is what she eats' (whether in the sense of oral or vaginal incorporation), she becomes the sticky mortal part of him from which he needs to distance himself" (Nussbaum 2001, 349). Nussbaum explains homophobia through such associations of ooziness, stickiness, and penetrability that help to mark homosexual men as objects of straight male disgust.[4] Miller makes a similar argument by stating that "semen has the extraordinary power conferred on it by patriarchy to feminize whatever it comes into contact with. In a sense, semen is more feminizing than the vagina itself. Whatever receives it is made woman" (Miller 1997, 103). This is certainly a strong statement.[5] Dworkin, Nussbaum, and Miller all address the symbolic filthiness of women in the framework of patriarchy—a concept that is easy to conceive of as a monolithic (even if historical and hence contingent) system of values, ideas, and practices. Although Dworkin sees women's bodies marked as filthy by default, both Nussbaum and Miller associate this filthiness with penetrability and the reception of male semen. The female body becomes a distorted mirror onto which male vulnerability and mortality can be projected. This happens not only through sex—attractive in its "dirty, bestial, smelly, messy, sticky, slimy, oozy" nature (Miller 1997, 127)—but through penises and semen that are seen as equally sticky, slimy, and oozy.

This seems almost too neat a framework for considering the fervor with which bodies—particularly female bodies—are lowered and rendered filthy in pornography, whether through coprophilic play, verbal denominators such as "filthy cocksucker," or visual motives like messy cumshots and bukkake galleries. It is evident that the generic conventions of heteroporn have been shaped largely by particular kinds of male desires revolving around female bodies as desirable yet somehow disturbing, disgusting, or even abject. At the same time, I am not suggesting that the affective dynamics of shame, disgust, and desire related to porn and its appeal are reducible to ideological systems such as patriarchy. They leak beyond the neat boundaries of categorical explanations, leaving their residual marks. To work through this residue, an even closer look at these affective registers is needed.

Lowly Solitary Desires

In a 1977 study on gender and sexual arousal, Donald L. Mosher and Paul R. Abramson showed undergraduate students two German films featuring masturbation, one with a male and another with a female performer. After seeing the films, the students were asked to evaluate their affective reactions and degrees of arousal. The results of the study are interesting (for example, the female respondents were as aroused as the males were by the films), but the researchers' affect adjectives are particularly noteworthy:

The seven affect categories, in addition to affective sexual arousal, were affective guilt, shame, disgust, depression, anger, anxiety, and calm. The adjectives for affective guilt were *guilty, sinful, blameworthy, conscience-stricken, repentant,* and *remorseful.* The adjectives for affective shame were *disgraced, degraded, humiliated, mortified, ashamed,* and *embarrassed.* The adjectives for affective disgust were *disgusted, nauseated, revolted, repelled, repulsed,* and *sickened.* The adjectives for affective depression were *depressed, melancholy, worthless, unhappy, sad,* and *hopeless.* The adjectives for affective anger were *grouchy, annoyed, resentful, angry, bad-tempered,* and *furious.* The adjectives for affective anxiety were *anxious, jittery, nervous, fearful, tense,* and *worried.* The adjectives for affective calmness were *calm, at ease, serene, relaxed, relieved,* and *composed.* (Mosher and Abramson 1977, 798; italics mine)

Other than the adjectives for affective sexual arousal (*passionate, sensuous, excited, lustful, aroused,* and *hot*) and for affective calm, the range of affects provided for students to choose from were in the negative register of guilt, shame, disgust, depression, anger, and anxiety. This register was almost synonymous with the negative affects in Tomkins's affect theory— anger/rage, disgust, dissmell (reaction to a bad smell), distress/anguish, fear/terror, shame/humiliation. The experiment did not offer any of the positive and neutral affects identified by Tomkins (enjoyment/joy, interest/excitement, or surprise/startle). I suggest that the centrality of negative affects in this 1977 study and its premises indicate not only the emphases (or biases) of this individual piece of research and the Puritan tendencies of North American culture but research assumptions that pornography is harmful and that its negative effects should be mapped (Bridges 2010, 35). Moreover, I see this study as emblematic of the affective dynamics, anxieties, and values attached to porn, masturbation, and solitary sexual arousal that have framed their objects in particular ways (for the actual topic of research was mediated images of solitary sex).

Although porn is also watched socially (in clubs, cinemas, and homosocial parties and together with partners), porn consumption is primarily a solitary activity aiming at sexual arousal that involves masturbation. According to Thomas Laqueur (2003), cultural taboos against "the sin of onanism" derive from a Judeo-Christian tradition that sees spilling one's seed as a crime analogous to bestiality or homosexuality. In all these cases, the sexual act is detached from procreation within the acceptable frame of heterosexual matrimony. In the eighteenth century, masturbation came to be seen not only as a morally dubious activity but also as hazardous to one's health. Leaflets and books addressed onanism, aiming to titillate their readers with depictions of excessive solitary sex and to market ointments for overcoming its curses. The literature that ensued defined masturbation as a morally deplorable and symbolically stigmatizing form of self-defilement that was seen to cause physical ills such as hairy palms, atrophic spine, bad posture, yellow and shallow skin, mental dullness, and poor eyesight.

According to Laqueur (2003, 64), masturbation came to be seen as a problem and a shameful secret since it conflicts with the ideals of the modern subject. Whereas the rational modern subject is in control of himself and his emotions, the masturbator turns inward and dwells in sexual arousal and pleasure, knowing no restraint or moderation. The masturbator requires no partner since his own imagination suffices to coin forever new figures of fantasy. These are practices with no "redeeming" social function (Laqueur 2003, 210–220, 232–233).[6] Masturbation has been disapproved of as a useless and immoderate form of sexuality, and pornography has fueled this excessiveness. The masturbator and the reader have been equated as figures who are prone to immersion in private fantasy worlds. Dwelling in the pleasures of sensuous reading, readers in the eighteenth and nineteenth centuries were seen as lost to the world as they turned inward toward their private desires and imagination (Schindler 1996). As Laqueur (2003, 308–309) notes, the female reader who was aroused by romantic fiction was established as a recurring visual and pornographic motif. These kinds of imageries point to both the literary content of the novels involved and also the ways in which the intimate act of reading was seen as a potential social peril (Laqueur 2003, 21). Caught in the fervor of "reading mania," women and girls—much like the lamented Internet porn addicts of today—were seen as seduced by novels, incapable of telling fiction apart from reality, and therefore impressed by the novels' "untruthful, exaggerated, or bizarre depictions" of love and romance (Schindler 1996, 67). The world of fiction was thought to affect readers in profound ways, corrupting their imagination and driving them to imitate the "dreams and passions of others" (Schindler 1996, 68). The figure of a masturbating porn consumer is intimately tied to this cultural imagery of self-indulgent sexuality, although the porn consumer tends to be gendered male (keeping in mind the "raincoated tossers, hairy-palmed no-mates" addressed in chapter 2).

The uses of pornography have been little studied outside of broad surveys. In addition to individual articles, notable exceptions include the Pornography in Australia research project, an overview of which is published as *The Porn Report* (McKee et al. 2008), and David Loftus's (2002) journalistic *Watching Sex: How Men Really Respond to Pornography*. The North American men that Loftus interviewed struggled constantly with shame to the degree that he sees shame as structuring the dynamics of porn consumption: "the only language we were given to describe our experience of porn was denial or confession: We hid or expressed shame" (Loftus 2002, 304). Although Loftus's informants were less dramatic in their statements, some of them did address sensations of shame and discomfort that followed from watching porn and masturbating to it. After ejaculation, the images ceased to be of interest, seemed ridiculous or even disgusting, and were hidden from view (Loftus 2002, 82–84). Tomkins (1995a, 401–402) notes how desire is oriented toward what is considered disgusting and shameful. Intense shame may well reinforce sexual desire or play a central role in evoking it. The lack of shame lessens excitement, interest, and the overall intensity of experience. In the examples provided by Loftus, the object of desire, its fascination, and the enjoyments derived from it were experienced as simultaneously disgusting, shameful, arousing, and titillating. In the affective dynamic of shame and disgust, the object of desire was both pulled closer to oneself and pushed further away again. This movement involving contingent and uneasy proximity gave rise to particular affective intensity and oriented the flow of desire.

Following Miller (1997, 112–113), sensations and articulations of disgust related to porn can be seen as functioning in two mutually supporting ways. First, disgust based on restriction and prohibition aims to ban access to objects deemed soiled, wrong, or dangerous. This is the case with moral, aesthetic, and political judgments of pornography as objectionable, filthy, and disgusting. Second, disgust may result from excess and saturation—for example, from masturbating and climaxing to pornography. After orgasm, the object may disgust rather than gratify, and one's own behavior may evoke a sense of shame. Miller (1997, 127) generalizes this reaction as reflecting the degree to which sexuality is marked by shame. The excess and surfeit of orgasm is followed by confusion, and one is left "empty, disgusted with one's own having desired." Although I doubt this to be the case with sexuality across cultures, it resonates with some of the Freudian undertones of heteroporn. Disgust and shame build a boundary between oneself and the object of disgust/desire, and this barrier then functions to intensify desire felt toward the object and its overall titillation. In a framework suggested by both Freud and Bataille, desire assumes that prohibitions and obstacles stand in its way, and acts of transgressing these prohibitions and obstacles become arousing in themselves: "It is always a temptation to knock down a barrier; the forbidden action takes on a significance it lacks before fear widens the gap between us and it and invests it with an aura of excitement" (Bataille 1986, 48). Unavoidably, the thing that disgusts and evokes shame also arouses, excites, and fascinates. The movement between disgust, desire, and shame feeds into the attraction of pornography as a forbidden fruit. If pornography and its users were freed or delivered from shame, as Loftus suggests should be done, the cultural position and the affective dynamic of the genre would be drawn in different ways. It could even be asked if anything would remain of pornography's titillation and attraction.

Social hierarchies and dynamics of desire articulated through disgust, shame, and degradation are central to the dynamics of porn as a popular genre (and to some its subgenres more than others). These affective dynamics tie into notions of transgression. Writing on taboo and sexuality, Bataille (1986, 256) argues that "desire in eroticism is that of transgression of the taboos. Desire in eroticism is the desire that triumphs over the taboo. It presupposes man in conflict with himself." Acts that transgress taboos give rise to inner conflicts that produce desire and pleasure that are impossible to grasp in the realm of language (Bataille 1986, 63–64, 107). Rather than losing their power or becoming undone in the acts of breaching, taboos become both stronger and redrawn, since transgression "suspends a taboo without suppressing it" (Bataille 1986, 36). The same argument could be made via Emile Durkheim, who argued that norms themselves give rise to deviance—that "policed boundaries of acceptability" come to face "contestation, resistance, and transgression" (Langman 2004, 193; also Jenks 2003, 16–32). Transgression refers to acts that both exceed and support the boundaries in question, for every "rule, limit, boundary or edge carries with it its own fracture, penetration or impulse to disobey. The transgression is a component of the rule" (Jenks 2003, 7). In porn, sexual taboos and the boundaries regulating decency and indecency exist in order to be transgressed: "transgressing the barrier itself produces the sense of excessiveness that provides pleasure as well as shame and disgust for it, all felt in some strange simultaneity, pleasure and aversion augmenting each other in a kind of ecstasy" (Miller 1997, 120). Addressing the role played by shame and disgust in the context of sexual taboos and transgressions helps to see how these rely on and support one another. They also play into the social status of pornography (as a genre synonymous with lowness), discussions concerning it, as well as the acts performed in it.

Sensations and articulations of disgust do not merely play into moral judgments over pornography as trash, filth, obscene, and hence something best hidden away or banned. They lay at the heart of pornography's imageries and their appeal. Investigating the complexities of shame and disgust is one means of breaking away from binary discussions of pornography (as either disgusting or pleasurable, bad or good) and of accounting for both the inner diversity of the genre and the affective dynamics that cut through it—the ways in which bad is good, filth is a marker of value, dirty sluts are more desirable than chaste maidens (although these do admittedly remain a popular porn trope in their own right), and nasty filth is highly titillating.[7] Nasty girls are the ones who transgress the boundaries of sexual norms, taboos, and even the boundaries of disgust. The desires that are magnetized to them revolve around the boundaries of the sexual and the embodied and the constant acts of transgressing and redrawing them.

At the Gross-Out Pantheon

Pornography knowingly explores the thresholds of titillation and disgust, and several scholars have identified contemporary pornography's tendencies to veer toward the extreme, the shocking, and the generally "gross" (Langman 2004; Jensen 2007; Maddison 2009; Jones 2010; Tyler 2010).

Boyle (2008, 45) notes that TV documentaries on porn often "seem to be constructed not for the purposes of arousal but of disgust." In the documentaries, female performers detail their experiences of working in the industry, list the acts that they will or will not perform (such as girl-on-girl sex, double-anal sex, and cumshot scenes with multiple men), and discuss issues such as rectal or vaginal damage while "directors recall fecal leakage on-set." This modality of grossness is equally evident in the behind-the-scenes clips that are discussed by Sanna Härmä and Joakim Stolpe (2010, 114). These are rife with toilet humor, farts, and talking anuses: performers give interviews while urinating, demonstrate the uses of the enema box, and make jokes over misplaced semen. Meanwhile, other bodily fluids, such as menstrual blood, remain unseen and unmentioned (Härmä and Stolpe 2010, 118). Nastiness and grossness are crucial to both the verbal and the visual registers of much contemporary porn, but they are conveyed through specific tropes and secretions.

What is seen as exceedingly disgusting—like "2 Girls 1 Cup"—in fact starts to fall outside of pornography proper. On the one hand, viral videos can be identified as pornography through their contexts of production: "2 Girls 1 Cup" is a trailer for a Brazilian fetish porn film titled *Hungry Bitches* produced by MFX Media, and "2 Guys 1 Horse" was shot by zoophiles as an amateur pornographic record. However, viral videos are not watched or experienced as pornography by the majority of their audiences. They also tend to fall outside the pornographic in their contexts of distribution. Like scat videos (Sargeant 2006), viral videos are not found on actual porn sites but on shock and gross-out sites. If the video is famous enough, it is likely to be hosted on a separate site. "2 Girls 1 Cup" can be seen on shock sites such as http://www.maniacworld.com, but it can also be accessed at a URL especially dedicated to it—http://www.2girls1cup.com.

In such circulation, the videos become part of broader gross-out pantheon. This pantheon features well-known characters such as Goatse, who is known primarily from one still image, "hello.jpg," which shows him stretching his anus with both hands and revealing the redness of his rectum and was displayed on the site goatse.cx from 1999 to 2004. The image has inspired a wide range of visual puns and fan art, including ASCII renderings of the image and allusions to its central features in advertisements, magazine covers, and objects of everyday life (figure 6.2). Tubgirl is another well-known gross-out meme, currently hosted at http://www.tubgirl.ca. It is a still image of a woman lying in a tub on her back, holding her legs behind her head, and squirting an orange enema liquid onto her masked face. As is the case in the viral video "Eel Soup," the genital area of Tubgirl is blurred, which suggests the conventions of Japanese porn (in which acts deemed extreme or bizarre by Western standards are shown, while genitalia and pubic hair may be effaced from view). The exemplary sentences associated with Tubgirl in http://www.urbandictionary.com frame the image firmly in terms of disgust: "Tubgirl is well beyond sick, twisted, and disgusting, and is well into the realm of just plain wrong"; "That is nastier than tubgirl!"; "i saw the tubgirl and vomited."[8] In comparison to Tubgirl, Lemon Party—a still image of three old men having oral sex featured on http://www.lemonparty.biz—seems rather tame. Although Goatse and Tubgirl both involve pushing the boundaries of the body and revealing its insides, Lemon Party is about "rendering the (homo)sexualized, elderly, or overweight body in

Figure 6.2
User submissions inspired by Goatse (http://knowyourmeme.com/memes/goatse)

terms of disgust and amusement" (Jones 2010, 128). All these images are "in your face" and invite certain visceral engagement, but they also involve distancing through both laughter and disgust. Laughter helps to create zones of safety around the object, and disgust implies stepping back and distancing oneself from it. In and through both of these gestures, the imageries and the people performing them are othered.

Like Internet memes, shock sites aim to trigger instantaneous and intense reactions that tend to revolve in the negative register. They are about gut reactions, disgust, and titillation. Their aim is to grab viewers, and this grab operates through the display of extremities. Such visceral address is part of the affective economy that is characteristic of contemporary popular interfaces on the Web. When viewers click on video and image links that promise shocking footage of puppies thrown off a bridge or animals cruelly treated by their owners—to cite two examples that I recently came across when reading a Finnish online newspaper—they expect to be shocked and appalled, disgusted and disturbed. Such footage is often decontextualized. It comes with little narrative framing and depicts events and instances that the user cannot change or influence (these shocking things have already taken place). The form of engagement with the footage is that of sharp gut reactions or even one of affective rush, and it is not uncommon for users to share the links with others in an act of inviting them to experience some of this visceral intensity. Other kinds of memes, such as those displayed on Cute Overload (http://cuteoverload.com) and Lolcats (http://icanhascheez-burger.com, http://lolcats.com) (figure 6.3), operate in the register of cuteness and fun, and users are also invited to upload their own examples of the exceedingly cute and cuddly (which, on Lolcats, often begins to border on the disturbing). Yet there is something of a family resemblance in the stickiness and titillation of both the shocking and the cute. The reactions they invite are seemingly clear—to be either appalled or endeared, to exclaim "ewww" or "awww," respectively. Users migrate to such site links in their search for particular kinds of fast affective rush. Although the gut reactions and sensations that the memes give rise to can be complex, this search for jolts and rushes characterizes their affective economy.

Shock sites featuring extreme porn need to be considered as part of this affective fabric of sharp gut reactions and affective jolts. Their resonance is one of shock in the sense of violent sensation or effect, emotional disturbance, and muscular spasm. On shock sites, the pornographic is meshed

Figure 6.3
"Awww!"—cuteness and fun (http://lolcats.com/view/9574)

in with a broader range of things sensational, vile, and gross, and hence their titillation is not only about the sexual. At the boundaries of the pornographic, possible sexual arousal is irrevocably meshed in with affective jolts of amusement, shock, and disgust. Titled as "shock and awe entertainment," http://www.m90.org displays "death videos, extreme porn & gore movies—brutal and nasty videos" (figure 6.4). Another shock site, http://www.newsfilter.org, provides similar videos that are defined in general terms as disturbing. Short captions describe both the contents of the videos and people's reactions to them in terms that refer to sexual arousal and the otherwise visceral (e.g., "Chewing on a slut's used tampon is the #3 leading cause of AIDS. And me puking up my breakfast" and "From sexy slut to raped, beaten, and brutally murdered all in 5 years. Get ready to puke everywhere . . . fuck"). Promising to be brutal, nasty, shocking, and disturbing to the degree of making the user vomit, the sites grab their users through the registers of disgust. At the same time, they also offer fairly mainstream humorous and pornographic images.

Figure 6.4

"Ewww!"—shock and awe entertainment (http://www.m90.org)

The Excessively Carnal

Stile Project (http://www.stileproject.com), established in 1999, is among the best-known shock sites, and it is advertised as "the best in free porn" with "free hardcore porn tube videos & XXX sex movies." The site features hardcore videos of the generic sort (in categories like "Amateurs," "Anal," "Big Dicks," "Blowjobs," "Creampies," "Teens") and of the niche variety ("BDSM," "Fatties," "Furries," "Insertions"). But users also can choose viral videos (with categories like "Goatse & Gapes" and "Funny Shit & Viral Videos"), gross-out images ("Barf," "Freaks of Nature," "Gore & Gross Shit," "Ultraviolence," and the aptly titled "WTF?"), or nonpornographic images (with categories like "Motor Sports," "Music," "Science & Nature," "Sports," and "Technology"). The videos submitted in the various subcategories are all about the extraordinary and excessive, including explicit attempts at gross-out, practical jokes, funny incidents, unlikely bodily performances, and unusual sexual preferences.

With the exception of pornographic content, the Stile Project videos resemble those shown in television shows such as *America's Funniest Home*

Videos and *World's Most Amazing Videos*. In the former, people share their private mishaps and incidents—people falling over, babies vomiting, pets and children misbehaving or being funny, and wedding rituals gone wrong. The videos tend to be low-tech, they are often dated, and they investigate the norms of "good taste" in their displays of the excessively carnal and embodied (Nikunen 2007, 29). In *World's Most Amazing Videos* (which resembles *Maximum Exposure*), the viewer is offered a marathon of random shocking incidents, including people who are run over by trains, cars, and trucks; storms, mudslides, and floods that demolish houses and trap people; police chases that lead to speeding and car accidents; people who catch fire; prisoners who maul each other; raging bulls that throw people around; and fatal accidents that take place in packed, collapsing football stadiums. *America's Funniest Home Videos* operates in the register of the mundane, whereas *World's Most Amazing Videos* offers spectacular and shocking video snippets harvested from around the world in which people are hurt, mauled, and even killed. The money shots in such videos are shown several times and in slow motion. Despite their mutual differences, both shows are connected in their displays of "ordinary" people and actual events. As is the case with pornography in a range of media, the videos selected for showing are based on incidents and action rather than language (Nikunen 2007, 31). They are therefore easy to distribute and understand across national and linguistic borders.

Television shows featuring amateur videos, surveillance camera shots, or videos shot by the police are all exemplary of striptease culture. Making a spectacle of the ordinary and showing the ordinary turned spectacle, the videos claim a documentary aura of authenticity, but their main goal is to amuse, astound, and shock. The Stile Project follows similar paths. In the category of "Animals," for example, its videos include domestic incidents ("Kitties fighting over a steak," "Toilet trained cat shits," "Moonwalking puppy," "Swearing parrot"), well-known Internet memes ("Dramatic Gopher," "Baby panda sneezes & surprises mom"), wildlife footage ("Walrus sucks his own dick underwater," "Octopus uses coconut shells for protection"), accidents and incidents involving people and animals ("Equestrian trick FAILS," "Cow drop kicks man in Pakistan," "Horse farts during interview recording"), and videos falling in the gross-out category ("Cat eaten by rats," "Pig gets castrated") (figure 6.5). The site brings together numerous online video genres from cute overload material starring kittens and puppies to YouTube celebrities, home movies, and found objects such as

Figure 6.5
Animal videos at http://www.stileproject.com

incidents once shown on TV. The videos often dwell on animal erections, masturbation, and defecation, particularly when these take place in front of or on top of surprised people. This is also where the modality of the site clearly departs from the television shows mentioned above. Although *World's Most Amazing Videos* offers abundant displays of real-life violence and bodily harm, it erases things sexual, the implication being that sex is more offensive and extreme than violence. Shock sites display what no light-hearted television show ever would, such as home videos of anal play, executions, and snipers hitting their marks. They borrow from the dynamics of TV video shows but take these to the extreme. This extremity is centrally played out on and through bodies, their insides, outsides, and the traffic in-between.

As a porn site, Stile Project presents a range of things from spectacular fetish scenarios to mundane incidents and, by doing so, encompasses a grandiose display of the bawdy, the physical, and the low. In spite of its visceral modality, the site invites a distanced mode of viewing as one subcategory after another promises extraordinary or otherwise fascinating incidents and sights to behold. Stile Project mixes body genres such as pornography, horror, and comedy in a variation of a mediated freak show. Pornography, however, dominates the landscape. The setting is not much different from what Kipnis (1999, 141) mapped out in her reading of *Hustler* as a magazine that zeros in on unsaid subjects and issues: "Things we would call 'tasteless' at best, or might even become physically revulsed by: the physical detritus of aborted fetuses, how and where the homeless manage to relieve themselves (not much social attention devoted to this little problem), amputation, the proximity of sexual organs to those of elimination, the various uses to which liposuctioned fat might be put—any aspect of how the material body fares in our current society" (Kipnis 1999, 142).

Shock and gross-out sites are equally involved and obsessed with the body, its inner spaces, and its fluid boundaries, and like *Hustler*, they dwell on the excessive and the residual with the aim of evoking visceral reactions in their consumers: their point is to shock and cause offense (Jones 2010, 123). As Steven Jones argues, shock sites harvest material from porn and combine it with medical imagery of injuries and physical abnormalities. Juxtaposing the titillating with the abject, shock sites valorize such combinations and frame representations of the exposed body that are "pushed beyond expected corporeal limits" in terms of repulsion, amusement, and more (Jones 2010, 124): "just as porn tries to sexually entice, the shock image may provoke physical revulsion or laughter, possibly in combination with, or repression, of sexual arousal. These are not simply images of disgust, even if their aim is to repel; they are situated between horror, amusement, desire, and morbid curiosity. Perhaps it is because of the mutability of what they signify—a propensity echoed in their contextual adaptability—that they are sought" (Jones 2010, 133).

Images of bodies stretched to the limits of their carnal capacity "reach out to viewing bodies and touch them so viscerally that they are likely to leave a mark, some form of a residue" (Kyrölä 2010, 122)—that is, images stick, and the sensations they evoke linger on. Whether they are experienced as waves of nausea, as a discomforting feeling in the pit of one's stomach, or as curious exhilaration, the imageries seen on shock sites remain with us long after the initial encounter. This can be a sensation of having been touched by a miasmic force or of having been soiled by disgusting vistas that one wants to step away from. The residue of the images conflates with the view of the images themselves as residue, waste, and dirt—in Mary Douglas's (1991, 35) terms, as "matter out of place." Disgust, however, may titillate and invite further watching. In this case, the residue of the images takes up a more seductive tone in its promises of jolts, sensations, and reverberations. Following Kristeva (1982, 1), this is a matter of abjection, a "twisted braid of affects" concerning what is experienced as repugnant, needs to be expelled from one's body (or the proximity of one's body), and yet fascinates, arrests attention, and refuses to go away. Abject is an issue of affective intensity and affective ambiguity—something that oscillates between excitement and disgust, joy and repulsion, and "does not allow itself to be dolled up in flowery sentences" (Kristeva 1982, 204).

Extremity and Ethics

Shock sites are about images and acts that are deemed extreme or even abject. They are about the images that are pornographic, obscene, and offensive,[9] including bodily waste, bestiality, and elaborate displays of BDSM. Although such material is circulated in newsgroups, P2P networks, and private messaging, shock sites remain the most visible and easily accessible platforms for imageries of extreme physicality (Jones 2010, 127). More recently, sites such as 4chan have taken over the role of Stile Project as a platform for sharing and witnessing Web curiosa and memes of all kinds, and many other sites exist for watching, sharing, and discussing extreme and shock pornographies. Among these are http://www.efukt.com, http://extremefuse.com, http://www.wtfpeople, http://www.uselessjunk.com, and www.nowthatsfuckedup.com, a site that was closed down in 2006 for violating Florida laws pertaining to obscenity and famous for publishing "trophy photos" of dead and mauled Iraqi insurgents that were uploaded by U.S. soldiers serving in Iraq (see Jacobs 2007, 122–124; Grusin 2010, 82–86). These sites highlight images and videos that are extreme, bizarre, and of low cultural status. Shock porn sites display videos where drunk sex workers are urinated on ("used as a human toilet bowl"), "fat girls" are forced into anal sex and the number of their cries is carefully documented, a "chick bangs a snake," young men are caught masturbating to cybersex, and a "crackwhore" with a "basketball-sized tumor hanging from her midsection" has sex with her son. The videos are predominantly grainy and amateurish (connoting home-made authenticity), and in one sarcastic caption after another, women are "destroyed" in sex acts.

Combining sexual titillation with disgust, shock, and disbelief, shock porn sites routinely border on so-called brutal pornography. Available also on specialized forums such as PunishTube (http://www.punishtube.com), "brutal" is a category for scenarios of humiliation and submission featuring gags, bondage, "cum showers," fucking machines, and sexual acts that are based on consent but discussed as torture. These sites make extreme BDSM imageries accessible to a mass audience. These imageries are not novel, but their wide visibility and broad circulation are. As BDSM imageries are rendered objects of consumption for a broad and mixed audience, they are cut loose from the sexual subcultures, ethics, and codes of their production. What appears as torture to one is, for another, an example of a domination-humiliation scenario based on consent, mutual desire, and shared codes (Jacobs 2009, 192–193). As these contexts become blurred and effaced, the imageries are also "marooned" by being relocated on sites featuring bodily abnormalities (cancerous tumors, stretched labia, miniscule and enormous penises) and instances of abuse (as in the examples of a sex workers urinated on or a woman forced to have anal sex). As sexual subcultures, codes, ethics, and practices become effaced at least for the noninitiated, it becomes possible to read BDSM imageries as instances of brutality or even torture.

Such realness begs for the status of presentation over representation—that is, of videos that involve mere showing rather than mediation or staged action. As discussed in chapter 3, in porn, the notions of realness, rawness, and amateurism all support one other. In addition to the properties of the images or the gut reactions that they evoke, realness also involves the conditions of their production. These involve ethical concerns, such as the abuse of sex workers, the mistreatment of animals, or the enticing of homeless people to hurt themselves or fight each other in return for money or alcohol (in the "bum-fight" videos circulated online since 2002). These videos give rise to gut reactions and jolts that are inseparable from their sense of realness and the unmediated. But what do such jolts then effect? The affective economy of Internet memes and shock sites is one of affect detached from considerations of ethics, meaning, or actual effects—namely, a straightforward interaction with the gross or the cute that gives rise to equally inconsequential effects (the "ewwws" and the "awwws"). Stripped of narrative and character construction, memes facilitate instant access to the visceral that is then experienced as bodily resonance. For me, this summarizes much of the memes' appeal, yet it is necessary to ask whether this is all that the jolts can affect and what their effects may be.

Following the work of Sianne Ngai and Katariina Kyrölä, it can be suggested that jolts are volatile in their effects, as well as inseparable from political and ethical considerations. The jolts experienced when faced with videos displaying cruelty to animals, for example, can both surface from and give rise to acute ethical concerns, and these jolts can then move one into action. The question of what kind of action this can be remains, however, for the videos tend to record what has taken place and can no longer be affected. Social networking sites such as Facebook offer the possibility of sharing and distributing the offensive images, and such action involves the circulation of shocks and jolts (as in the case of the 2007 news item of a Costa Rican artist who allegedly starved a stray dog to death in a gallery in the name of art, which inspired online protests and petitions). This kind of circulation increases the general stickiness and affective intensity of the images. It spreads the affect but offers no possibility of influencing the acts or conditions behind the images. Even so, the unease and jolts brought forth by the images can move people to action in their everyday surroundings as a way of making connections and considering their interconnections to other bodies and the world.[10] As Kyrölä (2010, 188) reminds us, the zones of affective engagement where media images and viewers' corporal locations and histories intertwine always involve something "that spills over, that mobilizes the relation between the imagined bodies and viewing bodies in ways that are not entirely unpredictable but which do not fall seamlessly into expected paths."

Networked Disgust

Although there is a family resemblance to their modalities, shock sites and viral videos differ dramatically from print forums such as *Hustler*. Magazines are products and ready-made commodities, whereas viral videos are better understood as "the mediating mechanisms via which cultural practices are originated, adopted and (sometimes) retained within social networks" (Burgess 2008, 102). Online, users upload content that is discussed and commented on collectively and then spread and redistributed as mash-ups and other remixes, whereas print media are based on editorial processes and provide far fewer possibilities for interaction. Web sites are dynamic in undergoing constant transformations as new content is added, code is rewritten, design is altered, and new users join the discussion and older ones leave. The sense of community and participation facilitated by the sites is crucial in terms of their affective dynamics, even if the overwhelming majority of users simply lurk. Both shock sites and *Hustler* dwell in the carnal and the low and give rise to a particular affective resonance in the process. Yet the sites involve much more viral and contagious kind of affective circulation—as users not only look at the images and videos but make and share them, frame them with descriptions, tag them, compare them to older and more recent uploads, and upload new content in response to what already exists and is of interest to others. As Henry Jenkins has pointed out, spreadable media content—such as viral videos—"gains greater resonance in the culture, taking on new meanings, finding new audiences, attracting new markets, and generating new value" through acts of reuse, reworking, and redistribution (in Burgess 2008, 102). Such involvements evoke specific kinds of networked resonances and forms of grab. The sites aim to grab their users, users grab video clips and circulate them with their descriptions and comments, and videos continue to grab new users and hold old ones in their grasp.

YouTube hosts numerous reaction videos of people watching viral shock porn videos for the first time. In fact, people are often asked to make and share such a video when first receiving the video link. In the reaction videos to "2 Girls 1 Cup," people typically watch the beginning of the video of the two women kissing and fondling each other with a smile, perhaps noting that they have seen similar things many times before. As one of the performers starts defecating in a cup (there has also been some dispute as to the actual contents of the cup, since some think it resembles chocolate fudge), the viewers begin to grimace and whimper in disbelief, and some hold their noses as if escaping the scent of excrement displayed on the screen. As the other woman begins to eat the excrement and especially as she vomits it into her partner's mouth, the sounds of disgust grow louder, and the viewers stand up, turn away from the screen, and cover their eyes (figure 6.6). Reactions are similar in the case of "2 Guys 1 Horse," with complaints such as "No way!" and "Ewww man!" Some viewers hide their faces, and others gag.

Reaction videos arouse curiosity about the original videos and encourage new viewers to record and share their own viewing experiences. Here,

Figure 6.6
Reaction videos to "2 Girls 1 Cup" (http://www.youtube.com)

interest and disgust are impossible to tell apart, and although the videos watched can be categorized as porn, the interests in question are not predominantly sexual. The social circulation of viral videos resembles that of coprophilic videos that are not watched merely by the fetishist but in far larger numbers by the curious, such as "teenage males trying to shock each other" (Sargeant 2006). As reaction videos are exchanged and accumulate online, affective reactions become social and shared. The reactions that are invited and shared are often of markedly performative and exaggerated disgust (rather than titillation or arousal of a different genre). Submitted on platforms such as YouTube, they move further away from the context of shock sites but still carry some of their registers of disgust, titillation, and wonder. Physical, exaggerated reactions of disgust attach the videos to one another, and the original videos become sticky with affect. Addressing such stickiness in the framework of Marx's theory of capital, Ahmed (2004, 194–195) suggests that affect results from the circulation of objects and signs. The more intense the circulation of signs, the higher the affective intensity or value an object gains and the stickier it becomes (Ahmed 2004, 45). Reaction videos, user comments, blog inserts, and newspaper columns addressing viral videos have increased their affective intensity, and this stickiness has attracted the attention of new curious people. Rather than being objects of titillation or gratification in themselves, viral videos become the means of social interaction. The shock, disgust, amusement, and surprise felt when watching them and in watching other people watch them structure the relations and communications taking place between people.

Pornography also can be considered a sticky object in a more general sense. Definitions and affective intensities of lowness, filth, disgust, and shame stick to porn, its performers, its consumers, and if Miller (1997, 22) is to be believed, porn researchers such as myself who seek out and take delight in the disgusting (cf. Ahmed 2004, 91). The metaphor of filth carries associations of contagion. Encounters with or observations of filth mean that some of the filth has already managed to stick on the observing subject (and one is therefore already soiled). Although the notions of filth, sleaze, and scum are efficient means of building social hierarchies, filthy or sticky encounters also make it more difficult to draw any clear boundaries between the self and the object of disgust—especially given the ways in which disgust and interest tend to interconnect and feed into one another (Cohen 2005, x).

In his consideration of bodily boundaries, Miller (1997, 127–128) argues that the person who gives permission for disgusting acts to take place is the one who is violating the boundaries of disgust: he or she is disgusting. Whereas Miller is concerned mainly with mundane and socially sanctioned breeches of bodily boundaries, such as French kisses or penetrative heterosex, the transgressions in "2 Girls 1 Cup" and "Eel Soup" are more drastic in nature. The videos are amazing partly because their performers— these extremely nasty girls—do not seem perturbed by feces, vomit, or eels. Articulations of disgust stick tightly to the female performers since they are both the ones giving permission to and the ones performing the extreme acts. The female performers in "Eel Soup" are Japanese, and the ones in "2 Girls 1 Cup" are Brazilian. From the perspective of Western viewers, they embody and represent ethnic and national differences. When writing on scatology and pornography, Sargeant (2006) notes how such videos "always come from 'elsewhere' of course, never close to home." This was the case with Tubgirl, "2 Girls 1 Cup," and "Eel Soup." "2 Guys 1 Horse," in contrast, was shot in Enumclaw, Washington. In the videos, dirt, filth, pollution, disgust, shamelessness, lowness, ethnicity, gender, sexuality, and otherness all stick to and reinforce one another. As these affective attachments and categorizations accumulate and sediment, they give rise and shape to social boundaries and categorizations. When the performers who are violating the boundaries of disgust are identified as "other" in terms of national and ethnic typing, the viral videos may be easier to distance from and laugh at. Affective stickiness, ethnic otherness, disgust, and distance facilitated by laughter are all evident in a 2008 *South Park* episode "Over Logging" and its references to "Japanese girls exchanging bodily fluids" and "Brazilian fart fetish porn." As extreme viral videos have circulated from the Internet to the broader media environment, they have grown increasingly sticky.

The reaction videos to viral porn feature expressions of disgust and disbelief, but acts of watching these reaction videos tend to be characterized by distancing laughter. When the initial reaction of disgust dissipates, "2 Girls 1 Cup" turns into a shared joke that involves exposing new viewers to the video in order to witness their reactions. Offense and amusement intertwine and become inseparable from one another, and "amusement can rise from being affronted or from *causing* offense to others" (Jones 2010, 129). Users may trick each other into visiting shock sites, or people may become curious after hearing of other people's reactions and descriptions of the videos as the most disgusting things ever made. In any case, the videos become sticky with affective intensity and contagious in their visceral force. Reaction videos involve encounters with the extreme and bizarre, and the reactions that people record on camera and share with others are ones of laughter, dismay, disbelief, disgust, and bemusement. All these reactions are built on and create a sense of distance toward what is being watched. The pornographic imageries are pushed away and held at a distance, and the self is marked as clearly separate from but (many times obviously and irrefutably) affected by the images witnessed. Such encounters are not marked by shame, sexual arousal, or articulations of (sexual) desire. Intimate encounters with online porn remain much more private. Although these may also be shared, this would be unlikely to happen on YouTube. Acts of watching the exaggerated gags, grunts, and moans expressed and performed in the reaction videos may be one of the few instances of accessing other people's affective reactions to pornography, yet this involves a limited affective register and rather staged and knowing performances of affect.

Too Close for Comfort

According to Nina K. Martin, viewers of pornography experience fundamental proximity and intimacy with the screen: "This closeness to the
image is replicated through a lack of aesthetic and intellectual distance
that might be undermined by the revelation of self-conscious performance
or artifice" (Martin 2006, 194–195). Martin argues that watching pornography involves, by definition, a lack of aesthetic distance and reflexivity.
The viewer is too close for comfort, is unable to distance herself from the
screen and things flickering on it, and does not recognize pornographic
images and performances as self-conscious or as displaying their artificiality—and if she does, then the closeness with the image will be lost. It is
unlikely that Martin is arguing that pornographic performances are not
self-conscious or that porn scenarios lack artificiality. This premise of lack
of aesthetic distance is understandable in a Kantian framework. Sociologist Pasi Falk has made a similar argument when stating that the loss of
distance—"the collapse of the representation back to the object," which
happens in encounters with porn—means that an aesthetic experience
"regresses" into a sensual and sexual one (Falk 1994, 194). Like Martin, Falk
sees proximity and aesthetic experience as mutually exclusive. The things
depicted on the screen become the object since the viewer can no longer distinguish between presentation and representation or between the
immediately present and the mediated. Falk also positions the sensual and
sexual lower in the experiential hierarchy—as something to regress to—
and implies that the engagement with the "lower regions" of the body is
indicative of lowness also in terms of value or morality. In Falk's view, "that
which *excites* by turning the representation into a mere stimulus-evoking
(bodily/sexual) response—even if by representational means (as is the case
of a pornographic representation)—excites *disgust* precisely because of the
resistance towards the abolition of the representative distance" (Falk 1994,
194, emphasis in the original). In this framework, sexual excitement effaces
aesthetic experience, and disgust disturbs the excitement: the relationship
of disgust and desire is one of conflict. As suggested above, the relationship
can, especially in the context of pornography, also be considered as one of
fundamental interconnectedness. What disgusts also excites and attracts,
and the oscillation between the two affective modes explains much of pornography's force and appeal.

It is also debatable whether aesthetics—as a "faculty of feeling" (Kennedy 2000, 12), as studies of perceiving and sensing the world, and as investigations into taste, style, and experiences thereof—is a matter of distance by default. Both Isobel Armstrong's (2000) theorizations of the "radical aesthetic" built on affective dynamics and Barbara M. Kennedy's (2000) theory of "the aesthetic of sensation" point to much more embodied, sensory, and affective conceptualizations of the aesthetic. Armstrong outlines a framework for understanding the role that affect plays in and for studies of literary texts. Departing from notions of distance and detachment, she argues that "close reading has never been close enough"' but has "always engaged with mastery" (Armstrong 2000, 95). That is, reading has been understood as something that the research performs on (or even forces onto) the text. Giving up the mastery of the reader over the text leads to a more dialogical relationship where the reader is "caught up with, imbricated in, the structure of the text's processes" (Armstrong 2000, 94). Armstrong addresses affect as a dynamic relationship between the text and the reader that stems from the analytical process, where sense and sensibility are impossible to tell apart. Since affective dynamics are contingent, the process of interpretation remains open as the interpreter becomes or does not become moved by what she studies. This motion affords insights and forms of knowledge and also sets limits to them. This is also the form of analysis that I propose for studying online porn and its carnal resonance.

The notion of distance remains central to eighteenth- and nineteenth-century considerations of beauty (characterized as something pleasing, satisfying, or harmonious) as an issue of reflective contemplation. Online porn is concerned with beauty mainly to befoul it one way or another. Beautiful faces become distorted in sexual arousal, pleasure, or physical discomfort, mouths are penetrated, and cheeks are smeared with semen. The female performers of viral videos are archetypical femininely attractive and young women who flaunt their abilities to engage in and enjoy (or pretend to enjoy) sexual acts that might deemed perverse by hegemonic notions of sexuality. For Bataille (1986, 145), physical desirability is central since the despoiling and profanation of physical beauty "is the essence of eroticism." In Bataille's view, female beauty and the beauty of the face, in particular, is smirched by exposing the woman's "secret parts" and then penetrating her body: "The greater the beauty, the more it is befouled" (also Kalha 2007a, 108). In online porn, beauty is befouled in facial cum shots (from singular to bukkake), ATM, and cum swapping. It also occurs in abundance on the rhetorical level of captions and terminology that clash beauty with its opposite—the ugly, vile, repulsive, disgusting, and offensive.

In Edmund Burke's aesthetic theory, the opposite of beauty was not the ugly, however, but the sublime. Both beauty and the sublime can be pleasurable, but the latter—the sensation of being overpowered, impressed, and overwhelmed by what one encounters—also involves fear, horror, uncertainty, and confusion. The sublime is frightening, expansive, and therefore attractive, while beauty is safe and contained. The sublime cannot be experienced at a distance. As Kant noted, it points to the limits of intelligibility, imagination, and sensibility (Olkowski 1999, 231–232; White 1997; Zuckert 2003). The sublime is monstrous and cannot be confined to the representational (Olkowski 1999, 70). The argument here is not that pornography is about the sublime rather than the beautiful. It need not be about either. But the dynamics of porn involve both contemplative distance and overwhelming proximity, and this does not render considerations of aesthetics impossible. It does, however, necessitate stepping away from eighteenth-century theories of aesthetics, their premises, and understandings of art that fail to grasp contemporary visual culture. Furthermore, aesthetics needs to be addressed in plural: porn involves different aesthetic registers, proximities, and distances.

Illegitimate Touchings

In her consideration of controversial and transgressive contemporary artworks, Allison Young (2005) addresses their "affective charge" and "jolt" and the ways in which the conflation of distance between an image and its viewers gives rise to sensations and articulations of disgust. According to Young (2005, 41), artworks such as Chris Serrano's *Piss Christ* or Marcus Harvey's *Myra* involve "endless illegitimate touchings" (of which the combinations of urine and a crucifix and a photo of a child killer and a hand of a child are the most illegitimate), "the sight of which creates shock, distress or queasiness in the viewer." Drawing their viewers to unbearable proximity, the works give rise to a shuddering sensation of "aesthetic vertigo." According to Young, visual proximity with representations (rather than with actual urine or the physical body of a child killer) gives rise to the imagined sensation of a touch that may be experienced as threatening or able to contaminate the viewer. This imagined sensation evokes disgust, which then leads to vertigo as disorientation. Visceral responses to such artworks "can be interpreted as the shudder arising from an image which transcends the cushioning effect of the fact of representation and threatens metaphorically to touch the spectator" (Young 2005, 42). For Young, disgust and the lack of distance give rise to aesthetic sensation and affective charge. These sensations are crucial to the ways that the artworks operate and the reactions of shock and aggression that they evoke.

Shifting the discussion from contemporary art to pornography of the extreme kind, I argue that despite crucial differences in terms of cultural position, contexts of production, distribution, and consumption, it involves similar experiences of "illegitimate touchings," vertigo, imagined sensations, and disgust. The representational "cushion" or distance disappears as people gag when faced with "2 Girls 1 Cup" and its scatological feast, experience visceral gut reactions when watching "2 Guys 1 Horse," or click through the "shock and awe" videos available on shock sites. Unbearable proximities, jolts, and moments of vertigo lay at the root of the attraction of shock sites and memes, for these images and videos do indeed threaten—or perhaps promise—to touch and move their viewers in visceral ways. Their displays of blurred bodily boundaries (gaping anuses, excrement consumed, bodies hurt and mauled) operate in a visceral register that resonates with the viewers in carnal ways. Invested with miasmic qualities, the videos get under one's skin and grab the viewer independent of her consent and initial orientation toward them. This affective density collapses the distance between the bodies on the screen, the files downloaded from a server situated somewhere across the globe, the moments in which the videos where shot, and the viewer's body. If this is an aesthetic—as Young proposes—then it is one of intimate proximity and visceral entanglement rather than distance or externality.

Encounters with Web sites and videos give rise to certain affective dynamics, resonance that varies in intensity, and that changes from one encounter to another. The aesthetic modality of porn has been located in its power to arouse sexually, to bring viewers close, and to drive them to masturbate and climax. However, given that there is more to its affective intensities than sexual arousal, porn is also experienced as disturbing in the gut reactions it evokes. In these, titillation is meshed in with disgust, shame, amusement, curiosity, and boredom. Armstrong (2000, 123) considers affect an ambiguous, alternating force that moves "between the destruction of representation, opening up an abyss in consciousness by violently breaking the barriers of repression, and appropriating, thieving, representation. It belongs to a chain of discourse and breaks it; it alternates between being bound and unbound, attached to signification and rupturing it." I interpret this to mean at least two things in terms of pornography. First, affect is not contained in the pornographic image or text as its inner property. As a force experienced in encounters with pornography, it touches and disturbs readers and viewers and makes them conscious of their gut reactions and orientations toward what they are viewing. At the same time, as a dynamic, affect cannot be uncoupled from the pornographic object since it surfaces in the interaction between the object and its users. Second, the secondary role of narrative or character construction in porn and its tendency to highlight the bodily and the visceral mean that there is not a great deal for affect to disrupt. The stage is always already set for gut reactions. As immediate sensory experiences and surprising intensities, affect escapes representation (visualization and narration in which it might be pinned down). Affective responses are knowingly evoked and aroused through camerawork, editing, music, performance, subject matter, captions, and comments. Extreme porn and shock sites are concerned with grabbing user attention and touching them viscerally: they disturb, upset, and arouse. Remembering Tomkins's argument that any affect can stick to any object, this arousal is full of surprises and frustrations. It cannot be preprogrammed or repeated as identical from one moment to another.

Materiality and Ethics

Realness begs for the status of presentation (mere showing) over representation (the mediated), and in porn, the notions of realness, rawness, and amateurism all support one other. In addition to the properties of the images or the gut reactions that they evoke, realness is also a question of production and its material conditions. In terms of ethics and pornography, the contexts for producing and circulating pornographic images cannot be avoided. All kinds of pornographies dwell on the materiality of bodies, the resonances between bodies, and the technologies of recording, circulating, and consuming media images. Addressing pornography as detached from the materiality of production or consumption results in a partial and selective perspective. Porn involves the organization and division of labor, and these forms of commodity production are hidden from view when conceptualizing the products as mere texts—that is, as a question of signification (Villarejo 2003, 10). At the same time, the contexts of labor are out of the grasp of those who study online porn through the interface rather than conducting ethnographic work on the locations of production. Porn is produced for glossy pay sites, it is distributed by amateurs for free in newsgroups and Web image galleries, images and videos are recycled on different platforms (portals and link sites), and they enter different forms of commodification and circulation in the process. The difficulties of contextualizing the working practices and principles of profit generation involved in the many practices associated with porn do not mean that questions of material production should not matter in the analytical work done on the topic. In all cases, materiality of production is a matter of both ethical considerations and methodological concerns. The focus is on the physicality of bodies that perform and consume pornography and also on the materiality of pornographic products that are distributed in particular media formats (such as photography, video, film, DVDs, Web sites, email messages, streaming videos) and that involve different resonance. It also means remaining sensitive to the different intentionalities of the images designed to sexually arouse, amuse, and disgust and the means through which these are carried out (the materiality of their production).

For some decades, antipornography discourse has argued for pornography as not "only words" but as interactions—and abuses—of a much more carnal nature. Following this line of reasoning, Catharine MacKinnon (1993) famously argued that pornography should not be protected under laws governing freedom of speech since it is a question of material acts. MacKinnon, like Andrea Dworkin, sees pornography as documentation of what has taken place—not as expression or interpretation but as mere showing, as indexical traces of what has taken place. In *Pornography Embodied*, social justice scholar Joan Mason-Grant argues for the value of MacKinnon's work in shifting the focus from speech to practice—from the linguistic to the lived, practiced, and embodied. For Mason-Grant (2004, 7), porn is a practice of subordination that words and images, as social forces, both effect and uphold. In her view, porn involves material acts, and research needs to account for this materiality of bodies acting and being acted upon. As bodily practice, porn is a form of corporeal training to recognize certain images and scenarios as arousing and to be moved by them. It is "erotic rehearsal of these sexual norms" (Mason-Grant 2004, 151).

The "education" that Mason-Grant addresses is very much of the carnal kind. By drawing on performative theories of gender, she sees pornography as reiterating sexual norms, codes, and hierarchies. It can be argued that pornographic imageries have highlighted certain sexual acts and, through this reiteration, mainstreamed them. Viewers have learned to enjoy conventions such as cum shots through viewing porn depictions as they have accumulated since the 1970s. In this sense, porn "educates" us to experience its imageries and settings as exciting (Dyer 2002a, 187). And as we become habituated to watching sex on the screen, we experience "our sympathetic relations to the sex of others as a kind of carnal knowledge felt in our own bodies" (Williams 2008, 311). When addressing the carnal learning involved in heteroporn, Mason-Grant defines it as corporeal interpellation into the ideologies of sexism, classism, and racism and the values of domination and submission (while, at the same time, remaining seemingly impervious to these effects herself). This is also where I depart from her argument, for as I have pointed out in the preceding chapters, the excessive modalities of porn cannot be accounted for in such categorical terms. Certain perspectives, titillations, and pleasures of heterosexual men do dominate the conventions of heteroporn, yet I would not associate this with ideological interpellation.[11] In a paranoid reading, we will always "know" that this is what pornography is and what it does: it will always be sexist, racist, classist, ageist, and ableist. At the same time, the hyperbolic, excessive, and exaggerated modalities of porn resist literal interpretations that help to grope at but do not quite grasp the dynamics at play between what is being presented, represented, sensed, and experienced.

As consumers of porn, we come to appreciate some styles and depictions and not others (Williams 2008, 6). The possibility of seeing bodies perform certain acts may or may not translate into a desire or an interest to repeat such acts with one's own body. The same images evoke different resonance in different people and give rise to different affectations, interests, orientations, and distastes. There is no reason to imagine that the affective complexities of shock porn sites and viral videos would automatically be experienced as sexually arousing or that people would relate to porn's imageries in a literal manner. The resonance of porn may well be an issue of shifting attraction and multiple modes of viewing from curiosity and disgust to distanced observation and up-close scrutiny.

In Mason-Grant's account, the physical fact of sexual arousal functions as material evidence of pornography's pedagogical force, which, again, echoes the material practices of porn production: "The woman being penetrated consecutively by several men in a gang-rape scene in video *really is* being penetrated consecutively by several men" (Mason-Grant 2004, 24). In other words, pornography documents sexual acts and turns them into commodities that are rife with indexical traces of what has been. With the centrality of realness and authenticity to hardcore, this is indeed the case. When watching hardcore porn, viewers expect to see sex acts actually played out rather than simulated (as might be the case in softcore porn). In the case of extreme and shock pornographies, this realness is inseparably tied to their visceral pull, jolt, and charge. At the same time, it is clear that a woman who is penetrated consecutively by several men in a gangbang scene is not being raped, unless the pornography is of the forbidden or extreme kind that might be found on the most extreme shock sites. She is performing under certain working conditions, with certain agreements, and for possible monetary compensation. This is a form of material, bodily labor (whether freely given or paid)—a series of physical performances that the performers have agreed to enact. It is also immaterial labor in the sense of giving rise to videos and affective labor in the sense of investing these videos with particular stickiness.

The failure to account for the agency of the individual performers of porn *as* performers means that analyses cannot account for the staged, choreographed, and indeed fictitious aspects of porn scenarios. Although these acts have actually been performed, they are not the only thing that has occurred at the place of shooting. The media of recording, editing, storing, and distributing these images do not function as windows on the world, yet interpreting pornographic representation as presentation (mere showing) presents them as such. The importance of the indexical in and for pornography need not lead one to conflate pornographic products (videos or images) with the acts conducted. Porn is not sex but a media genre. Porn is always mediated and underpinned by the affordances and specificities of both media technology and genre. Porn is posed, scripted, and edited. People act out roles, and generic conventions have a perpetual presence of their own. This applies also to amateur porn performed for the camera as more spectacular variations of domestic play. When using examples of shock videos involving abuse (of women, men, and animals) as exemplary of pornography as a genre, these specificities and distinctions disappear from sight. All kinds of pornographies revolve around a play between presentation and representation, authenticity and artifice, realness and fiction, and they do so in different ways. Consequently, the forms and implications of this play need to be part of the analytical agenda.

Affective Rhetoric

Online shock pornographies have, particularly in their violent variations, contributed to and reanimated feminist antipornography activism (Jones 2010; Dines et al. 2010). Feminist analyses and critiques of pornography continue to matter, especially in their emphasis on the material conditions of production and the social contexts of pornographic imageries. However, given that antiporn rhetoric has drawn on both strong articulations of distaste and definitions of pornography as violence and degradation of women for several decades, shock porn steps in with optimal examples of the disgusting, which can then be generalized as characteristic of the genre as a whole. Finnish sociologist Sari Näre does something of this kind when quoting Ragnhild Bjornbekk and Tor Evjen's description of niche pornographies as descriptive of online pornography that involves "wounding and penetrating genitalia with objects or fists, bondage and torture with various objects, strangulation and suffocation, rape, defecation, urination, eating and drinking feces, sexual abuse of bodies and animals, execution at war, other murder and mutilation, presentation of dead and mutilated children and fetuses" (in Näre 2002, 230). A posting in a 2007 online discussion of Robert Jensen's antipornography article relies on similar rhetorical force:

Twenty two years ago, feminists visited "adult bookstores" and found whole units devoted to "MUTILATION." Anyone who has studied the progression of porn since the '70s and '80s finds a MARKED increase in both physical and psychological brutality, example RAPE, TORTURE, MURDER. Women do NOT get aroused (unless they are very sick) by pictures of them being URINATED on, physically BRUTALIZED and very degraded, e.g., with terms like "SLUT" "Whore" etc., while being beaten and RAPED.[12]

In both these examples, the extreme becomes representative of online porn. Both excerpts make use of affective triggers (in the latter case, these are spelled out in capital letters) that are intended to orient the reader's interpretation by evoking gut reactions and jolts of shock, disgust, and anger. The hyperbolic lexicon of porn is read literally as evidence of pornography's focus on violating and degrading women. These rhetorical and affective modes of address have a lively tradition in antiporn feminism, as in evident in Dworkin's (1989, 2000a) forcefully emotional writing built on sorrow and rage and in MacKinnon's (1993) ways of addressing her readers in the second person as victims of pornographic depiction. In addition to affective triggers of the textual kind, antipornography feminists have drawn centrally on visual examples used as evidence of pornography's sexism and violence. Antiporn slideshows have been screened since the 1980s, and they continue to be used in helping women in particular to "recognize immediately that they are looking at raw, visceral contempt for women" when faced with porn (Rebecca Whisnant, in Dines et al. 2010, 17). When discussing such slide shows, Carole S. Vance (1989, 16) notes that images are experienced as more overpowering than text: "The emotion aroused by an image is easily attached to rhetorical arguments, overwhelming more subtle analysis and response, and the audience." Images experienced as disturbing or even shocking can then be "effectively used to propel viewers to the desired conclusion." The images of porn—whether mainstream or extreme—have considerable force, and their affective jolts and shocks can be channeled into antiporn purposes without difficulty because they balance at the border of sexual arousal and disgust and continuously flirt with extremity.

My point is not to deny or undermine the importance of critical analysis of shock or extreme pornography but to argue that categorical generalizations of porn as violence make it difficult to distinguish between consensual BDSM scenarios and instances of actual sexual violence and abuse and to intervene in their circulation. The hyperbolic rhetoric of shock holds considerable affective power and appeal, and discussions about it may turn out to be counterproductive in framing the object of pornography in partial ways. Ultimately, analyses of shock porn cannot be isolated from considerations of the range and diversity online pornography, sexual subcultures, Internet memes, and the interconnections of disgust and arousal in pornography.

The Visceral Smell of the Forbidden Fruit

Online porn is mundane and ubiquitous. At the same time, its status as forbidden fruit triggers public disapproval and secrecy (Kalha 2007b, 29–31).

As Annette Kuhn (1994, 23) notes, "in order to maintain its attraction, porn demands strictures, controls, censorship. Exposed to the light of day, it risks loss of power. Pornography invites policing." Walter Kendrick (1996) has also elaborated on the intimate ties of pornography and secrecy. According to Kendrick, the pornographic has, since the nineteenth century, been mapped out as something necessitating regulation, secrecy, and limited access. In the process of regulation and censorship, porn has been embedded in a discourse of filth, smut, depravity, garbage, and sewage and defined as "utterly loathsome stuff with no redeeming qualities of any kind" (Kendrick 1996, 212). In addition, as pointed out in chapter 2, this sewage has been invested with the power to galvanize people, particularly young and impressionable people, into debauchery (Kendrick 1996, 261). Rejection, banning, and silencing—of the kind expressed in moral, religious, aesthetic, and political objections to pornography—add to the overall appeal and attraction of porn and even function as its preconditions: "Wherever arguments in favor of elite culture are made, they seem unable to resist invoking pornography (or its kissing cousin, masturbation), to represent the dangerous thing that has to be resisted. What this means, of course, is that pornography ends being spoken about more and more frequently, and becomes even more culturally indispensable" (Kipnis 1999, 178).

Disapproval and censorship make pornography thrive, and porn knowingly feeds this disapproval through its commitment to what is deemed shameful, repulsive, or disgusting. I agree with many of Kipnis's points and seldom fail to enjoy the "affective voice" (Gregg 2006) of her writing. But I have reservations about her view of porn as a form of civic disobedience and transgressive political theater that maps out of "culture's system of taboos and myths" (Kipnis 1999, 164, 206). According to this idea, porn—as low culture—disrupts and mocks the high, which tries in vain to control it. This game of the hegemonic and the repressed reads as a political class allegory, and porn becomes property of the lower classes and the queer against the norms and conventions of the heteronormative and the bourgeois. Kipnis's reading is based on examples of transgender and fat porn that disrupt normative codes governing legible bodies, physical desirability, and sexuality and examples from *Hustler* as the flipside of *Playboy*'s glossiness. Had Kipnis taken more mainstream material into consideration, it would have been difficult to define porn as a transgressive force. Kipnis's project of complicating interpretations of pornography remains crucial, but it is structured by the dynamics of the porn wars and does not engage with the full complexity and paradoxes of pornography as an internally split and diverse genre. Pornography risks becoming a metaphor for transgression, an unruly social fantasy pointing to the struggle of the high and the low. This almost structuralist prism makes it more difficult to account for the changing positions of high and low in terms of pornography's social visibility and cultural role, as well as pornography as forms of labor.[13] The last point is paradoxical since Kipnis's analysis is concerned with the forces and dynamics of capitalism.

As argued in the chapters above, the boundaries of so-called mainstream and alternative pornographies are malleable and elastic, yet these categories are frequently evoked as points of reference and markers of distinction in discussions on porn. A similar problem surfaces with the notion of transgression. It seems self-evident that pornography is transgressive in its breeches of the social boundaries of race or class, norms of good taste, and bourgeois body ideals. Such statements actually tell little of what such breeches may affect and what their significance may be. Transgression threatens to become a reference that is void of actual content or relevance—a marker of the subversive without reference to what is subverted, how, and to what effect.[14] The transgression of taboos—concerning social categories, appropriate or "normal" sexual acts, and the boundaries of the body—is standard fare in porn. They are expected and hence they require little uncovering. The visceral body aesthetics of porn go against the grain of those deployed in most other popular genres, yet it does not subvert them. Porn has its own conventions, modalities, and forms of display that do not make it transgressive in any general sense.

The cultural role and position of pornography have undergone important transformations since the 1990s. Pornographic styles and gestures are circulated in so-called mainstream media (for example, in advertising and music videos), and hardcore pornography is an increasingly accessible and mundane part of the media landscape. Porn has been domesticated in both its softcore and hardcore variants (albeit in different ways). Rick Poynor (2006, 132) argues that "by covering porn, the media borrows some of its dirty glamour and sense of danger, while in turn it confers legitimacy, making porn a topic of interest and discussion like any other." McNair (2002, 70) similarly argues that porno-chic—that is, ways of flirting with and borrowing from porn in other realms of popular culture—"aims to transfer the taboo, transgressive qualities of pornography to mainstream cultural production." Herein lies a paradox: given that the attraction of porn lies in its violations of public morality and taste, much of its power would be lost if it were to become accepted, mainstreamed, and familiar (McNair 2002, 42). In the context of such mainstreaming, shock pornographies can be seen as pointing at the limits of domestication.

As fetish videos, "2 Girls 1 Cup" and "Eel Soup" push the traditional definitions of the pornographic in the sense that display of genitalia or penetrative sex plays no central part in them. At the same time, they help to maintain the associations with dirt, filth, shame, and disgust related to porn on which its cultural status and attraction draws. Viral videos and the public attention they gain support the boundaries between lower and higher culture (for example, as articulated in the separation of the pornographic from the erotic). By evoking disgust, they help to mark pornography as being apart from more mainstream media culture at the very moment when such distinctions have become increasingly elastic. Something of this kind is at play in the ads for Farm Girls that claim to contain "Forbidden XXX hardcore" that is "Banned in over 51 states." Disapproval and dismay intensify the scent—or smell—of pornography as a forbidden fruit. By doing this, they reinforce the dynamic of shame, desire, and disgust that pornography targeted at heterosexual couples, publications insisting on notions of quality (such as *Playboy*), political lesbian pornography, and erotic entertainment for female consumers have done their best to dispel. Shock porn cannot be domesticated or mainstreamed, for it is too extreme, nasty, and filthy to become "a topic of interest and discussion like any other." And if the role and status of pornography necessitates censorship and articulations of disgust and disapproval, then it can be domesticated only to a degree. As such, shock sites and viral videos stand for what is outside of domestication and refuses to be housebroken.

7   Conclusions: The Tactile Grab of Online Pornography

My best friend at the age of eight had a sister and two brothers, all her senior by at least a decade. She was the baby of the family, and she performed the part by talking to her parents with a high-pitched baby voice. We went to school (third grade), had sleepovers, and played in the woods nearby. In those days, paper recycling was less organized than it is today. A few times a year, people gathered their old magazines to be collected by youth organizations that sold them for small amounts of money. Sitting on the stairs outside my friend's house in suburban Helsinki, we looked through the piles of magazines discarded by her family, really looking for one thing—the older brothers' hardcore porn magazines, which generally were stashed in the middle of the pile so that they would not be easily found. When we located these magazines, sitting on cold concrete steps (it always seems to be winter in these recollections), we contemplated their exotic images with attention and curiosity. These probably were not the first pornographic images that I ever saw—similar magazines were sold in most shops and kiosks with their covers easy to see—but they are the first ones I recall.

This was in 1983, the year the Finnish porn magazine *Erotica* gained publicity by publishing an issue that came "with smell" (*"mukana haju"*). The magazine's editor later claimed that the scent was achieved by mixing a foul perfume acquired from a bazaar in Cairo with printing ink and by storing magazines overnight in a sausage factory. The stunt was successful. Newspaper agents publicly complained of the smell, and the issue sold out (Korppi 2002, 111–116). Having heard of this wonder, my friend and I sniffed magazines in vain, perhaps looking for some odor of sex, adult pastimes, or forbidden things, but we managed to catch merely the smell of ink and paper. Some ink remained on our fingers, as if—suspected of misconduct—we had had our fingerprints taken. The sense of the secrecy of our activities added considerably to the titillation. The magazines were at times confusing, but we were not appalled. As part of the world of teenage boys and adults, the magazines were not meant for us to see, and they made us giggle nervously.

After several magazine collections, my friend's mother noticed what we were up to. Upset, she phoned my mother, who was more amused than horrified. My parents subscribed to the porno-chic discourse of the 1970s, and they have often told the story of screening Super 8mm porn films imported from Germany on the living room wall of their new house with their friends before even setting up the curtains to keep away the curious eyes of neighbors. After my best friend and I were caught, my friend's mother at some point suggested that my friend should spend less time with me. Although the magazines were not the central reason that our friendship slowly disintegrated, I was left feeling that I had somehow corrupted my friend, the baby of the family—oddly enough, with her brothers' magazines that were sitting by the door of their house.

For some readers, this narrative may seem like a feminist "coming to consciousness story" that develops from childhood fascination and subjection to sexist fantasies to feminist revelation—an awakening from false consciousness. But although the body aesthetics of 1980s porn may not be my cup of tea, my relationship to porn continues to be marked by interest and curiosity. The adult lure of pornography may have long since disappeared, yet different kinds of affect remain, and pornography has the power to move me. For other readers, this story may be read as one of childhood soiled and even of parental neglect that made it possible for children to encounter pornographic materials. For still others, this anecdote may be another piece of evidence that the Nordic countries are a realm of sexual and pornographic abundance.[1] My point is that I grew up in a culture or at least a family where pornography was a mundane issue, although definitely something not meant for children. I may have been a white, middle-class girl with blond hair and a penchant for pink clothes, but—unlike my best friend in her parents' eyes—I would not have passed for a "hapless cherub" of the sort discussed in chapter 2. I probably came across more as an exemplar of Freud's polymorphous perverse child. As Lee Edelman notes, the figure of a child is a creature separate from empirical children, a cultural ideal of a kind. Factual children are interested in the world beyond the constraints set by this ideal and are fascinated by the "gross" and the sexual (Lamb 2001). There is a considerable difference between intentionally encountering sexually explicit materials and being violated by them. The story makes evident the centrality of context and framework for encounters with porn. My early explorations were characterized by the lack of an explanatory framework. Those in the know could find porn, which, fascinating as it was in its adult appeal, left me rather clueless. The titillation of porn was increased by the risk of being found out and potentially punished. Porn—this forbidden fruit of crumbled magazines—gained some transgressive force through the setting of limits, especially since the logic of these limits demarcating proper behavior was never explained.

Without continuing further on this autobiographical detour, I would like to point out some things arising from it. First is that of framework: although I write on pornography in English, the cultural context from which I come and where I continue to live is not one where pornography is necessarily considered a social ill, nor are discussions concerning it predominantly marked by moral panics. I believe that entering studies of porn from the framework of Finnish discourses on sexuality that emphasize "sexual health" (as active sexuality, see Paasonen 2009) rather than the "tired binary" (Juffer 1998, 2) of antiporn and anti-antiporn positions makes it easier to investigate questions such as appeal, mixed feelings, and passionate discourse. Second, my autobiographical narrative points to the appeal of the forbidden fruit, as discussed throughout this book—to the attraction of the prohibited and the dirty, which, for me, explains a great deal of pornography's cultural status and appeal. Third, there is the broad question of pornography and pedagogy—porn as a site and form of learning. Fourth is the question of tactility, media, and mediation. This final chapter revisits the two last issues, in particular—the relationship of porn and habits and the notions of tactility (the modalities and pull of online porn, its grab and resonance).

Familiarity and Habit

In the previous chapters, online porn has been addressed as balancing documentary realism and authenticity (of bodies, acts, and pleasures). These are supported by the promises of directness that are associated with the Internet as a medium, and the ubiquitous modalities of excess, hyperbole, and spectacle (desires knowing no bounds, taboos transgressed, and sexual acts performed in abundance). Aiming to grab the attention of its viewers, porn plays knowingly with the modality of filth, scum, and nastiness, highlights it, associates it with sexual acts and the people performing them, and meshes notions of disgust with those of titillation and pleasure. Familiar porn conventions and recognizable "types" (such as the housewife, MILF, and coed) give rise to a strong sense of familiarity, repetition, and predictability. This is also why examples that do not comply with such conventions or somehow disrupt them stand out. The grab of porn is dependent on seemingly omnipresent conventions and formulas.

Mariah, a Finnish porn performer and producer with a decade-log career (1996–2006), noted in a radio show that we did together that she wanted to alter the routine choreography of heteroporn in her videos but that this had not been easy. For the videos to appeal to their customer base, which represented middle-of-the-road porn rather than a specialized niche, certain things needed to be included. Even seemingly minor alterations—such as not having female performers wear high heels—required negotiation. This is telling of how deeply sedimented some porn conventions remain: no matter how randomly they have come about, high heels and cum shots assumedly need to occur for porn to feel like porn. These conventions are contingent—new technologies push the boundaries of how porn can be produced, distributed, and consumed, new numbers are introduced, and body styles alter—yet much also remains the same.

There is an often repeated truism, "Porn is boring," that is articulated by people who study, make, and consume porn. Paradoxically, a genre intending to arouse though visceral gut reactions regularly fails as its repetitive and predictable features give way to a feeling of *déjà-vu* that flattens the affective dynamics involved in watching it. Drawing on Vivian Sobchack's synesthetic conceptualization of experiencing film through the senses beyond vision, Linda Williams (2008) frames experiences of on-screen sex as bodily pedagogy. *To habituate* means to accustom by frequent repetition or prolonged exposure: it is a matter of practice and process. Habit stands for a recurrent, often unconscious pattern of behavior acquired through repetition. Sexual practices are also a matter of habit—routines and choreographies that are repeated and tested. Although habits are contingent, they are not simply matters of choice. Marked by orientations, preferences, experiences, memories, traumas, dialogic relations, the desires of intimate others, things seen and read, fantasies, and carnal resonances, they are part and parcel of what we are and the somatic archives that we live with.

Following Peirce's theory of signs, Teresa de Lauretis (1994, 300) identifies three different effects of signs—emotional (intensities of feeling), energetic (mental or muscular effort or exertion), and habit change (modification of one's tendencies toward action on the basis of past experiences). Adapting this discussion to experiences of pornography, the two first effects describe affective states, gut reactions, and feelings evoked by porn (from disgust, interest, and shame to sexual arousal and attempts to curb it), and the third to the habits, habituations, and habit changes that they inspire. According to de Lauretis (1994, 301–302), habit change "makes sense out of the emotion and muscular/mental effort that precedes" it as the result of a somatic-mental process of sensing and making sense of the world. In encounters with pornography, one's somatic archives remain open to habit changes and also orient the directions that such changes may take. Encounters with images and moments of being moved and disturbed entail volatility and potentiality of change. Watching porn, we habituate to its images, but we also take more pleasure in some images and ignore and resist others. As viewers, we oriented ourselves toward the images, and as these orientations change, so do the resonances involved.

In the work of both Williams and de Lauretis, encounters with cultural images are simultaneously somatic and semiotic. They are felt in the body and also involve acts, histories, and conventions of representation. This book is premised on the inseparability of sensing and making sense, the affective and the semiotic. Affect involves and forges relations between people, texts, values, norms, and artifacts. And since affect and touch, texture and sensation go hand in hand, the "feel" and grab of porn images are not minor concerns. Affective intensities such as resonance and dissonance are matters of materiality—how and which bodies resonate and what kinds of materializations these resonances involve.

Material Resonance

As digital pornography circulates—through films purchased on DVD, streaming video, clips and longer videos, and files (transferred in P2P networks, zipped, saved on hard drives, or burned on a DVD)—it both materializes in different ways and facilitates particular kinds of affective encounters.

Paraphrasing Karen Barad with some liberties, pornography involves intra-actions between bodies producing and consuming images, bodies perform-ing and depicted, the technologies used in creating and mediating porn, images previously seen and experienced, the circulation of money, notions of cultural value, taste, and social hierarchies, and practices of regulation. This nexus is rife with inner contradictions and tensions. Meaning is not a property of pornographic images, texts, or videos but is something that is made possible through specific material practices (Barad 2007, 148)— of theorizing, choosing examples for analysis, juxtaposing and comparing images with others, interrogating regulatory discourses, and considering affective resonances and intensities. The media do much more than "medi-ate" (as a channel of some kind). They involve different materializations of what is encountered on a screen or page.

The Consider, for example, the porn magazines mentioned in the beginning of this chapter. These early memories are impossible to decouple from the feel of the glossy pages (slightly moist and sticky from their exposure to the natural elements), the smell of ink and paper, and the sounds made when the pages were turned. In these memories, texture, sensation, fascination, and pictorial content stick firmly together and give rise to a particular sense of materiality. In fact, I recall the haptic and the olfactory more clearly than the subject matter of the images. Encountering the same magazines today would be a different matter altogether. They would have different kind of materiality and resonance. Encountering the magazines' images online, I probably would be unable to make the connection.

The carnal resonance of pornography is a question of subject matter but also one of tactile and material feel. Luciana Parisi and Tiziana Ter-ranova (2001, 124) argue that digital culture "presents an intensification of the material qualities of the image." The materiality that the authors are referring to is not the texture of images as tangible objects but rather their affective intensity—their power to move between and affect various bodies. Understood in this vein, digital images become sensed "as matter (a matter of information), and matter as dynamic or 'informational'" (Clough 2003, 362, emphasis in the original) and are always in a state of becoming in encounters with bodies, forces, and images. For Parisi and Terranova (2001, 125), the intensification of the material qualities of digital images is due to their relative autonomy from the regimes of representation and identifica-tion. Unlike photochemical records, they are no longer tied to notions of the real. I agree with the point on identification, yet because the appeal and materiality of porn are linked closely to its indexical and iconic aspects (that is, its promise to act as a document and proof of what has been), this definition does not apply to considerations of online porn.

Digital files go through considerable transformations as their format and properties change. Consequently, they also materialize in different ways. The spam email archive serves as a good example. My decision to archive the advertising messages as screen captures has limited my ability to contextualize their origins and locations since I have no way of knowing what URLs the messages were actually linked to. The porn sites advertised in the spam messages may not be the ones doing the spamming, since spammers recycle the images, texts, and layouts of porn sites' "free tour" sections to generate traffic to their own sites with the aid of email, links, redirected URLs, and pop-ups (Chun 2006, 125; Bonik and Schaale 2007). Whether the spam messages were used for these ends is impossible for me to know, since they are cut off from their links and circulation. Having initially been sent as emails coded in HTML and including active hypertext, links, and, in some cases, animated GIFs, the files have been captured as screen shots and archived as JPG and TIFF files. In other words, I have grabbed the messages in a rather concrete way and, by doing so, altered them. Although the image resolution remains the same (72 dpi), they have been fundamentally transformed in the act of archiving. These are no longer email messages but static still images—representations—of emails. The animated features or hyperlinks no longer work. The long messages that required scrolling down have been archived as several files, which adds to the sense and feel of discontinuity.

Over the years, this spam archive has been stored on several computers, external hard drives, and flash drives. The files have been exhibited on computer screens and projected onto larger screens when embedded in slides. Storage formats, modes and spaces of display, and screen settings and resolutions have all altered the ways that viewers can experience and make sense of the material. These transformations make evident my own active role in crafting my research material. Rather than simply archiving what was there and transparently making it available for future revisiting, I have actively molded the material. The current static condition of the spam material contrasts with the dynamic and viral nature of spam email more generally: it is of different materiality and resonance. The spam archive is heavy with traces of my multiple practices of engagement. Following Barad (2007), intra-action and entanglement with one's object of research are part of the phenomena produced.

My scholarly accountability first involves having created the research material (as a sample and an archive) as one with particular properties. It also extends to making evident the affordances and effects of different research methods—that is, the ways in which my deployment of different methods and approaches "performs" the spam material into being as a certain kind, gives rise to different relationships between the researcher and the material, and facilitates certain analytical paths (as is evident in chapters 4 and 5, in particular). My accountability equally involves accounting for the ways in which the phenomenon of pornography is performed into being in the course of research. With intra-action, Barad (2007, 139) refers to activity through which "the boundaries and properties of the components of phenomena become determinate" and "particular concepts (that is, particular material articulations of the world) become meaningful." In other words, my intra-actions with the porn spam email messages, porn sites, images, videos, and stories discussed in this book have given shape to online pornography as a phenomenon with particular properties, intensities, boundaries, and modalities.

The Grab of Media

Carnal resonance in pornography is not simply about bodies resonating with one another since there is always the aspect and activity of mediation to consider. Images do not have structure (in the sense of grammar or syntax), yet the practice of putting videos and photos together involves rules and conventions, including framing, focus, panning, zooming, and a variety of editing styles. When considering the resonance at play in online porn, it is therefore necessary to consider how the images have been put together, what kinds of representational conventions have been used, and how these may have evolved and traveled from one medium to another. This leads to questions concerning the properties of the media addressed, the uses that they facilitate, and the forms of experience that they afford. The process of mediation is intimately connected with the technological horizons of possibility—that is, different media technologies afford and enable some activities and not others. It involves acts of production, whether scripting, haphazard and automated practices of recording, and the modalities and intensities of media and their mutual differences. Networked platforms, for example, differ from VCRs and print in their experiences of use and inter-action possibilities. Mediation is also about the sensations of connection, presence, and realness that surface in encounters with pornography.

The forms and experiences of using the Internet involve engagements and tactile interactions that are not directly comparable to, say, choosing a television channel or engaging with cinematic fiction. One can watch TV shows and films online, and the qualities of streaming media resonate with other screen-based practices. Considered from the perspective of represen-tation, online porn is closely connected to magazines, videos, photos, and films. The same content is repurposed and circulated, and acts, poses, and positions are reenacted in one medium after another. The differences are on the level of media forms, technological makeup, communication forms, and the intensities and sensations of usage. Users do not merely choose a video to watch, as one might do with VHS, DVD, or a pay channel. Instead, they search, browse (through sites, listings, and directories), bookmark, click, download, upload, leave comments, rate, log in, and compare. At the same time, Internet usage is not constant discussion, posting, rating, and uploading but largely, especially in the case of online porn, just look-ing. As Michele White (2006, 8–9) argues, lurking, reading, and viewing are the most common modes of user engagement. However, even "when 'just viewing' or 'lurking,' one actively sends and receives data (all spectators are still visible—the degree of their visibility, or more properly their trace-ability, is the issue)" (Chun 2006, 98). When searching for, reading, and looking at something, we make our movements and choices visible. We are in the network even when we do not actively upload files, post on forums, log in, or interact with other users.

When addressing the pleasures and frustrations involved in searching for porn, Zabet Patterson (2004, 109) argues that "the structure of many porn sites seems to be to direct and cater to the viewer's desires for delay and deferral by allowing the process of searching to exist under the aegis of the goal of 'getting what they want,' but in excess of it." In Patterson's view, the act of searching involves promises of both novelty and perfect satisfac-tion. Since each image and video ultimately remains inadequate in relation to one's fantasies and the utopian state of satisfaction, one keeps search-ing. This future tense of potentiality and possibility is central to porn, yet

I feel that Patterson's analysis downplays the visceral sensations derived from porn that is searched for, downloaded, and consumed. Desire may be impossible to satisfy—being a dynamic of perpetual intensity—yet sexual arousal and momentary gratification are much easier to accomplish. Rather than delay and deferral, I see the uses of online porn as a matter of tactile engagement, grab, rhythm, and resonance. It involves user activity: users download videos, grab documents and files with bookmarks and in screen grabs, occasionally interact with one another, and grab themselves (hence the "grab your dick and double-click" in the musical *Avenue Q* and the *World of Warcraft* machinima video discussed at the beginning of chapter 2). At the same time, the question is equally one of the grab, pull, and force of pornography to move and touch those interacting with it through rhythm and resonance.

Laura Kipnis makes use of the notion of grab when describing the power of porn as something that "grabs us and doesn't let go. Whether you're revolted or enticed, shocked and titillated, these are flip sides of the same response: an intense visceral engagement with what pornography has to say. And pornography has quite a lot to say" (Kipnis 1999, 161). This visceral grab, discussed throughout this book as resonance, cuts through pornographies that are produced and distributed in a range of media. Porn disturbs and gets on and under one's skin, although I would not identify this resonance as speech. Porn does not speak for the reason that the semantic and the linguistic remain secondary to its fleshy depiction and appeal. Calling its affective dynamics speech undermines its specificity and directs analytical attention toward language at the expense of visceral intensities. As argued in chapter 5, although porn involves representation and meaning, its resonances cannot be reduced to them, for visceral (and hence extra-linguistic) excess is perpetually present.

This book has tried to account for the particular grab and pull of online porn, centrally through Theresa M. Senft's definition of *grab* as a characteristic of the dynamics of looking and being seen online. According to Senft (2008, 46), to "grab is to grasp, to snatch, to capture. Grabbing occurs over the Web in different ways during each stage of production, consumption, interpretation, and circulation." Images and videos are grabbed (or ripped) from their original contexts of distribution, circulated on other forums, altered, and commented on. Digital images are impossible to control in their circulation and "social afterlife" (Klastrup 2007) as they are grabbed and reused. Grabbing, as discussed by Senft, refers to clutching with the hand—that is, to tactile interaction—and it is effected by both online materials and their users. To grab is "to command attention, to touch—often inappropriately, sometimes reciprocally" (Senft 2008, 46)—as on porn sites aiming to grab users by the eyeballs by showcasing novelties, extremities, and oddities. This attention economy of perpetual novelty and curiosity results in affective intensities of interest, shock, titillation, disgust, and curiosity. The grab of porn images is felt in the body—at times as inappropriate and at other times as reciprocal.

As they use the Internet—browsing through thumbnail galleries, clicking on links to other sites, reading descriptions of available torrents,[2] trying to find arresting images, and tagging videos and downloading them—porn users are seeking what grabs them and what they want to grab in return (figure 7.1). When doing so, their IP addresses are being grabbed, and their movements tracked. Although they can remove cookies and clear their browsing history, traces of their routes through and within sites linger on through agents such as Google that constantly archive and analyze massive amounts of user data. The arresting sensation of being grabbed (by porn and by the Internet) and the catching gesture of grabbing are quintessentially

Figure 7.1
Torrents to grab and download (http://www.porntorrents.ws)

ones of resonance. *Resonance* and *grab* are my preferred terms for addressing the power and force of pornography to move those watching. Both concepts frame this movement as two-directional: as involving the orientations and activities of users and the appeal of sites, videos, images, and networked communication. This affective dynamic is contingent and often disturbing. It attaches people, images, and media technologies together, draws them apart, grabs our attention, resonates with our somatic archives, and allows us to grab digital files in return.

Notes

Chapter 1

1. http://rulesoftheinternet.com/index.php5?title=Main_Page.

2. The history of pornography is more complex than one sentence can possibly convey. Some of these historical developments and connections are addressed in the following chapters, but this is not primarily a book on the histories of pornography. For such treatises, see Hunt (1996), Kendrick (1996), Williams (1989), O'Toole (1998), and Sigel (2005).

3. See Jacobs (2007) and Jacobs et al. (2007) for discussions of fringe, niche, artistic, activist, and subcultural online pornographies.

4. This is partly the case because artistic and experimental pornographies speak to the interests of scholars studying porn while such rapport may be more difficult to establish with commercial and mainstream agents. Florian Cramer (2006, 134) argues that the "interests of art and commercial enterprise, of artists and sex workers, of sex industry and cultural criticism seem to blend into each other" as porn performers present in academic seminars and researchers analyze their works. As Cramer points out, this leads to a general lack of conflict, and the potentially provocative elements of such interactions disappear from view.

5. It is not warranted to categorize the work of scholars such as Richard Dyer (1993), Annette Kuhn (1994), or Stuart Hall (1997) with notions of mirroring or judgment. Considerations of popular media's ability to move and touch its audience cut across Dyer's work, while Kuhn exemplifies self-reflexive scholarly agency, and Hall remains very much concerned with the mutually constitutive forces of material realities, histories and systems of representation, and ways of perceiving oneself and others. The tradition of British cultural studies that these scholars represent is not alien to an understanding of representation as a question of both meaning and doing (Abel 2007, 58), and it does not obtain unaffected objectivity.

   In *The Matter of Images: Essays on Representations*, Dyer points to the limitations of "word politics" that focus on discourse and the social construction of reality. Such work has broken with "tendencies to think of reality as out there, separate from consciousness and culture," but it risks considering words and discourses as all that there is and "forgetting that words and discourses are attempts to make sense of what are not themselves words and discourses: bodies, feelings, things" (Dyer 1993, 9–10). This is not a representationalist take on images and words as separate from the world but is one interested in how they matter and the material and emotional consequences that they have. By emphasizing the effects of cultural images and the analytical and political work concerning them, Dyer addresses the emotional, embodied, and extralinguistic (an emphasis that is also evident in his more recent work on film music). Although it would be possible to trace representationalist echoes in the separation of bodies, feelings, and things as not discourse (for, following Barad via Foucault, discourse is not merely a question of language but one of material conditions), I take it to mean that there is more to the world than language and words—for example, feelings and bodies—that we interact with and that matter (an antirepresentationalist claim).

6. Realizing this to be the case, Abel identifies the critical practice as one moving "*through* the work that representation does." Because it is impossible to break away from figuration and narrative, such practice "may perhaps be best thought of as the preconscious of representational criticism—representational criticism operating at a different speed or on a different level of intensity" (Abel 2007, 28).

7. This, again, is as much about forgetting as about remembering. Sara Ahmed (2008) argues that for authors to claim that corporeality has been reduced to social constructivism, critics need to ignore earlier scholarship on embodiment, materiality, and biology. The move to affect necessitates a move "from." What we are assumedly moving away from tends to be depicted in simplified terms as caricature (Ahmed 2008, 36). As Hemmings (2005, 555) eloquently puts it, in "the search for 'the new' that bears no resemblance to the past, the identifying features of that past are inevitably overstated, and the claims for that new embellished in ways that must at the very least fall short of rigorous."

8. This is also the case with Abel's (2007) proposal for a critique "after representation" that shifts attention away from semantics, representation, mediation, and meaning and toward affective, asignifying intensities. Contrary to his mode of masocriticism that heeds the "irreducible singularity" of the event (of the image), "representationalist judgement itself begins from outside the object or event to be judged, and the judging subject sits safely situated afar or above—unaffected and, allegedly, objective" (Abel 2007, 219). This criticism is targeted at specific forms of textual analysis, yet throughout Abel's book, it is presented as descriptive of studies of representation. Such apparently clear demarcations make it difficult to account for the diversity of approaches to representation and theorizations of sensation and interpretation outside of, or beside, the more "Deleuzian" ones.

9. Wendy Chun (2008, 323) similarly points out that, arguably, "digital media's biggest impact on our lives is not through its interface, but through its algorithmic

procedures." In other words, we do not experience technology or its effects directly, and from the perspective of users, Internet technologies remain something like black boxes.

10. My uses of the term also come close to how Adi Kuntsman (2009, 234) defines *reverberation* as movement between and through bodies, spaces, and emotions. There is also a partial connection to Jennifer Barker's (2009, 3) discussion on the affective resonances of cinema.

11. See definitions at http://www.thefreedictionary.com/resonance.

12. The cultural position of pornography has gone through evident transformations with the introduction of digital production tools, online distribution platforms, and the accumulation of pornographic images available for consumption. The last decade has witnessed an increase in the public visibility of all kinds of pornographies—centrally through and on online platforms—and also in public debates spanning from scholarly diagnoses on the mainstreaming of porn and sex (McNair 1996, 2002; Attwood 2006, 2009; Paasonen et al. 2007) to (primarily North American) nonfiction titles investigating contemporary culture as "pornified," "porned," or "raunchy" (e.g., Paul 2005; Levy 2005). Advertising borrows from the conventions of softcore porn, select porn stars gain celebrity status, and vintage porn films are released as collector's editions available from mainstream vendors. Such developments, identified as porno-chic (McNair 2002) and pornification (Paasonen et al. 2007), affect softcore and hardcore pornographies in different ways. Although popular culture flirts with the conventions of pornography, the hardcore can be mainstreamed or domesticated only to a degree. Generalized debates on pornification risk conflating these developments into one master narrative at the moment when the range and volume of pornography is inflating. For analyses of such mainstreaming to have critical edge and political relevance, they need to be specific and based on an understanding of the dynamics and media forms in question. Spaces for critical engagement with the imageries and economies of pornography remain crucial, yet they cannot be built on categorical criticisms of pornography as an assumedly fixed entity.

13. This said, people studying porn tend to do so from a distance and under the guise of invulnerability. By doing so, they fight the power of porn to get under one's skin and disturb. This position also characterizes some of my own early attempts at studying porn. The discomfort experienced in being touched or moved by the porn one studies is paradoxical in the sense that this is what the genre aims to achieve (Dyer 2002b, 138–139). Sobchack (2004, 56) notes that while physical thrills—from THX vibrations felt in the body to tears evoked by melodrama—are a central aspect and attraction of cinema-going, film theorists "seem either embarrassed or bemused by bodies that often act wantonly and crudely" and tend to efface these from their considerations of cinematic experience. This goes against the ways in which films work and are felt. A similar argument can be made for pornography outside the

framework of cinema—in still images, video clips, thumbnail galleries, webcam
streams, and stories.

14. In her criticism of the term *reflection*, Barad attaches it to a representationalist
understanding of scholarship and language as merely mirroring the world rather
than being practices located in, and shaping the world. Juxtaposing *reflection* with
diffraction at some length and depth, Barad (2007, 89–90) defines the former as
involving sameness and the latter differences, the former "reflecting on representations" and the latter "accounting how practices matter." Perhaps ironically, in the
tradition of feminist media and cultural studies that I have been trained in, representation is understood as practices that matter, and scholarly agency is seen as an
issue of accountability and implicatedness rather than outside objectivity. With self-
reflexivity, I am not pointing to acts of endless (self-)mirroring but to the role that
sensing pornography plays in making sense of it. Working with online porn, the
level of mediation—the role and effects of specific technological assemblages, histories, conventions, and practices of creating media images, the forms of experience
that the media facilitate, and tactile engagements that users have with it—is impossible to do away with. This, again, is a question of representation. Although for
some, representation is seen as a matter of imitation, likeness, and mirroring, for
others it involves embodiment, exhibition, practices of imaging, imagining, and
communication. It can be stated that contemporary critical theory is product of
reflexivity of the kind that Barad discusses as diffraction (see Hayles 1999, 8–9).

15. Browsing through the spam archive tends to reveal that a sense of the repetitive
and the formulaic dominates. Although site concepts vary and change, spam ads all
resemble one another. Most spam is repetitive in terms of the acts depicted, the terminology employed, its layout, and its use of headers, slogans, collage, links, and
image galleries. Many sites use literally the same templates. Some analytical fatigue
has been involved in my habit of archiving messages with titles such as "sameold.
jpg," "generic.jpg," and "this_again.tiff." In such instances, my intellectual agility
may indeed have suffered.

16. When criticizing studies of mediation, Brian Massumi points out the lack of the
sensing body in considerations of "reading" and "decoding," resistance and subversion, as practiced in cultural studies: "The body was seen to be centrally involved in
these everyday practices of resistance. But this thoroughly mediated body could
only be a 'discursive' body: one with its signifying gestures. Signifying gestures make
sense. If properly 'performed,' they may also unmake sense by scrambling signification already in place. Make and unmake sense as they might, they don't *sense*. Sensation is utterly redundant to their description " (Massumi 2002, 2).

I agree that theories of bodies as "text," embodied practices of signification, or
performative acts of gender (partly conceptualized through speech-act theory) have
tended to treat the body less as a biological and organic entity and more as a social
construction of one kind or another (also Barad 2007). On the one hand, a focus on
signifying bodies is necessary in studies of media, whose imageries and narratives

are conveyed with, through, and in performing bodies on the level of representation. On the other hand, a focus on the level of the screen cannot accommodate considerations of the thick materiality of bodies made of guts, bones, nerves, and blood.

17. Here my project is close kin to Katariina Kyrölä's (2010) work on body images as affective zones of contact between images and bodies in which the representational and the material cannot be distinguished from each other.

Chapter 2

1. http://www.google.com/support/websearch/bin/answer.py?answer=510.

2. A similar dynamic can be identified in academic explorations into porn. Mark Jones and Gerry Carlin (2010, 187–188) discuss their class titled "Unpopular Texts" in which they taught porn along with other examples deemed offensive, such as Enid Blyton's novel *The Three Golliwogs* and white supremacist texts. This selection made sense in terms of the aim of the class—to explore the boundaries of acceptability and the practices of policing them. At the same time, the framing of unpopularity and offensiveness fixes porn (in its multiple subcategories, styles, and local incarnations) as extreme, problematic, potentially disgusting, and even dangerous. Independent of what is said of pornography in this context, the lines of discussion have been already drawn. However, as argued throughout this book, pornography is not something already known—a stable category or a point of reference—but rather something that is continuously transforming and being mapped out in our attempts to make sense of it. If framed as both unpopular (paradoxically, in spite of its considerable and lasting popularity) and offensive, it is also pinned down, homogenized, and simplified in ways that block much of this mobility and contingency.

3. http://www.searchengineguide.com/wordtracker/top-500-search-engine-key-words-of-the-we-7.php.

4. http://mashable.com/2009/12/19/porn-toddlers.

5. The first Web browser with a graphical user interface was the little-known Erwise (1992). ViolaWWW, launched in 1991, started gradually supporting graphics. The beta version of Mosaic was launched in the spring of 1993, and it developed into Netscape Navigator (by the same developers) in 1994. Microsoft launched its Explorer in 1995.

6. People may be asked to download a special plug-in when looking at porn online (as in a thumbnail gallery), and Trojan horses and worms have been circulated in files suggestive of porn (such as "Porno Screensaver britney.scr," "Teen Porn 15.jpg.pif," or "XXX hardcore pics.jpg.exe" (see Bilogorskiy 2006).

7. As Wendy Chun (2006, 94–96) points out, children abused by the people they encounter online tend to be adolescents motivated by curiosity or rebellion rather

than "agentless" young children. In addition to parents, people convicted of child abuse tend to be "schoolteachers, coaches, and priests"—that is, people working with and trusted by children who have little need for networked communications to interact with them.

8. http://www.amazon.com/Porn-Nation-Conquering-Americas-Addiction/dp/B002PJ4NMA/ref=sr_1_1?ie=UTF8&s=books&qid=1269432263&sr=8-1.

9. Gail Dines suggests that one reason that Christian sources associate porn with addiction is that many religious men are addicted to porn (in Dines et al. 2010, 28). According to Benjamin Edelman's recent study, there are more U.S. users who subscribe to porn pay sites in states "that have enacted conservative legislation on sexuality," "where surveys indicate conservative positions on religion, gender roles, and sexuality," and "where more people agree that 'I have old-fashioned values about family and marriage' and 'AIDS might be God's punishment for immoral sexual behavior,'" with Utah topping the chart (Edelman 2009, 219).

10. Writing in 1994, Marcia Pally noted that, according to the American Library Association, AIDS and sex education information most commonly trigger acts of censorship (Pally 1994, 15).

11. In many Asian countries, pornography is associated with Western cultural dominance and the erosion of traditional values. According to Shohini Ghosh (2006, 273), in India, the word "'pornography' has rarely been used to denote the *genre* of pornography, that is, sexually explicit material produced specifically for sexual arousal. It has been used to describe material that *connotes* sex, like film songs, advertisements, cover girls, rape sequences, consensual sex and even beauty pageants." Similarly, the "porn laws" debated in Indonesia have had less to do with porn than the regulation of clothing and demeanor, such as public displays of affection (Lim 2006).

Chapter 3

1. The term has been quickly picked up as shorthand for self-made pornography that does not confine itself to the generic conventions of mainstream porn, its economy, or its distribution (Hardy 2009, 12–14).

2. http://www.seemygf.com/submit/submit-gf.php.

3. According to the terms of use:

By agreeing to this Agreement and submitting your video, or other visual or audio data (collectively, Content) to www.seemygf.com, you are granting See My GF Entertainment Inc., a Ontario based Corporation and its successors, assigns, and licensees and parent, subsidiary and other affiliated entities (See My GF), an option to elect to either (a) purchase all right, title and interest in and to the Content (Purchase); or (b) receive a non-exclusive, fully-paid, world-wide, royalty-free license (License) to publicly display, publicly perform, distribute, and reproduce your Content, portions or derivative works thereof in any manner and in any medium, including, without limitation, through physical copies such as still photos, videos, and CDs, on merchandise such as T-shirts, posters and assorted paraphernalia, by television by any means, on or via the Internet, including, without limitation, the World Wide Web, and any other two-way transmission control protocol / internet protocol (TCP/IP) based distribution network or similar networks or technologies now known or hereafter to become known, including, but not limited to, delivery via such a network to personal computers, hand-held devices, and television set-top boxes through telephone or cable lines, or wirelessly through broadband, satellite, cellular or terrestrial broadcast networks and other similar networks or technologies whether now existing or hereafter developed. You understand that the Purchase gives to See My GF, at a minimum, all of the rights granted by the License. 2. You agree that no obligation of any kind is assumed by or may be implied against See My GF because of See My GFs receipt or potential or actual review of the Content or any discussions or negotiations you may have with See My GF.

4. The concept and site and title of You.porn.com are similar to video-sharing sites (such as YouPorn) that have provided platforms for uploading and downloading amateur content along with clips of the more professionally produced kind. Established in 2006, YouPorn was identified as the largest free porn site the following year, and it has been currently listed among the 100 top sites (70 in Alexa ratings and 47 on http://mostpopularwebsites.net; the figures for PornHub are 49 and 59, respectively).

5. This can be seen as an intensified form of immaterial labor of the kind that Mark Coté and Jennifer Pybus (2007) address in the context of social media as "immaterial labor 2.0."

6. Here a personal anecdote may be in order. *Hygeia Revisited*, a 1998 Net art project that I executed with Tapio Mäkelä and wrote a large part of the HTML for, was included in the book *Web Site Graphics Now! The Best of Global Site Design*. Edited by Mediamatic and published by Thames & Hudson in 1999, the book showcased the cutting edge of contemporary site design. The site was made with basic (yet at that time, novel) JavaScript of mouseovers, rollovers, and a couple of drag and drops. All this required little technical skill (I was not then and am not now an advanced programmer), but it evidently invested the site with enough cutting-edge credibility to qualify as exemplary of global elite design at the time. This level of excellence would be exceedingly difficult to produce a couple of years later.

7. http://ideepthroat.com/aboutme.htm.

8. http://wifebucket.com/blog/staff-bios.

Chapter 4

1. Taking the notion of porno script further, porn—as a reservoir of gestures, acts, scenarios, and moves—might be considered more broadly through the notion of scripting, as used in studies of romance. According to this idea, expressions of romantic feeling are tied in with culturally available scripts concerning settings, situations, articulations of love, tenderness, and passion. These are drawn from literary and cinematic fiction, television, guidebooks, journalism, and cultural narratives

and are negotiated in practices of courtship. One thus "writes oneself into love" by associating intimate moments, events, emotions, and experiences with such scripts. Acts such as romantic walks in the moonlight are about the intermeshing of representations (romantic fiction) and lived experienced (Stacey and Pearce 1995, 13–15; Langford 1999, 142; Duncombe and Marsden 1995).

The notion of porno scripts points similarly to the blurred boundaries of the personal and the social and cultural. Explicit chat (like cybersex) tends to involve onomatopoetic typing ("ooohhh . . .") but also terms, suggestions, and expressions reverberating with the lexicon and generic elements of porn ("you're so hard"). Like "talking dirty" or setting the table for a romantic candlelight dinner, this can be seen as a script that is open for rescripting, variation, and alteration and that involves no small degree of reflexivity. The concept of scripting may be helpful in grasping aspects of legibility. A romantic moment becomes (or materializes in) one when interfacing with romantic scripts. Amateur porn feels and is recognized as porn when certain acts, phrases, or positions occur. Such incorporation of acts, moments, gestures, and scenarios into one's lived experiences is recognizable enough, and it may also help to explain some of pornography's appeal. "Scripting" is nevertheless limited in its emphasis on signification. The embodied, the affective, and the visceral are downplayed and even ignored by focusing on script as narrative and "instructive."

2. Close-up shots bring body parts in close view while framing out the rest of the body. As Jack Sargeant (2006) points out, this results in the body being shown as a "collection of zones and areas" rather than an organic whole. In his view, body parts each have their own signifying practices. Patricia MacCormack (2004) similarly argues that "genitals signify gender, skin race, entrails the forbidden chamber of the self. No part of the body fails to be invested with meaning, location, function and attached social value." Orifices such as mouth, vagina, and anus carry different connotations of cleanliness, and acts of penetrating them (or one after the other, as in the ATM shots that Sargeant addresses) involve different notions of extremity or filth. At the same time, all this exceeds the registers of signification. Reactions of disgust are in excess to the semantic and translate into language only with some effort and residue. Meanings are attached to body parts and sexual acts, yet this is only one level of activity and interaction taking place, and its forms and results are by no means fixed. As argued in the following chapters, the ways of experiencing pornography do not merely result from "acts of signification" or from decoding a set of meanings encoded in the images in their processes of production.

3. Advertisements for Black Cocks White Sluts depict the faces and bodies of white female performers engaged in penetrative sex while framing out the bodies of black men except for their penises, hands, thighs, or abdomen—a visual register already suggested by the site title. Mapping heterosexual structuralism onto notions of racial difference, the ad features images of fellatio embedded into the shapes of a black and white jigsaw puzzle. The ad for White Pussy Black Cocks, again, presents a gal-

lery of twelve images both in color and in black and white, altering in size and partly merging with text fields. The largest image on the top left shows the hands and penis of a man and the head of a blonde woman. Her eyes are closed, her lips slightly apart, and she is pushing her chin forward. The man is holding her head down with his left hand and holding his penis, connected to the woman's mouth by a trail of semen and saliva, in the right. Although the other images in the ad present the visual juxtaposition of black penises with pink vulvas, this cum shot presents the viewer with an ambiguous racialized spectacle. The hue of the man's skin is only slightly darker than the woman's and could well exemplify the convention of depicting white men as masculine, strong, and always slightly darker than their female counterparts (Dyer 1997, 57, 132–140). In this instance, race is articulated verbally rather than visually: the verbal mark of blackness sticks to the skin and turns it into a sign of difference.

4. The figure of the huge and hard black penis taps into racialized dynamics and a contingent reservoir of cultural stereotypes (see Bhabha 1994; Gilman 1985). Although Fanon's analysis was historically specific, his observations have been frequently applied to readings of pornography that has been produced in a variety of frameworks (e.g., Fung 1991; Mercer 1994; Williams 2004b). For Kobena Mercer (1994, 134, 149), the intertwining of white fears and fantasies in the figure of the "monstrous" black penis explains some of its centrality in pornographic imagery.

5. Discussing the film *Let Me Tell Ya 'bout White Chicks* (1984), which presents black men as pimps and thieves lusting after white women, Williams (2004c, 281–284) recognizes its use of regressive stereotypes but argues that its displays of sex between black men and white women is a fantasy and that this fantasy is not solely the property of white men. In her analysis of the film's spin-off, *Let Me Tell Ya 'Bout Black Chicks* (1985), Mireille Miller-Young proposes a slightly different interpretation. The Dark Brothers, who made both films, addressed their interracial video porn to white consumers and did so by knowingly depicting black characters as caricatures. According to Miller-Young (2007, 38, 40), this resulted in a particular kind of racial political theater that was both produced and consumed by white men. Rather than reworking the complex dynamics of sexuality, race, and gender in the United States, the film rendered black women as markers of racial difference, taboo, and sexual excess. As Miller-Young's analysis shows, the question is not what the meanings of the videos are (as "fantasy," "racist," or something else) inasmuch as what their reverberations are with both histories of representation and the social hierarchies lived, performed, and experienced.

6. Following Stuart Hall (1996, 21, 24; 1997), it can be suggested that the visual signs of blackness are constructed through fantasy and equally through the discourse of racism and that the two may be impossible to decouple. The excessive sexualization of black men and women can be identified as a historical trope drawing on colonialism, slavery, and racism. This trope has been molded for a number of different uses, including that of the figure of the black macho (aggressively sexual,

hard, and dangerous) in the black power movement. As Michele Wallace (1999, 35) points out, this was a figure of authority and power, a superheterosexual man who was freed from histories of slavery: "Here was a black man with an erect phallus, and he was pushing it up in America's face" (Wallace 1999, 36). The figure of the black macho lives on in gangsta iconography and in pornographic niches such as hip-hop porn (Härmä 2007).

Advertisements for Gangbang Squad, with the slogan "We're packin' rods lookin' for victims," hark back to the figure of black macho when outlining sexual inner-city adventures. These ads feature both African American and Latino performers, whereas its verbal markers of blackness are (once again) more certain: "Mereisa has a boyfriend, but that didn't stop her from taking on 4 big black cocks in all her holes." In contrast to whiteness, a category policed with some vigilance, blackness has historically been a highly protean and elastic category signifying the nonwhite (Dyer 1997, 25). As if following this maxim, the category of blackness in Gangbang Squad is flexible and works to construct sociability, even group identity. The term *gangbang* has become synonymous with *group sex* or *orgy* and is routinely used in porn sites. At the same time, *gangbang* still connotes *rape*, and this innuendo is supported by the terminology of *hunters* and their (willing) *victims*. While referencing the stereotype of black men as sexual predators, the ad displaces it by posing female participation as voluntary and motivated by desire, pleasure, and money.

7. Cf. Said (1995, 207–208, 222) and Sawhney (1995, 200–202). The notion of genital jewels can be traced back to Denis Diderot's *Les bijoux indiscrets* (1748): here the "indiscreet jewels"' are vaginas telling the truth about female sexuality.

8. Marcia Pally (1994, 39) aptly points out the fluidity and contingency of such definitions by asking, "Is a woman inviting intercourse subordinate, in love, or commanding? Is oral or anal sex 'normal'?"

9. The makers of stag films were similarly "pornified": *Wonders of the Unseen World* (1927) was "Seduced by A. Prick," "Directed by Ima Cunt," and "Photographed by R. U. Hard," while the team of *A Free Ride* (1915) included A. Wise Guy (director) and Will B. Hard (photographer) (Di Lauro and Rabkin 1976, 50–51).

10. For example, http://www.efukt.com/2362_Intruder_Alert.html.

11. Sontag has been justly criticized for dismissing the gay histories of camp. Her emphasis is on the individual experiences and pleasures of "camping," and the essay fails to address gay camp beyond "a peculiar affinity and overlap" between camp and homosexuality and discussing authors such as Isherwood and Wilde (Sontag 1999, 64; see Frank 1993; Meyer 1996; Cleto 1999, 10, 17–18). Authors following Esther Newton (1972) tied the notion of camp in with gay urban histories, while others, like Mark Booth (1983, 20), criticized Sontag for popularizing the "unhelpful" idea of camp's gay origins. Another point of Sontag's that has gathered much criticism and for the same reasons is her definition of camp as "disengaged, depoliti-

cized—or at least apolitical" (Sontag 1999, 54; see Bergman 1993; Meyer 1996). Contrary to what many camp practitioners understand themselves to be doing, Sontag frames out political uses of camp. In his introduction to *The Politics and Poetics of Camp* (a book bearing a veritable 1990s cultural studies title, post Stallybrass and White), Moe Meyer (1996, 7) accuses Sontag of having killed off "the binding referent to Camp—the Homosexual—and the discourse began to unravel as Camp became confused and conflated with rhetorical and performative strategies such as irony, satire, burlesque, and travesty." In Meyer's view, camp is queer by definition and engaged with queer visibility.

12. This is a recurring theme. Consider, for example, The Bait Bus (www.baitbus.com), a gay reality site where "guys" are lured into a minivan with promises of sex with an attractive woman on camera. Blindfolded, they soon realize that they are in fact having oral sex with a man. The upset "victims" are then promised money, and the action proceeds to anal sex (with the "victim" on top). After the cum shots have been recorded, the van stops, and the man is pushed out. Claiming to bring "straight boys over to the dark side," Bait Bus is part practical joke and part fantasy that plays with the contingency of straightness and straight male identity in particular:

So what is it about straight boys that makes us want to corrupt them sooo badly?? I digress. . . . I don't mean corrupt. I mean defile. I mean make them switch teams on their knees in the dugout. And the million dollar question of what will it take to get this straight boy to see the light at the end of the dark tunnel? Well, alot (sic) less than you . . . may . . . think. And that then begs the question. . . . if it was this easy to turn you, then maybe you always really wanted it. Yeah, you wanted it . . . cowboy. . . .

13. http://thesaurus.com/browse/straight.

14. In her analysis of Annabel Chong's star image, Celine Parreñas Shimizu (2007, 164) argues that, by initiating the gangbang in the 1995 film, she took the hypersexuality associated with Asian women to the extreme in an embrace of whoredom as a feminist practice. Shimizu unravels representations of Asian American women, including the nineteenth-century figure of a female Chinese prostitute, Japanese and Korean war brides, more recent mail-order brides and sex workers, and histories of stage shows, stag films, and porn films with their dragon ladies, prostitutes, and dominatrixes. For Shimizu (2007, 176–181), Chong's athletic performance fulfills "the extreme perverse expectations for racialized sexuality" while also facilitating critical agency (even if seriously weakened by the fact that Chong was never fully paid for the work she did). In this framework, excess becomes a way of working through the racialization and hypersexualization of Asian porn performers.

Chapter 5

1. Reality Kings sites and gonzo porn in general tend to be focalized through the perspective of white, predominantly American men (the *me* and *I* also performing in the videos), as is also the case with Captain Stabbin:

Me and my crew go out to find hot young backdoor virgins and get then aboard SS Stabbin for some fun in the sun. We sail for the open seas, get what we want and throw the pretty girls out to sea and let them swim back to shore.

In this homosocial fantasy, women are lured onboard to have sex with men, and when the (male) climax is over and recorded, the women are disposed of. The concept is presented with some humor, and the narrative is somewhat fantastic. The first advertisement for the site in my archive is dominated by a large image of a naked woman being pushed off a boat, accompanied by a headline text "Captain Stabbin: fucking girls in the ass on the open seas and making them walk the plank." The photograph is complete with drawings of shark fins—a visual motif that is artificial, excessive, and sadistic. In the ad, the "plunge" is presented as a climax equal to anal penetration and money shots. The narration of Captain Stabbin is in the first-person singular, and the ad is focalized and anchored in the figure of the captain himself—a white man in his late forties or early fifties wearing a white captain's hat, sunglasses, black shorts, and a white t-shirt covering his wide midriff. The captain and his crew, "1st mate Pounder" and "2nd mate Hunter," invite users to follow the action and the "newest booty." In contrast to the exclusive use of male narrators, the message sender names are female. The subject lines are brief descriptions of the events from the female performers' perspective, some of them involving direct invitations to the recipient: "When he whipped out his big fat schlong I told him to put it in my assh [sic]" (from Wendy Aspump); "He said my ass was so fine he wanted to do me anal on his boat" (from Kammy Bootie); "He marveled at my tight tanktop and I gasped when he put it in the butt" (from Leslie Nutcruncher); "If you shove it in my p00per, I'll lick it when you unload" (from Monica Sweetpoo); "Feeling him slide in and out of my butt made me climax" (from Marsha Modik).

2. In contrast, high-production-quality videos make repeated use of villas, outdoor swimming pools, and expensive cars as settings and props for sexual acts, creating a pornotopia of wealth and affluence.

3. Fragmentation and close-up shots are clearly an issue of explicitness. This representational convention has been identified as characteristic of hardcore. For example, in 1988, Rautakirja, the main distributor of magazines in Finland, ruled that it would allow porn magazines in its selection to feature images of intercourse only when the partners' bodies were not cropped (Kontula and Kosonen 1994, 270; Korppi 2002, 172–173). Meat shots would not be distributed.

4. Film scholar John Ellis pointed out some three decades ago that the directness of pornographic imagery (close-ups of labia) questions the basis of Mulvey's argument that revolves around castration anxiety and women's lack of a penis: "Yet in every other respect, current visual pornography maintains the kind of textual structure that Mulvey associates with fetishism" (Ellis, 1980, 98–99; also Williams 1989, 82).

5. This is something that Mulvey herself has expressed some concern over (see White 2006, 40).

6. In her *The Body and the Screen* (2006), Michele White argues for Internet usage as spectatorship—looking and reading—contrary to visions of users in control of the medium actively discussing and creating content. Drawing on feminist cinema and television studies, White charts the representational aspects of the Internet, the ways in which users are positioned and addressed, the kinds of dynamics of looking (and the gaze) that are involved, and the ways that social categories tied in with the representational continue to matter. This analysis highlights certain aspects of Internet usage and the visual experiences that it involves, yet it does not fully allow for investigations of the material and the affective as something that comes into being and is sensed in interactions with online platforms and digital media.

7. Similarly, the form of narrative cinema continues to function as an internal norm in studies of pornography because film scholars have been particularly active in investigating the genre, its history, and its development. Linda Williams (2008, 312) identifies developments such as the video porn of the 1980s and the online porn of the 2000s as involving little interest in narrative, aiming mainly to make their users "come," and hence marking a departure from the "big screen" pornography of the 1970s. This definition is apt, yet I would argue that the lack of interest in narrative and the intention of facilitating sexual climax are characteristic of pornography both before and after the era of 35mm porn films, from porn magazines to interactive webcam chats. As I see it, rather than representing a golden age of pornographic style and form, narrative cinema has been merely one form among many others. It is by no means given that films with narrative and character construction would be "good porn" in the sense of sexually arousing their viewers and aiding them to climax.

8. Video has not fared well in comparisons between the eras and aesthetics of film and video pornography. According to adult filmmaker Ed Peroo, for example, "film had soul; video has nothing. . . . It flows like water, but film had a texture, a feeling, something you could grab onto and feel" (in McNeil and Osborne 2005, 369; also Kleinhans 2006, 155; Paasonen and Saarenmaa 2007, 30). The image quality of early video porn was grainy, and its sound was harsh. In the late 1990s, video cameras allowed an image quality that approximated the standards of broadcast TV, and the quality of streaming video lagged clearly behind. Files buffering slowly and timing out were more the rule than the exception until the era of broadband connections in the 2000s. The current increase in high-definition online pornography has further challenged the status of DVD distribution, while the "classic works" of film pornography are enjoyed as collectors' editions.

9. Using the form of narrative cinema as a point of departure is not very helpful for anyone who is untangling these connections. This point is illustrated in the chapter on "small screen sex" in Williams's otherwise insightful book, *Screening Sex*. This concluding chapter on sexuality and cinema broadens to investigate interactive DVD pornography and online porn, yet it does not explore their specific properties.

This results in a somewhat anecdotal treatment of interactive pornography that I find difficult to map onto my own encounters with online pornography. On the basis of these I would for example contest the argument that online porn "sacrifices arresting spectacles of nudity, masturbation, and sex for more everyday activities like brushing hair and primping" (Williams 2008, 316). Such remarks stand out in unflattering contrast to the careful film analyses presented elsewhere in the book.

10. This is a matter of taste. In the interviews carried out during the Pornography in Australia research project, female porn users were more likely to identify narrative and credible characters as criteria of good porn, whereas others argued that stories were unimportant and got in the way of their viewing pleasures (McKee et al. 2008, 42–43).

11. In subgenres such as hip-hop pornography (Härmä 2007), music and the rhythm of the sexual acts are edited into a coherent choreography.

12. On the one hand, Barthes (1981, 43) claims that "*punctum* shows no preference for morality or good taste" and "can be ill-bred." On the other hand, his dismissal of the pornographic as not having the power to truly move its viewers seems to be derived from preconceived cultural hierarchies of value (that are embedded in notions of good taste).

13. Feminist authors writing about their own porn watching have found it easier to account for disturbing rather than arousing experiences (e.g., McClintock 1993). Following Sobchack's call for an embodied relation to films, Linda Williams (2008, 24, 124) addresses films that have "literally and figuratively 'made sense'" to her "as forms of carnal knowledge"—or, as in the case with *Deep Throat*, turned her on. In *Netporn*, Katrien Jacobs (2007) writes about her fondness for particular kinds of pornographies. Mark McLelland (2006) writes on what he perceives as the best Web site for men who have sex with men. It is telling of the difficult balance between personal writing and the legacy of the porn wars that not many other examples of scholarly fondness for particular kinds of pornographies spring readily to mind.

14. I have previously written on moments of being touched and imprinted by the porn that I study. These have been the exceptional incidents, such as an image of "sneaker fucking" that Sergio Messina archived from an alt.fetish newsgroup and that I have, since 2005, had an intimate fascination with (Paasonen 2010a) and examples of porn spam advertisements that fail to conform to the bulk (Paasonen 2007). These investigations have made it evident that there is more to the visual properties of porn than the neat divisions of punctum and stadium or the optic and the haptic allow for. These frameworks are helpful in grasping the ways in which we are moved by images but far less impressive if taken as "structural guidelines" for categorizing them.

15. I am indebted to Leif Dahlgren for this point on craft.

Chapter 6

1. In Ana J. Bridges's (2010, 46) content analysis of contemporary hardcore hetero-porn, as many as 41 percent of all scenes included ATM.

2. I address spam email advertisements for animal porn sites, the boundaries of the human and the animal, and the ethical issues involved in bestiality in Paasonen (forthcoming). Because this material is not representative of the mainstream, I have excluded it from the materials discussed in this book.

3. The story of Mr. Hands is depicted in the semidocumentary film *Zoo* (USA 2007, directed by Robinson Devor).

4. Dean (2000, 130, 156–157) sees both pornography and gay male bodies as symbolic violations of the social body and hence objects of nausea.

5. In their discussion on the fetishization of ejaculate in contemporary porn, Lisa Jean Moore and Juliana Weissbein (2010, 86) posit semen as "ultimately toxic" for the same reasons.

6. In general, sex involves the possibility of losing control. As Miller (1997, 103) notes, the facial expressions and spasmic movements of those abandoning to physical pleasure are not representative of the model of a self-controlling rational modern subject. All this involves the risk of shame.

7. The nasty girl and the chaste maiden can be seen as further variations of the figures of Justine and Juliette scripted by Marquis de Sade, which Angela Carter (1978) interprets as the two key hyperbolic pornographic archetypes. Justine is the victim, the woman who is constantly in tears and who invites further violation and victimization from her tormentors, whereas her sister, Juliette, is the harlot who is proud of her sexual skills and who is willing to sell her services in return for money. Justine stands for virtue, and Justine for vice (see also Jacobs 2007, 86–88).

8. http://www.urbandictionary.com/define.php?term=tubgirl.

9. See YouTube's terms of use at http://www.youtube.com/t/terms.

10. In antipornography slide shows, affective jolts involved in disturbing imagery are tied to the possibilities for political action.

11. But many others would (e.g., Jensen 2007).

12. http://www.alternet.org/sex/47987.

13. By focusing questions of meaning and reading, Kipnis's book also cuts short discussions of materiality as other than that of viewers' gut reactions or the carnal displays they encounter. The materiality of production seems to evaporate as one connected to ethics—which is a recurring tendency of textual analysis.

14. Critical inquiry has been focused on the dynamics of discipline and transgression, power and resistance, norm and subversion for a number of years. The analytical movement involved in such a dualistic concept is tied to a continuous uncovering of prohibition, ideology, and power that are—as Sedgwick points out—postulated to start with (Hemmings 2005, 553).

Chapter 7

1. The Nordic countries have enjoyed a pop cultural reputation as a "sanctuary for sexuality and pornography" (particularly in the United States) (Schröder, 1997; Sabo 2005, 37). However, although Denmark deregulated audiovisual pornography in 1969 and Sweden in 1971, the other countries in the region did not follow suit. Finland had strict legislation concerning pornography up to the late 1990s. I believe that this history of regulation explains something of pornography's enduring and increasing popularity in Finland in comparison to the other Nordic countries (Paasonen 2009, 590; Haavio-Mannila and Kontula 2001). At the same time, Finland is a Lutheran country, but it does not share the Puritan traditions of North America or the United Kingdom. With the casual social nudity involved in Finland's sauna culture and the state-mandated discourse of sexual health as active responsible sexuality (Helén and Yesilova 2006), the issues of nudity or sexuality are framed in a different manner. Porn is objected to as being commercial and sexist, but debates concerning it have been relatively tame, and Christian and other religious voices have remained subdued.

2. BitTorrent is a P2P protocol for file sharing: torrent files store metadata and divide the target file into smaller pieces that can be downloaded from a number of peer users; BitTorrent then reassembles the pieces of files.

References

Abel, Marco. 2007. *Violent Affect: Literature, Cinema, and Critique after Representation*. Lincoln: University of Nebraska Press.

Adorno, Theodor. 2001. *The Culture Industry: Selected Essays on Mass Culture*. Edited by J. M. Bernstein. London: Routledge.

Ahmed, Sara. 2000. *Strange Encounters: Embodied Others in Post-coloniality*. London: Routledge.

Ahmed, Sara. 2001. "Communities That Feel: Intensity, Difference and Attachment." In *Conference Proceedings for Affective Encounters: Rethinking Embodiment in Feminist Media Studies*, edited by Anu Koivunen and Susanna Paasonen, 10–24. Turku: University of Turku. http://www.utu.fi/hum/mediatutkimus/affective/proceedings.pdf.

Ahmed, Sara. 2004. *The Cultural Politics of Emotion*. Edinburgh: Edinburgh University Press.

Ahmed, Sara. 2006. *Queer Phenomenology: Orientations, Objects, Others*. Durham: Duke University Press.

Ahmed, Sara. 2008. "Imaginary Prohibitions: Some Preliminary Remarks on the Founding Gesture of 'New Materialism.'" *European Journal of Women's Studies* 15, no. 1:23–39.

Ahmed, Sara. 2010. "Creating Disturbance: Feminism, Happiness and Affective Differences. In *Working with Affect in Feminist Readings: Disturbing Differences*, edited by Marianne Liljeström and Susanna Paasonen, 33–46. London: Routledge.

Ahonen, Johanna. 2010. "Nomadic Bodies, Transformative Spaces: Affective Encounters with Indian Spirituality." In *Working with Affect in Feminist Readings: Disturbing Differences*, edited by Marianne Liljeström and Susanna Paasonen, 118–131. London: Routledge.

Albury, Kath. 2002, *Yes Means Yes: Getting Explicit about Heterosex*. Crows Nest: Allen & Unwin.

Albury, Kath. 2003. "The Ethics of Porn on the Net." In *Remote Control: New Media, New Ethics*, edited by Catharine Lumby and Elspeth Probyn, 196–211. Cambridge: Cambridge University Press.

Altman, Rick. 1999. *Film/Genre*. London: BFI.

Armstrong, Carol. 1998. *Scenes in the Library: Reading the Photograph in the Book, 1843–1875*. Cambridge: MIT Press.

Armstrong, Isobel. 2000. *The Radical Aesthetic*. Oxford: Blackwell.

Arthurs, Jane. 2004. *Television and Sexuality: Regulation and the Politics of Taste*. Berkshire: Open University Press.

Arvidsson, Adam. 2007. "Netporn: The Work of Fantasy in the Information Society." In *C'lick Me: A Netporn Studies Reader*, edited by Katrien Jacobs, Marije Janssen, and Matteo Pasquinelli, 69–76. Amsterdam: Institute of Network Cultures.

Attwood, Feona. 2002. "Reading Porn: The Paradigmatic Shift in Pornography Research." *Sexualities* 5, no. 1:91–105.

Attwood, Feona. 2006. "Sexed Up: Theorizing the Sexualization of Culture." *Sexualities* 9, no. 1:77–94.

Attwood, Feona. 2007. "No Money Shot? Commerce, Pornography and New Sex Taste Cultures." *Sexualities* 10, no. 4:441–456.

Attwood, Feona. 2009. "Introduction: The Sexualization of Culture." In *Mainstreaming Sex: The Sexualization of Western Culture*, edited by Feona Attwood, xiii–xxiv. London: Tauris.

Attwood, Feona. 2010a. "Conclusion: Toward the Study of Online Porn Cultures and Practices." In *Porn.com: Making Sense of Online Pornography*, edited by Feona Attwood, 236–243. New York: Lang.

Attwood, Feona. 2010b. "Introduction: Porn Studies—From Social Problem to Cultural Practice." In *Porn.com: Making Sense of Online Pornography*, edited by Feona Attwood, 1–13. New York: Lang.

Barad, Karen. 2007. *Meeting the Universe Halfway: Quantum Physics and the Entanglement of Matter and Meaning*. Durham: Duke University Press.

Barcan, Ruth. 2002. "In the Raw: 'Home-Made' Porn and Reality Genres." *Journal of Mundane Behavior* 3, no. 1.

Barker, Jennifer M. 2009. *The Tactile Eye: Touch and the Cinematic Experience*. Berkeley: University of California Press.

Barron, Martin, and Michael Kimmel. 2000. "Sexual Violence in Three Pornographic Media: Towards a Sociological Explanation." *Journal of Sex Research* 37, no. 2:161–168.

Barthes, Roland. 1981. *Camera Lucida: Reflections on Photography.* Translated by Richard Howard. New York: Hill & Wang.

Barthes, Roland. 2007. *Criticism and Truth.* Translated and edited by Katrine Pilcher Keuneman. London: Ahtlone Press.

Bataille, Georges. 1986. *Erotism: Death and Sensuality.* Translated by Mary Dalwood. San Francisco: City Lights.

Bell, Jennifer Lyon. 2001. "Character and Cognition in Modern Pornography." In *Conference Proceedings for Affective Encounters: Rethinking Embodiment in Feminist Media Studies*, edited by Anu Koivunen and Susanna Paasonen, 36–42. Turku: University of Turku. http://www.utu.fi/hum/mediatutkimus/affective/proceedings.pdf.

Benjamin, Andrew. 2006. *Pornification.* New York: Falls Media.

Bennett, David. 2001. "Pornography-Dot-Com: Eroticising Privacy on the Internet." *Review of Education, Pedagogy and Cultural Studies* 23, no. 4:381–391.

Bennett, Jane. 2010. *Vibrant Matter: A Political Ecology of Things.* Durham: Duke University Press.

Bergman, David. 1993. "Introduction." In *Camp Grounds: Style and Homosexuality*, edited by David Bergman, 3–16. Amherst: University of Massachusetts Press.

Bergson, Henri. 2007. *Matter and Memory.* Translated by Nancy Margaret Paul and W. Scott Palmer. New York: Cosimo.

Berlant, Lauren. 2006. "Cruel Optimism." *Differences: A Journal of Feminist Cultural Studies* 17, no. 3: 20–36.

Bhabha, Homi K. 1994. *The Location of Culture.* London: Routledge.

Bhattacharyya, Gargi. 2001. "Flesh and Skin: Materialism Is Doomed to Fail." In *Contested Bodies*, edited by Ruth Holliday and John Hassard, 36–47. London: Routledge.

Bilogorskiy, Nick. 2006. "Click Me: Social Engineering in Malware." http://www.nickolay.ca/docs/click.me.pdf.

Boler, Megan. 2008. "Introduction." In *Digital Media and Democracy: Tactics in Hard Times*, edited by Megan Boler, 1–50. Cambridge: MIT Press.

Bolter, Jay David, and Richard Grusin. 1999. *Remediation: Understanding New Media.* Cambridge: MIT Press.

Bonik, Manuel, and Andreas Schaale. 2007. "The Naked Truth: Internet-Eroticism and the Search." In *C'lick Me: A Netporn Studies Reader*, edited by Katrien Jacobs, Marije Janssen, and Matteo Pasquinelli, 77–88. Amsterdam: Institute of Network Cultures.

Booth, Mark. 1983. *Camp*. London: Quartet Books.

Bourdieu, Pierre. 1984. *Distinction: A Social Critique of the Judgement of Taste*. Translated by Richard Nice. Cambridge: Harvard University Press.

Boyle, Karen. 2008. "Courting Consumers and Legitimating Exploitation." *Feminist Media Studies* 8, no. 1:35–50.

Boyle, Karen. 2010. "Porn Consumers' Public Faces: Mainstream Media, Address and Representation." In *Everyday Pornography*, edited by Karen Boyle, 134–146. London: Routledge.

Braidotti, Rosi. 1991. *Patterns of Dissonance: A Study of Women in Contemporary Philosophy*. New York: Routledge.

Braidotti, Rosi. 2002. *Metamorphoses: Towards a Materialist Theory of Becoming*. Cambridge: Polity.

Bridges, Ana. 2010. "Methodological Considerations in Mapping Pornographic Content." In *Everyday Pornography*, edited by Karen Boyle, 34–49. London: Routledge.

Brown, Bill. 2000. "Thing Theory." *Critical Inquiry* 28, no. 1:1–22.

Bruns, Axel. 2008. *Blogs, Wikipedia, Second Life, and Beyond: From Production to Produsage*. New York: Lang.

Burgess, Jean. 2008. "'All Your Chocolate Rain Are Belong to Us?' Viral Video, YouTube and the Dynamics of Participatory Culture." In *The Video Vortex Reader: Responses to YouTube*, edited by Geert Lovink and Sabine Niederer, 101–110. Amsterdam: Institute of Network Cultures.

Burnett, Ron. 2005. *How Images Think*. Cambridge: MIT Press.

Butler, Judith. 1993. *Bodies That Matter: On the Discursive Limits of "Sex."*. London: Routledge.

Buzzell, Timothy. 2005. "Demographic Characteristics of Persons Using Pornography in Three Technological Contexts." *Sexuality and Culture* 9, no. 1:28–48.

Califia, Pat. 2000. *Public Culture: The Culture of Radical sex*. 2nd ed. Pittsburgh: Cleis Press.

Calvert, Clay. 2000. *Voyeur Nation: Media, Privacy, and Peeping in Modern Culture*. Boulder: Westview Press.

Capino, José B. 2006. "Asian College Girls and Oriental Men with Bamboo Poles: Reading Asian Pornography." In *Pornography: Film and Culture*, edited by Peter Lehman, 206–219. New Brunswick: Rutgers University Press.

Carter, Angela. 1978. *The Sadeian Woman and the Ideology of Pornography*. New York: Pantheon Books.

Chalfen, Richard. 2002. "Snapshots 'R' Us: The Evidentiary Problematics of Home Media." *Visual Studies* 17, no. 2:141–149.

Chancer, Lynn S. 1998. *Reconcilable Differences: Confronting Beauty, Pornography, and the Future of Feminism*. Berkeley: University of California Press.

Chun, Wendy Hui Kyong. 2004. "On Software, or the Persistence of Visual Knowledge." *Grey Room* 18:26–51.

Chun, Wendy Hui Kyong. 2006. *Control and Freedom: Power and Paranoia in the Age of Fiber Optics*. Cambridge: MIT Press.

Chun, Wendy Hui Kyong. 2008. "On 'Sourcery,' or Code as Fetish." *Configurations* 16, no. 3:299–324.

Citron, Michele. 1999. *Home Movies and Other Necessary Fictions*. Minneapolis: Minnesota University Press.

Cleto, Fabio. 1999. "Introduction: Queering the Camp." In *Camp: Queer Aesthetics and the Performing Subject—A Reader*, edited by Fabio Cleto, 1–42. Ann Arbor: University of Michigan Press.

Clough, Patricia Ticineto. 2003. "Affect and Control: Rethinking the Body 'beyond Sex and Gender.'" *Feminist Theory* 4, no. 3:359–364.

Clough, Patricia Ticineto, and Jean Halley, eds. 2007. *The Affective Turn: Theorizing the Social*. Durham: Duke University Press.

Cohen, William A. 2005. "Introduction: Locating Filth." In *Filth: Dirt, Disgust, and Modern Life*, edited by William A. Cohen and Ryan Johnson, vii–xxxviii. Minneapolis: University of Minnesota Press.

Connor, Steven. 2006. "The Menagerie of the Senses." *Senses and Society* 1, no. 1:9–26.

Cooper, Alvin, Dana E. Putnam, Lynn A. Planchon, and Sylvain C. Boies. 1999. "Online Sexual Compulsivity: Getting Tangled in the Net." *Sexual Addiction and Compulsivity* 6, no. 2:79–104.

Coopersmith, Jonathan. 2006. "Does Your Mother Know What You *Really* Do? The Changing Nature and Image of Computer-based Pornography." *History and Technology* 22, no. 1:1–25.

Coté, Mark, and Jennifer Pybus. 2007. "Learning to Immaterial Labour 2.0: MySpace and Social Networks." *Ephemera: Theory and Politics in Organization* 7, no. 1:88–106.

Cowie, Elizabeth. 1993. "Pornography and Fantasy: Psychoanalytic Perspectives." In *Sex Exposed: Sexuality and the Pornography Debate*, edited by Lynn Segal and Mary McIntosh, 132–152. New Brunswick: Rutgers University Press.

Cramer, Florian. 2006. "Sodom Blogging: 'Alternative Porn' and Aesthetic Sensibility." *Texte zur Kunst* 16, no. 64:133–136.

Cramer, Florian, and Stuart Home. 2007. "Pornographic Coding." In *C'lick Me: A Netporn Studies Reader*, edited by Katrien Jacobs, Marije Janssen, and Matteo Pasquinelli, 159–171. Amsterdam: Institute of Network Cultures.

Cranor, Lorrie Faith, and Brian A. LaMacchia. 1998. "Spam!" *Communications of the ACM* 41, no. 8:74–83.

Cronin, Blaise, and Elizabeth Davenport. 2001. "E-rogenous Zones: Positioning Pornography in the Digital Economy." *Information Society* 17, no. 1:33–48.

Dahlqvist, Joel Powell, and Lee Garth Vigilant. 2004. "Way Better Than Real: From Manga Sex to Tentacle Hentai." In *Net.seXXX: Readings of Sex, Pornography, and the Internet*, edited by Dennis D. Waskul, 91–103. New York: Lang.

Davison, W. Phillips. 1983. "The Third-Person Effect in Communication." *Public Opinion Quarterly* 47, no. 1:1–15.

Dean, Carolyn J. 2000. *The Frail Social Body: Pornography, Homosexuality, and Other Fantasies in Interwar France*. Berkeley: University of California Press.

De Lauretis, Teresa. 1994. *The Practice of Love: Lesbian Sexuality and Perverse Desire*. Bloomington: Indiana University Press.

Deleuze, Gilles, and Félix Guattari. 2009. *Anti-Oedipus: Capitalism and Schizophrenia*. Translated by Robert Hurley, Mark Seem, and Helen R. Lane. New York: Penguin Books.

Dery, Mark. 2007a. "Naked Lunch: Talking Realcore with Sergio Messina. In *C'lick Me: A Netporn Studies Reader*, edited by Katrien Jacobs, Marije Janssen, and Matteo Pasquinelli, 17–30. Amsterdam: Institute of Network Cultures.

Dery, Mark. 2007b. "Paradise Lust: Pornotopia Meets the Culture Wars." In *C'lick Me: A Netporn Studies Reader*, edited by Katrien Jacobs, Marije Janssen, and Matteo Pasquinelli, 125–148. Amsterdam: Institute of Network Cultures.

Dery, Mark. 2007c. "'Sex Times Technology Equals the Future'—J. G. Ballard." *Psychopathia Sexualis* blog. http://markdery.com/?p=68.

DeVoss, Danielle. 2002. "Women's Porn Sites: Spaces of Fissure an Eruption or "I'm a Little Bit of Everything." *Sexuality and Culture* 6, no. 3:75–94.

Di Lauro, Al, and Rabkin, Gerard. 1976. *Dirty Movies: An Illustrated History of the Stag Film 1915–1970*. New York: Chelsea House.

Dines, Gail, Linda Thompson, and Rebecca Whisnant, with Karen Boyle. 2010. "Arresting Images: Anti-pornography Slide Shows, Activism and the Academy." In *Everyday Pornography*, edited by Karen Boyle, 17–33. London: Routledge.

Douglas, Mary. 1991. *Purity and Danger: An Analysis of the Concepts of Pollution and Taboo.* London: Routledge.

Dovey, Jon. 2000. *Freakshow: First Person Media and Factual Television.* London: Pluto Press.

Duggan, Lisa. 1995. "Introduction." In *Sex Wars: Sexual Dissent and Political Culture,* edited by Lisa Duggan and Nan D. Hunter, 1–14. New York: Routledge.

Duggan, Lisa, Nan D. Hunter, and Carole S. Vance. 1995. "False Promises: Feminist Antipornography Legislation." In *Sex Wars: Sexual Dissent and Political Culture,* edited by Lisa Duggan and Nan D. Hunter, 43–67. New York: Routledge.

Duncombe, Jean, and Dennis Marsden. 1995. "'Can Men Love?': 'Reading,' 'Staging' and 'Resisting' the Romance." In *Romance Revisited,* edited by Lynne Pearce and Jackie Stacey, 238–250. London: Lawrence & Wishart.

Dworkin, Andrea. 1989. *Pornography: Men Possessing Women.* New York: Dutton.

Dworkin, Andrea. 2000a. "Against the Male Flood: Censorship, Pornography, and Equality" (1994). In *Feminism and Pornography,* edited by Drucilla Cornell, 19–38. Oxford: Oxford University Press.

Dworkin, Andrea. 2000b. "Pornography and Grief." In *Feminism and Pornography,* edited by Drucilla Cornell, 39–44. Oxford: Oxford University Press.

Dyer, Richard. 1993. *The Matter of Images: Essays on Representations.* London: Routledge.

Dyer, Richard. 1997. *White.* London: Routledge.

Dyer, Richard. 2002a. *The Culture of Queers.* London: Routledge.

Dyer, Richard. 2002b. *Only Entertainment.* 2nd ed. London: Routledge.

Edelman, Benjamin. 2009. "Red Light States: Who Buys Online Adult Entertainment?" *Journal of Economic Perspectives* 23, no. 1:209–220.

Edelman, Lee. 2004. *No Future: Queer Theory and the Death Drive.* Durham: Duke University Press.

Edwards, Elizabeth, and Janice Hart. 2004. "Introduction: Photographs as Objects." In *Photographs, Objects, Histories: On the Materiality of Images,* edited by Elizabeth Edwards and Janice Hart, 1–16. New York: Routledge.

Ellis, John. 1980. "Photography/Pornography/Art/Pornography." *Screen* 21, no. 1:81–108.

Elsaesser, Thomas. 1998. "Digital Cinema: Delivery, Time, Event." In *Cinema Futures: Cain, Cabel or Cable? The Screen Arts in the Digital Age,* edited by Thomas Elsaesser and Kay Hoffman, 201–222. Amsterdam: Amsterdam University Press.

Epley, Nathan Scott. 2007. "Pin-Ups, Retro-Chic and the Consumption of Irony." In *Pornification: Sex and Sexuality in Media Culture*, edited by Susanna Paasonen, Kaarina Nikunen, and Laura Saarenmaa, 45–57. Oxford: Berg.

Esch, Kevin, and Vicki Meyer. 2007. "How Unprofessional: The Profitable Partnership of Amateur Porn and Celebrity Culture." In *Pornification: Sex and Sexuality in Media Culture*, edited by Susanna Paasonen, Kaarina Nikunen, and Laura Saarenmaa, 99–111. Oxford: Berg.

Ess, Charles. 1996. "Philosophical Approaches to Pornography, Free Speech, and CMC: Cyberspace as Plato's *Republic*—or, Why This Special Issue?" *CMC Magazine* 3, no. 1. http://www.december.com/cmc/mag/1996/jan/ed.html.

Falk, Pasi. 1994. *The Consuming Body*. London: Sage.

Fanon, Frantz. 1967. *Black Skin, White Masks*. New York: Grove Press.

Filippo, Jo-Ann. 2000. "Pornography on the Web." In *Web.studies: Rewiring Media Studies for the Digital Age*, edited by David Gauntlett, 122–129. London: Arnold.

Foucault, Michel. 1990. "An Introduction." Translated by Robert Hurley. *The History of Sexuality*. Vol. 1. London: Penguin.

Foucault, Michel. 1998. *Aesthetics, Method and Epistemology: Essential Works of Foucault 1954–1984*. Vol. 2. Edited by James D. Faubion and Paul Rabinow. New York: New Press.

Frank, Marcie. 1993. "The Critic as Performance Artist: Susan Sontag's Writing and Gay Cultures." In *Camp Grounds: Style and Homosexuality*, edited by David Bergman, 173–184. Amherst: University of Massachusetts Press.

Freeman-Longo, Robert E. 2000. "Children, Teens, and Sex on the Internet." *Sexual Addiction and Compulsivity* 7, no. 1–2:75–90.

Fried, Michael. 2005. "Barthes' *Punctum*." *Critical Inquiry* 31:539–574.

Fung, Richard. 1991. "Looking for My Penis: The Eroticized Asian in Gay Male Porn." In *How Do I Look? Queer Film and Video*, edited by Bad Object-Choices, 145–160. Seattle: Bay Press.

Gallop, Jane. 1988. *Thinking through the Body*. New York: Columbia University Press.

Gallop, Jane. 2005. "The Liberated Woman." *Narrative* 13,no. 2:89–104.

Gates, Henry Louis, Jr. 1986. "Introduction: Writing 'Race' and the Difference It Makes." In *"Race," Writing, and Difference*, edited by Henry Louis Gates Jr., 1–20. Chicago: University of Chicago Press.

Genette, Gérard. 1986. *Narrative Discourse: An Essay in Method*. Translated by Jane E. Lewin. Oxford: Basil Blackwell.

Ghosh, Shohini. 2006. "The Troubled Existence of Sex and Sexuality: Feminists Engage with Censorship." In *Gender and Censorship*, edited by Brinda Bose, 255–285. New Delhi: Women Unlimited.

Gilman, Sander L. 1985. *Difference and Pathology: Stereotypes of Sexuality, Race, and Madness*. Ithaca: Cornell University Press.

Gitelman, Lisa. 2006. *Always Already New: Media, History, and the Data of Culture*. Cambridge: MIT Press.

Greenberg, Joshua M. 2008. *From Betamax to Blockbuster: Video Stores and the Invention of Movies on Video*. Cambridge: MIT Press.

Greenfield, Patricia M. 2004. "Inadvertent Exposure to Pornography on the Internet: Implications of Peer-to-Peer File-Sharing Networks for Child Development and Families." *Applied Developmental Psychology* 25, no. 6:741–750.

Gregg, Melissa. 2006. *Cultural Studies' Affective Voices*. Houndmills: Palgrave.

Griffin, Susan. 1981. *Pornography and Silence: Culture's Revenge against Nature*. New York: Harper & Row.

Griffiths, Mark. 2000. "Does Internet and Computer 'Addiction' Exist? Some Case Study Evidence." *Cyberpsychology and Behavior* 3, no. 2:211–218.

Grindstaff, Laura. 2002. *The Money Shot: Trash, Class, and the Making of TV Talk Shows*. Chicago: University of Chicago Press.

Gronow, Jukka. 1997. *The Sociology of Taste*. London: Routledge.

Grosz, Elizabeth. 2005. *Time Travels: Feminism, Nature, Power*. Durham: Duke University Press.

Grosz, Elizabeth. 2006. "Naked." In *The Prosthetic Impulse: From Posthuman Present to a Biocultural Future*, edited by Marquard Smith and Joanne Morra, 187–202. Cambridge: MIT Press.

Grosz, Elizabeth. 2007. "Chaos, Territory, Art: Deleuze and the Framing of the Earth." Wellek Library Lectures in Critical Theory, University of California, May 2005. http://va-grad.ucsd.edu/~drupal/files/Grosz_on_Choas_Territory_and_Art.pdf.

Grusin, Richard. 2010. *Premediation: Affect and Mediality after 9/11*. New York: Palgrave.

Haagman, Dan, and Byrne Ghavalas. 2005. "Trojan Defence: A Forensic View." *Digital Investigation* 2:23–30.

Haavio-Mannila, Elina, and Osmo Kontula. 2001. *Seksin trendit meillä ja naapureissa*. Helsinki: WSOY.

Halavais, Alex. 2005. "Small Pornographies." *ACM SIGGROUP Bulletin* 25, no. 2:19–22.

Hall, Stuart. 1996. "The After-Life of Frantz Fanon: Why Fanon? Why Now? Why *Black Skin, White Masks?*" In *The Fact of Blackness: Frantz Fanon and Visual Representation*, edited by Alan Read, 12–37. London and Seattle: ICA and Bay Press.

Hall, Stuart. 1997. "The Work of Representation." In *Representation: Cultural Representations and Signifying Practices*, edited by Stuart Hall, 15–64. London: Sage and Open University.

Hardt, Michael, and Antonio Negri. 2001. *Empire*. Cambridge: Harvard University Press.

Hardt, Michael, and Antonio Negri. 2004. *Multitude: War and Democracy in the Age of Empire*. London: Penguin.

Hardy, Simon. 2009. "The New Pornographies: Representation or Reality?" In *Mainstreaming Sex: The Sexualization of Western Culture*, edited by Feona Attwood, 3–18. London: Tauris.

Härmä, Sanna. 2007. "Bitch Is (Talking) Back: Gangsta Rap ja pornon narttuilevat naisräppärit." In *Pornoakatemia!*, edited by Harri Kalha, 338–375. Turku: Eetos.

Härmä, Sanna, and Joakim Stolpe. 2010. "Behind the Scenes of Straight Pleasures." In *Porn.com: Making Sense of Online Pornography*, edited by Feona Attwood, 107–122. New York: Lang.

Hayles, N. Katherine. 1999. *How We Became Posthuman: Virtual Bodies in Cybernetics, Literature, and Informatics*. Chicago: University of Chicago Press.

Hayles, N. Katherine. 2003. "Translating Media: Why We Should Rethink Textuality." *Yale Journal of Criticism* 16:263–290.

Hayles, N. Katherine. 2009. "Digital Arts and Cultures and the Humanities: Challenges and Opportunities." Paper presented at the *After Media: Embodiment and Context* conference (DAC'09), University of California Irvine, December 12–15.

Heins, Marjorie. 2001. *Not in Front of the Children: "Indecency," Censorship, and the Innocence of Youth*. New York: Hill and Wang.

Helén, Ilpo, and Katja Yesilova. 2006. "Shepherding Desire: Sexual Health Promotion in Finland from the 1940s to the 1990s." *Acta Sociologica* 49, no. 3:257–272.

Hemmings, Clare. 2005. "Invoking Affect: Cultural Theory and the Ontological Turn." *Cultural Studies* 19, no. 5:548–567.

Higgins, Charlotte. 2007. "The Art of Seduction: Sex through the Ages, from Every Possible Angle." *The Guardian*, October 10.

Hillis, Ken. 2009. *Online a Lot of the Time: Ritual, Fetish, Sign.* Durham: Duke University Press.

Hunt, Lynn. 1996. "Introduction: Obscenity and the Origins of Modernity, 1500–1800." In *The Invention of Pornography: Obscenity and the Origins of Modernity, 1500–1800,* edited by Lynn Hunt, 9–45. New York: Zone Books.

Jacobs, Katrien. 2004. "The New Media Schooling of the Amateur Pornographer: Negotiating Contracts and Singing Orgasms." http://www.libidot.org/katrien/tester/articles/negotiating-print.html.

Jacobs, Katrien. 2007. *Netporn: DIY Web Culture and Sexual Politics.* Lanham, MD: Rowman & Littlefield.

Jacobs, Katrien. 2009. "Make Porn, Not War: How to Wear the Network's Underpants." In *The Spam Book: On Viruses, Porn, and Other Anomalies from the Dark Side of Digital Culture,* edited by Jussi Parikka and Tony Sampson, 181–194. Cresskill, NJ: Hampton Press.

Jacobs, Katrien, Marije Janssen, and Matteo Pasquinelli. 2007. "Introduction." In *C'lick Me: A Netporn Studies Reader,* edited by Katrien Jacobs, Marije Janssen, and Matteo Pasquinelli, 1–3. Amsterdam: Institute of Network Cultures.

Jameson, Fredric. 2002. *The Political Unconscious: Narrative as a Socially Symbolic Act.* New edition. New York: Routledge.

Jancovich, Mark. 2001. "Naked Ambitions: Pornography, Taste and the Problem of the Middlebrow." *Scope: An Online Journal of Film and TV Studies* (June). http://www.scope.nottingham.ac.uk/article.php?issue=jun2001&id=274&section=article.

Jansen, Bernard J., and Amanda Spink. 2006. "How Are We Searching the World Wide Web? A Comparison of Nine Search Engine Transaction Logs." *Information Processing and Management* 42, no. 1:258–259.

Jenkins, Henry. 2006a. *Convergence Culture: Where Old and New Media Collide.* New York: NYU Press.

Jenkins, Henry. 2006b. *Fans, Bloggers and Gamers: Exploring Participatory Culture.* New York: NYU Press.

Jenkins, Henry. 2007. "Porn 2.0." http://henryjenkins.org/2007/10/porn_20.html.

Jenkins, Philip. 2001. *Beyond Tolerance: Child Pornography on the Internet.* New York: NYU Press.

Jenks, Chris. 2003. *Transgression.* London: Routledge.

Jensen, Robert. 2007. *Getting Off: Pornography and the End of Masculinity.* Cambridge: South End Press.

Johnson, Jennifer A. 2010. "To Catch a Curious Clicker: A Social Network Analysis of the Online Pornography Industry. In *Everyday Pornography*, edited by Karen Boyle, 147–163. London: Routledge.

Jones, Mark, and Gerry Carlin. 2010. "'Students Study Hard Porn': Pornography and the Popular Press." In *Everyday Pornography*, edited by Karen Boyle, 179–189. London: Routledge.

Jones, Steven. 2010. "Horrorporn/Pornhorror: The Problematic Communities and Contexts of Online Shock Imagery." In *Porn.com: Making Sense of Online Pornography*, edited by Feona Attwood, 123–137. New York: Lang.

Juffer, Jane. 1998. *At Home with Pornography: Women, Sex, and Everyday Life*. New York: NYU Press.

Kalha, Harri. 2007a. "Halu alennuksessa: Sigmund Freud ja matalan vetovoima." In *Pornoakatemia!*, edited by Harri Kalha, 78–113. Turku: Eetos.

Kalha, Harri. 2007b. "Pornografia halun ja torjunnan kulttuurissa." In *Pornoakatemia!*, edited by Harri Kalha, 11–76. Turku: Eetos.

Kangsvuo, Jenny. 2007. "Insatiable Sluts and Almost Gay Guys: Bisexuality in Porn Magazines." In *Pornification: Sex and Sexuality in Media Culture*, edited by Susanna Paasonen, Kaarina Nikunen, and Laura Saarenmaa, 139–150. Oxford: Berg.

Kappeler, Susan. 1986. *The Pornography of Representation*. Minneapolis: University of Minnesota Press.

Kendrick, Walter. 1996. *The Secret Museum: Pornography in Modern Culture*. 2nd ed. Berkeley: University of California Press.

Kennedy, Barbara M. 2000. *Deleuze and Cinema: The Aesthetics of Sensation*. Edinburgh: Edinburgh University Press.

Kibby, Marjorie, and Brigid Costello. 2001. "Between the Image and the Act: Interactive Sex Entertainment on the Internet." *Sexualities* 4, no. 3:353–369.

Kipnis, Laura. 1999. *Bound and Gagged: Pornography and the Politics of Fantasy in America*. Durham: Duke University Press.

Klastrup, Lisbeth. 2007. "From Texts to Artefacts: Storytelling Version 3.0." Paper presented at the NordMedia 2007 conference, University of Helsinki, August 16–19.

Kleinhans, Chuck. 2004. "Virtual Child Porn: The Law and the Semiotic of the Image." In *More Dirty Looks: Gender, Pornography and Power*, 2nd ed., edited by Pamela Church Gibson, 71–84. London: BFI.

Koivunen, Anu. 2001. "Preface: The Affective Turn?" In *Conference Proceedings for Affective Encounters: Rethinking Embodiment in Feminist Media Studies*, edited by Anu

Koivunen and Susanna Paasonen, 7–9. Turku: University of Turku. http://www.utu.fi/hum/mediatutkimus/affective/koivunen.pdf.

Koivunen, Anu. 2010. "The Affective Turn? Reimagining the Subject of Feminist Theory." In *Working with Affect in Feminist Readings: Disturbing Differences*, edited by Marianne Liljeström and Susanna Paasonen, 8–29. London: Routledge.

Kolnai, Aurel. 2004. *On Disgust*. Translated and edited by Barry Smith and Carolyn Korsmeyer. Chicago: Open Court.

Kontula, Osmo. 2008. *Halu & intohimo: Tietoa suomalaisesta seksistä*. Helsinki: Otava.

Kontula, Osmo, and Kati Kosonen. 1994. *Seksiä lehtien sivuilla*. Helsinki: Painatuskeskus.

Korppi, Timo. 2002. *Lihaa säästämättä: 30 vuotta suomalaisen pornobisneksen etulinjassa*. Helsinki: Johnny Kniga.

Kotamraju, Nalini P. 1999. "The Birth of Web Design Skills: Making the Present History." *American Behavioral Scientist* 43, no. 3:464–474.

Kozel, Susan. 2007. *Closer: Performance, Technologies, Phenomenology*. Cambridge: MIT Press.

Kristeva, Julia. 1982. *The Powers of Horror: An Essay on Abjection*. New York: Columbia University Press.

Kuhn, Annette. 1994. *The Power of the Image: Essays on Representation and Sexuality*. London: Routledge.

Kuhn, Annette. 1995. *Family Secrets: Acts of Memory and Imagination*. London: Verso.

Kuipers, Giselinde. 2006. "The Social Construction of Digital Danger: Debating, Defusing and Inflating the Moral Dangers of Online Humor and Pornography in the Netherlands and the United States." *New Media and Society* 8, no. 3:379–400.

Kulick, Don. 1998. *Travesti: Sex, Gender and Culture among Brazilian Transgender Prostitutes*. Chicago: Chicago University Press.

Kulick, Don. 2005. "Four Hundred Thousand Swedish Perverts." *GLQ: A Journal of Lesbian and Gay Studies* 11, no. 2: 205–235.

Kuntsman, Adi. 2009. *Figurations of Violence and Belonging: Queerness, Migranthood and Nationalism in Cyberspace and Beyond*. Bern: Lang.

Kyrölä, Katariina. 2010. *The Weight of Images: Affective Engagements with Fat Corporeality in the Media*. Turku: University of Turku.

Laine, Tarja. 2010. "*The Diving Bell and the Butterfly* as an Emotional Event." *Midwest Studies in Philosophy* 36:295–305.

Lamb, Sharon. 2001. *The Secret Lives of Girls: What Good Girls Really Do—Sex Play, Aggression, and Their Guilt.* New York: Free Press.

Lane, Frederic S., III. 2001. *Obscene Profits: The Entrepreneurs of Pornography in the Cyber Age.* New York: Routledge.

Langford, Wendy. 1999. *Revolutions of the Heart: Gender, Power and the Delusions of Love.* London: Routledge.

Langman, Lauren. 2004. "Grotesque Degradation: Globalization, Carnivalization, and Cyberporn". In *Net.seXXX: Readings of Sex, Pornography, and the Internet,* edited by Dennis D. Waskul, 193–216. New York: Lang.

Laqueur, Thomas. 2003. *Solitary Sex: A Cultural History of Masturbation.* New York: Zone Books.

Largier, Niklaus. 2007. *In Praise of the Whip: A Cultural History of Arousal.* Translated by Graham Harman. New York: Zone Books.

Laukkanen, Anu. 2010. "Hips Don't Lie? Affective and Kinaesthetic Dance Ethnography." In *Working with Affect in Feminist Readings: Disturbing Differences,* edited by Marianne Liljeström and Susanna Paasonen, 126–139. London: Routledge.

Lazzarato, Mauricio. 1996. "Immaterial Labour." http://www.generation-online.org/c/fcimmateriallabour3.htm.

Leach, Edmund. 2004. "Concerning Trobriand Clans and the Kinship Category 'Tabu.'" In *Kinship and Family: An Anthropological Reader,* edited by Robert Barkin and Linda Stone, 148–175. Oxford: Wiley-Blackwell.

Leadbeater, Charles, and Paul Miller. 2004. "The Pro-Am Revolution: How Enthusiasts Are Changing Our Economy and Society." *Demos.* http://www.demos.co.uk/files/proamrevolutionfinal.pdf.

Leahy, Michael. 2008. *Porn Nation: Conquering America's #1 Addiction.* Chicago: Northfield.

Lehman, Peter. 2006. "Revelations about Pornography." In *Pornography: Film and Culture,* edited by Peter Lehman, 87–98. New Brunswick: Rutgers University Press.

Levi-Strauss, Claude. 2004. "Structural Analysis in Linguistics and in Anthropology." In *Kinship and Family: An Anthropological Reader,* edited by Robert Barkin and Linda Stone, 145–157. Oxford: Wiley-Blackwell.

Levy, Ariel. 2005. *Female Chauvinist Pigs: Women and the Rise of Raunch Culture.* New York: Free Press.

Levy, Neil. 2002. "Virtual Child Pornography: The Eroticization of Inequality." *Ethics and Information Technology* 4, no. 4:319–323.

Liljeström, Marianne, and Susanna Paasonen. 2010. "Introduction: Feeling Differences—Affect and Feminist Reading." In *Working with Affect in Feminist Readings: Disturbing Differences*, edited by Marianne Liljeström and Susanna Paasonen, 1–7. London: Routledge.

Lillie, Jonathan James McCreadie. 2002. "Sexuality and Cyberporn: Towards a New Agenda for Research." *Sexuality and Culture* 6, no. 2: 25–47.

Lillie, Jonathan James McCreadie. 2004. "Cyberporn, Sexuality, and the Net Apparatus." *Convergence* 10, no. 1: 43–65.

Lim, Merlyna. 2006. "Democracy, Conspiracy, Pornography: The Internet and Political Activism in Indonesia." Keynote paper presented at the IR 7.0 Internet Convergences Conference, Brisbane, September 28.

Lindgren, Simon. 2010. "Widening the Glory Hole: The Discourse of Online Porn Fandom." In *Porn.com: Making Sense of Online Pornography*, edited by Feona Attwood, 171–185. New York: Lang.

Loftus, David. 2002. *Watching Sex: How Men Really Respond to Pornography*. New York: Thunder's Mouth Press.

MacCormack, Patricia. 2004. "Perversion: Transgressive Sexuality and Becoming-Monster." *Thirdspace* 3, no. 2. http://www.thirdspace.ca/articles/3_2_maccormack .htm.

MacDougall, David. 2006. *The Corporeal Image: Film, Ethnography, and the Senses*. Princeton: Princeton University Press.

MacKinnon, Catharine. 1987. *Feminism Unmodified: Discourses on Life and Law*. Cambridge: Harvard University Press.

MacKinnon, Catharine. 1993. *Only Words*. Cambridge: Harvard University Press.

Maddison, Simon. 2009. "'Choke on It, Bitch!': Porn Studies, Extreme Gonzo and the Mainstreaming of Hardcore." In *Mainstreaming Sex: The Sexualization of Western Culture*, edited by Feona Attwood, 37–54. London: Tauris.

Maddison, Simon. 2010. "Online Obscenity and Myths of Freedom: Dangerous Images, Child Porn, and Neoliberalism." In *Porn.com: Making Sense of Online Pornography*, edited by Feona Attwood, 17–33. New York: Lang.

Magnet, Shoshana. 2007. "Feminist Sexualities, Race and the Internet: An Investigation of Suicidegirls.com. *New Media and Society* 9, no. 4:577–602.

Manoff, Marlene. 2006. "The Materiality of Digital Collections: Theoretical and Historical Perspectives." *Portal: Libraries and the Academy* 6:311–325.

Marcus, Steven. 1964. *The Other Victorians: A Study of Sexuality and Pornography in Mid-nineteenth-Century England*. New York: Basic Books.

Marks, Laura U. 2000. *The Skin of the Film: Intercultural Cinema, Embodiment, and the Senses*. Durham: Duke University Press.

Marks, Laura U. 2002. *Touch: Sensuous Theory and Multisensory Media*. Minneapolis: Minnesota University Press.

Martin, Nina K. 2006. "Never Laugh at a Man with His Pants Down: The Affective Dynamics of Comedy and Porn." In *Pornography: Film and Culture*, edited by Peter Lehman, 189–205. New Brunswick: Rutgers University Press.

Mash, Taylor. 2004. "My Year in Smut: Inside Danni's Hard Drive." In *Net.Sexxx: Readings on Sex, Pornography, and the Internet*, edited by Dennis D. Waskul, 237–258. New York: Lang.

Mason-Grant, Joan. 2004. *Pornography Embodied: From Speech to Sexual Practice*. London: Rowman & Littlefield.

Massumi, Brian. 2002. *Parables for the Virtual: Movement, Affect, Sensation*. Durham: Duke University Press.

McClintock, Anne. 1993. "Gonad the Barbarian and the Venus Flytrap: Portraying the Female and Male Orgasm." In *Sex Exposed: Sexuality and the Pornography Debate*, edited by Lynn Segal and Mary McIntosh, 111–131. New Brunswick: Rutgers University Press.

McKee, Alan. 2006. "The Aesthetics of Pornography: The Insights of Consumers." *Continuum: Journal of Media and Cultural Studies* 20, no. 4:523–539.

McKee, Alan, Katherine Albury, and Catharine Lumby. 2008. *The Porn Report*. Melbourne: Melbourne University Press.

McLelland, Mark. 2006. "The Best Website for Men Who Have Sex with Men: Cruisingforsex.com. In *Beautiful Things in Popular Culture*, edited by Alan McKee, 79–86. Oxford: Blackwell.

McNair, Brian. 1996. *Mediated Sex: Pornography and Postmodern Culture*. Oxford: Oxford University Press.

McNair, Brian. 2002. *Striptease Culture: Sex, Media and the Democratization of Desire*. New York: Routledge.

McNeil, Legs, and Jennifer Osborne. 2005. *The Other Hollywood: The Uncensored Oral History of the Porn Film Industry*. New York: Regan Books.

McWilliams, Brian. 2005. *Spam Kings: The Real Story behind the High-Rolling Hucksters Pushing Porn, Pills, and @*#?% Enlargements*. Beijing: O'Reilly.

Mehta, Michael D. 2001. "Pornography in Usenet: A Study of 9,800 Randomly Selected Images." *Cyberpsychology and Behavior* 4, no. 6:695–703.

Mehta, Michael D., and Dwaine Plaza. 1997. "Content Analysis of Pornographic Images Available on the Internet." *Information Society* 13, no. 2:153–161.

Mercer, Kobena. 1994. *Welcome to the Jungle: New Positions in Black Cultural Criticism.* New York: Routledge.

Messina, Sergio. 2006. "Realcore: The Digital Porno Revolution." http://www.sergi omessina.com/realcore.

Meyer, Moe. 1996. "Introduction: Reclaiming the Discourse of Camp." In *The Politics and Poetics of Camp*, edited by Moe Meyer, 1–22. London: Routledge.

Miller, Nancy K. 1991. *Getting Personal: Feminist Occasions and Other Autobiographical Acts.* New York: Routledge.

Miller, Richard B. 1989. "Violent Pornography: Mimetic Nihilism and the Eclipse of Differences." In *For Adult Users Only: The Dilemma of Violent Pornography*, edited by Susan Gubar and Joan Hoff, 147–161. Bloomington: Indiana University Press.

Miller, William Ian. 1997. *The Anatomy of Disgust.* Cambridge: Harvard University Press.

Miller-Young, Mireille. 2007. "'Let Me Tell Ya about Black Chicks': 1980s Interracial Video Porn." In *Pornification: Sex and Sexuality in Media Culture*, edited by Susanna Paasonen, Kaarina Nikunen, and Laura Saarenmaa, 33–44. Oxford: Berg.

Mosher, Donald L., and Paul R. Abramson. 1977. "Subjective Sexual Arousal to Films of Masturbation." *Journal of Consulting and Clinical Psychology* 45, no. 5:796–807.

Moore, Lisa Jean, and Juliana Weissbein. 2010. "Cocktail Parties: Fetishizing Semen in Pornography beyond Bukkake." In *Everyday Pornography*, edited by Karen Boyle, 77–89. London: Routledge.

Mowlabocus, Sharif. 2007. "Gay Men and the Pornification of Everyday Life." In *Pornification: Sex and Sexuality in Media Culture*, edited by Susanna Paasonen, Kaarina Nikunen, and Laura Saarenmaa, 61–73. Oxford: Berg.

Mowlabocus, Sharif. 2010. "Porn 2.0? Technology, Social Practice, and the New Online Porn Industry." In *Porn.com: Making Sense of Online Pornography*, edited by Feona Attwood, 69–87. New York: Lang.

Mulvey, Laura. 1988. "Visual Pleasure and Narrative Cinema". In *Feminism and Film Theory*, edited by Constance Penley, 57–68. London: Routledge and BFI.

Munster, Anna. 2006. *Materializing New Media: Embodiment in Information Aesthetics.* Hanover: Dartmouth College Press.

Munt, Sally. 2007. *Queer Attachments: The Cultural Politics of Shame.* Aldershot: Ashgate.

Näre, Sari. 2002. "Kyberseksin ja -pornon muistijäljet nettisukupolvessa." In *Tieto ja tekniikka: missä on nainen?*, edited by Riitta Smeds, Kaisa Kauppinen, Kati Yrjän-heikki, and Anitta Valtonen, 228–240. Helsinki: TEK.

Newton, Esther. 1972. *Mother Camp: Female Impersonators in America*. Chicago: University of Chicago Press.

Ngai, Sianne. 2005. *Ugly Feelings*. Cambridge: Harvard University Press.

Nikunen, Kaarina. 2007. "Kompuroivat perheet hajoilevissa taloissaan eli tavallisuuden representaatiot *Hauskoissa kotivideoissa.*" *Lähikuva* 20, no. 2:27–45.

Nikunen, Kaarina, and Susanna Paasonen. 2007. "Porn Star as Brand: The Intermedia Career of Rakel Liekki." *Velvet Light Trap* 59:30–41.

Nussbaum, Martha. 2001. *Upheavals of Thought: The Intelligence of Emotions*. Cambridge: Cambridge University Press.

Olkowski, Dorothea. 1999. *Gilles Deleuze and the Ruin of Representation*. Berkeley: University of California Press.

O'Reilly, Tim. 2005. "What Is Web 2.0: Design Patterns and Business Models for the Next Generation of Software." http://oreilly.com/web2/archive/what-is-web-20 .html.

O'Riordan, Kate. 2002. "Windows on the Web: The Female Body and the Web Camera." In *Women and Everyday Uses of the Internet: Agency and Identity*, edited by Mia Consalvo and Susanna Paasonen, 44–61. New York: Lang.

O'Toole, Laurence. 1998. *Pornocopia: Porn, Sex, Technology and Desire*. London: Serpent's Tail.

Paasonen, Susanna. 2007. "Strange Bedfellows: Pornography, Affect and Feminist Reading." *Feminist Theory* 8, no. 1:43–57.

Paasonen, Susanna. 2009. "Healthy Sex and Pop Porn: Pornography, Feminism and the Finnish Context." *Sexualities* 12, no. 5:586–604.

Paasonen, Susanna. 2010a. "Disturbing, Fleshy Texts: Close Looking at Pornography." In *Working with Affect in Feminist Readings: Disturbing Differences*, edited by Marianne Liljeström and Susanna Paasonen, 61–86. London: Routledge.

Paasonen, Susanna. 2010b. "Good Amateurs: Erotica Writing and Notions of Quality." In *Porn.com: Making Sense of Online Pornography*, edited by Feona Attwood, 138–154. New York: Lang.

Paasonen, Susanna. 2010c. "Labors of Love: Netporn, Web 2.0 and the Meanings of Amateurism." *New Media and Society* 12, no. 8:1297–1312.

Paasonen, Susanna. Forthcoming. "The Beast Within: Materiality, Ethics, and Animal Porn." In *Controversial Images*, edited by Feona Attwood, Vincent Campbell, Ian Hunter, and Sharon Lockyer. New York: Palgrave.

Paasonen, Susanna, Kaarina Nikunen, and Laura Saarenmaa. 2007. "Pornification and the Education of Desire." In *Pornification: Sex and Sexuality in Media Culture*, edited by Susanna Paasonen, Kaarina Nikunen, and Laura Saarenmaa, 1–20. Oxford: Berg.

Paasonen, Susanna, and Laura Saarenmaa. 2007. "The Golden Age of Porn: History and Nostalgia in Cinema." In *Pornification: Sex and Sexuality in Media Culture*, edited by Susanna Paasonen, Kaarina Nikunen, and Laura Saarenmaa, 23–32. Oxford: Berg.

Pally, Marcia. 1994. *Sex and Sensibility: Reflections on Forbidden Mirrors and the Will to Censor*. New Jersey: Ecco Press.

Parikka, Jussi. 2005. "Digital Monsters, Binary Aliens: Computer Viruses, Capitalism and the Flow of Information." *Fibreculture* 4. http://journal.fibreculture.org/issue4/issue4_parikka.html.

Parikka, Jussi, and Tony Sampson. 2009. "On Anomalous Objects of Digital Culture." In *The Spam Book: On Viruses, Porn, and Other Anomalies from the Dark Side of Digital Culture*, edited by Jussi Parikka and Tony Sampson, 1–18. Cresskill, NJ: Hampton Press.

Parisi, Luciana, and Tiziana Terranova. 2001. "A Matter of Affect: Digital Images and the Cybernetic Re-wiring of Vision." *Parallax* 7:122–127.

Patterson, Zabet. 2004. "Going On-line: Consuming Pornography in the Digital Era." In *Porn Studies*, edited by Linda Williams, 104–123. Durham: Duke University Press.

Patton, Cindy. 1991. "Visualizing Safe Sex: When Pedagogy and Pornography Collide." In *Inside/out: Lesbian Theories, Gay Theories*, edited by Diane Fuss, 373–386. New York: Routledge.

Paul, Pamela. 2005. *Pornified: How Pornography Is Damaging Our Lives, Our Relationships, and Our Families*. New York: Owl Books.

Pearce, Lynne. 1997. *Feminism and the Politics of Reading*. London: Arnold.

Peirce, Charles Sanders. 1991. *Peirce on Signs: Writings on Semiotic*. Edited by James Hoopes. Chapel Hill: University of North Carolina Press.

Penley, Constance. 1997. *NASA/TREK: Popular Science and Sex in America*. New York: Verso.

Penley, Constance. 2004. "Crackers and Whackers: The White Trashing of Porn." In *Porn Studies*, edited by Linda Williams, 309–331. Durham: Duke University Press.

Perdue, Lewis. 2002. *EroticaBiz: How Sex Shaped the Internet*. New York: Writers Club Press.

Phillips, Douglas. 2009. "Can Desire Go On without a Body? Pornographic Exchange as Orbital Anomaly." In *The Spam Book: On Viruses, Porn, and Other Anomalies from the Dark Side of Digital Culture*, edited by Jussi Parikka and Tony Sampson, 195–212. Cresskill, NJ: Hampton Press.

Plummer, Ken. 2003. *Intimate Citizenship: Private Decisions and Public Dialogues*. Seattle: University of Washington Press.

Poynor, Rick. 2006. *Designing Pornotopia: Travels in Visual Culture*. New York: Princeton Architectural Press.

Probyn, Elspeth. 2000. *Carnal Appetites: Food, Sex, Identities*. London: Routledge.

Probyn, Elspeth. 2005. *Blush: Faces of Shame*. Minneapolis: University of Minnesota Press.

Provos, Niels, Dean McNamee, Panayoiotis Mavrommatis, Ken Wang, and Nagendra Modadugu. 2007. "The Ghost in the Browser: Analysis of Web-based Malware." *Proceedings for HotBots'07 Workshop*. http://www.usenix.org/events/hotbots07/tech/full_papers/provos/provos.pdf.

Putnam, Dana E., and Marlene M. Maheu. 2000. "Online Sexual Addiction and Compulsivity: Integrating Web Resources and Behavioral Telehealth in Treatment." *Sexual Addiction and Compulsivity* 7, no. 2:91–112.

Radway, Janice. 1984. *Reading the Romance: Women, Patriarchy, and Popular Fiction*. Chapel Hill: University of North Carolina Press.

Ray, Audacia. 2008. "Power to Pornographers: A Naked Revolution?" http://www.hotmoviesforher.com/guest-blogs/audacia-ray-from-waking-vixen/power-to-the-pornographers-a-naked-revolution.html.

Reading, Anna. 2005. "Professing Porn or Obscene Browsing? On Proper Distance in the University Classroom." *Media Culture and Society* 27, no. 1:123–130.

Richardson, Diane. 1996. "Heterosexuality and Social Theory." In *Theorising Heterosexuality: Telling It Straight*, edited by Diane Richardson, 1–20. Buckingham: Open University Press.

Rimm, Martin. 1995. "Marketing Pornography on the Information Superhighway: A Survey of 917,410 Images, Descriptions, Short Stories, and Animations Downloaded 8.5 Million Times by Consumers in over 2000 Cities in Forty Countries, Provinces, and Territories." *Georgetown Law Journal* 83, no. 5:1849–1934.

Rival, Laura, Don Slater, and Daniel Miller. 1999. "Sex and Sociality: Comparative Ethnographies of Sexual Objectification." In *Love and Eroticism*, edited by Mike Featherstone, 295–322. London: Sage.

Rooke, Alison, and Mónica G. Moreno Figueroa. 2010. "Beyond 'Key Parties' and 'Wife Swapping': The Visual Culture of Online Swinging." In *Porn.com: Making Sense of Online Pornography*, edited by Feona Attwood, 217–235. New York: Lang.

Rose, Gillian. 2007. *Visual Methodologies: An Introduction to the Interpretation of Visual Materials*. London: Sage.

Ross, Andrew. 1989. *No Respect: Intellectuals and Popular Culture*. New York: Routledge.

Rubin, Gayle. 1989. "Thinking Sex." In *Pleasure and Danger: Exploring Female Sexuality*, edited by Carole S. Vance, 267–319. London: Pandora.

Rubin, Gayle. 1995. "Misguided, Dangerous and Wrong: An Analysis of Anti-pornography Politics." In *Gender, Race and Class in Media: A Text Reader*, edited by Gail Dines and Jean M. Humez, 244–253. London: Sage.

Russell, Diana E. H. 2000. "Pornography and Rape: A Causal Model." In *Feminism and Pornography*, edited by Drucilla Cornell, 48–93. Oxford: Oxford University Press.

Sabo, Anne G. 2005. "The Status of Sexuality, Pornography, and Morality in Norway Today: Are the Critics Ready for Bjørneboe's Joyful Inversion or Mykle's Guilt Trip?" *Nora: Nordic Journal of Women's Studies* 13, no. 1: 36–47.

Said, Edward W. 1994. *Culture and Imperialism*. London: Vintage.

Said, Edward W. 1995. *Orientalism: Western Conceptions of the Orient*. London: Penguin.

Sargeant, Jack. 2004. "Hot, Hard Cocks and Tight, Unlubricated Assholes: Trangression, Sexual Ambiguity, and 'Perverse' Pleasures in Serge Gainsbourg's *Je t'aime moi non plus*." *Senses of Cinema* 30. http://www.sensesofcinema.com/2004/30/je_taime_moi_non_plus.

Sargeant, Jack. 2006. "Filth and Sexual Excess: Some Brief Reflections on Popular Scatology." *M/C Journal* 9, no. 5. http://www.journal.media-culture.org.au/0610/03-sargeant.php.

Sassoon, Joanna. 2004. "Photographic Materiality in the Age of Digital Reproduction." In *Photographs, Objects, Histories: On the Materiality of Images*, edited by Elizabeth Edwards and Janice Hart, 186–202. New York: Routledge.

Sawhney, Sabina. 1995. "The Jewels in the Crotch: The Imperial Erotic in *The Raj Quartet*. In *Sexy Bodies: The Strange Carnalities of Feminism*, edited by Elizabeth Grosz and Elspeth Probyn, 195–210. London: Routledge.

Scarry, Elaine. 1985. *The Body in Pain: The Making and Unmaking of the World*. Oxford: Oxford University Press.

Scharrer, Erica. 2002. "Third-Person Perspective and Television Violence: The Role of Out-Group Stereotyping in Perceptions of Susceptibility to Effects." *Communication Research* 29, no. 6:681–704.

Schindler, Stephan K. 1996. "The Critic as Pornographer: Male Fantasies of Female Reading in Eighteenth-Century Germany." *Eighteenth Century Life* 20, no. 3:66–80.

Schneider, Jennifer P. 2000. "Effects of Cybersex Addiction on the Family: Results of a Survey." *Sexual Addiction and Compulsivity* 7, no. 1:31–58.

Schröder, Stephan Michael. 1997. "More Fun with Swedish Girls? Functions of a German Heterostereotype." *Ethnologia Scandinavica* 27:122–137.

Schulze, Hendrik, and Klaus Mochalski. 2009. *Ipoque Internet Study 2008–2009.* http://www.ipoque.com/study/ipoque-Internet-Study-08-09.pdf.

Sedgwick, Eve Kosofsky. 2003. *Touching Feeling: Affect, Pedagogy, Performativity.* Durham: Duke University Press.

Senft, Theresa M. 2008. *CamGirls: Celebrity and Community in the Age of Social Networks.* New York: Lang.

Serres, Michel. 2008. *The Five Senses: A Philosophy of Mingled Bodies.* Translated by Margaret Sankey and Peter Crowley. London: Continuum.

Shah, Nishat. 2007. "PlayBlog: Pornography, Performance and Cyberspace." In *C'lick Me: A Netporn Studies Reader*, edited by Katrien Jacobs, Marije Janssen, and Matteo Pasquinelli, 31–44. Amsterdam Institute of Network Cultures.

Shamoon, Deborah. 2004. "Office Sluts and Rebel Flowers: The Pleasures of Japanese Pornographic Comics for Women." In *Porn Studies*, edited by Linda Williams, 77–103. Durham: Duke University Press.

Shaviro, Steven. 1993. *The Cinematic Body.* Minneapolis: University of Minnesota Press.

Shelton, Emily. 2002. "A Star Is Porn: Corpulence, Comedy, and the Homosocial Cult of Adult Film Star Ron Jeremy." *Camera Obscura* 17, no. 3:115–146.

Shimizu, Celine Parreñas. 2007. *The Hypersexuality of Race: Performing Asian/American Women on Screen and Scene.* Durham: Duke University Press.

Shohat, Ella, and Robert Stam. 1994. *Unthinking Eurocentrism: Multiculturalism and the Media.* London: Routledge.

Sigel, Lisa Z., ed. 2005. *International Exposures: Perspectives on Modern European Pornography 1800–2000.* New Brunswick: Rutgers University Press.

Skeggs, Beverley. 1997. *Formations of Class and Gender: Becoming Respectable.* London: Sage.

Skeggs, Beverley. 2005. "The Making of Class and Gender through Visualising Moral Subject Formation." *Sociology* 39, no. 5:965–982.

Slater, Don. 1991. "Consuming Kodak." In *Family Snaps: The Meanings of Domestic Photography*, edited by Jo Spence and Patricia Holland, 49–59. London: Virago.

Slater, Don. 1998. "Trading Sexpics on IRC: Embodiment and Authenticity on the Internet." *Body and Society* 4, no. 4: 91–117.

Slayden, David. 2010. "Debbie Does Dallas, Again and Again: Pornography, Technology, and Market Innovation." In *Porn.com: Making Sense of Online Pornography*, edited by Feona Attwood, 54–68. New York: Lang.

Snyder, Donald. 2000. "Webcam Women: Life on Your Screen." In *Web.studies: Rewiring Media Studies for the Digital Age*, edited by David Gauntlett, 68–73. London: Arnold.

Sobchack, Vivian. 2004. *Carnal Thoughts: Embodiment and Moving Image Culture*. Berkeley: University of California Press.

Sontag, Susan. 1999. "Notes on 'Camp.'" In *Camp: Queer Aesthetics and the Performing Subject—A Reader*, edited by Fabio Cleto, 53–65. Michigan: University of Michigan Press.

Sontag, Susan. 2002. *Styles of Radical Will*. New York: Picador.

Spink, Amanda, Helen Partridge, and Bernard J. Jansen. 2006. "Sexual and Pornographic Web Searching: Trend Analysis." *First Monday* 11, no. 9. http://firstmonday.org/htbin/cgiwrap/bin/ojs/index.php/fm/article/view/1391/1309.

Spinoza, Baruch. 1992. *The Ethics, Treatise on the Emendation of the Intellect and Selected Letters*. Edited by Seymour Feldman and translated by Samuel Shirley. Indianapolis: Hackett.

Stacey, Jackie. 1994. *Star Gazing: Hollywood Cinema and Female Spectatorship*. London: Routledge.

Stacey, Jackie, and Lynne Pearce. 1995. "The Heart of the Matter: Feminists Revisit Romance." In *Romance Revisited*, edited by Lynne Pearce and Jackie Stacey, 11–45. London: Lawrence & Wishart.

Stapleton, Adam. 2010. "Child Pornography: Classifications and Conceptualizations." In *Porn.com: Making Sense of Online Pornography*, edited by Feona Attwood, 34–53. New York: Lang.

Stein, Arlene. 2006. *Shameless: Sexual Dissidence in American Culture*. New York: NYU Press.

Storr, Merl. 2003. *Latex and Lingerie: Shopping for Pleasure at Ann Summers Parties*. Oxford: Berg.

Taormino, Tristan. 2008. Presentation at the Sex Work in Industry and Academe workshop at the Console-ing Passions 2008: An International Conference on Television, Audio, Video, New Media, and Feminism, University of California, Santa Barbara, April 24–26.

Terranova, Tiziana. 2000. "Free Labor: Producing Culture for the Digital Economy." *Social Text* 18, no. 2:33–58.

Terranova, Tiziana. 2006. "On Sense and Sensibility: Immaterial Labour in Open Systems." In *Curating, Immateriality, Systems: On Curating Digital Media*, edited by Geoff Cox, Joasia Krysa, and Anya Lewin, 27–36. New York: Autonomedia.

Thornburgh, Dick, and Herbert S. Lin. 2002. *Youth, Pornography, and the Internet*. Computer Science and Telecommunications Board, National Science Council. Washington, DC: National Academy Press.

Thrift, Nigel. 2008. *Non-representational Theory: Space / Politics / Affect*. London: Routledge.

Toepfer, Karl. 1991. *Theatre, Aristocracy, and Pornocracy: The Orgy Calculus*. New York: PAJ.

Tola, Miriam. 2005. "Re-routing the (A)sex Drives of Big Dickie: Interview with Katrien Jacobs." http://networkcultures.org/wpmu/netporn/press/interview-with-katrien-jacobs.

Tomkins, Silvan. 1995a. *Exploring Affect: The Selected Writings of Silvan S. Tomkins*. Edited by E. Virginia Demos. Cambridge: Cambridge University Press.

Tomkins, Silvan. 1995b. *Shame and Its Sisters: A Silvan Tomkins Reader*. Edited by Eve Kosofsky Sedgwick and Adam Frank. Durham: Duke University Press.

Twitchell, James B. 1989. *Forbidden Partners: The Incest Taboo in Modern Culture*. New York: University of Columbia Press.

Tyler, Imogen. 2006. "Chav Scum: The Filthy Politics of Social Class in Contemporary Britain." *M/C Journal* 9, no. 5. http://journal.media-culture.org.au/0610/09-tyler.php.

Tyler, Imogen. 2008. "Methodological Fatigue and the Politics of the Affective Turn." *Feminist Media Studies* 8, no. 1:85–90.

Tyler, Megan. 2010. "'Now, That's Pornography!' Violence and Domination in *Adult Video News*." In *Everyday Pornography*, edited by Karen Boyle, 50–62. London: Routledge.

Uebel, Michael. 1999. "Toward a Symptomatology of Cyberporn." *Theory and Event* 3, no. 4. http://muse.jhu.edu/journals/theory_and_event/v003/3.4uebel.html.

Vance, Carole S. 1989. "Pleasure and Danger: Toward a Politics of Dexuality." In *Pleasure and Danger: Exploring Female Sexuality*, edited by Carole S. Vance, 1–27. London: Pandora.

Van Doorn, Niels. 2010. "Keeping It Real: User-Generated Pornography, Gender Reification, and Visual Pleasure." *Convergence* 16, no. 4:411–430.

Villarejo, Amy. 2003. *Lesbian Rule: Cultural Criticism and the Value of Desire*. Durham: Duke University Press.

Villarejo, Amy. 2004. "Defycategory.com, or the Place of Categories in Intermedia." In *More Dirty Looks: Gender, Pornography and Power*, 2nd ed., edited by Pamela Church Gibson, 85–91. London: BFI.

Wallace, Michele. 1999. *Black Macho and the Myth of the Superwoman* (1978). London: Verso.

Warner, Michael. 2000. *The Trouble with Normal: Sex, Politics, and the Ethics of Queer Life*. Cambridge: Harvard University Press.

Waskul, Dennis D., ed. 2004. *Net.seXXX: Readings on Sex, Pornography, and the Internet*. New York: Lang.

Whisnant, Rebecca. 2010. "From Jekyll to Hyde: The Grooming of Male Pornography Consumers." In *Everyday Pornography*, edited by Karen Boyle, 114–133. London: Routledge.

White, Michele. 2003. "Too Close to See: Men, Women, and Webcams." *New Media and Society* 5, no. 1:7–28.

White, Michele. 2006. *The Body and the Screen: Theories of Internet Spectatorship*. Cambridge: MIT Press.

White, Richard. 1997. "The Sublime and the Other." *Heythrop Journal* 38, no. 2:125–143.

Williams, Linda. 1989. *Hard Core: Power, Pleasure, and the "Frenzy of the Visible*. Berkeley: University of California Press.

Williams, Linda. 1991. "Film Bodies: Gender, Genre, and Excess." *Film Quarterly* 44, no. 4:2–13.

Williams, Linda. 2004a. "Porn Studies: Proliferating Pornographies on/Scene: An Introduction." In *Porn Studies*, edited by Linda Williams, 1–23. Durham: Duke University Press.

Williams, Linda. 2004b. "Second Thoughts on *Hard Core*: American Obscenity Law and the Scapegoating of Deviance." In *More Dirty Looks: Gender, Pornography and Power*, 2nd ed., edited by Pamela Church Gibson, 165–175. London: BFI.

Williams, Linda. 2004c. "Skin Flicks and the Racial Border: Pornography, Exploitation, and Interracial Lust." In *Porn Studies*, edited by Linda Williams, 271–308. Durham: Duke University Press.

Williams, Linda. 2008. *Screening Sex*. Durham: Duke University Press.

Woida, Chloe. 2009. "International Pornography on the Internet: Crossing Digital Borders and the Un/disciplined Gaze." Plenary presentation at the DAC'09 conference on After Media: Embodiment and Context, University of California Irvine, December 12–15.

Young, Alison. 2005. *Judging the Image: Art, Value, Law*. London: Routledge.

Zimmermann, Patricia. 1995. *Reel Families: A Social History of Amateur Film*. Bloomington: Indiana University Press.

Žižek, Slavoj. 1998. "From Sublime to Ridicule, or, Sexual Act in Cinema. *Lähikuva* 4:19–35.

Zuckert, Rachel. 2003. "Awe and Envy: Herder contra Kant on the Sublime." *Journal of Aesthetics and Art Criticism* 61, no. 3:217–232.

Index

"2 Girls 1 Cup," 209–210, 212, 214, 222, 233–236, 240, 249
"2 Guys 1 Horse," 210, 212, 222, 233, 235, 240
4chan, 1, 230
8Tube, 6, 34, 66, 121

Abel, Marco, 9–10, 133, 193, 194, 195, 264n6
Abject, 58, 212, 214, 216, 229
  abjection, 230
Abramson, Paul R., 217
Addiction, 45
  and Internet porn, 2, 33, 48–49, 63, 67
  and religion, 268n9
Aesthetics, 52, 102, 237–240
  amateur, 81, 98, 104, 112, 113, 172, 196
  body, 73, 82, 121, 149, 248
  and camp, 142, 143
  and judgment, 43, 56
  of pornography, 3, 6, 14, 51, 61, 62, 71, 81, 137, 140, 145, 183, 185
Affect
  autonomy of, 26, 193, 194
  categories of, 217
  definitions of, 22–23, 54–55
  and emotion, 26–27
  and interpretation, 8–10, 13, 15, 18, 20–21, 24, 63, 132–134, 136, 144, 189, 190, 192–195, 197–198, 199–200, 238

and representation, 8–11, 27, 187, 205, 241
  as synesthetic, 203
  theory, 62, 211, 212, 217
Affectation, 23, 25, 133, 174, 188, 192, 194, 196, 197–198, 243
Affection, 91, 97, 103, 202
Affective. *See also* Resonance
  address, 52, 189, 197–198, 224, 246
  circulation, 2, 3, 54–55, 232–234
  complexity, 8, 16–17, 109, 188–189, 230
  dynamics, 19, 22, 24–25, 61, 105, 211, 215–216, 218, 219–221, 231, 233, 238, 254, 260, 262
  economy, 66, 90, 91, 224, 231
  intensity, 2, 10, 14, 25, 33, 75, 112, 143, 164, 188, 236, 240, 255–256, 261
  investment, 21, 90, 133, 209
  jolts, 27, 199, 224–225, 230, 231–232, 239–241, 244, 245–246
  labor, 21, 22, 90–92, 94–97, 244
  rhetoric, 45–48, 54, 59, 245–246
  stickiness, 60, 198–199, 200, 209, 215, 232, 234–236, 244
  turn, 10–11, 12, 264n7
  voice, 247
Agency
  and labor, 244
  of objects, 25, 103
  scholarly, 23, 258, 266n14